The
Rider's
Problem Solver

**YOUR QUESTIONS ANSWERED:
HOW TO IMPROVE YOUR SKILLS,
OVERCOME YOUR FEARS, AND
UNDERSTAND YOUR HORSE**

JESSICA JAHIEL

Illustrations by Claudia Coleman

 Storey Publishing

The mission of Storey Publishing is to serve our customers by publishing practical information that encourages personal independence in harmony with the environment.

Edited by Deborah Burns and Lisa Hiley
Art direction and text design by Cynthia McFarland
Cover design by Kent Lew
Text production by Erin Dawson
Cover photograph by ©Arnd Bronkhorst Photography/www.arnd.nl
Indexed by Susan Olason

Printed in the United States by Versa Press
10 9 8 7 6 5 4 3 2 1

Library of Congress Cataloging-in-Publication Data

Jahiel, Jessica.
    The rider's problem solver : your questions answered : how to improve your skills, overcome your fears, and understand your horse / Jessica Jahiel ; illustrations by Claudia Coleman.
      p. cm.
    Includes index.
    ISBN-13: 978-1-58017-838-9; ISBN-10: 1-58017-838-3 (pbk. : alk. paper)
    ISBN-13: 978-1-58017-839-6; ISBN-10: 1-58017-839-1 (hardcover : alk. Paper)
  1. Horsemanship—Miscellanea. 2. Horses—Behavior—Miscellanea. I. Title.
SF309.J364 2006
798.2'3—dc22

                                              2005031351

CONTENTS

I'm Uncomfortable Mounting from the Ground • My Horse Won't Stand Still for Mounting • Holding the Reins and Saddle While Mounting • Dismounting: Should I Jump Off or Slide Off? • Emergency Dismounts

Rider Leg Position • What Is Correct Knee Position? • Rider's Tight Upper Body • I Lean Sideways, and My Horse Does Too

How Should I Move My Arms at the Walk? • Soft Hands at the Walk • Young Horse Won't Walk, He Jogs • Lengthening a Short Walk Stride • My Horse Anticipates Walk-Trot Transitions

Help! Can't Master Posting Trot! • How Do I Learn Diagonals? • I Can't Sit the Trot • Please Provide Sitting Trot Image • First Lengthenings at Trot and Canter • What *Is* Correct Trot Lengthening? • Trot Lengthening or Medium Trot?

Canter Phobia • My Horse Won't Canter • Problems with Right Lead • Smooth Canter Depart • Rider's Leg Swinging at Canter • Better Canter for Rider and Horse

Explain Crest Releases, Please • I Can't "See My Distance" • Losing Stirrups over Jumps • Learning to "Fold" over Jumps • Hunt Seat Compared to Cross-Country Position • Strong Legs for Cross-Country Jumping?

Trail Riding in Balance • Galloping on Trail Ride • Riding Down Hills • Essential Equine Trail Skills

DEDICATION

▼

To Edwin and Lenrose Jahiel — two extraordinary teachers

AND

To the readers!

No book can teach you to ride, but by offering analysis, explanations, and possible solutions, a book can help you achieve additional insights and give you some ideas to discuss with your instructor, all of which helps improve your riding and your relationship with your horse.

My overall ambition, in my writing and my teaching, has always been to enable horses and riders to understand each other better and enjoy each other more. Life is too short for any one of us to make all the possible mistakes and discoveries on our own. It's essential for us to be able to learn from other people's experiences — that's what this book is all about.

ACKNOWLEDGMENTS

No book is ever the creation of a single individual.
In the case of this book, several individuals (and one large
group of people) stand out for their special contributions:

Madelyn Larsen, agent and friend, who found the ideal
publisher for a series of *Horse-Sense* books.

Deb Burns and Lisa Hiley, my editors at Storey,
and Candace Akins, copyeditor.

Claudia Coleman, whose superb artistic talent continues
to be a source of amazement and delight.

Karen Fletcher, aka "Web Goddess,"
without whom the *Horse-Sense* mailing list and
Web site would never have become a reality.

Last but not least: the *Horse-Sense* readers who have
been asking questions and telling their stories over the last ten
years. Thank you all for wanting to improve your riding and
thus improve the relationships you have with your horses.
There are too many of you to list, but you know who you are.

FOREWORD

THIS IS A "HOW-TO" BOOK for people with a deep interest in improving their riding. A firm believer in the principles of classical training, Jessica Jahiel has worked with thousands of horses and riders in her lifetime. Multitudes of riders, from occasional trail-riders to full-time professionals, have written to her *Horse-Sense* e-mail newsletter asking for help with an enormous variety of problems relating to horses and riding. From these questions she has built this book, which follows her successful *Horse Behavior Problem Solver* and has the same accessible Q&A format.

Jessica writes clearly and well, and her book is easy to read. The questions follow the logical sequence of learning to ride. One thing I particularly like about this book is that in answering each question she gives one or more wrong approaches to correcting the problem, explains why they won't work and then presents the right approach and explains why it *will* work. Though this book is not technically about teaching riding, you will learn a lot about good riding instruction before you are finished.

Another fine aspect of this book is Jessica's consistent and persistent emphasis on kindness to both horse and rider. Most of us already know the advantages of using kindness, but it does only good to keep that in front of us.

SALLY SWIFT
Author of *Centered Riding*

PREFACE

REGARDLESS OF WHERE THEY LIVE, what sort of horses they ride, and what riding disciplines they follow, riders everywhere share the same worries and frustrations, wrestle with the same problems, and experience the same joys.

Riders of all ages, all over the world, ask similar questions about all aspects of riding. All are concerned with learning the physical skills of riding: balance, coordination, and the application of the aids. All are concerned with finding suitable tack and clothing, locating good instructors, and getting the greatest benefit from lessons and clinics. Issues of position and balance, tack and clothing, confidence and fear, comfort and discomfort, exist for all riders. Even riders who ride only once or twice a month, and can never be sure that they will be assigned the same horse for two consecutive lessons, want and need to know what they can do to improve their understanding, their skills, and their comfort and security in the saddle.

Riders want to know how to deal with all of these issues and more. They want to know how to handle fatigue, anger, frustration, and fear. They want to know how they can make progress when they are busy, less fit than they would like to be, and unable to ride on a regular schedule.

All riders want to know how to overcome the problems presented by their horse's conformation, fitness level, aptitude, and attitude, and they also want to know how to overcome the problems presented by their *own* conformation, fitness level, aptitude, and attitude. Many of them have questions they don't feel comfortable asking their instructors ("Should I let other people ride my horse?"; "Should I be riding a lot of different horses in my lessons, or just one?").

Riders want to know everything, and most of all they want to know the things that they haven't been taught. They want to know how to mount easily and safely, especially if they are older and less flexible than they once were. They want to know how to hold their reins correctly and how to post the trot without making a huge effort and feeling unbalanced. They want to know how to get their horses to pick up a canter smoothly and they want to know how to sit the canter comfortably. They want to know whether their instructors are good, how to evaluate a clinician, and how and when and why to use whips and spurs.

Some riders want to overcome the fear that is keeping them from enjoying their horses. Riders with pain from injuries or illness want to know what they can do to go on enjoying their sport. All of them want to feel competent and confident, and all of them want to enjoy their horses more.

The purpose of this book is not to teach riders how to train or school their horses; that will be the subject of a future book. *The Rider's Problem Solver* is all about riders and their problems and concerns. Its primary purpose is to provide riders with information, advice, and suggestions that will help them improve their riding skills whether they ride their own horses, lease horses, borrow horses, or only ride a few times a year on holidays or at a local rental stable. It is intended to help riders deal with *riding* problems and to help them to ride more comfortably and effectively.

The titles of the chapters are simple and self-explanatory; the questions are real questions submitted to the *Horse-Sense* newsletter by riders of all ages and skill levels from all around the world.

JESSICA JAHIEL
Summerwood Farm

Mount Up and Ride

CHAPTER 1

Getting On and Off

MOUNTING AND DISMOUNTING are two activities often dreaded by riders and neglected by instructors. Riders with weak ankles, painful knees, or stiff hips often find mounting both painful and embarrassing. Some riders give up riding because of the physical and emotional strain of clambering painfully upward while praying that the horse won't move and the saddle won't slip. Meanwhile, many horses also experience back pain and physical damage when riders mount awkwardly.

There are various ways to solve the problem of difficult and painful mounting and dismounting. Sometimes the solution is better technique; sometimes it's a taller mounting block. Dismounting is usually less challenging, but it's a moment at which the rider is particularly vulnerable. Careful, smooth, *safe* mounting and dismounting should be every rider's habit.

I'm Uncomfortable Mounting from the Ground

Q Although I have ridden many times, I still have trouble mounting from the ground. I always seem to need a mounting stool. Is there anything that could possibly help me in mounting? Maybe a special technique or some little thing that I haven't learned will make it easier for me.

A It's a good idea to know how to mount from the ground; every rider should be able to do this. But once you've learned how, and can do it if you have to, I suggest that you do it only on those occasions when you have no other choice. It's easier for you and your horse if you use a mounting block. (See page 361 for directions on building a sturdy four-step version.)

Be creative. A mounting block doesn't have to be a purpose-built device in an arena. If there's no mounting block, look for something else that might serve. An overturned bucket, a chunk of log, a large rock, a fire hydrant — I have personally used all of these at one time or another. If there is *nothing* for you to stand on, try standing your horse on the low side of a slope or in a ditch.

Stand as close to your horse as you can. Trying to climb on from even a short distance away puts an incredible amount of torque on your horse's back, on your saddle tree, and on your own back.

As for how to mount: Think about getting up and out of a swimming pool when there are no steps or ladder. I'm sure you've done this before! The key is to stand as close as you can to the edge of the pool, put your hands on the edge, and push yourself straight up. As soon as your body begins to rise, lean forward slightly, so that your body weight is over your hands and arms. If you swim, try this, then move back just an inch or two from the edge and try it again. It works only when you stand right at the edge and lift yourself straight up, shifting your weight forward onto your hands right away.

The basic idea behind mounting is exactly the same: You want to push off with your legs so that your body is balanced over your *hands,* over the saddle.

1. Stand at your horse's shoulder, as close to him as possible, facing to the rear. Hold the reins and a handful of mane in your left hand, just in front of the withers. Your right rein should be slightly shorter than your left rein.

2. Using your right hand, twist the stirrup until you can put the toe of your left foot into it. When the ball of your foot is on the stirrup, turn your toe in toward your horse's girth. If your toe digs into your horse's body as you mount, he may, quite reasonably, interpret this as a signal to move. If your toe digs into the girth, it won't bother him as much and he is more likely to stand still.

3. Put your right hand on the waist, or twist, of the saddle — that's the narrowest part of the seat, just behind the pommel. Bend your right knee so that you can bounce once or twice if you need to, then, keeping your toe turned into the horse's girth and your own body as close as possible to your horse's body, *jump up* from the ground.

As soon as you jump, your number one priority is to get your weight up and balanced over the top of your saddle. Do this as quickly and smoothly as you can, so that you are supporting your weight *on your hands* at the top of your jump. Your left foot will be in the stirrup, but you'll put very little weight on that foot.

NOTE: Don't put your right hand on the cantle for two reasons: It twists the saddle tree, and it will also put your own right hand and arm just exactly where your body will need to be in another second! You need to go straight up without pausing, so don't stop until your weight is on your hands and arms.

4. As your body comes *up*, slide your right hand down until you are gripping the skirt of the saddle on the right (the skirt is the little flap that covers the stirrup bar). When you've got it in your hand, push *down* with your right arm as though you were pushing the right side of the saddle away from you. This will help you get up and over while keeping the saddle in place. (If you are riding in a Western saddle, put your right hand on the swell, just to the right of the saddle horn, and push down.)

5. With your weight on your hands and arms, you are free to swing your right leg over the saddle. When your leg is on the right side of the saddle, pick up your right stirrup with your foot and balance your position before you sink softly into the saddle. It may seem easier to sit down first and then pick up your offside stirrup, but don't give in to that temptation. When you pick up both stirrups and balance your weight *before* you lower yourself softly into the saddle, your backside will have a controlled descent, not an abrupt, forceful impact that can hurt the horse's back.

This sounds complicated, I know, but it all makes sense, and you'll find that it takes you much less time to do than it did to read about doing it. If you're in a situation where you must mount from the ground, it's important that you do it well so that your horse won't be uncomfortable. If he knows that mounting is going to be unpleasant for him, he'll quickly learn to back away or swing his hindquarters away from you in an effort to avoid the unpleasantness.

My number one suggestion about mounting from the ground remains: Try to avoid it if possible! Doing most, if not all, of your mounting from a mounting block will protect your horse's back, your saddle tree, and your own back.

Use a strong, tall, sturdy mounting block to protect and preserve your horse's back, your own back, and your saddle tree.

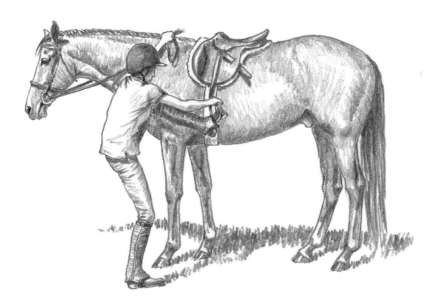

It's useful to know how to mount from the ground, but try to avoid it if you can.

My Horse Won't Stand Still for Mounting

Q When I put the mounting block beside my 5-year-old Arabian mare and step up on it, she backs up or moves sideways. I spent a day teaching her to stand still by gradually working up to mounting — stepping up and down off the box; stepping up, putting my left hand on her crest, stepping down; eventually putting my foot in the stirrup; and then getting on. I praised her and gave her a treat when she stood still, and if she moved I quietly said "no" and moved her back into position. She did really well that day, and for two or three days afterward she stood perfectly still while I got on. Now she's backing up again.

Do you think I just need to spend another day on the "standing still" lesson? I spent about half an hour on it that day. I make sure not to jab her with my toe, I take little or no contact with her mouth while mounting, and the saddle fits her well, so I don't think I'm doing anything that could make her uncomfortable. Once I get on, she stands still and waits for me to ask her to walk forward. She's *very* laid-back, and I always have to encourage her to go forward at the walk, but she is quite forward at the trot. She's comfortable and happy with me on her back, stretches her head and neck down, and is doing great. If she moved forward while mounting I could take contact with her mouth to make her stop, but because she's moving backward, I'm not sure what to do. I tried standing her with her rear end in a corner, but she always wriggles her way out somehow.

A This isn't an unusual problem, and there are several things you can do. First, though, be sure that your saddle isn't pulling or shifting in a way that makes your mare uncomfortable when you mount. Very few riders have access to a tall enough mounting block to enable them to step across onto the horse's back. Most mounting blocks serve only to make the rider a little taller, so even *with* a mounting block, it's important to show consideration for the horse by mounting in a way that creates the least amount of pressure and torque on the horse's back.

Also, be certain that your mare is standing in balance before you mount. If her own weight is unevenly supported because her legs are too close together or too far apart, the addition of your weight, especially while you mount, will force her to shift and take a step or two just to keep upright. If you teach her to stop and stand square for mounting, she'll be much less likely to shift out of position.

If you're sure that she's comfortable, then the problem is likely to be one of communication. She doesn't understand that she is expected to stand still and that she *must* stand still! You will have to convince her that standing still is easier and more fun than the alternatives.

Because what you have done in the past worked, you might return to it; one afternoon's practice won't last a lifetime. You have to be consistent in your requests and your praise. Think back and remember exactly what you did to teach her to stand for mounting, and then watch yourself carefully and notice whether you are doing something differently now. You may find that you are giving her a signal without meaning to do so.

Try teaching a verbal command — "Stand!" is quite useful. Use the word whenever she *is* standing quietly, and she will soon learn to associate the word with what she is doing.

Sometimes, just putting the horse back into position isn't enough. Not all horses respond in the same way, so here is another option for you to try.

If your horse steps sideways, away from you, use the stiff fingers of your right hand or the butt end of your whip to prod her barrel lightly while your other hand leads her a little forward. What you are going to do here is to turn her evasion (moving her hindquarters sideways) into an exercise (moving her hindquarters sideways while moving forward on a small circle). Just do one or two or three circles, with your left hand keeping her nose tipped a little toward you and your body sending her *forward* on a small circle, while your right hand is giving her a gentle poke in the ribs and asking her to step underneath herself and reach across under her body with her inside hind leg. This is also quite a useful gymnastic exercise for suppling your horse — in dressage, it's the beginning of in-hand work.

> *You will have to convince the horse that standing still is easier and more fun than the alternatives.*

Similarly, if her evasion is to walk backward, use your fingers or the butt of your whip to prod her chest gently and ask her to back, calmly and in a straight line, for five or ten steps. Then when you lead her back to the block and put her into position and tell her to stand, she may decide that standing still is the best choice.

Remember that you aren't punishing her; you are educating her. Work very calmly and quietly without getting angry. When you ask her to move sideways or backward, don't jerk her to punish her; ask her gently to move off correctly and energetically, so that she has to *work*. At first you may need to ask her multiple times, but you won't have to do this for long. If she's a clever mare, which she probably is, she will figure it out for herself and teach herself the lesson without the two of you ever having a fight of any kind.

One more thing to think about: There's no such thing as a onetime "standing still lesson." If you want your horse to stand still every time, you need to be ready and willing to take a few minutes to remind her what you want her to do every time. If you're careless and start to mount while she's standing in an unbalanced position, you're effectively asking her to move. If you're in a hurry and you mount even though she starts to move when you don't want her to, you're effectively saying "It's fine with me if you move." Be very clear about where you want her to stand and what you expect her to do and correct her whenever she does something else. Training is always a work in progress, not a permanent fix.

You've done well so far — after all, just half an hour's practice resulted in several days of standing still. But what she understands right now is "This is something I *can* do" rather than "This is something I *must* do." It will take much more practice before standing quietly becomes something that she does automatically, without wondering whether you want her to do it every time.

Holding the Reins and Saddle While Mounting

Q I've taken up riding again after 20 years, and either I'm remembering things wrong or there have been a lot of changes in what's considered right. When I rode at camp as a child, the riding counselor had a certain way that she wanted us to hold our reins and saddles when we mounted the horses. Then when I was 12 and started taking regular lessons, the instructor had a different way that he wanted us to hold our reins and saddle. I thought that maybe the camp way was for little kids and the new way was the right way. But my current instructor is asking me to do it a third way!

Here are the three ways: At camp, I was told to hold the pommel in my left hand and the cantle in my right hand, face the back of the saddle, and keep the reins tight. In my regular lessons from when I was 12 to about 16, the instructor told me to hold the mane in my left hand and the cantle in my right hand, face the front of the saddle, and keep the left rein tighter than the right so that if the horse tried to get away from me he would step away from me and not step on me with his hind feet.

Now my instructor says you should *never* face the front when you mount. She wants me to hold the mane in my left hand and hold the pommel with my right hand, face the back of the saddle, hold the reins just barely tight with the *right* rein tighter than the left one, and never touch the cantle. Her way seems to work fine, but why are there three ways to mount and which way is really the right way? Also, I definitely remember that we were always told to mount and dismount only from the left side, and my new instructor wants me to learn to mount and dismount from both sides.

A Your new instructor's way makes more sense than the other ways you describe, and there are reasons for everything she asked you to do.

It's okay to face front when using a mounting block, but she doesn't want you to face front when you mount from the ground because it's not safe. In that position, you can't see what the horse's hind legs are doing, and a surprise kick could hurt you very badly. The horse wouldn't have to be kicking at you — he could be kicking at a fly, but if you were in the way, you would be sorry. Even if the horse never kicked, he might startle, jump, buck, or just begin to walk off as you mount, and if you're facing his head, you'll miss the moment when he begins to move and may have a difficult time stopping him.

There's another good reason for facing backward and looking at the horse's hock when you mount. If you are standing by the horse's belly, facing forward, and he takes a step forward, he'll be too far ahead of you for you to catch up and

When you hold the outside rein more tightly than the inside rein, it's easier for the horse to swing his hindquarters toward you than away from you. If he moves while you are mounting, he'll move toward you, making it easier for you to mount.

mount. If your foot is already in the stirrup, you might find yourself falling off the mounting block or hopping along after him for a step or two and then falling. Standing at the horse's shoulder and doing a hop-and-swing into the saddle is much safer, because if the horse takes a step while you are halfway up his side, his movement will swing you *into* the saddle instead of away from it.

Holding the mane in your left hand along with your reins helps steady your hand and protect your horse against being jerked in the mouth. Holding the reins loosely might inspire your horse to walk off, but holding them tightly will make him uncomfortable and nervous. Or, depending on how he has been trained, it might make him think that you are asking him to walk backward. It makes more sense to hold the reins so that they are neither loose nor tight.

Uneven tension on the reins makes sense, too. If your horse doesn't step forward but tends to swing his hindquarters away from you or even take a step sideways, be sure that when you pick up your reins in preparation for mounting, you shorten the right rein slightly. Horses find it easier to move their hindquarters away from a bend, so asking for a slight neck bend to the right means that he will find it easiest to swing his hindquarters to the left, which will move the saddle toward you instead of away from you. If you are in the process of mounting, having the horse move toward you makes your job easier.

Telling you that you should never touch the cantle is good advice. With one hand on the horse's withers and the other just behind the pommel, you're in a good position to shift your weight to your hands as you mount. If both of your hands are holding the saddle, you're likely to put far too much weight in your left stirrup, and that, especially if you are holding the cantle, makes it likely that you will pull the saddle out of position. Even a large, solid Western saddle can slide out of position and end up sideways or even under the horse. If the person who pulls the saddle over when she's mounting puts all of her weight in the left stirrup, just imagine where she and that saddle could end up.

Finally, it's a very good idea to learn to mount and dismount from both sides. Not all horses accept being mounted from the right, so always ask before you attempt this. The unfamiliar sensation can cause reactions ranging from mild curiosity to a startled leap.

Tradition and convention are the only reasons we still mount and dismount from the left. When was the last time you saw someone mounting a horse while wearing a long sword? That was the last time you saw a rider with a really compelling reason to mount and dismount only from the left side.

Dismounting: Should I Jump Off or Slide Off?

Q When it's time to dismount at the end of a ride, I never know quite how to do it. I ride English and Western, so maybe I need to learn two different ways to dismount. When I ride English, I usually swing my leg over and hold myself up with my arms (one hand on the withers and one on the saddle seat, just like mounting, only in reverse), and then I kick my left foot out of the stirrup and slide down the horse's side. When I was younger I used to jump down instead of sliding down, but now that I'm (a lot) older I find that it really jars my feet and knees and back. I've started riding with a friend who always jumps off, and she says it's important to jump and push yourself away from the horse instead of sliding down because if you slide you could get something caught, like your shirt or your necklace. Which way is right?

Also, what about stepping down? I dismount from my Western saddle pretty much the same way that I do from my English saddle. When I was young I used to lean forward and swing my right leg over the horse's back and slide down to where my right foot was on the ground, then take my left foot out of the stirrup and put it on the ground. I can't do that anymore; it's too uncomfortable. I feel like I'm doing the splits. Is it okay to dismount without stepping down?

One more question: I've seen riders get off by taking their feet out of the stirrups and lifting their right leg over the saddle so that they're sitting sideways in the saddle facing left, and then they just slide down with their back to the horse. Is that a good way to dismount? I never used to worry about this, but I guess now that I'm 40 years old, I'm getting more nervous. I make lists for everything these days and I think I need a checklist for dismounting.

A Dismounting *is* mounting in reverse — you're absolutely right about that. The safety considerations are much the same: You want your horse to stand quietly, you want to dismount smoothly without kicking your horse as you bring your right leg across his croup, and whether you're riding English or Western, you want to have *both* of your feet free of the stirrups before you take your weight off your arms and slide or jump down.

Sliding down is usually preferable to jumping down, because it keeps you closer to your horse and able to take a little support from the saddle as you dismount. If you're riding Western, however, don't lean too close to your saddle as you slide down! Your friend's warning is accurate: Shirts and necklaces can get caught. You can avoid that situation by keeping your shirt tucked in and leaving your necklace at home. That's a good idea in any case — for safety's sake, jewelry for riding really should be limited to small stud earrings. But if you wear your shirt or T-shirt loose and floating, you may want to jump down instead of sliding down. It can be very awkward to start sliding down your horse's side and then realize, too late, that while you are on your way to the ground, the front of your shirt (and perhaps even your bra!) seems to be attached to the saddle horn.

Apart from those considerations, whether you slide down or jump down depends on the height of your horse, the length of your arms, the condition of your feet, ankles, knees, and hips, and your own preferences. Either way, remember to bend your knees a little on the way down, so that you won't land stiff-legged and feel the impact all the way up your spine.

If you're young and athletic, push yourself away from the horse's neck and jump down.

For most riders, a slow, gentle slide down the horse's side is easier. Whichever your preference, be sure to have both feet out of the stirrups before you begin your descent.

Stepping down by leaving your left foot in your stirrup until your right foot is on the ground is a practice best left to tall cowboys on short horses. Riding safety involves giving some thought to "What if?" questions. Ask yourself what would happen if something startled your horse while you were dismounting. With both feet out of the stirrups and both legs together, you have a reasonably good chance of landing on your feet and perhaps pushing yourself away from the horse. With your left foot still in the stirrup (and high in the air if your horse is tall), you would be in a very precarious position. It would be hard for you to keep your balance if the horse moved, difficult for you to stop the horse, and quite possible that you could be dragged.

Swinging your leg over the horse's neck and sliding down with your back to the saddle may seem slick and sophisticated, but it's actually risky and rather silly. No matter how it's done, dismounting always puts the rider into a vulnerable position for the second or two between sitting in the saddle and standing on the ground. This form of dismounting puts the rider in a particularly vulnerable position. If the horse should jump or throw his head up suddenly, as your leg was passing over his neck, you would be likely to land on your back with your head very close to the horse's hooves.

Practice this safety exercise: When you've jumped up and are supporting all of your weight on your hands, kick your foot out of the stirrup and drop back to the ground instead of getting on. This can quite literally be a lifesaver.

Here's your dismounting checklist:

1. Bring your horse to a balanced, square halt.
2. With both reins in your left hand, put your left hand on the horse's neck just in front of the saddle and your right hand on the pommel.
3. Stand up in your stirrups.
4. Drop your right stirrup, begin putting your weight onto your hands and arms, and swing your right leg as high as you can over your horse's rump.
5. With your legs together, still supporting yourself on your hands, take your left foot out of the stirrup and slide or jump to the ground.
6. Run up your stirrups, loosen the girth, and pat your horse.

One final thought: Many riders train their horses to line up and stand quietly next to the mounting block for both mounting and dismounting. If you own or lease the horse you ride, and if you have access to a heavy, sturdy mounting block, this option might suit you very well.

Emergency Dismounts

Q   Would you please explain what emergency dismounts are and how to do them? I have a terrible fear of falling and would love to learn some way to "bail out" safely if I am in a situation where staying on the horse would be dangerous. I have heard of horses bolting into traffic or machinery or fences, and I dread something like that happening to me. I think I would feel better if I knew some way to get off the horse other than falling (I also have a terrible fear of being dragged).

A   When you first get on a horse, you spend some time learning to mount. Often, you don't learn how to *dismount* until the end of the ride and then you don't really think about it much. Many riders aren't very comfortable dismounting and they need to practice until both mounting and dismounting are easy. In Pony Club, we eventually require our riders to mount and dismount from both sides.

Until you are quite comfortable mounting and dismounting, and can do both easily, don't attempt to practice emergency dismounts. If you are stiff because you are out of shape, have physical limitations, or are tense, you will need to become fitter and more flexible before you begin practicing emergency dismounts. Improving your physical fitness is a good idea anyway, for all riders! The improved fitness, flexibility, and balance will help your riding and will make you less likely to come off, suddenly or otherwise.

When we were children, we all knew how to fall and roll — we rolled in the grass, we rolled down hills when we could find them, and we delighted in our ability to do somersaults and the like. It was easier for us to keep our balance, and we didn't worry when we *lost* our balance. But for many of us, that was a long time ago, and now that we are older and stiffer and more afraid of falling, we've forgotten how to break a fall by curling up and rolling. We stiffen and fall flat in exactly the way that you don't want to hit the ground.

Learning how to fall off a horse can be useful. For one thing, it might lessen your fear of falling off! For another, it can give you a safer option in the event that you *need* to get off suddenly, without stopping, either because you have lost your balance completely or because the horse is no longer under control and is going somewhere you do not want to go with him (into traffic, say, or into a wire fence). But the emergency dismount shouldn't be a rider's first reaction to anything slightly nervous-making — it's not the answer to every minor loss of balance or an appropriate reaction to every small leap, buck, or spook. There are times, depending on the situation and terrain, when it makes much more sense to stay with your horse.

If you determine that you do *not* want to stay with the horse, you need to know more than just how to get off in a hurry. You need to know how to come off, when to come off, and what to do after you come off: run with the horse, stop the horse, let the horse go, or roll as far away from the horse as possible. If you're a jockey in a race, you'll want to stay on until you can't stay on any longer, and then roll up in a ball and stay in one place, hoping that the horses following yours will be able to avoid you. If you're riding at slower speeds and in less dangerous circumstances, you have more choices.

Here is a common form of the emergency dismount.

1. Drop your stirrups.
2. Lean forward and look up and out, ahead of the horse.
3. Wrap your arms around the horse's neck.
4. Straighten your legs, swing your right leg over the horse's back, *look up,* and slide off.

NOTE: Some instructors advise doing this with no reins; others suggest keeping hold of the reins. I tend to prefer keeping hold of the reins, because that, plus keeping the head up, can help a rider land upright and looking forward. At that point, you can still drop the reins and let the horse go if you need to!

If you *do* opt to hold on to the reins, you'll need to add two final steps to your emergency dismount:

5. Land with your knees slightly bent.
6. Immediately run a couple of steps with the horse before you let him go or try to stop him.

To get this right, you must practice! You don't even have to involve a horse at first — you can use a barrel (brace it so it won't roll). Just be sure that you have a soft surface to land on, and don't wear your best clothes.

When you practice on a horse, start at a standstill, then at a walk, and eventually, if you can, the trot and canter. You'll have to be quite a good rider to achieve this, not because it's difficult to come off at trot and canter but because it can be very difficult to keep your horse moving at trot or canter once you initiate the dismount process. School horses are especially good at slowing to a walk or halt as soon as (in their minds) you begin to lose your balance. It's part of their job to keep you on board, and they know it.

You can practice at the walk and trot by setting up two cones in your arena, about 30 feet apart. When you pass the first cone, drop your stirrups and lean forward, putting your arms around your horse's neck. At the second cone, reach as far around his neck as possible and straighten your body, bringing your legs up. Swing your right leg over his back and slide off.

When you land feet down, head up, and facing forward, you should be able to grab your horse's rein and run along with him for a few steps, after which you can ask him to stop, if he's moving slowly enough, or you can let the rein — and the horse — go. Your fitness, comfort, and circumstances will factor into your decision, but for safety's sake, if vaulting off and rolling away from the horse isn't a realistic option for you, this is a practical way to keep your feet down and your head up and to remain next to your horse, instead of under his legs, as you dismount.

The dismount described above works even for riders who are older and stiffer. If you're more athletic, you can vault off (and this too should be practiced first on a barrel and then on a standing horse). When you vault off, drop your stirrups but don't wrap your arms around the horse's neck. Instead, drop your reins, put your hands on the horse's withers, lower your chest, bring your right leg over the horse's back, and push down strongly with your hands as you swing your body away from the horse's left side. This method requires more upper body strength and will help you land farther from the horse. It encourages tucking and rolling instead of trying to land on your feet and running with the horse.

If you don't know how to tuck and roll, don't try to learn that skill during an emergency dismount! Practice the "tuck and roll" part *without* the horse or the fall. If you take a basic gymnastics class, your instructor may have suggestions or variations of her own to suggest, and she knows you, your body, and your ability.

Some instructors worry that their students will begin to perform emergency dismounts at the slightest provocation, leaping off and perhaps endangering themselves unnecessarily each time a horse stumbles or snorts. I've found the opposite to be true: When riders know that they can come off the horse in a more controlled manner, they don't worry as much about coming off in an *uncontrolled* manner. They stay more relaxed and cope better with sudden movements and temporary losses of balance.

CHAPTER 2

Staying On:
What's Your Position?

"POSITION" IS A TERM that's often misunderstood by riders. Rider position does not refer to a fixed, stiff pose; correct rider position is constantly shifting and adjusting. The rider's body remains balanced and flexible, flowing easily from one position to another in response to the horse's movements. These are tiny adjustments, and a nonrider observing a good rider would probably notice no movement whatsoever.

Many riders have difficulty achieving a balanced position in the saddle. Others manage adequately at a standstill, but not when the horse is in motion; many exhaust themselves by gripping the saddle with knees or thighs. Riders will find it easier to keep a centered seat and an upright, relaxed upper body if their feet are supported by correctly adjusted stirrups.

Rider Leg Position

Q I have been riding seriously for about two years now. I have a wonderful trainer (certified by the British Horse Society) who has been working with me once a week on my seat. I also have been half-leasing a Thoroughbred-Trakehner mare that I ride three days a week. When my folks came to visit me and took pictures of me riding without stirrups, I was horrified to see that I have this drastic wing foot tendency when riding without stirrups! I try to keep the flat of my thigh against the saddle but I guess I'm not trying hard enough. Will riding without stirrups, and posting without stirrups, help? Is there an exercise I can use to stop this heel-jabbing habit? I'm so glad I wasn't wearing spurs!

A Don't be too frustrated — it sounds as though you're doing well for only two years of serious riding. Your "wing foot" problem is shared by many other riders, and it's fixable.

Instead of doing a lot of work without stirrups, I suggest that you put the stirrups back on the saddle for now and work *with* them. Work without stirrups is beneficial only if the rider can maintain the same position and the same contact without stirrups as with them. If working without stirrups causes you to ride with the back of your calf against the horse, then all you are doing is creating and reinforcing a bad habit. Work with stirrups (I'll suggest some exercises for you) and then go back to occasional brief work without stirrups when your leg position is more secure and will stay unchanged when you remove the stirrups.

The best single exercise to help you develop a secure, correct leg is work in a half-seat (also known as a two-point position). Begin by checking that your stirrups are at the correct length. Let your legs hang comfortably with your feet out of the stirrups. You may need someone on the ground to help you make the adjustments. The ground person can bounce the stirrup tread lightly against your leg to determine where it reaches. Correct stirrup length for dressage, flatwork, and very low jumps has the tread hitting your anklebone. For higher jumps, take the stirrups up so the tread hits your leg just above the anklebone. If you are doing flatwork only and feel that you need a slightly longer stirrup, let the tread hit you just below the anklebone, but no lower. Too-long stirrups will weaken your legs and seat instead of strengthening them and will put you into all manner of incorrect, unbalanced postures.

Once you've found the correct stirrup length, begin incorporating a lot of work in half-seat position into your regular riding. If you do most of your warm-

Your leg should be in the same position, and be just as effective, whether you're riding with stirrups or without them.

up and cool-down in a half-seat, your legs will become much more stable, and your horse will be grateful.

Leg stability and position come from *balance,* not from *grip.* Trying to hold on to the saddle by force with any part of your leg will damage your position. Your legs must be able to sink softly around your horse's barrel, with the stirrups supporting the ball of your foot so that your weight can drop unimpeded through your thigh, knee, and calf into your heel. You may need to review your position every few minutes as you ride, just to remind yourself not to grip! Don't worry, though. After a few weeks of constant reminders, you'll be on your way to building a good habit.

Here's a revolutionary thought: *Rider toes are not always going to face forward, and rider feet are not always going to be perfectly parallel to the horse's sides.* It's nice when this ideal position comes easily, but if it doesn't, don't try to force it. Each rider's conformation is a little different, and one rider's toes may point straight ahead while the toes of an equally proficient rider may point away from the horse at a 10-degree angle.

The toe position only matters insofar as it reflects the total leg position. The question is not "Are my toes pointed straight forward?" but "Do I have contact with the saddle and horse throughout my leg?" In other words, ask yourself, "Is my inner thigh resting against the saddle? Is my inner knee resting against or near the saddle? Is my inner calf resting against the horse?" If the answer in each case is "yes," then your position is right *for you,* even if your feet are not perfectly parallel to the horse's sides.

If the only problem you notice involves your feet, you will probably try to correct it by twisting your feet inward. Don't do this! You'll strain your ankles and knees in the short term, which will damage them in the long term. Instead, look at your entire leg and see whether or not you are in contact with your saddle and horse.

If you can see that your toes turn out *and* your knee is far from the saddle *and* the fronts of your inner thighs are turned away from the saddle, then you do have a leg-position problem, but it's not originating with the feet, and you shouldn't try to solve it by "fixing" your feet. If your entire leg is opening away from the horse, you need to fix the problem where it begins: in the hips. Riding well means rotating the hips so that the legs can hang easily and adhere softly to the horse's sides. Work on rotating your legs from the hips, and you'll find that your legs fall readily into position, with your knees pointing forward and your toes aligned more or less below your knees.

If you've ever taken ballet lessons, you know how to rotate your hips in one direction; now you'll need to learn to rotate them the other way. Riding position requires a rotation that's the precise *opposite* of ballet turnout — I call it "dressage turn-in."

The key to all of this is to maintain a soft, supple leg that bends easily at all joints: hips, knees, and ankles. If you remove your stirrups and try to hold your horse by gripping with the thighs, you effectively immobilize your hips — try it! This isn't good for your riding. If you try to "correct" a turned-out foot by forcing the foot inward, you effectively immobilize your ankles *and* your knees. Try it! In fact, try all of these positions, but keep bringing yourself back to the one in which your legs are relaxed and correctly aligned and all your leg joints can flex.

After a month or two of regular, conscious position adjustment and a lot of work in a half-seat, remove your stirrups and try again. I think you'll find that it's much easier than before and that your feet won't be as likely to stick out at right angles.

What Is Correct Knee Position?

Q I have mostly ridden Western, but in the past year I sold my saddle and bought an English saddle — a Wintec Endurance. It fits my horse well, is comfortable for me, and easy to clean. I am interested in competitive trail riding, endurance, and possibly jumping in the future, so I figured it was a good all-round saddle. And it's so much lighter than my Western saddle!

When I sit in the saddle, however, I have noticed that my knees are not completely touching the saddle. I would have to squeeze the saddle with my upper thigh in order for them to touch, which I don't think is the right thing to do. Are my knees supposed to be like this? There are removable/adjustable knee blocks under the saddle flap; should I maybe move these higher?

A Don't worry at all if your knees are not in contact with the saddle. Certain areas of your leg should be in contact with the saddle, but these are the inner thigh and the inner calf, not the knees. Don't focus on your knee position in isolation. Instead, ask yourself these questions:

- ▸ Are my inner thighs in contact with the saddle?
- ▸ Are my inner calves in contact with the saddle?
- ▸ Are my knees pointing forward?
- ▸ Are my toes more or less under my knees?

If you can answer yes to all these questions, your knees are just fine, even if they are never in contact with the saddle at all.

If your knees are pointing so far out to the sides that the backs of your calves, rather than the inside of your thighs and calves, are in contact with the saddle, then your knees are too far from the saddle, but that's just a symptom of the problem, not its cause. The cause is almost certainly tightness in the hips and an inability to rotate the hips in. Correcting the hips will correct the position of the thighs and calves, and the knees will then be as close to the saddle as they are going to be naturally. Leave them alone and don't try to force them closer.

For most women and many men, trying to keep the knees in contact with the saddle requires a contorted position in which the hips are locked and stiff, the seat bones are out of the saddle, and the lower legs are pushed completely away from the horse. Any one of these makes it difficult to be comfortable or effective, and the combination of all of them makes it utterly impossible for a rider to be anything but an inconvenient and uncomfortable passenger, so you can see why trying to keep the knees in contact with the saddle is a bad idea.

Trying to force your knees onto the saddle will cause all sorts of problems with your position, your balance, and your ability to give coherent aids to your horse. In the short term, this practice puts far too much strain on knees and hips; in the long term, it can also hurt your lower back. If you want your leg to lie flatter and closer to the saddle, you'll need to do exercises to loosen your hips and facilitate your hip rotation. Yoga can help a great deal, and so can Pilates.

You might also want to evaluate the fit of your riding clothes. Riding pants can make a big difference in your ability to place your leg flat against the saddle. If too-tight breeches, jeans, or riding tights are combining with a round thigh to create a sort of sausage-casing effect, you'll have tight, rounded "tubes" of leg that will curve in all directions, including toward the saddle. You can't possibly keep your knees anywhere near the saddle, or have a secure seat, if your riding pants are too tight around your thighs.

If your saddle's knee rolls are moveable, try them in different positions and at different heights until you find a place where they help you — or a place where they don't interfere. Knee rolls in jumping and all-purpose saddles are intended to give the rider some security when jumping. When the stirrups are shorter and the rider's knees come more forward onto the forward-cut saddle flaps, knee rolls can provide some support for the knees and/or serve as a position reminder. Knee rolls and thigh blocks in dressage saddles are meant, depending on their size, to (a) fill in the otherwise inevitable gap between knee and saddle, supposedly for the benefit of the judge at the competition, or (b) encourage the rider to keep the leg from creeping forward, or (c) by sheer size and bulk, prevent the rider's leg from creeping forward.

Some riders are happier without knee rolls or prefer pencil-thin ones, while the comfort and happiness of other riders seems to be in direct proportion to the size of their knee rolls and/or thigh blocks. There's no right or wrong here — it all comes down to individual rider conformation and preference.

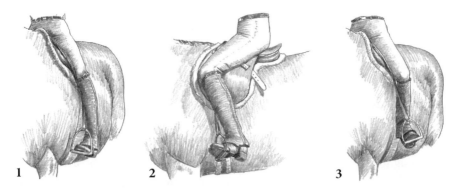

1. *The first leg, softly draped around the horse's barrel, is relaxed and can be used effectively.*
2. *The second leg is tense, gripping with the knee, and the lower leg and foot are pushed away from the horse. 3. The third leg is tight and gripping with the back of the calf — see how the inner thigh and knee and calf, not just the toe, are all turned away from the horse!*

Rider's Tight Upper Body

Q I recently took a lesson that didn't go well at all. My lower leg was wiggling, I was sitting too far forward, my shoulders were forward, and my hands were down too low and spread wide apart. Halfway through the lesson, my teacher got fed up and told me to make my hands touch and to bend my elbows. (Apparently they were straight.) I did as I was told, and my position completely fixed itself. My legs didn't move at all, my seat and legs were independent, I sat up and back, and my horse's head went down. My teacher said the difference was incredible. Although this was all good, my upper body was so tense that it became rigid and unmovable. I was wondering how I could keep this position without being so stiff and tense. I tried to relax, but then my hands went right back down, and my position went wrong again. What can I do?

A The secret is good posture and body awareness, both on and off the horse. I'm sure that you would find Centered Riding books, videotapes, and clinics very helpful. The Alexander Technique, the Feldenkrais Method, yoga, Pilates, and tai chi are all excellent resources for riders who want to improve their balance, breathing, and body awareness. Some of these may be taught locally — find out! In the meantime, here are some things you can think about and work on.

The first things to look at are your seat and legs. You won't be able to do much about your hands until your upper body is where you want it to be, and your upper body won't *stay* where you want it until you've managed to achieve a solid, steady, relaxed position with your seat and legs.

If your instructor has a longe horse, or if your horse is reliable on the longe line, ask her to give you some lessons in posture and exercises on the longe. This will let you work on your upper body while your lower body follows the horse's movement. Sit straight and tall, stretch your upper body up, and do arm circles, torso twists, neck rolls, shoulder rolls, and anything else that you or your instructor can think of.

If your instructor doesn't do longe lessons or if your horse isn't suitable or experienced, it's better not to try this. But with or without longe lessons, you can improve your posture dramatically just by doing things to help yourself at home, off the horse.

Riding with round shoulders and your head dropped forward has several effects on your riding, all of them bad. First, it pulls your seat out of your saddle, and you can't sit deep and relax onto your seat bones if you are tipping forward. Just dropping your head shifts your weight in the saddle and rocks you forward. Second, shifting your weight forward tells your horse to speed up, which is usually not what you had in mind, so you end up fighting with him, which makes you even more stiff and tight. Third, it takes away that lovely soft leg contact that goes all the way from inner thigh down to inner calf. Riding with round shoulders and a lowered head also rolls you forward onto your knees, which then become pivot points, causing your lower legs to swing. Fourth, it makes it impossible for you to sit straight, breathe deeply, and look where you're going. Does this sound familiar?

The solution sounds simple: sit up, stretch your legs down around your horse and your upper body upward, and look up. But if you're in the habit of keeping your head down and shoulders rounded, it's very likely that your back muscles have become weak from constant stretching, and your chest muscles have become tight from never stretching. Your riding will improve much more quickly if you do some exercises at home — with no weights or light weights at first, then with slightly heavier weights as your muscles develop.

Anything that strengthens your abdominals will improve your strength and your posture and your back and your riding. Do pelvic tilts and all the various crunches that work on your obliques. Lat pull-downs are wonderful for your back, shoulders, and arms, so if you have access to a machine that will let you do lat pull-downs, use it. For your arms, shoulders, and chest, you can begin resistance training with a good book or video on the subject (check the shelves at your local library) and a pair of one-pound weights. Useful exercises for riders include flys, arm raises, triceps rows, extensions, and curls.

Even 10 or 15 minutes of this every other day will very soon make an incredible difference to your riding. Be sure to always warm up first, then stretch, then do your resistance training, then stretch again, then cool down. You want to condition and build your muscles, not tear them!

You can work on your posture at home, at the office, on the horse, and every little bit of work will have a big payoff. And not just for *your* position: You'll be surprised how much a little more strength and flexibility, a slightly straighter back, and a bit of deep breathing on your part will do for your *horse's* performance.

No, I didn't forget about your hands. Don't worry about them. Focus on strengthening and suppling your abs, back, chest, shoulders, and arms and on keeping your legs long. If you keep your eyes up and your chest open, and remember to breathe deeply, you won't have low, pulling hands anymore.

Looking down tilts your head and neck forward, rounds your shoulders and back, and collapses your chest, making it impossible for you to breathe deeply.

Trying to force your heels down only stiffens your body, tightens your chest muscles, and puts your feet "on the dashboard."

Looking up and allowing your weight to drop into your heels has a very different result: You can be correct, balanced, and relaxed in the saddle.

I Lean Sideways, and My Horse Does Too

Q I have a 13-year-old Thoroughbred who raced for a while and then was used for endurance. His owners didn't have time for him, and he was ridden only sporadically for a couple of years. He was used for children's camps and as a spare horse whenever he was needed.

I have had him for two years now, and we get along great. At first I only hacked him on the weekends or when I could get the time. More recently, I've been riding four days a week and have done quite a bit of schooling in the arena. One of the other riders has been helping me, and we are doing pretty well (considering his prior training and that I haven't ridden since my long-ago Pony Club days).

Anyway, I'm taking occasional lessons now, and my teacher tells me I lean *way* too much, as if I'm riding a motorcycle. She rode my horse and said that he is very heavy and leans way over. She thinks that perhaps he has always done that, and I've just learned to lean with him. I try and try to catch myself doing it, but it is second nature to me now.

She told me that each time I ride, I should do some work without stirrups and some small circles at sitting trot, and that over time, I'll be able to catch myself and correct myself when I start leaning. Are there any other exercises that will help us? I think if we can correct this, our lives will become easier. Are there things we can do while we hack, since the nice weather is coming and we are looking forward to getting outside again?

A This is a common problem with horses and riders who haven't learned to bend and balance correctly. Don't worry, you *can* learn to stay straight and balanced on your horse, and your horse *can* learn to bend and balance around his turns instead of leaning into them like a motorcycle.

A horse that leans into turns is unbalanced. Instead of bending his body and keeping his weight over all four feet, he overbalances his body to the inside of the turn. His body weight, and yours, is then just over his inside legs, with much less weight on the outside legs. If a horse in this position puts a foot wrong or if the rider shifts her position suddenly, the horse can go down. It's not safe, it's not comfortable, and every turn puts a lot of strain on the horse's inside legs.

One thing that will help is for you to learn to evaluate your balance *off* the horse. Yoga is wonderful for this; so is tai chi. For your balance *on* the horse, try some of the Centered Riding exercises in Sally Swift's books and videotapes,

Centered Riding and *Centered Riding II*. Take a Centered Riding clinic if you can find one in your area.

On your own, practice sitting up straight and standing tall and doing "torso twists" — extend both arms out to the sides at shoulder height, look straight ahead, and swivel your entire torso to the right, then to the left, and so forth. Maintain your balance and your position while you do this: Keep the arms up and straight, and look straight ahead, so that your head is in line with your torso and the two move together. This will help your riding quite a bit.

I don't think that working on small circles is a good idea. Instead, work on large circles, perhaps by riding around the arena and making a large circle at each end. It will be easier for you to make the necessary corrections and changes on a larger circle, because the correct bend will be a more gradual, gentle one. This will be easier on you mentally and physically and *much* easier on the horse. Remember that you will be asking him to use his body in a new and different way and that he may get a little sore at first. Gradual, incremental changes will be easiest for both of you.

By improving your own position and balance, you can make a big change in your horse's position and balance. Horses have a lovely way of keeping themselves directly under our weight, whether our weight is in the right place or not. Take advantage of this when you practice your new balanced position on horseback. Think about the way your horse should be bent on a curve — his inside shoulder will be slightly behind his outside shoulder. Then think about the fact that your shoulders should always parallel your horse's shoulders, and you'll know that when you are ready to begin your circle or turn, you will want to bring your own inside shoulder back to match the position of your horse's shoulder and to match his balance. Practice the "torso twists" on

A rider who collapses over her inside hip and shoulder and leans inward on the turns, as if she's on a motorcycle, will find that her horse will lean inward too, like a motorcycle. It's easier than bending.

horseback at a standstill at first, then at a walk, until you are comfortable with the action. Then practice making turns and circles by *turning* your body instead of *leaning* to one side.

Think about drawing a circle on the ground. You want your horse to follow the track of that circle exactly, with his inside feet on the inside of the line, his outside feet on the outside, and his balance distributed equally. As you reach the end of the arena, be conscious of your balance in the saddle, and as you ask your horse to bend and turn, keep even pressure on your seat bones and stirrups and just swivel your torso slightly so that your eyes look around your circle and your inside shoulder comes back to match your horse's. If you need to, and you feel safe doing it, close your eyes for a moment and focus on where your weight is. You'll learn to notice when you are leaning in, because you'll feel much more weight on your inside seat bone and inside stirrup. This will help you learn to correct your balance by redistributing your weight.

Another helpful hint is to find something in the arena that is at eye level when you are sitting straight and balanced. Then keep your eyes at that same level when you make your turns and circles. If you notice that you are looking straight at a *lower* level whenever you circle or turn, you're leaning in!

One of the first things you will notice when you start doing this correctly is that your circles will be more consistent. When you stop leaning in and your horse stops moving in to stay under your weight, your circles will stop getting steadily smaller. Then you can practice shifting your weight slightly to the outside to make your circles larger and to the inside to make them smaller. This will show you exactly how much effect even a tiny weight shift has on the horse.

It will take a little time for you and your horse to learn how to do turns correctly, and turning correctly will feel wrong at first because the position and sensation will feel unfamiliar. Keep paying attention to your own position and to your horse's, and remember that what you are trying to do, for *both* of you, is build a new pattern of movement and a new habit. You will get there in time, so be patient with yourself and with your horse.

CHAPTER 3

At the Walk

RIDERS TEND TO MAKE one of two mistakes at the walk. They either do too little, attempting to keep their bodies motionless and thus interfering with the horse's natural movement, or they do too much, kicking and squeezing constantly with their legs and pushing with their seats. To ride the walk really well requires time, focus, thought, breathing, and the ability to sit quietly in balance.

Teach yourself to sit softly and quietly, relaxing and allowing yourself to become aware of each movement the horse makes, and of how each of the horse's movements affects your own body. It may not seem like exercise, but sitting, breathing, and allowing the horse to move your body will improve your balance, muscle tone, and neuromuscular reflexes.

How Should I Move My Arms at the Walk?

Q I have always tried to keep my hands very still, positioned just over the front of my saddle. I thought this was the right way to ride with "quiet hands." When I first started riding, there was a very advanced dressage rider at our stable, and I used to watch her ride every day. Her hands never seemed to move at all, and I have always tried to be like her.

Yesterday I had my first real dressage lesson with a new instructor, who said I could come early when she was schooling her horse so that I could watch her ride. Her hands moved all the time! So did her arms; I could see them going back and forth. When I asked her about it, she looked very surprised and said, "Oh, I'm just following the horse's movement." To me, it looked as if her arms were very busy, but I must say that her horse looked comfortable and pretty, although he moved his head up and down quite a lot.

When I got on my horse, she told me that I was hanging on the reins and should go with the horse's movement. My horse barely moves his head when he walks, so I think it would be bad for his mouth if I tried to "row a boat" with my arms the way she seemed to be doing. This instructor is well-recommended, and her horse is beautiful and seems happy, so I want to trust her, but I *know* that the rider I used to watch was a true upper-level expert, and if this instructor is one too (she is supposed to be), I don't understand why there is such a difference between the way they use their hands and arms.

Please clear this up for me! Which way is correct riding? Should I "row" with my arms and hands or keep them still? And if "rowing" is correct, how can I teach myself to do it? I have spent many years being careful to keep my elbows at my sides, and this "rowing" just seems so unnatural.

A The difference in the two riders is probably a direct reflection of the age and stage of training of their horses. The woman you admired so much, the one with the still hands, was riding an older, upper-level horse; when you watched your new instructor ride, she was schooling her young horse.

A horse moves his head and neck when he walks and canters to help himself balance. The head and neck reach forward and down, then come up and back, then reach forward and down again, as long as he is walking or cantering. Young horses and green horses make much bigger movements with their heads and necks because their balance is not yet as good as it will someday be. Older, more developed, fully trained horses work more from behind, carrying their front ends, and are much better balanced, so they can walk and canter with minimal head and neck movement.

A rider can have still hands on any horse, but "still" doesn't mean "hands that stay in the same place." It means "hands that are still in relation to the horse's mouth" — in other words, hands that follow the horse's movement. Similarly, "following the horse's movement" doesn't mean pushing the reins or "rowing a boat." It means allowing the horse's head and neck movements to take your hands forward and down, up and back, forward and down again, and so forth.

If you fix your hands in one place, which is what happens when you keep your elbows glued to your sides, then the horse cannot use his head and neck to balance himself. He will quickly learn that reaching forward and down means a painful bump in the mouth from the bit, so he will keep his head and neck as still as possible. The stillness of a balanced, upper-level horse is very different, because that horse isn't having its movement restricted.

I think that what you have been practicing, because you had no way to know that it was incorrect, is keeping your hands still in relation to the saddle, which isn't at all the same thing. By holding your hands just above the front of your saddle and not allowing your arms to move with your horse's head and neck movements, you cause two things to happen. First, you keep yourself from "following," or going with the flow of your horse's movements. Second, you prevent or discourage your horse from making those natural balancing movements, and he will typically begin to move more stiffly, with shorter strides.

As you "follow" your horse's head and neck movements at the walk, there will always be a straight line from your elbows to your horse's mouth.

"Quiet" hands aren't necessarily "still" hands, and "fixed" hands are another matter entirely. I think that when you watched your instructor, you saw quiet hands in action. If her horse moved freely, seemed happy, and showed a lot of head and neck movement, you can be sure that his rider wasn't restricting him.

If you've been riding with your elbows clamped to your sides, it can be difficult to learn to go with the horse's movement, but here are two exercises that will help you.

The first is to close your eyes from time to time as you ride so that you can feel (not see!) what your horse is doing with his head and neck. This may make it easier for you to relax and allow your horse's head and neck to move your hands and arms.

The other is a multipurpose exercise for riders (yes, plural — you are certainly not the only one!) who don't find it easy to learn a quiet, following hand. It works for both walk and canter, and it's also brilliant for riders who are having difficulty learning how to fold their upper bodies and let their arms extend to follow their horse's head and neck movement over jumps.

Start by leaning forward a little so that you can put one hand on each side of your horse's neck, at least 12 or 15 inches in front of his withers, preferably about halfway between his withers and head. Then walk, trot, and canter. You will feel your arms moving forward and back and your elbows automatically opening and closing at walk and canter. Let the sensation become familiar, and then try to recapture the same feeling when you're sitting up and no longer have your hands on your horse's neck. Whenever you lose the feeling and catch your hands becoming stiff and "fixed," just go back to your hands-on-the-sides-of-the-neck exercise and find the feeling again. In time, you'll be able to let your arms move easily as your horse moves.

> *"Quiet" hands aren't necessarily "still" hands, and "fixed" hands are another matter entirely.*

Try not to think of the movement in terms of "rowing." When you row a boat, you push the oars forward and pull them back. If you want to imagine yourself in a rowboat, you'll need to pretend that someone else is rowing the boat and that you are sitting directly behind that person, resting your hands on his arms. Your hands and arms will move, but you're not pushing or pulling or even initiating the movement — you're just relaxing and letting your hands and arms go with the flow.

Soft Hands at the Walk

Q I want to have soft hands because my Arabian mare is sensitive and has a very soft mouth. My instructor tells me to keep contact with Kira's mouth and to close my hands on the reins. I prefer to hold the reins with just my fingers so I can be softer, and because I want to ride with the reins loose most of the time so that I only have to use them if I want Kira to stop or turn. This is so that I can be very soft with her.

I know how sensitive she is because she flips her head a lot even though I am so gentle with my hands. I'm afraid that if I do what my instructor says and use a lot of contact, Kira will go crazy and rear or something. She likes to nod her head way down when she walks, so I try to stay out of her way and keep the reins loose, whatever she does. If I try to have contact when she is walking and nodding, I am sure it will hurt her mouth.

A By trying to be extra gentle with Kira, you are actually being much harder on her, and you are confusing her. Let me explain.

Soft hands are nice, but softness isn't the same thing as throwing the horse away. Softness doesn't come from opening the fingers or from letting the reins hang loose. Kira *needs* contact — she has to know where you are and what your hands and her bit are telling her. I'm going to assume that you've already checked her mouth and her bit, and that her teeth are fine, and her bit is suitable and fits well. If you haven't checked these things yet, begin there.

Softness comes from *good* contact, which means always having enough tension in the reins that you can feel the right side of her mouth with your right rein and the left side of her mouth with your left rein. You're not *pulling*, you're *following*, but you do have constant contact with your horse's mouth. You can give her a long rein when she needs a break and still keep the contact. You can shorten the reins after the break without losing the contact and without grabbing her.

If you ride her with steady contact, which can be very light and soft, she will be able to relax and she'll stop flipping her head. If the reins are loose most of the time, you have no contact with her mouth and when you pick them up to ask her to turn or stop, she gets a sudden, surprising, painful bump in the mouth. This makes her worry all the time, and she flips her head when you pick up the contact because it's an uncomfortable surprise.

"Puppy dog" hands with loose, open fingers aren't soft hands, they're sudden, unpredictable, pain-causing hands.

With a firm, steady grip on the reins, you can "talk" to your horse with tiny, gentle finger movements instead of hurtful grabs.

If your fingers are closed on your reins in a soft fist (not clenched and gripping but with the ends of your fingers just touching your palms), then you can be *soft* with your hands. You'll be able to add a little pressure by closing your fingers more tightly and you'll be able to release the pressure by moving your hands forward slightly or relaxing your fingers even more, just for a moment. But when you hold the reins loosely in your fingertips, you can't *give* with them or use them to talk to Kira or respond to her, you can only *take,* and when you do, it's sudden and unpleasant for her.

Try riding her with your reins shorter and your fingers closed, and let her move your arms at the walk. Don't push the reins back and forth, just relax, let your upper arms hang straight down from the shoulders, and allow your elbows to open and close as the reins follow Kira's head and neck movements. Your instructor can help you with this.

I think that you and Kira will both be happier (and I know your instructor will be happier!) once you've learned to ride her on contact with a following hand. Try it your instructor's way for a few weeks, and see how Kira responds. I think you'll like the results.

Young Horse Won't Walk, He Jogs

 Two months ago, I was given a 3-year-old gelding named Barney. He is big and sweet, and I think that he could be a nice horse for me someday, but we are not off to a very good start. Because he is so young, I just ride him for about twenty minutes every other day in our 4-acre pasture, which is a little bit hilly but has pretty nice footing.

My problem is that when I ride Barney, he walks for a few steps, then he wants to trot. When I make him walk, he walks for just a little bit and then he tries to trot again. This makes me nervous, and I end up holding the reins tighter and shorter, which I know is not good. I try not to fight with him, but things are getting pretty tense between us. I obviously cannot allow him to trot when I want him to walk. If he won't do what I want at the walk, how can I expect him to do what I want at the trot? So I need your help to make Barney walk. My neighbor says I ought to use a twisted bit and jerk it hard whenever he trots so he'll learn to take me seriously. I know that would be wrong, but I don't really know what my other options are here.

A You're right that you shouldn't be holding the reins tight and short, and you shouldn't be fighting with your horse. Your instincts are good: your neighbor's method will do nothing but create a very unhappy, sore horse that will quickly learn to hate the whole idea of being ridden. That's not the way to handle a horse. Ignore your neighbor's advice. If you don't feel comfortable doing that, you can smile, say "Thank you for sharing," and *then* ignore his advice.

Barney is very young; he's only about half-grown and still finding his own balance. This isn't easy for him without a rider, and with one, it's very difficult. There are many reasons for a horse trying to trot instead of walk. In this case, I think you can cross "deliberate disobedience" and "ill will" off your list. Instead, consider the possibility that Barney, like any other young horse trying to balance his constantly changing body, is simply unable to walk well in a hilly pasture while carrying a rider.

Horses that feel unbalanced will do whatever they feel will improve their balance and security. When a horse feels unbalanced, he feels endangered. The solution to feeling unbalanced at the walk is to trot. If you watch young horses move around rough terrain on their own, you'll notice they don't walk at a consistent, even pace. They walk a few steps, slow down, speed up, slow down, put their heads down, stretch their necks out, and, yes, trot whenever they feel the need to do so to restore their balance. And that's without riders! When you add a rider, a young horse is going to become unbalanced much more quickly, be much more unbalanced, and stay unbalanced much longer, unless the rider is experienced and secure enough to ride the youngster on a very long rein, allowing him to use his head and neck for balance.

At this point in Barney's training and development, it's not a question of him doing what you want at the walk, it's a matter of allowing him to learn how to carry himself *and* you at the walk and trot. That's quite a job in itself. During these early days of Barney's training, you shouldn't be very demanding about precise steering, consistent speed, or even maintaining the same gait at all times. When he loses his balance, which he is likely to do frequently, he'll trot. If you accept this and ride the trot without grabbing at the reins, you'll be able to bring him back to a walk without fuss or fear on either side. But to do this well, considering your own nervousness, you should probably look for an enclosure, either an arena or a large (70 feet wide or larger) round pen, with safe fencing and safe footing. With a barrier to turn Barney, you won't have to worry about where he will go and what he will do if he loses his balance and trots.

If you don't have a suitable enclosure, consider borrowing someone else's arena or round pen. It may seem silly to trailer a horse some miles from home just to ride him in an arena, but if doing that will allow you to relax and let Barney move forward comfortably on a long rein, do it. The two of you will build a much more successful partnership if you begin with kindness and understanding instead of nervousness and grabbing at the reins. So even if you're looking at half an hour of driving to get somewhere to ride for twenty minutes, it will be well worth the extra effort of getting there and back. (Not to mention the valuable experience you'll both gain in loading and trailering.)

Twenty minutes every other day sounds like a fine program for Barney, but you'll both be happier and more comfortable if you can bring yourself to let him have all the rein he needs to walk comfortably. If he has a longer rein, he'll be able to balance himself and walk for longer periods before losing his balance and needing to trot. Also, when he does trot, why not just let him trot? It's easier for him to maintain his balance under you if he's trotting, because at the trot, his head and neck are steady instead of constantly moving. At the trot, you can set your hands on his neck, stop worrying about following his head, stop feeling guilty about shortening your reins out of fear, and just allow yourself to relax and stay balanced in the saddle so that Barney will have a chance to stay balanced under you.

Another point to think about is that when you get nervous and shorten the reins and hold them tight, you are probably also holding your breath and gripping with your legs. This is a fairly effective way of telling a horse that you want him to trot! Barney may be doing his very best to give you what he thinks you want, and what he thinks you want may be what you're *asking* him to do, although it may not be what you would *like* him to do. If your brain is thinking "walk" but your body language and balance are saying "trot!" Barney is going to trot. So whenever you wonder why he isn't doing what you want him to do, give him the benefit of the doubt and check your own balance and signals to be sure that what you want and what you're asking for are the same.

Lengthening a Short Walk Stride

Q My mare Fancy is a 4-year-old Quarter Horse. My problem is she won't use her neck, and she takes little tiny steps. Before I got her she didn't have any training, and now she is good about saddles and bridles and riding, but she just doesn't seem to know what I want her to do. My instructor says to make her go more forward and to get after her, but when my instructor rode Fancy the same thing happened, so I don't think I'm the problem. Do you think I can ever ride Fancy in hunter shows and go on trails? Or am I crazy to think about hunter shows on a Quarter Horse? Is it just natural for a Quarter Horse to have a really short stride? I don't want to get after her with spurs and a whip.

A You're not crazy at all. Many Quarter Horses make nice show hunters, some make good field hunters, and I've never yet seen one that couldn't learn to do trails. And unless your mare has been injured, she should be able to achieve a more normal stride length.

For now, don't worry about her neck. I know what you mean about her not using it, but your *first* priority has to be getting Fancy to use her rear end and back more. If you can do that, she will automatically use her neck. The engine is in the rear and has to be engaged before anything else will work. You'll have to engage it, not just once, but every time you get on her, and every step, at least for a while.

Because Fancy wasn't ridden before you bought her, you know that she hasn't been ruined by bad riding. From the sound of it, she just hasn't learned to move freely under a rider. If she moves well on her own, and if your vet and farrier don't find anything wrong with her, there's a great deal you can do. And you can do most of it at a walk, without using a whip or spurs.

Walking her up and down slopes would build her strength, but if you don't have access to any hills, there are things you can do on flat land or even in an arena. Transitions will help her a lot. She needs to learn to reach under herself with her hind legs, use her rear end, and lift her back. When those things happen, she will naturally stretch her neck all by herself. She needs to be physically developed to the point where she *can* do what you want and she needs to understand what you want and how to do it. You can teach her all of this.

Start by doing transitions within the walk. Begin by riding her normal walk, on steady contact, with your legs stretched long and draped around her belly so that you can feel how it shifts from side to side as she walks. Once you've got that feeling, drop your heels a little farther down and add a little leg pressure with alternating legs, so that each leg in turn "pushes" her belly as it swings away from you. This is asking her to take bigger steps with her hind legs.

The engine is in the rear and has to be engaged before anything else will work.

As soon as she begins to take those bigger, longer steps, you will feel a little more weight in your hands and she'll make your arms move a little more as she takes her head farther forward and down. Go with her. After eight or ten steps like this, relax your legs and let her come back to her normal, shorter walk, keeping the contact with her mouth. Do eight strides of normal walk, then ask for another longer walk and do that for eight strides.

You can keep this up indefinitely, in the arena and on the trail. It's no-impact and low-stress and it will help build her muscles and use her neck. It will also teach her that soft steady rein contact is a guarantee; that no matter how much or how little she needs to use her head and neck for balance, you're going to keep up with her. As she gets better at the exercise, you'll feel more and more difference between her ordinary walk and her longer walk.

Once she is smooth and reliable at the walk, lengthening her stride when you put your leg on (which is one of the main points of the exercise), you'll be able to do an exercise with poles on the ground. Put a pole on the ground on either side of the arena (hexagonal or octagonal poles, so they won't roll) and just walk around and around the arena, so that she has to step over the poles whenever she comes to them. She'll want to stretch down and look at each pole, maybe even sniff it. That's fine; it's exactly what you want her to do. Just keep your legs on, encourage her to keep moving forward, and let her stretch her neck. After she has sorted out where the poles are, you can continue to walk around on contact, inviting her to stretch down. She will, which is one point of this exercise.

The other point is that it teaches her to reach forward with her front legs as well as her hind legs! Because she won't always get to the pole in position to step over it easily, you'll need to be ready to add a little leg squeeze if she shortens her stride as you approach the pole. At first, be happy if you can just keep her going at her normal walk and have her step over the pole without sucking back and taking baby steps. Once she goes over without hesitating, ask her to take longer steps. When you have the option of a long, reaching step over the pole or an extra short step before it, ask her to take the long step.

You'll eventually be able to do similar exercises at trot and canter, but for now, don't be in a hurry. Take the time you need to make your horse strong and supple; you'll have a better hunter and a better trail horse in the long run and you'll be a better rider. If Fancy is a typical Quarter Horse, she's smart and balanced and sensible and she will respond very well to good training.

My Horse Anticipates Walk-Trot Transitions

Q My horse has a nice walk when she is relaxed, but whenever she thinks I am going to ask her to trot, she gets antsy and begins trotting before I ask. The first few times she did this I thought it was cute and told everyone that she could read my mind. Now I think it's annoying, and I want her to just walk until I ask for a trot.

My instructor thinks that I am asking my horse to trot but I know I'm not. For example, if I'm coming up on the arena gate and I think "Okay, I'll ask for a trot just when we get to the gate," she starts trotting right then, before we're at the gate. What can I do to make her stop doing this and listen to me?

A I think she *is* listening to you! Even if your *mind* is thinking, "I'm going to ask my mare to trot when we get to the gate," your *body* responds by changing its balance and position so that it will be ready for the trot. These changes — a little tip forward with your upper body, a little more grip with your calves, a little tighter hold on your reins — are so small that you may not notice them, but your mare notices and she reacts.

Your nice, responsive mare pays close attention to everything you do. She's not reading your mind, she's reading your body, and when your body tells her to do something, she does it. To keep her in walk until you *want* her to trot, you'll need to be able to control what your body is doing in response to your thoughts or you'll need to be able to control your thoughts.

To control your body: At the walk, relax and feel your legs shift from side to side as her belly swings right and left. Feel your hips and seat bones move forward *with* the saddle, one at a time. Sit tall, breathe deeply, and feel the way your arms move forward and back as they follow the movements of your horse's head and neck. Now think about asking her to trot, and notice how your posture and movement change. Those changes are telling your mare to trot.

Deep breathing exercises will help you stay relaxed in the saddle. If you can keep your body relaxed and your breathing deep and regular, without tensing, gripping, and shifting forward, even incrementally, you'll be able to keep your mare at a walk until you deliberately change your posture and actions to ask her to trot.

Rider position at walk: upper body straight, tall, and relaxed; arms moving with the horse's head and neck movement.

Rider position at rising trot: upper body inclined slightly forward, hands steady to reflect the unchanging position of the horse's head and neck.

CHAPTER 4

At the Trot

WHEN RIDERS DISCUSS TROTTING, the four subjects that seem to cause the most frustration are the posting trot, the sitting trot, diagonals, and lengthening the horse's stride. Very often, simply gaining a fuller understanding of the correct body movements can create an "aha!" moment for a rider.

In most cases, the riders who become the most frustrated are those who are working too hard and trying to do too much. Learning to trot successfully is best accomplished by two apparently contradictory concepts: The rider must gain core strength and good control over her own body, and then the rider must learn to relax and let the horse do most of the work.

Help! Can't Master Posting Trot!

Q I own a horse but haven't had any riding experience since childhood. I have forgotten everything I learned about trotting. I know how to control my horse, and she responds really well to me, but as soon as we try to trot I get nervous and have to stop her.

I know it is my fault, as my horse is 13 years old and very gentle and patient, but when she starts to trot, I almost get bounced right out of the saddle and I just can't seem to manage a rising (posting) trot at all. I have heard and read all sorts of advice about doing the rising trot, such as gripping with your thighs and rising that way or rising and falling in rhythm with the horse's shoulder, but I still just can't quite bring it all together.

I get bored just walking around with my horse and am very keen to progress, but I feel that if I can't manage this I may as well not keep her.

A As you've discovered, rising to the trot is one of those skills that can be difficult to master initially. Keep working at it, and know that when you finally have that moment when it all comes together, you will find rising easy and you will never, ever forget how to do it.

Good lessons on a longe line would be ideal. Longe lessons let you focus exclusively on yourself, because someone else is responsible for the horse's direction and gait. But if you don't have access to a good instructor, you can master the rising trot on your own. Just be patient with yourself and take it a step at a time.

Work in an enclosure of some sort so that you can put your mare "on her honor" to go around the school while you focus on yourself. Now for some general ideas and some specific suggestions that may help you.

First, make sure your stirrups are correctly adjusted. To achieve an effective leg, you need to ride with your stirrups at the correct length. If they are too short, you will pop up and down like a jack-in-the-box because your knee cartilage won't be able to tolerate the compression. If they are too long, you won't be able to sit or rise easily or with any security, because you'll have no bend in your knee.

To adjust your stirrups: Sit in your saddle with your feet out of the stirrups and your legs hanging softly at your horse's sides. In this position, bump the stirrup gently against your foot and leg. Where does the stirrup tread contact your body? For a correct stirrup length, the tread should bounce against your anklebone. If the tread is much above your anklebone, the stirrups will be too high for you to be comfortable; if the tread is much below your anklebone, the stirrups will be too low for you to ride comfortably or effectively.

If you can't adjust your stirrups to precisely optimum length, and you have to choose between a slightly high or a slightly low stirrup position, select the slightly *higher* position. You'll have more control over your leg and your balance and you'll be able to begin stretching your legs and confirming your balance by working in a half-seat (two-point) position.

If your main interest is dressage and you want a "long leg," you'll still need to follow the above instructions. There is no way to achieve a "long leg" by adjusting the stirrups too low. Begin with your stirrups at a correct length, spend a lot of time in the saddle, do your balancing exercises, and be patient. Over time, you may find that your correct length becomes longer, so that you eventually need to drop your stirrups a little lower. The treads should *still* contact your anklebones when you hang your legs as described above, though. A "longer leg" doesn't mean a straighter leg — you will still have the same bend at the knee. The extra length comes from the loosening and stretching of your hip ligaments, which allows you to sit deeper into your saddle.

Standing up and sitting down don't come into posting and neither does "up-down." The key to successful posting is balance.

Now that your stirrups are the right length, walk your horse and notice how you are sitting: You should be upright, with your seat bones in contact with the lowest part of the saddle and your weight distributed between your seat bones and thighs. This position (full-seat or three-point position) isn't just for walking, it's also for cantering and it's the position that you will use half of the time when you are rising to the trot.

What *is* rising to the trot?

The words we use are not always accurate descriptions of what we are doing, and "rising" trot is a perfect example of this. I've heard so many riders complain that it's terribly hard to learn this skill because they have to stand, sit, stand, sit while their instructors yell "Up-down-up-down!" This doesn't work, not because you're stupid but because it's wrong. Standing up and sitting down don't come into this and neither does "up-down." The key to successful posting is *balance*.

Whenever you are on a horse, whether you are at a halt or at a canter, your balance must always be over your own feet. There's an old and true saying that riding position is not a sitting but a *standing* one. Stand on the ground or, better yet, in an arena with a soft surface (so that you can have your heels lower than the balls of your feet). Stand balanced with legs apart, knees bent, and heels low. This is your riding position. If you bend your knees a lot, you have to shift your hips back to keep your balance. If you straighten your knees, you have to keep your body upright above them to keep your balance. But the thought you need to keep in mind at *all* times is this: If your horse suddenly disappeared from underneath you, would you land on your feet, knees bent, body balanced? The answer should always be yes.

At posting trot you'll spend half of your time in a full seat, balanced over your feet with your legs, crotch, and seat bones in contact with the horse. You'll spend the other half of your time in a half-seat, with your crotch and seat bones *out* of the saddle. Rising to the trot means alternating rhythmically between full seat and half-seat (three-point and two-point).

When you can sit comfortably in a balanced full seat at a walk, practice your half-seat (two-point position) at a halt, at a walk, and at a trot until it is easy and comfortable for you. When you ride in a half-seat, your legs should be relaxed, knees bent, heels low, head up with eyes looking forward, and hands forward holding the mane or a neck strap (essential to helping you learn to keep your balance without hurting your horse's mouth).

If you feel stiff and the horse's movement jars you, you are probably standing up too high and straightening your knees. Don't. Your ankles, knees, and hips all function as shock absorbers, but they can't work if your legs are tense and rigid.

If you find yourself falling forward onto your horse's neck, two things happened: You stood on your toes, letting your heels come up, and you brought your upper body too close to your horse's neck. (Hint: You are no longer balanced over your feet.)

If you sit down suddenly and hard (*poor horse!*), it's because your legs are swinging forward. (Hint: You are no longer balanced over your feet.)

Checklist for your half-seat:

- Reins shorter, hands holding mane or strap, head up, eyes looking forward
- Knees bent, legs relaxed, weight dropping into low heels
- Shoulders slightly ahead of hips, back straight (eyes up!)

Once you've mastered the half-seat, the posting trot will be much easier to learn. An effective half-seat allows you to balance easily without gripping with your legs or pinching with your seat.

If you're a visual learner, try this: Imagine that you are riding with your underwear outside your breeches. Today's choice of underpants is a pair of bright yellow boxer shorts with red hearts on them — very eye-catching. Now, when you post, remember that *only* the part of your body inside those shorts is doing the work — hips, pelvis, and to a lesser extent the lower back and upper thigh. Your body from the waist up will be quiet; your legs from the middle of the thigh to your low heels will be quiet and steady.

There are really three components to your movement at a rising trot: up, down, and forward. Only one of these is your job. Don't worry about going up; that's the horse's job, and his movement will bump you upward. Don't worry about coming down; gravity will take care of that. All you have to do is remain balanced so that your descent is controlled and not sudden — a deep knee bend that just barely puts your seat into contact with the saddle for a brief moment.

The forward part is the only component for which you must take full responsibility, and it's not complicated. When your horse's movement bumps your body upward, move your hips and pelvis *forward*.

Now for that forward movement! Ask your horse to trot and be ready. With your head up, eyes looking ahead, and legs long and stretched so that your weight

The "up" part of posting isn't really rising; it's shifting your hips forward as the horse's movement lifts you up. And the "down" part of posting isn't really sitting; it's a deep knee bend. Let your boxer shorts do the posting!

drops through them into your heels, feel the movement as the horse bumps you up and, as you go up, push your hips forward, toward your hands.

Exaggerate the hip movement at first — try to take your hips so far forward that your crotch clears the pommel, then relax and let your body sink down so that your crotch touches down, softly and briefly, just behind the pommel. Then the horse will take you up, and you'll shift your hips forward again, and so on.

Posting is *not:*
- ▶ Pushing against stirrups with feet
- ▶ Pushing against stirrups or horse with legs
- ▶ Standing up and sitting down

Posting *is:*
- ▶ Shifting the pelvis forward when the horse bumps you up
- ▶ Touching down lightly just behind the pommel when gravity takes you down
- ▶ Shifting forward again as the horse takes you up

Your legs should stay under you, heels down, relaxed and stretched, lying against the horse's sides but never gripping. If you grip with your thighs or knees or calves, you'll exhaust yourself without improving your posting trot at all. Thinking "hips toward hands" or "belly button toward mane" or even "hip sockets forward" is useful, because all of these concepts will help you post forward instead of trying to stand up and sit down.

NOTE: For the sake of your horse's mouth and your own balance, find a way to keep your hands absolutely still. When you shorten your reins to trot, move your hands forward onto your horse's neck and take a pinch of mane with each hand. If your horse has no mane, put a stirrup leather or a piece of soft rope around his neck so that you can hold that along with your reins. If you have an SOS strap (a short strap attached to the D-rings on either side of your pommel) on your saddle, you can use that. It's important to have steady hands so that your horse can trot forward confidently without worrying about being pulled. If you hold his mane or a neck strap or neck rope, you'll be able to help yourself balance without doing it at your horse's expense.

How Do I Learn Diagonals?

Q I have been riding Western on and off for about six years and now I am beginning to take English equitation lessons. I have been doing really well, but I just can't seem to figure out which diagonal I'm on. My instructor says I have good rhythm and I stay on the same diagonal, but I don't know which one it is or when I'm on the right one.

My instructor also says that my biggest problem for just basic riding is that I look down too much. She says that I am telling my mare there is something there to look at and making her nervous. So looking to see which diagonal I'm on is not a great idea since I am trying to break that habit. Do you have any ideas that might help me out?

A Diagonals can be tricky when you're first learning to ride, especially if you're riding a horse that has a smooth trot and is equally comfortable on both diagonals. There are some things that will help, though.

Your instructor is right about looking down — when you do that, the weight of your head and neck rounds your shoulders, pulls your seat up out of the saddle, and makes you hold with your knees while your lower legs loosen up! You need to look where you are going to keep your own position and balance, and to help your horse keep hers.

But, you're thinking, how can I possibly know what diagonal I'm on if I don't look? At first, *you can't know,* so you will need someone else to look and tell you. Ask your instructor if she will spend an entire lesson, or a good section of your next four or five lessons, working on this with you. If you can begin posting and then have someone else say, "That's it" or "Change diagonals," you won't have to look down. You'll be able to know for sure that you're on the correct diagonal and then you can focus on how it feels. If you feel comfortable, close your eyes for a few strides and focus on the feel. (Tell your instructor what you're going to do so that she can alert you to anything that you would actually need to see, such as another horse coming into the arena). Closing your eyes cuts out a lot of distractions and lets you focus entirely on what you feel.

You can also practice this without your instructor. Ask a friend or fellow student to stand in the arena and tell you if you're on the correct diagonal. If the person who is willing to help doesn't know much about diagonals, you can use an old Pony Club trick: Wrap your horse's legs in different colors, say red for one diagonal and blue for the other. That makes it easy for someone on the ground to see whether you're rising with the outside foreleg.

At your lessons, ask your instructor to help you learn to *glance* down at your horse's shoulder — this is an art in itself, because to do it correctly you can't change your position or balance. This means you drop just your eyes, not your whole head. Another Pony Club trick is to put a small piece of brightly colored tape, such as masking tape or duct tape, on the lower end of your horse's outside shoulder to make it easier to drop your eyes for just a moment and check your own diagonal. If that piece of tape goes *forward* as you are rising, good for you. If not, sit an extra beat and then come up so that you can post the outside diagonal, or as we say in Pony Club, "Rise and fall with the leg on the wall."

Do a lot of trotting on turns and circles. If you have a patient horse, circle and practice changing your posting diagonal while you are still on the circle. You should be able to tell immediately that posting on the outside diagonal (rising as the outside foreleg and inside hindleg are coming forward) lets your horse circle more easily, more smoothly, and in better balance, whereas posting on the inside diagonal (rising as the inside foreleg and outside hind are coming forward) will make the circle less smooth, and you will feel your horse lean in slightly as your weight shifts to the inside and unbalances him a little.

If your instructor can put you on the longe line to practice this, you will learn the feel even more quickly because you'll be able to focus entirely on the movement without being responsible for your horse's speed or direction. When you begin trotting and your instructor asks, "Which diagonal are you on?" you'll be able to tell from the way it feels.

An old Pony Club trick is to wrap your horse's legs in different colored leg wraps, one color for each diagonal pair.

I Can't Sit the Trot

Q My problem with sitting trot is that I cannot seem to get the "independent" seat. Occasionally, in my last few lessons, now that my horse is rounding up nicely, we've had a very definite feel that we were actually moving together at the trot, but it's only for a few strides. Most of the time, I'm still having a hard time keeping my knees down, sitting back, and "driving" with my seat bones. Most of the time my seat bones aren't even connected to the saddle! Are there any exercises I can do?

A Before I explain how to sit the trot, I need to say this: Never "drive" with your seat. Your legs should encourage the horse to go forward; your seat should *allow* the horse to go forward. "Driving", "pushing", "grinding" — no matter how you describe the forceful action of the rider's back, the effect is the same: It interferes with the horse's ability to move comfortably.

There are two secrets to sitting the trot. The first concerns the rider. Sitting the trot is an active process, not a passive one. Most problems at sitting trot are caused by the down motion — as the saddle drops away from the rider, the rider doesn't move with it but instead begins to drop down just as the saddle is moving back up toward the rider, with a resulting "whack!" to the rider's seat and the horse's back. The rider stiffens, and the next "whack!" is even harder as the horse stiffens in response and drops his back, making the trot impossible to sit.

To sit the trot, you need to be able to *chase* the saddle as it drops away from you and, just to make it more complicated, you need to chase it softly, with one seat bone at a time. If you can find a hard wooden kitchen chair and straddle it with the back of the chair in front of you, you can practice this. First, just sit as you would in a saddle and feel both seat bones in contact with the chair seat. Your seat bones are in pads of muscle, and you should be able to tighten and relax those muscles at will. You can practice alternating sides so that while sitting astride the chair, you lift one seat bone and drop the other one. It isn't easy at first, but persevere. If you find this difficult, ask yourself why — you may have trouble isolating the muscles that lift and drop your seat bones, or your hips and lower back may be tight.

Once you've learned the feeling, you'll be able to practice in the saddle. Your lower back and hips need to be strong and flexible so that you can follow the saddle with your seat bones; your upper back needs to be tall and balanced over your hips and seat (think about a stack of building blocks, all in place) so that your spine can absorb the movement of your horse's trot.

I'm sure you've seen people who round their backs while sitting the trot — they are the ones whose heads bounce up and down in exaggerated nods at each stride because the movement of the horse isn't absorbed by their backs. The "blocks" are out of alignment, and the movement all comes out at the very end of the spine: the neck and head.

If your knees won't stay down and back, that's a sign that your hips are tight and/or your building blocks are out of alignment. If you sit on your bottom instead of your seat bones, your knees will begin to rise. If you try to push your knees down, your legs will become stiff, and you will no longer have flexible hips. Your hips must be flexible so that you can bring your legs back and underneath you and let them hang naturally *from the hip.* Then you can follow the movement of the horse.

The second secret is that you cannot, and should not, sit the trot until and unless your horse is ready. He must be warmed up, relaxed, engaged, and *offer* his back to your seat. If his back is lifted and swinging, you will be able to sit easily. The second he feels uncomfortable and drops his back, the trot will become difficult, if not impossible, to sit, and you should *not* sit it!

Make your horse's topline a priority by developing the muscles that will allow him to carry you at a comfortable, swinging trot. The best exercise for this is simply to alternate sitting and posting. When your horse offers his back, sit and pay attention to subtle signals. As soon as he hesitates or begins to drop his back,

Sit the trot only when your horse is relaxing and stretching his topline and "offering" his back to your seat.

begin to rise to the trot and continue until he relaxes forward and offers his back again. Then sit for as many strides (possibly three or four) as his back remains *up*, beginning to post just as soon as he becomes even slightly uncomfortable. If you pay very close attention, you will learn to recognize a tiny hesitation in your horse's stride just before he becomes uncomfortable. Begin posting at that moment, before your horse shows any overt sign of discomfort. If you work with him in this way, you won't give him any reason to become tense and stiff, and you will help him to become stronger. Eventually those few strides of sitting trot will become 8 or 12 or 20 strides! Take your time, be aware of what is going on underneath you, and *never* sit to the trot until your horse offers his back.

Please Provide Sitting Trot Image

Q I've been riding for a number of years. About 10 years ago I was intro- duced to Centered Riding. I feel my riding improved greatly from that point, since I use imagery to learn any sport I play, and it makes great sense to me. I have a wonderful new instructor, and we get along great. I have slightly stumped her, and I haven't figured it out myself yet, so on to my question: Do you have a good image for the sitting trot? I feel I understand the movement of the horse, yet I can't seem to link an image to the movement. I can sit the trot, but I feel I could do it better if I could have an image in my mind.

A The best image I know for the sitting trot may or may not work for you, but here it is: think about doing the hula. Really. No joke.

A lot of movement needs to take place in *your* body to absorb and reflect the movement of the horse's body. At the trot, his hips lift and drop, his hind legs drive forward, and his back lifts and drops, and your body needs to accommodate all of that movement.

Your hips need to move quite a lot — not just up and down but also for- ward and back, almost as though you were sitting in (and pushing) a swing. Your abdominal area must be relaxed and able to follow the horse's back *down*. If you have an image of yourself "bouncing the horse" as you would bounce a basketball with your hand, that's a close approximation.

You can't do this with a tight, tense abdomen and you can't do it by pushing hard with a tense back, although many riders try. This brings us back to the hula image.

Think of a line of dancers doing the hula. They're not thin and they're not "sucking in" their bellies, in fact their tummies tend to pooch out a little at times, but they're obviously using lots of muscles everywhere from their lower rib to their knees, which, oddly enough, is also the area we speak of as the "seat." Think about the coordination, the rhythm, and the free, flexible movement. Think *hula,* have fun, and let all your body parts work together while you're dancing with your horse.

First Lengthenings at Trot and Canter

Q I have a question about getting those first lengthenings in dressage. My mare is working very well at Training Level, and we have been getting scores in the 60s pretty consistently. I would like to move her up but I am worried about getting lengthenings. I can get them pretty easily at walk, but trot and canter are confusing to her. We end up going faster and faster until she canters (if she's trotting) or I pull her up (if she's cantering). Please help us. I don't want to stay at the same level forever like so many of the riders I see at shows!

A Lengthenings won't be difficult for your mare once she understands what you want her to do. Right now, it sounds as though she isn't certain what you're asking for and so she offers what comes most easily: an increase in speed.

I think it's easier to begin with the canter, asking for a lengthened stride on the long side. Come around the short side in a good, round, balanced canter and then come down the long side maintaining the *same tempo* while asking for more stride with brief, pulsing leg pressures. Keep a light contact with her mouth, letting her lengthen the reins by an inch or two during the time you're asking her to lengthen her stride. But be careful to keep your balance unchanged and your head up as you ask for the lengthening, and let *her* lengthen the rein along with her stride.

If you try to take the initiative and throw the rein at her, she will lose her rhythm and probably increase the tempo to "catch" herself. Also, if you look down at the reins or at her neck while you are allowing the reins to lengthen, your balance will shift forward and instead of a lengthened stride, you'll just get a horse on the forehand.

Once your mare understands lengthening at the canter, the trot lengthenings will come more easily to both of you. The key to a good trot lengthening is to have the horse well balanced before the lengthening. Begin with a 10-meter circle in one corner of the arena. To achieve a rhythmic, relaxed 10-meter circle, your mare has to demonstrate the same balance she'll need to perform a trot lengthening.

From the circle, go down the long side or across the diagonal (the latter will give you more room), keeping the same rhythm, balance, and tempo for the first few strides. Then, without changing your balance or looking down, ask with your legs and allow with your hands and seat. Notice and reward *any* tiny increase in stride length.

First lengthenings are incremental and gradual. Prepare carefully by putting your horse into a balanced, rhythmic, energetic trot.

This rider is allowing (not forcing) her horse to stretch his back and neck and increase the length of his stride.

Like so much else in riding, what matters most about creating a lengthening is the preparation! A balanced, energetic, rhythmic, round horse can lengthen his stride without losing any of those qualities; a horse lacking any of those qualities cannot. As you prepare for your lengthenings, run through a little checklist in your mind and ask only when you know that everything is a go.

What *Is* Correct Trot Lengthening?

Q I've been looking in the United States Equestrian Federation (USEF) rulebook and asking judges about what exactly is correct trot lengthening. So far I've had no luck. One judge said that it's not in the rulebook but she knows it when she sees it, which didn't help me much! Can you help?

What exactly should my horse be doing, and what will the judge be looking for? I think I understand about extensions, but I'm a long way from doing any of those! Are there some exercises that I could do with my horse to get real lengthening? My best friend is working on the same thing, so maybe there is something we can do together. We really want to get this lengthening thing down by summer if we can, but we also want to do it correctly even if it takes longer than that.

A Lengthening isn't terribly complicated, and you can certainly develop your own eye to the point where you'll be able to see it when it happens. I'm glad that you and your friend want to do it right — that's much more important than doing it as soon as possible. You should probably begin by checking the USEF rulebook again; this time, go to "Dressage" and look under "DR 104." It's true that the term "lengthening" isn't used as a header, but the descriptions of the various trots make it quite clear what's involved.

When you and your friend work together, I suggest that you take turns watching each other ride so that the watcher can say, "Yes, that's it" or "No, it's not happening." Then the rider can focus on noticing exactly how the horse feels when the watcher says, "Yes, that's it!" Working together, the two of you can teach yourselves to see and feel lengthenings.

A lengthening is somewhere between a working trot and a medium trot. To lengthen its stride, a horse must step under itself more deeply (push and reach a little more with its hind legs) and reach a little more with its forelegs. The horse should already be on the aids and should remain there during the lengthening.

The rider, having asked for the lengthening with brief, increased pressure from both legs, should *allow* the lengthening by sitting (or rising) quietly. At the same time, the rider should give the horse a little more rein. For the horse to lengthen his stride correctly at trot, keeping the same tempo and clear, one-two trot rhythm, he will have to reach slightly more forward and down with his head and neck. This isn't a plunge onto the forehand or a dive toward the arena footing; the horse is reaching forward and showing a slightly longer neck while putting his nose a little more in front of the vertical.

Whoever is watching the horse and rider should be looking for a horse that is balanced, rhythmic, and showing both definite forward movement and clear impulsion originating in the hindquarters, all of which should be visible *before* the rider asks for a lengthening. Without balance and power and engagement, the horse won't be able to lengthen.

The watcher should keep an eye out for these problems:

Without balance and power and engagement, the horse won't be able to lengthen.

If the horse loses his balance and falls on the forehand, the rider may be throwing the reins at him instead of allowing another inch or two of rein to slide through her fingers. (Rider: There's also a good chance that you looked down at your hands, at the horse's neck, or at the horse's head. Before you ask for your lengthening, find an eye-level spot on the wall or in a tree at the other end of the arena, and keep looking at it while you ask your horse to lengthen.)

If the horse speeds up instead of reaching, the rider may have forgotten to give him any rein at all.

If the horse's front legs seem to be reaching much more than his hind legs, watch carefully to see where the front feet land. The horse should reach out with each foreleg, placing the hoof on the ground at the far end of the stride. When the leg swings forward, the hoof should point at a specific spot on the ground and then land on that spot. If the watcher sees the horse's front legs swing forward, point at the ground, then drop back or "hang" for a moment, so that the front feet touch down *behind* the spot at which they were pointing, this means that the horse is losing his balance.

Correct lengthenings always come from behind. A horse that "flips" his front feet or "hovers" with his front legs at the trot is not stepping under himself and reaching out and up, but is pushing himself along with the hind legs and flinging his front legs out in front — not at all the same thing and not what you want. Watch the horse's hind leg, too. The hocks should bend, then straighten as the horse pushes off, then bend again and come forward as well as up. You'll learn to see the difference between a horse using his hind legs to step under himself (good) and one that is using his hind legs to push back against the ground and shove himself forward (bad). This may be hard to see at first, but keep watching! You'll learn to recognize the signs of a horse losing balance and tempo.

Rider, you'll have to use your "feel" from the saddle to notice whether the horse's back is lifting under your seat or dropping away from it. If the horse is using his hind legs and belly muscles well, and there is no interference from rider or tack, the hind legs will drive under and the back will lift. If the horse is using his hind legs incorrectly, and his belly muscles not at all, you'll feel his back dropping away from you as his hind legs begin to trail behind his body.

You'll also need to develop your personal sense of timing so that your internal metronome will warn you when the horse's tempo changes. A true trot lengthening will affect only the horse's length of stride so that he covers more ground in fewer strides. As long as the rhythm of the trot stays pure and the tempo remains unchanged, with the horse neither speeding up nor slowing down, you can be sure that your horse is doing his best even if the lengthenings are small.

Remember that lengthenings are *not* extensions, and that your horses are not yet developed to the point at which they could offer a true medium trot, let alone an extended trot. I make this point because it's easy for riders to get over-enthusiastic when they have seen upper-level horses make a smooth, fast transition to a medium or extended trot. Well-trained, well-conditioned, strong, athletic horses that are working at the upper levels and have had plenty of practice can make such transitions quickly.

Your horses are not able to make the transition from working trot to lengthened trot instantly, or even in two or three strides. Give them plenty of preparation and plenty of room before you ask. If you are working in an arena, you can prepare for the lengthening, then ask for it as you come across a long diagonal. It may take half of that distance for your horse to begin to lengthen. This is normal, so don't become anxious. It will take time and correct practice for your horse to develop the necessary strength to lengthen properly. Each correct lengthening, no matter how small, will help your horse become stronger and more enthusiastic. Ask often, expect little, and never forget to praise and reward!

Trot Lengthening or Medium Trot?

Q I'm finally about to move up to First Level in dressage! I've been going to shows and watching the upper-level riders, but I'm having a very hard time telling the difference between a trot lengthening and a medium trot. They look about the same to me, except the medium is with the horse in more of a frame. I know that I need to practice the lengthening, but I always like to look forward to the future, and maybe someday I'll be ready to do the medium too! So could you please tell me, first, what exactly is the difference, and second, do you have any tips for me about riding trot lengthenings? I was wondering if I could maybe practice both of them now?

A There's a logical progression to dressage training, and there's a very good reason for you to begin working on lengthenings early (First Level) and leave the medium trot until later. At this stage in your horse's physical and mental development, lengthening is quite enough work! A true medium trot requires a lot of pushing and carrying power. This will come with time and correct training (the system is progressive, remember?), but pushing and carrying require muscular development that your horse simply doesn't have at this stage. The different demands of the working, collected, medium, and extended trots will be easier for you to understand if you'll take the USEF rulebook and look up the paragraphs that specifically refer to the various forms of the trot: "DR 104."

The beauty of dressage training is that each step prepares the horse, both mentally and physically, for the next step so that the process of learning is a pleasant one, and progress comes easily and naturally. The process is simple: preparation, suggestion, and discovery. That is, you prepare your horse for each new step and when he is ready, you suggest and indicate what you want and allow him to figure it out and discover that he can do it. Then you develop the new skill, amplify it, refine it, and build on it until your horse is ready for the next step. So you're ready for a trot lengthening. This isn't complicated: You simply begin with your horse's working trot (a tempo with which you should be quite familiar by now) and, without changing the tempo or, heaven forbid, the rhythm, you *allow* (not force!) the horse to stretch a little so that his stride becomes longer. His frame will become slightly longer too.

At this fairly early point in your horse's training, making a nice, clear, balanced transition into and out of each lengthening should be your main goal.

Don't push for too much of a lengthening — keep the rhythm and tempo steady, keep your horse balanced, and try to create enough interest and energy in him that he will lengthen automatically when you increase your leg pressure slightly (and briefly) and allow your hands to move very slightly forward. Keep your own position steady as well. Your horse won't be able to lengthen if he falls on his forehand, which he will do if you ask him for a lengthening and then drop your head in an attempt to see whether he's given you one. Trot lengthenings are like touch-typing: You have to look straight ahead and feel what's happening underneath you, because if you look down, whatever was happening will stop happening.

The best advice I can give you is to keep your horse sufficiently balanced, energetic, and forward (in body and attitude) so that he feels good in himself and *wants* to lengthen his stride. When that's the case, a slight squeeze of the leg and a little more rein will be enough to tell him that he has your permission to lengthen (nice forward transition), and a closing of your fingers will be enough to tell him that it's time to come back now.

When the time comes for you to begin working on a medium trot, you'll be glad that you spent time working on correct lengthenings! Every good lengthening will help your horse become stronger and better muscled, and he will need those muscles to perform a medium trot. Lengthening involves a longer stride and a longer frame; medium trot involves much greater power from behind because in medium trot the horse does more than just lengthen frame and stride. He also has to push much harder from behind, not just to send his body forward in a longer frame and with a longer stride but also to send it *upward* in a longer frame and with a longer stride.

Next time you're watching upper-level riders, pay particular attention to the physical development of the horses that are performing medium trot and notice how their bodies differ from those of the horses that are still learning to perform lengthenings. It's a whole different phase of muscular development, and you'll notice that those horses are not only in more of a frame but that they are, overall, balanced differently, carrying more weight behind, and moving more uphill. All of this begins with correct lengthenings.

CHAPTER 5

At the Canter

CANTER IS A SENSITIVE SUBJECT for a good many riders. Fear of cantering is quite common; some riders are afraid of going too fast, while others fear the feeling of the horse being out of control. Even a single plunging canter depart is enough to put many riders off the whole idea of cantering, sometimes for years, sometimes forever. Some riders are not afraid of cantering but are frustrated by their inability to persuade their horses to pick up a canter or to canter on a specific lead. Others can get their horses to canter but want to improve the quality of the canter, and the ease and comfort with which they ride it.

Canter Phobia

Q I am deathly afraid of cantering. I've ridden for about five years; I was an adult beginner. I ride a couple of times a week, have my own horse, and love everything about riding except this one area where I'm terrified. I have cantered successfully several times, but each time something intervened. The last time I tried was more than a year ago; I was riding a horse I trusted, he had a nice forward canter, and we were fine on a 20-meter circle. It was fun and I was feeling great. Then he spooked at a baby powder container and I hit the dirt; I haven't been able to make myself canter since. I would welcome any suggestions; it's to the point that if I don't start cantering I want to sell my horse and quit riding.

A Cantering can be an intimidating prospect, and you've had some bad experiences already, so it's natural for you to be nervous and worried. Don't give up, and don't force an artificial deadline on yourself. By *my* rules, you aren't allowed to canter until you are physically and psychologically ready to canter. My beginner riders don't canter until they are balanced and secure and begging to be allowed to canter. Is it the canter itself that frightens you or the prospect of falling off?

If you're afraid of falling off, then it may help you quite a lot to practice some emergency dismounts. Ask your instructor to teach you these. You can practice at the halt and the walk, and even at the trot if the horse will cooperate. I say that because most school horses feel responsible for keeping riders in the saddle. They will often stop trotting as soon as you lose your balance, or if they *think* you are losing your balance, so it sometimes can be very difficult to persuade a school horse to allow you to perform an emergency dismount at the trot!

In any case, learning how to fall can take away a lot of the fear of falling, and learning how to bail out can take away much of the fear of loss of control. If the horse is out of control, you know exactly how to jump off and let it be out of control *without* you.

If it's the canter itself that you find frightening, you need to enlist the help of your instructor and a quiet, reliable school horse with an easy, rhythmic canter. Ask to be put on the longe line for a while and work at walk and trot until you feel totally comfortable, whether you are riding with or without stirrups.

Do exercises on the longe; not just physical movements of your arms and legs and back, but deep breathing exercises. You can even sing (it doesn't matter if you're awful), because it helps to relax you and keep you breathing regularly.

When you are ready, you can practice your first canters on the longe line. This is why you want a horse with an easy rhythmic canter, perhaps even a flat, hunt seat equitation-style canter that doesn't jar the rider at all.

Some riders worry about cantering because they associate cantering with speed. That's not necessarily the case. A good school horse's trot and canter may be exactly the same speed; they're just different ways of arranging the horse's feet.

Stand next to your instructor while she longes the horse and watch as he goes from a balanced trot to a balanced canter. Watch the saddle and see how it moves more dramatically in trot than in canter. Canter is actually easier to sit! Watch as your instructor sends the horse from trot to canter and back to trot and remember that she will be able to bring the horse back from canter to trot just as easily when you are in the saddle.

When you're mounted, the same thing applies. If the trot is balanced and rhythmic and the horse is carrying himself well, the transition to canter should be smooth, and the canter itself should be equally balanced and rhythmic.

Cantering on the longe means that the instructor is still in charge of the speed and the steering; all you have to do is relax your back and breathe. Asking for the canter shouldn't involve any change in position and it doesn't mean speeding up the trot until the horse falls into a canter, since that kind of canter *will* be fast and

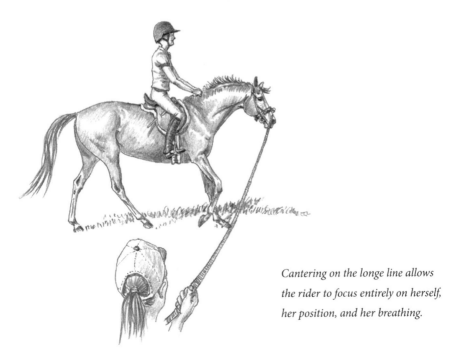

Cantering on the longe line allows the rider to focus entirely on herself, her position, and her breathing.

rough and disjointed! You can't pick up a smooth, round canter from a trot unless the trot is smooth and round.

Post to the trot until your horse is offering a rhythmic, steady, smooth trot. Then sit for one or two strides so that you can ask for the canter from a smooth sitting trot. Your instructor will be able to show you how this works as you ride on the longe line — you should *signal* to ask for the canter, not overbalance or "pump" the horse into the new gait. The transition from trot to canter is not scary, once you know how to ask for the canter from a balanced trot. The same is true of the transition from canter to trot, so practice both types of transitions on the longe. If you take a deep breath before the transition and then *exhale* during the transition, your muscles will be relaxed and it will be easier for you to follow the horse's motion.

If you're on a trained school horse, it may be easier for you to canter from the walk. This is a logical transition, and an easy one because, as with the transition from sitting trot, your position doesn't change and neither do your movements. From walk to canter, almost nothing changes: Your bottom and lower back follow the motion; the horse's head and neck move your arms back and forth.

Talk to your instructor, make a plan, and then work at each step until you are ready for the next one. You need a lot of easy transitions and short, pleasant canters so that you'll have some good experiences to draw on and then cantering won't be a phobia anymore. For the first few weeks, it may help if you recite this list to yourself, over and over, while you canter:

- ▸ Breathe deeply and *smile*
- ▸ Look up and *smile*
- ▸ Inside leg on, outside leg back, and *smile*

My Horse Won't Canter

Q I am having trouble getting my horse to take a canter. He doesn't respond consistently to my leg aids for greater impulsion or change of gait, but when he does, he reacts by raising his head, shortening his neck backward, and doing "one-tempi trot changes" so that he just takes canter departs and then trots again. This gets frustrating, and I am at a loss as to how to help him.

When we were working in an indoor arena he would take a canter occasionally, but then tear around like a maniac or drop back into trot. His trot is good, balanced, and regular. But he does not seem to have the "oomph" to start cantering or the balance to stay calm and reasonably paced at the canter. I cue him by moving my outside leg back somewhat and using the verbal cue "can-*ter!*" When he does respond, his head comes up, and he rushes into a canter or does the things I described above. I have a hard time sitting this rough and jarring mess, so eventually I end up taking him back to the trot in disgust! I have this elusive image of the two of us cantering happily across a pasture or along the rail, but I have been trying for long enough to think I need help if that is ever going to happen.

A I think that your "elusive image" is perfectly attainable, so let's try to figure out a good way to get you and your horse into that picture.

First, your horse needs to learn to move forward from your leg *consistently.* You can practice at the walk and trot, asking for, say, eight steps of his usual walk, then eight steps of lengthened stride at the walk, then eight steps of his usual walk, and so on. When he's responsive to your aids at the walk, start doing the same thing at the trot until he's balanced and responsive, and you can send him from a short, energetic trot to a long-strided trot without any change in the *tempo* (longer should *not* be faster, just longer!). When you can add leg and know that he will automatically reach forward from behind, lift his back, and stretch his neck forward, you'll be ready to start playing with canter departs and canter work.

Here's a system that works nicely. Make sure your horse is thoroughly warmed up and supple before you begin.

1. Pick up a balanced, energetic trot and make a 20-meter circle at one end of the arena, let's say at C.
2. When your circle brings you back toward M, sit the trot but keep it at the same balanced, energetic level.
3. Soften your inside hand and leg-yield into the corner between M and C.
4. Half-halt as you come out of the corner by deepening your seat, adding leg, and, as you feel your horse step up farther under himself, squeezing your hands for a second, then *releasing.*
5. Half-halt again at C, in exactly the same way, and *release.*
6. With your inside leg still at the girth, bring your outside leg back a little, half-halt again, and release as your outside leg asks for the canter. *Exaggerate the release — loosen the inside rein.*
7. When you ask, your horse should jump *up* into your soft inside hand and canter.

If you get a quick, fast trot instead, don't get upset; just regroup and begin the circle again with your balanced, energetic posting trot. Check your own position and be sure that you are *releasing* after each half-halt and that you are sitting deep into the saddle, with your back straight and tall. Your position, from sitting trot into canter, should not change. If you lean forward as you ask for the canter, you are almost guaranteed to get a trot instead, or to get a canter strikeoff followed almost instantly by a trot as your weight overbalances your horse onto his forehand and your legs and seat cease to be effective.

When you get the canter, praise your horse and let him canter on for a bit so that he knows that you did *want* the canter after all. Let him do this even if he

If your horse is unbalanced and inattentive at the trot, no amount of pushing with your body will create a balanced canter.

At a steady, balanced trot, if you sit a stride or two and put yourself into a good position to ride a balanced canter, then ask, *you're likely to get the response you want.*

offers the wrong lead at first. If you bring him back to trot immediately, he will think that he was mistaken and that you didn't really want him to canter. Take your time, wait until he's balanced and ready, check your own position and aids, and then ask. You'll get it!

Problems with Right Lead

Q I have a 9-year-old, 14.2-hand, grade Quarter Horse gelding named Junior. He is quite good, considering his owner could use some lessons. Until this spring, I've never concentrated on what lead he was on, especially since I never had lessons to know about leads and never had an arena to work with him. With the help of videotapes and your clues to look for the inside leg leading, I now see that he is always taking his left lead. This is true on a longe line as well as under saddle, so it's not completely the rider's fault (although I'm sure I contributed because I never corrected him before). I have been able to get the right lead once in six to eight tries. If he does it, I immediately tell him he's a good boy and let him come down to a walk on a loose rein. It never seems as comfortable as his left lead, which is very smooth. It's amazing how well he can countercanter to the right.

Could there be physical reasons? When he had his spring shots, I had the vet check his right hind, and he had a small reaction to the flexion test. He was also tracking wide with this leg. Since we have been working, that tendency has gone away, and he seems to be tracking correctly in both directions on the longe line. My farrier seems to think the left front is off, causing some problems in the right hind. Before he had front shoes on, I noticed Junior was wearing his left front hoof more to the outside than his right front. The farrier suggested I have the vet look at it the next time he is here.

I would like to narrow down this problem and try to separate behavior from physical. If possible before the vet comes, are there certain tests that could be done to give him a clue where to start? I hate to get him here and have no clue. If you could give me a list of possibilities, it would be great!

A It's always a good idea to talk to your vet, but it sounds as though Junior is in good shape and may simply not be in the habit of using himself equally in both directions. That's a matter of training, and as long as he seems sound and comfortable, it would be a good idea to try some training solutions to what may very well be a training problem! If retraining doesn't get you anywhere, you'll have something else to tell the vet. In the meantime, he can tell you if there's any overt physical reason why your horse would have difficulty taking his right lead.

Many horses have this problem, often because they haven't been systematically developed through exercises that stretch and strengthen both sides equally. Junior has been cantering on only his left lead for years, so he's very good at it, but he's *not* very good at cantering on his right lead. Many horses have a preferred lead and a preferred diagonal at the trot, and unless the rider is aware of the difference and determined to work on both leads and both diagonals, the horse frequently does all his cantering on one lead, and convinces his rider to post on one particular diagonal, because the rider wants to be comfortable.

It's normal for a horse's canter to be much more comfortable in one direction (usually to the left) than in the other. The horse's muscles are less flexible on his left side, and it's easier for his right side to stretch, as it must do for him to flex to the left. When you take him to the right, his less flexible left side has to stretch, which takes more effort.

The fact that he does the same thing on the longe tells you that he is used to cantering only on one lead. This doesn't mean that he can't learn to use the other lead, but he will need a lot of practice, and it won't be as comfortable at first, for him or for you. You'll have to be patient. Since you're getting your right-lead canter once in six to eight tries, you know he *can* do it, so he just needs to do it more often, and do more of it, and understand that he can do it, and that this is what you want and what you expect.

Start by doing a lot of preliminary work to the right — circles are great. Walk-trot-walk transitions are also very useful.

Whenever you work to the right, be sure that his nose is just slightly to the inside — not much, but enough for you to see his inside eyelashes and nostril. As you work on a large circle at the trot, think about keeping Junior evenly bent like a banana from nose to tail through his whole body (not just a bent neck attached to a straight body). And remember that this is *work* for him, so let him stretch his head and neck down every few minutes. You can do this at the walk and at the trot.

If he gets too strung out and onto the forehand at the trot, he won't be able to pick up his right lead at the canter and will fall into it on his preferred lead. This is where half-halts come in. As you trot, help him stay round and energetic by rebalancing him with half-halts. Once or twice on each circle (and more often if you can do it comfortably), stretch your legs down around him and add a little pressure. You should feel his response immediately: He should step up under himself and lift his back a little more. When you feel that extra energy, close your fingers tightly for a moment (don't move your hands back, just squeeze your fists), and then relax them again. That tells him to step up, rebalance, and keep moving forward in his new, rounder frame. Never close your fists until you feel that energy surge, and always relax your hands after that one-second squeeze.

As you work on a circle in either direction, remember to bring your inside shoulder *back,* so that your shoulders parallel your horse's shoulders, with the outside shoulder ahead of the inside one.

When you can keep your horse in an energetic, rhythmic (try singing while you trot!), forward trot and keep him softly bent on a circle, practice sitting a few strides, then posting, then sitting, then posting. You'll need to sit before you ask

Instead of letting him walk again immediately when you've asked for and gotten a right lead canter, praise him, pat him, and keep cantering!

for canter, but it's important to sit sometimes when you are *not* going to canter. Otherwise, Junior will anticipate a canter each time you sit for a few strides of trot. If he does this, he will canter because you *sat,* not because you asked for the canter, and he will probably strike off on his preferred left lead!

When he is comfortable with your going smoothly back and forth between posting and sitting trot, you can ask him to canter. For a right-lead canter, start with a trot circle to the right. Half-halt a couple of times on the circle to get your best possible balanced trot, then sit again, half-halt again, and this time, as you relax your hands, bring your outside leg back and ask him to strike off with that left hind leg. If you get the wrong lead, bring him back to a trot, get your best possible trot again, and calmly try again. When you get the right-lead canter, sit up, keep your legs long, rock along with the movement, and *praise your horse!*

One thing I'd like you to do a little differently is this: Instead of letting him walk again immediately when you've asked for and gotten a right-lead canter, praise him, pat him, and *keep cantering!* He may not know that you were happy to get that canter, so he needs to do enough of it to be sure he understands that a canter was indeed what you wanted. If you walk right away, he won't think he's being rewarded for cantering on the right lead. He'll think that he made a mistake and that you actually wanted him to walk, which will make it harder to get the canter next time, because if he's a clever horse, he'll probably try to go directly to walk.

Keep your own position in mind throughout: straight and tall, with your inside shoulder back. A horse that's stiff to the right, ridden by a rider who is also stiff to the right, is going to take some work and some time to fix. Most riders, like most horses, are one-sided — I'll bet that *you* find it easier to bring your left shoulder back than to bring your right shoulder back.

Smooth Canter Depart

Q Sometimes I have trouble getting a smooth transition from a trot into a canter. I'll think I have my horse collected, but when I use outside leg and rein, he'll go into a faster trot instead. I seem to have better luck going into a canter from a walk! What could I be doing wrong?

A There may be several things happening here, so let's just run through the most common possibilities. First, when you say that he feels collected but your canter aids just make him trot faster, guess what? If he's truly on the aids, your canter aids should produce a canter. If he doesn't understand that you want a canter, he should offer you a longer stride at the trot, not a faster trot.

You already know that going from trot to canter doesn't mean going faster, it just means changing to a different sequence of footfalls. Now let's figure out how to make that clear to your horse.

If your horse is trotting in balance and with impulsion (*controlled* forward movement, not *speed*), he can take the canter easily. If he is on the forehand and inverted (topline dropped instead of lifted, and hind legs not coming up underneath his body), he will find it almost impossible to reach far enough under himself to canter. He will trot faster and faster, and eventually fall into a canter, but it won't be the canter you wanted because a horse can't go into a nice balanced canter from an unbalanced trot. He *can* go into a horrible, long, strung-out, four-beat canter, but that isn't what you want.

When your horse speeds up, he's telling you either that he isn't balanced enough to go into a canter (because he isn't sufficiently balanced at the trot or because he loses his balance during the transition) or that he honestly thought that you *wanted* him to speed up.

If he isn't balanced during the trot, help him by doing a lot of transitions from walk to trot and back again, as well as transitions from shortened trot to normal trot to lengthened trot and back again. All of this will keep him attentive and more balanced, and will make the trot-canter transition easier for him.

If it's the transition itself that's the problem, it's interesting that he takes the canter more easily from the walk. That generally indicates that the rider is in a better position to ask for and get the transition when the horse is walking. This makes sense, as your walk and canter position are similar: upright, seat in the saddle, hips moving with the horse, arms following the movement of the horse's head and neck. It's very natural for a horse at the walk to move into the canter since the rider doesn't have to change anything about her position.

I'm assuming that you are doing a posting trot. The first thing you need to do, after balancing your trot, is to sit the last few strides before you ask for the canter. That's because before you ask for the canter, you have to begin to ride the canter: sit deep into your saddle, straighten your shoulders, lengthen your legs, and half-halt. Squeeze with both legs and when you feel the horse step more deeply under himself (without falling on the forehand!), squeeze your fingers and then relax your fingers again. Repeat as necessary — never prolong a half-halt, just repeat it.

*This horse is balanced, energetic, and attentive; his rider should
be able to ask for and get a forward, energetic, balanced canter.*

When you feel that your horse has become more balanced (the purpose of a half-halt, after all!), half-halt again, but this time, after you squeeze your fingers relax only the inside hand while bringing back your outside leg to ask your horse to strike off into canter. Keep your eyes up, looking ahead of you, and as your horse begins to canter, give softly with that inside rein. You aren't going to drop him on his nose or throw the rein away, but horses use their heads and necks to balance themselves at the canter, just as they do at the walk, and you must be ready to follow his movements.

Don't lean forward as you ask because that simply asks the horse to keep trotting and go more onto his forehand, and negates the effect of your half-halts. Stay perpendicular to the horse and ask him to jump into canter.

If he doesn't canter immediately, stay perpendicular to him, repeat your half-halts, regroup, and ask again. When he does it, even if he doesn't take the correct lead, praise him and let him canter for at least 10 strides. It's important for him to understand that you *wanted* a canter and that you are pleased with him. If you bring him back to a trot too quickly, he may think that he was mistaken and you didn't want a canter after all.

Once he is cantering, run down this mental checklist:

▸ Inside leg at the girth
▸ Outside leg just behind the girth to keep the hindquarters from falling to the outside
▸ Body quiet (hips and seat following, not pumping)
▸ Inside hand asking for just enough bend for you to see his inside eyelashes, not his whole eye or his forehead
▸ Inside shoulder back so that his shoulders and yours are parallel
▸ Contact, rhythm, and balance appropriate to the gait and to the figure (straight line? circle?) on which you are working him

Rider's Leg Swinging at Canter

Q I can manage to sit quietly at the canter whenever my instructor makes me drop both stirrups, but when I use my stirrups my legs begin to swing, and my outside leg in particular moves constantly. She can't figure out why I do this, and I don't know how to make it stop. How can I quiet my legs, especially my outside leg, at the canter?

A   Many riders have a tendency to collapse over their inside hip and put more weight into the inside seat bone and leg when they canter, particularly on a curve or circle. This unbalances their weight, and the outside seat bone becomes very light in the saddle, sometimes coming off the saddle entirely, which causes the outside leg to swing.

The fact that you lose your swinging outside leg when you drop your stirrups tells me that when you canter *with* stirrups, you are almost certainly putting far too much weight in your inside stirrup and probably dropping your inside shoulder as well! When you work *without* stirrups, your instinctive balance takes over at the canter and you sit up straight and stretch your legs down evenly in self-defense. This isn't a physical problem; it's just a matter of habit, inattention, and balance.

My advice is to begin by checking your tack to see that your stirrup leathers are the same length and that your saddle tree isn't twisted in any way. Occasionally someone will have this sort of cantering problem in one direction only, generally because of uneven stirrup leathers (don't just count the holes, by the way; take them off the saddle and compare lengths!) or because a twisted saddle tree is causing them to ride with one leg ahead of the other. This is comparatively rare, and your tack is probably fine, but it won't hurt to have a look and be certain.

Next, check your stirrup leathers again, this time to be certain that they are adjusted to a suitable length. If you sit in the saddle and allow your legs to hang down naturally out of the stirrups, the stirrup treads should hit you, as nearly as possible, on your anklebones. If you try to ride with too-long leathers, you will have a terrible time balancing at canter because this tends to put your weight onto your crotch rather than your seat bones and deprives you of the shock-absorbing effects of flexed ankles and knees. If you try to ride with too-short leathers, your body will want to straighten and you will pop up like a jack-in-the-box!

Finally, ask your instructor to put you on a longe line so that you have no concerns about directing or guiding the horse and can focus entirely on your own position. Then (after a suitable warm-up) begin canter work.

Practice sitting very tall and straight, with your legs underneath you and the stirrups resting under the balls of your feet. Heavy pressure in the stirrups will cause you to collapse over your inside hip, so just use the stirrups to help keep your toes up while your weight flows down into your heels. Canter without stirrups and focus on your sensations from the seat bones *up*, then pick up your stirrups and try to recapture the same sensations in your seat and upper body.

Use your head not just for thinking but also for balance. Looking in the direction of movement is a useful habit, but *dropping* your head in the direction of movement causes problems for both you and your horse! When you are cantering a circle on the left rein, look ahead perhaps a quarter of the way around your circle, but look straight ahead, not *down* and ahead. If your head tips to the inside, your spine won't be straight and your upper body will tend to collapse over your inside hip, putting you into a position that will tend to create a loose, swinging outside leg.

If your horse is quiet and has a soft canter, so that you can do these exercises with your arms held out to the sides at shoulder height, so much the better. It's wonderful for keeping you balanced. If your horse isn't that reliable, or you can't arrange to be longed, you can still do this work on your own, although it may take a bit longer. Try to find someone to help you from the ground who can tell you if your shoulders are even or if you're leaning in.

Working on your posture and balance off the horse will carry over to your riding. And you can help yourself by doing some exercises to improve your hip flexibility. Some riders, like some horses, are extremely one-sided and have terrible difficulty doing things equally in both directions.

Be patient with yourself: Changing a habit takes time and effort because the only way to do it is to build an entirely new habit! So, practice correctly and as often as possible, and don't allow yourself to be sloppy when you canter, and it will come right.

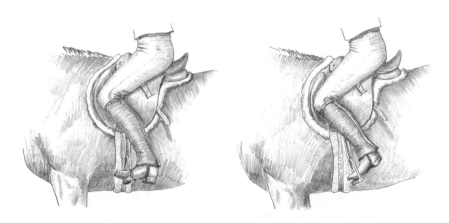

To take your leg back correctly, move the whole leg back from the hip (left). If you swing it back from the knee, your heel will come up and you may lose your stirrup (right).

Better Canter for Rider and Horse

Q My horse is a 9-year-old Azteca (Andalusian and Quarter Horse cross), very sweet and willing and pretty well balanced. I rode him Western Pleasure for three years, then he was off for a year because of a tendon injury, and I ended up taking hunt-seat lessons on a friend's horse for a year. It was a good year, but now that Chico is sound again, I don't want to do any more Western Pleasure. I didn't think it was a good idea to jump a horse with a tendon problem, so I've started taking dressage lessons. I'm having a good time and Chico likes it too.

Our canter problems are probably my fault. When I rode Western Pleasure I had to stay totally stiff and so did the horse, and then when I rode hunt seat I always got up in a two-point position to canter, so I don't know how to sit a canter because I've never had to. Chico is not a lazy horse, but the change to dressage is probably pretty hard on him, and I'd like to make it easier.

When I ask him to canter and I stay in my saddle, he either doesn't want to pick up the canter, or he picks it up and then right away goes back to a trot. He does this even when I lean forward and give him plenty of rein. I should probably use my legs more but I don't want to push him too hard or make him go too fast because of his tendon. I know it's my fault because sometimes he does pick up the canter, and then I get scared and tense because it feels like his back is coming up much more than it used to. I start to grip with my legs and hands, and then he trots. What can I do to ride better and make Chico's canter better?

A If Chico has been cleared by the vet for canter work, I think you can safely ask him for a little more energy. This isn't the same thing as asking him to go faster. What you want from Chico, both going into the canter and during the canter, is *impulsion,* not speed. You want him to be moving with enough energy and bounce to give you the feeling that instead of making him canter or asking him to canter, all you have to do is *allow* him to canter.

During his Western Pleasure years, Chico probably learned to do a flat, four-beat gait that was called a "lope" but had nothing to do with an actual lope or canter. It sounds as though he's trying to offer you a real canter now, which is probably why you're getting scared and why it feels as though his back is "coming up so much more than it used to." (Good description, by the way!) This is a good sign. If he's built like most Aztecas, he'll probably turn out to be a very nice mover, and from your description, I'd say he's already on his way to better movement. It's getting more comfortable for him to use his belly, lift his back, and move correctly, which is great, but now you have to learn how to sit quietly and allow him to do those things.

I think your problems have come from the way you've been asking for and riding the canter. It sounds as though you are unbalancing your horse on the transition, then becoming nervous whenever he *does* manage to pick up the canter, at which point you sit up, clamp your legs, and haul on the reins. If you become nervous and grip with your legs, your seat pops right out of the saddle, and if you're holding the reins hard, even though what you're really saying is "I'm scared and I don't know how to sit this canter," what Chico hears, through your legs and reins, is "Trot, please, I don't want you to canter!"

When you give your canter aids from the walk, don't change your body position at all.

Here are some things you can do. Leave your seat *in* the saddle when you ask for the canter. When you ride the canter, don't get up, don't go anywhere, just *sit.* Practice sitting in the saddle at a walk. When you know you're in a balanced position, sit quietly and just breathe. Feel how your hips move up and down and back and forth, and how your seat bones lift and drop, one at a time, as Chico's hind legs take turns moving forward. Let your hips and pelvis do all the moving; your seat should stay softly in the saddle and your back should remain straight. When you find that you're doing this easily and automatically at the walk, you'll be ready to try it at the canter.

You'll find it easiest to ride the canter if you ask your horse to canter from the walk, since you're working to improve your own position and movement. If you do walk-canter transitions and you're riding the walk correctly, you'll find that your position in canter will be the same and the movements of your hips and pelvis will change hardly at all.

If Chico is offering you a nice, forward, energetic walk, he should have the necessary impulsion for a good canter transition and a nice canter. If he is offering a flat, short-strided walk, don't bother with the canter until you've worked on his walk for a while. He needs to get into the habit of "using himself" at the walk — in other words, putting some movement and energy into it.

Be sure that your aids are very clear, so that he knows which lead you want. If you're out in a big field, you can concentrate just on getting the transition from walk to canter on either lead. That's probably the best way to begin, because when you're teaching a horse to offer an energetic transition up into the canter, you don't want to be bringing him back to a trot right away for any reason, so it's better to put yourself into a situation where you don't need to worry about whether he's on a particular lead.

When you give your canter aids from the walk, don't change your body position at all. Shifting your outside leg back to ask for the canter is all you'll need to do, because if he's walking well, your hips and arms will already be moving with him correctly. The action you've described — leaning forward and giving him rein — actually interferes with his canter transition. He needs to be balanced to step *up* into the canter, and how can he stay balanced under you if you suddenly lean forward, throwing away the contact and dumping your weight (and his) on his forehand? Try to sit very softly and quietly, so that Chico can keep his balance and make the good transition you want.

As he takes that first canter stride, feel your hips and pelvis moving, just as you did when he was walking. As long as you can keep your rear end in the saddle and your hips moving with your horse, you'll know you're not interfering with him or confusing him, and you should find the canter quite easy to sit. But be sure you can feel your hips and pelvis moving — if they aren't, something is wrong. Hint: If you grip with your legs or tighten your buttocks or lift your seat out of the saddle, your hips and pelvis will stop moving, the canter will feel very rough and bumpy, and you will feel as if you're slapping into the saddle.

Since you have someone to give you lessons, is there any chance you could take a couple of longe lessons on one of the instructor's horses? It would be very good for you to learn to sit the canter without worrying about steering or speed or your horse's tendon. Even just a couple of longeing sessions would help you by letting you focus on yourself and not your horse. You would have a chance to get the feel of transitions and of sitting in the saddle quietly (but not stiffly) during the canter. If you can possibly set up a couple of lessons on the longe line with a good instructor, you won't be sorry.

CHAPTER 6

About Jumping

RIDERS ARE USUALLY EXCITED and pleased when they begin learning to jump. Younger riders generally want to know how soon they can jump and then how high they can jump. Older riders worry more about whether they are doing it right, whether they are getting in their horses' way, and just how much strength they need to get around a course of stadium or cross-country jumps.

No jumping clinic goes by without several riders asking for help with their various releases. Others are concerned with their ability to get their horse to the ideal takeoff point by "finding a distance" or "seeing a spot." Riders also worry about their own bodies and about what they should be doing before, during, and after each jump.

Explain Crest Releases, Please

Q I've been riding hunt seat for about a year, but I can't get the whole "crest release" idea clear in my head. Can you explain exactly what a crest release is, what it's for, and the difference between short and long and automatic releases? I think I could jump a lot better if I could make sense of these ideas. I don't see the point of putting my hands up in the air above the horse's neck. Does this really help him jump better?

A The idea of a crest release is simple: Going over a jump, the rider's hands are pressed into the crest of the horse's neck. This provides the rider with upper body support and allows the horse enough rein to reach with his head and neck as he needs to do when he jumps. Because the crest release supports and stabilizes the rider, it also helps protect the horse against being caught by the bit on landing, as can happen if the rider straightens up too soon.

The first release you're likely to learn is the "long release," which involves pushing your hands halfway up the horse's neck. As you become more advanced, you'll progress to the "short release," which involves placing your hands just a short distance up the horse's neck, between the withers and the crest. An "automatic release" is for *really* good riders, who are secure and balanced in their saddles and can fold down and sit up without disturbing their horses' balance or pulling on their horses' mouths. An automatic release doesn't involve the crest at all but means that the rider's hands follow the horse's mouth, maintaining light contact through the entire jumping process.

If your hands barely touch his neck, or float above his neck, then that's not a crest release; it's an annoying, pointless, show-ring affectation. Real hunt seat riders progress from the long release to the short release to the automatic release, which is the only truly effective release if you're riding over a complex course at speed.

Long crest release: This rider's hands are on, and pressing into, the horse's neck.

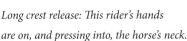

Short crest release: This more advanced rider is pressing her hands just a few inches in front of her horse's withers.

Automatic release: This rider needs no support from the horse's neck; her independent seat allows her to maintain soft contact with his mouth over the jump.

I Can't "See My Distance"

Q I am in my second year of eventing after four years at a hunter barn. I have just moved up to Training Level. My trainer is happy with me and my horse, but I am concerned about something. I've always had a problem "seeing my spot" to a jump, which really worries me on cross-country. I would like to go Prelim some day, but I'm already worried about the cross-country jumps at Training, because they are bigger and more dangerous to hit if we come into them wrong. My instructor keeps saying that I'll learn to see my spot, but it still hasn't happened. A related concern is what I should do when I really misjudge a fence and my horse takes off before I am "with" him! What can I do to keep us both safe?

A This is a very common problem, and there are several ways to approach it. One is to explain to your instructor just how much this worries you and ask for some exercises that will help you learn to see your spot.

It may help if you realize that "seeing a spot" or "seeing a stride" is not a matter of *seeing* anything but more a matter of knowing your horse's stride and feeling it's rhythm. If you can develop an ability to feel when you need to push on a little and when you need to hold back a little, you'll be well on your way.

Not everyone goes around the cross-country course "seeing a spot" at every jump, but everyone who wants to take the trouble can do something that's just as useful. You can canter with a good rhythm between jumps and bring your horse into each jump straight, with good impulsion and balance, going energetically *forward* at a round, bouncy canter. This will help your horse jump each obstacle well, even if he doesn't come in on the perfect stride. He'll be able to make any necessary adjustments and take you both over the fence safely.

If the worst happens and you feel your horse take off when you are not "with him," stay over his back, stretch your legs down with your heels low, move your arms forward to slip him the reins, and *look up*. If it's physically possible, your horse will get both of you over the obstacle once you've freed him to make the effort. If you try to make corrections and changes during or after takeoff, you might injure yourself or your horse.

Losing Stirrups over Jumps

Q My 16-hand Arabian gelding loves to jump. He's very careful, but his jump is so powerful, and he has such a round bascule, that I often get popped out of the saddle! If we get to a perfect takeoff spot it's not so bad, but when approaching a single fence from several strides away, we often end up taking off too far away and then he makes a huge effort to clear the fence. He doesn't rush, and he always manages to avoid knocking the fence down, but my feet lift right out of the stirrups and I have to slip the reins to avoid bumping his mouth. Then, of course, everything falls apart, and I have to pull up and try again.

When we go trail riding he insists on jumping the ditches instead of walking through them! It's amazing to see him clear these, but again, I get shaken loose! He has a round barrel, and I don't have the nice long legs I wish I had, so maybe that contributes to my troubles. The highest I've jumped is 2'6", but he's free-jumped 4'6" with ease. He even jumped the arena fence once and then came running back to get a treat! Please help; he's so wonderful and the love of my life, and I feel terrible when I don't give him a good ride.

A It sounds to me as though you need to do some grid work with your horse so that you can practice your jumping position without worrying about takeoff spots. It's not easy to jump a horse with a big bascule, and because of that you'll need to do a lot of work on your seat and stability.

I suspect you aren't ready for the size and "bounce" of your horse's jumping effort, and when he takes off, you find yourself grabbing the saddle with your knees. This is a guaranteed way to lose your stirrups — your gripping knees become pivot points, your lower legs lift and swing, and your feet, as you so accurately put it, "lift right out of the stirrups." As a result, you become top-heavy and unstable just when you should be sinking down around your horse with your seat barely out of the saddle and your bottom sliding back toward the cantle.

If you let your horse lift you out of the saddle as he takes off, while you keep your balance over your legs and allow your weight to settle into your heels, you won't get jumped out of the saddle or lose your stirrups. But to achieve this balance, you'll need to spend a lot of time in two-point on the flat and a lot of time jumping down small grids, with your legs relaxed and your weight in your heels.

First, be sure that your stirrups are at a good length for jumping. When you sit in the saddle with your feet dangling out of the stirrups, the treads should be level with, or a fraction of an inch above, your anklebones.

Second, spend as much time as you can in two-point — during your warm-up, at walk and trot, at canter. There's nothing quite as effective for strengthening your leg and stabilizing your position.

Third, set two small cross rails 10 to 12 feet apart (narrow it to 9 feet if your horse has any trouble bouncing through). Trot to the first one: Your horse will jump in, then jump out. Add more cross rails, one at a time, until you have five or six of them in a row, set at a comfortable distance for your horse to bounce through. Then put your horse on his honor and ride through them, just focusing on yourself. Keep your eyes up, your back straight, and your body balanced over your legs, and keep your legs long and soft and relaxed so that your weight drops a bit more into your heels with each successive jump. When you have a habit of gripping with the knees, the only way to change it is to learn to jump while *relaxing* the knees and then do it again and again until you've built a new, stronger habit of jumping correctly.

One more thing — on the road, make him walk into and out of the ditches unless you *ask* him to jump. It's nice that he is an eager jumper, but it's not safe to have him making that decision on his own. Get him into the habit of listening to you

On the way to the jump: Leaning forward and gripping with the knees causes the lower legs to swing back and the heels to come up.

This rider's balanced body and low heels will help her stay in control of her horse before, during, and after the jump.

now, so when the day comes that he wants to jump the ditch and you really don't want him to because you see something dangerous (a car coming? broken glass where he's going to land?), he'll listen. Someday, this could save both your lives.

Don't worry about giving him a good ride; he seems to be enjoying your time together. Practice, work on your leg flexibility and relaxation, and don't cut flatwork in favor of work over jumps. When you do begin jumping, don't be in a hurry to raise the jumps; first perfect your skills over the small ones. There will be plenty of bigger jumps later on, when you're ready to enjoy them together.

Learning to "Fold" over Jumps

Q I love jumping and I want to get good at it, but I'm having terrible trouble with something that is very basic. In fact, it is so basic that my instructor can't explain it to me; all she can do is demonstrate, over and over again. I've seen her "fold" over a jump at least 200 times, but it isn't helping me figure out how to do it. She tells me to close my hip angle, and I think I'm doing this, but when I see a photo of myself jumping, my bottom is up in the air over the saddle and my upper body is halfway up my horse's neck. I've tried closing my hip angle a little and a lot and everywhere in between, but I just can't get it right.

A You've actually already figured out what's wrong and you are very close to figuring out what to do about it. The key word is "fold." The trouble with the expression "close the hip angle" is that it makes perfect sense on the flat, where your rear end remains in or just above the saddle and your torso is straight or slightly inclined depending on your hip angle. Over jumps, however, you need to do more than just close your hip angle or you'll end up in exactly the position you're seeing in your photos.

You can practice folding over jumps without even being on a horse. Assume your basic riding position: Stand on the ground, with your feet apart (approximately the width of a horse), bend your knees, and keep your balance over your feet. You shouldn't have any trouble staying balanced in this position.

Now close your hip angle until you begin to lose your balance. This is what happens over jumps! If *all* you do is close your hip angle, your torso will tip forward and you will fall on your nose, unless you compensate by (on the ground) throwing your arms out to catch yourself or (in the saddle) by opening your knee angle, which lifts your bottom away from your saddle and into the air, and pushing your arms against your horse's neck to keep from falling over his shoulder.

This rider is standing in her stirrups, interfering with her horse's ability to jump.

This rider is folding correctly, enabling her horse to jump much more easily.

The secret to folding over jumps is that you don't *just* close your hip angle. As your upper body inclines forward, your bottom shifts *back,* toward the cantle. This lets you fold and remain balanced over your feet.

When I teach eventing clinics and jumping clinics, I would say that most jumping problems I see are caused by riders getting ahead of their horses and unbalancing them. In almost every case, the cause is the same: Instead of folding, the riders close their hip angles, lean forward, and climb their horses' necks.

The solution to this problem is both simple and easy. Stay in balance at all times so that you can be sure that if the horse disappeared from underneath you, you would still land on your feet. If you can find an old-fashioned ironing board somewhere, open and close it several times: *That* is the kind of folding you need to do over jumps!

Hunt Seat Compared to Cross-Country Position

Q You once wrote "Your eventual cross-country position will *not* be the same as the position you would assume in a hunt seat equitation class." Can you elaborate on these differences and on the hunt seat equitation position? I have recently been exposed to hunt seat equitation after moving back to the States a few months ago, and I often feel confused about the two-point position because I only learned jumping position (hips back and shoulders down). Now I am trying to keep a two-point with my shoulders up and farther back.

I have become more and more serious about beginning eventing next year and I would like to understand more about how the galloping position differs from the two-point in hunt seat. I often feel, and this may be due to my particular trainer, that in hunt seat lessons I am being taught to stay off the horse's back and interfere as little as possible, which frankly doesn't seem like the kind of riding I want to do. Is this usual in hunt seat equitation?

A That's an excellent question with a complicated answer. There are two issues here: one of definition and one of quality. First, the definition: Hunt seat equitation is strictly an American phenomenon. It has nothing to do with hunting or with riding cross-country. The name tends to confuse people from other countries because "hunt seat" or "hunter seat" sounds as though it ought to have something to do with hunting.

But the real issue is one of quality. When hunt seat riding is taught well, it establishes a rider position that is both elegant and functional. Done correctly, it's the basis for our American jumping style; it is much admired, and emulated, by jumper riders in other countries. *Good* hunt seat training can be very good, but it can also be hard to find.

The downside is that hunt seat is very often done incorrectly. It's a style that is too often taught as an end in itself and too often taught by people who are concerned only with show ring success. Instead of creating soft, elegant, balanced riders, these teachers produce stiff, perched, posed passengers who don't so much ride their horses as float above them, staying out of their way while the horses "perform" as they have been taught to do. Success in equitation classes depends partly on the appearance of the rider (clothing and body as well as position) and partly on the choice of horse! "Equitation" horses are not the sort of horses that you would choose for eventing, for instance. The ideal equitation horse is a daisy-cutter, a flat mover with as little knee action as possible and *no* bascule over a fence, because riders can maintain their pose more easily on a horse that jumps flat, without using his back.

The sort of riding rewarded by these standards can look attractive to the casual observer but isn't actually very practical. Perching and posing can be maintained only if the horse is working on smooth, flat footing and only as long as the horse's balance isn't compromised.

Eventing is another matter. A good event horse shows more knee action, is more versatile, has an active, strong back, and possesses the intelligence and agility to get himself out of trouble. With an event horse, looks matter less than performance.

In eventing, the rider must participate actively, not just stay on top of the horse. Riding up and down hills, through water, and across uneven terrain and variable surfaces makes a lot of demands on the balance of both horse and rider. An event rider who tries to "perch" with an overarched back may not last through the cross-country phase — either rider and horse will part company at some point or the rider will come through the final flags sore and exhausted (and so will the horse, having had no help from the rider). As courses become more difficult and demanding, the rider needs to become more supple and strong; eventually, most riders find that the best galloping position for cross-country involves staying close to the horse. The rider position with the body just a little behind the leg is definitely less stylish than an equitation position, but staying very slightly behind the leg is a useful security precaution.

I agree that the riding you're doing at the moment doesn't sound like the kind of riding you want to do if you're going to event. Your interests (and your safety) would probably be best served if you were working with a competent instructor who teaches eventing rather than hunt seat equitation. If there isn't a qualified professional in your area, I suggest that you go to a few events, look at the riders who seem most proficient and whose horses seem the best prepared and most comfortable, find out who trains those riders, and approach that person about lessons. A truly good lesson every two or three months will allow you to make steady progress, whereas an indifferent, poor, or inappropriate lesson every week will do nothing to help you improve.

This rider is demonstrating a good hunt seat equitation position on a flat-moving horse cantering over level ground.

This rider's position offers greater safety when galloping over uneven terrain.

Strong Legs for Cross-Country Jumping?

Q I am training with a former dressage rider who is now teaching hunt seat. We have been working on keeping my upper thighs loose and open when I ride, in order to "give my gelding's back somewhere to go." This works wonderfully on the flat, for the most part, but when I start to jump, one of two things happens: Either my thighs close around him or my open thigh doesn't stabilize me; consequently, I either fall back or fall forward.

All the books I've ever read say that a strong, tight leg keeps you on your horse during cross-country riding and jumping. How can I keep on my horse if he bobbles, yet still give his back some room to round in? I'm very confused. My instructor says that it is your lower leg and heel that keeps you on your horse, but with some of the fences I've seen, you would need a death grip (which the horse would interpret as a "GO!!!" command — not what I want for control purposes!) or a blessing from the Pope himself. What can I do?

A You need to relax and let your weight sink down through your legs into your heels when you're riding cross-country, just as you do when you're riding a stadium course. Riding cross-country does require strong legs but *not* tight, gripping ones. Riding cross-country makes demands on your leg muscles, and you need to prepare for those demands by exercising and strengthening your legs (ankles, calves, quadriceps, and hamstrings) and your back and your abdominal muscles.

Spending a portion of every ride working in your two-point position will help a lot. It's also a nice way to start the ride: Let your horse walk and trot gently on a long rein to warm up while you two-point and relax into position.

The term "grip" can be confusing. For riding purposes, leg grip is not an active, tensing-the-legs process; it's a *friction* grip, which is something else entirely. You achieve a good friction grip by sitting correctly and letting your legs stretch down the horse's sides so that all of your inner thigh and inner calf is in soft contact with your saddle and horse. Soft contact doesn't mean *squeezing!* You have to ride by balance, not by force. Consider this: During your ride, you may need to use your legs to give signals to your horse. How can you possibly give your horse a soft squeeze with your calves to signal, "Jump coming, alert!" if your legs are already squeezing him nonstop? And how long do you think you *could* keep squeezing actively? Not long enough to jump an entire course!

When you try to grip hard with your legs, two things generally happen. Most often, you will find that you are gripping mostly with your knees, turning them into pivot points and sending your lower legs flopping backward or forward, where they can't help your stability or your balance. Sometimes you will find that your entire lower body becomes rigid because you are gripping so hard. Gripping locks your ankles, your knees, and your hips, and makes you completely unable to balance over your horse and sink softly into and around your saddle. If you try to gallop or jump — particularly downhill — in either of these positions, you will undoubtedly come off.

Your lower leg and heel help to keep you on, but not because you are holding tightly with them. They keep you on because they are directly under your weight, and you are carrying as much of your weight as possible in your thighs, calves, and heels, allowing your relaxed legs to stretch down with each stride. If your body is tense and rigid, and you are perched above your pommel, no amount of lower-leg grip will keep you on your horse for very long. If, however, you can achieve a position that depends on balance and controlled relaxation, you can sink softly into your saddle and wrap your legs softly around the horse. Active grip only comes into play occasionally, for an instant, in an emergency. And the better your balance and your ability to follow the movements of your horse, the fewer emergencies you will have.

Riding cross-country does require strong legs but not tight, gripping ones. Soft contact doesn't mean squeezing! You have to ride by balance, not by force.

If you do have to hold with your leg for a moment, think of *how* you would like to hold and with which part of your leg. The upper leg? No, because that's holding the upper, round portion of the horse; gripping with that part of your leg will just push you up out of the saddle! But holding for an instant with the lower leg is another story. Your low heels and long, relaxed lower leg can wrap around the lower part of the horse, below his widest point, and gripping your horse briefly with this part of your legs will help pull your seat a little closer to the saddle. The key, always, is to be correctly balanced over your legs and not pinching with any part of the leg.

I would guess that your instructor doesn't really want you to keep your thighs loose. She is probably just (a) trying to break you of the habit of using them to grip the saddle and (b) trying to help you stay flexible in the hips. Your eventual cross-country position will *not* be the same as the position you would assume in a hunt seat equitation class. Cross-country means just that: across the country, over changing terrain and different footings. You will be more secure on the cross-country course if you are accustomed to riding in balance with the horse at all times, at all gaits, uphill and downhill as well as on the flat.

Ask your instructor to help by setting up some low grids that you can jump through without reins or stirrups. This will help you learn exactly when to rock forward with the horse and fold over his back as he jumps, and it will teach you (in self-defense!) to keep your legs long, your heels down, your back flat, and your eyes up.

You can work on this alone too, by setting up a "course" to ride — not jumps, but pairs of standards to ride between as though you were jumping. Make it interesting, with twists and turns, and then practice going through it at walk, trot, and canter, focusing on your body position throughout. Because you won't have to worry about actual jumps, you can work on your timing and go from sitting or two-point to jumping position (your bottom shifts backward and your upper body folds down as your hip angle closes, which keeps you in balance over your legs). Once you're used to this, add rails between the standards. When your instructor comes out for a lesson, she'll be able to make you an actual small course so that you can try out your new skills.

As a beginning eventer, you'll spend the first year or two jumping low courses — the jumps won't even be three feet tall, and they may be a good deal smaller, so don't worry about needing a death grip at any point. If your position is good and you're in balance with your horse, you'll be fine. This is where you have to rely on your instructor to prepare you properly and not take you to a competition until you are quite, quite ready. With any luck, you won't have to ask the Pope to become involved until you're doing three-day Prelim and your horse stumbles at a gallop. . . !

CHAPTER 7

On the Trail

TRAIL RIDING IS A FULL-TIME ACTIVITY for some riders. For others, it's a welcome break from their usual routine involving indoor and outdoor arenas. Riders who are new to trail riding are often concerned with issues such as maintaining their balance in the saddle and helping their horses maintain *their* balance, especially over uneven terrain; coping with trails at speed; and dealing with hills, which are rarely found in either indoor or outdoor arenas. Like every other sort of riding, trail riding is much more enjoyable when both riders and horses possess the necessary skills.

Trail Riding in Balance

Q My husband and I are in our 40s and fairly new riders, about two and a half years. We took lessons (Western) to get started, and I still do occasionally to improve my balance and build my confidence. I don't have a "natural" seat — I have to concentrate on sitting deep, soft eyes, relaxed legs, and so forth.

We are fortunate to own two great trail horses: Quarter Horse mares, one 23 and the other 13 years of age. They neck-rein and follow leg aids, and both are unflappable as far as cars, four-wheelers, wildlife, and such. My husband uses a Western roping saddle, and I use a Tucker endurance saddle (I like the light weight and closer feel). Both saddles are high quality, have been evaluated for fit on our horses, and seem fine.

I hope you can tell me how we should be riding over varied terrain on the trails. I suspect we'd be doing our horses a favor to change position at certain times, such as going up or down a steep incline or crossing over logs. Should we change position at all or just sit through everything? Our horses seem to go well under any circumstances, but if we could help by leaning forward, leaning backward, standing in the stirrups, or other variations to ease the burden on their backs, we'd be happy to. This really hit home to me recently when my mare essentially bounded up a long, steep incline, bless her heart; I wanted to help her out! As with motorcycles, I'm not sure the rider's instinct for "helping out," for example by leaning or putting down a foot, is always right. Or am I overthinking this whole thing?

A What a wonderful question! Your horses are lucky. Many people ride for years without ever thinking that changing the way they sit or lean could make their horses more comfortable on the trails.

There are times when it's right to sit and times when it's right to get up and off your horse's back. If your trails are fairly flat, you'll be sitting most of the time. If your trails are hilly, you will probably spend a good bit of your time in a half-seat (two-point position). Either way, it's good to know what will make life easier for your horse.

On the flat at walk and jog: You can sit, but remember that "sitting" on horseback isn't like sitting in a chair; it's much more like standing on the ground, legs apart, knees bent. Spend at least a few minutes in your half-seat position while you're warming up and repeat this at intervals during any ride. It will help you develop a good leg and improve your balance on horseback. Even when you are riding a slow, easy-to-sit jog, spend some time in a half-seat.

On the flat at trot: You could sit, but your horse would be much happier if you didn't. Posting to the trot is a useful skill. Don't worry about changing your posting diagonal every time your trail bends or twists, but *do* make it a point to change diagonals reasonably often, so that you aren't spending more time posting on one than on the other. If you always post on the same diagonal, both you and your horse will develop unevenly.

On the flat at canter: Again, you could sit, but your horse would probably be happier if you spent at least half of your canter time in a half-seat. And again, spending time in a half-seat is a wonderful way to develop your leg and balance.

As you ride, whether you are "sitting" the walk or jog or canter, rising to the trot, or staying slightly out of your saddle in a half-seat, from time to time ask yourself where you would land if your horse disappeared in a puff of smoke. If the answer is

Stay balanced and stay out of the horse's way so he can do his job.

"on my feet with my knees bent," then you're doing fine. If the answer is either "oops, on my face in the mud," or "oops, on my back in the mud," then you need to spend more time in a balanced half-seat to learn to stay *over,* not in front of or behind, your feet.

Up and down hills: The horse is a rear-engined animal that uses his head and neck to help himself balance. If you keep this in mind, you won't make many mistakes on hills. Give your horse his head, as much as you possibly can, so that he can balance himself while climbing and descending. Don't make any big movements or any significant changes to your own position *during* an ascent or descent. To free your horse's back and let his hindquarters work effectively, stay very slightly out of your saddle and balanced over your feet no matter whether you're going uphill or downhill.

Take your hills straight, unless you are following a near vertical trail that incorporates switchbacks, in which case you should stay on the trail. Coming down at an angle can cause a horse to fall. To stay balanced while coming down a slope, a horse needs to keep his hindquarters directly behind the rest of his body, not off at an angle. When you're coming down a hill and you are *most* tempted to

*By riding in your half-seat, you can make it easier for your horse to go
up and down hills. A handful of mane can help you keep your balance.*

choke up on the reins and look down, don't — instead, let the horse have a little
more rein, and keep looking up. It will help both of you stay balanced.

Going uphill, don't hesitate to get into a half-seat, give your horse a long rein,
and let him do the work. Sitting and kicking just make the horse's job harder.
Horses can canter up hills more easily than they can walk or trot, so keep that in
mind. If your horse offers a canter up a steep hill, don't panic and assume that
he's running away — he may just not have the strength required to trot uphill. If
you have difficulty keeping your balance, grab a handful of mane, which is also a
good way to ensure that your arms move with your horse's head and neck.

Over obstacles: The way you sit will tell your horse whether you expect to
walk over a log or a ditch or a trickle of water, or jump over it, so make up
your mind before you reach it. Horses can walk over surprisingly large and wide
items. If you feel the horse gathering himself for a jump, grab a double handful
of mane, about halfway up the horse's neck, and use the same balanced-over-the-
feet, weight-in-the-heels, crotch-barely-off-the-saddle position that you would
use going up or downhill. Hold the mane tightly, *look up,* and leave the reins loose
enough so that the horse can make the jumping effort without getting hurt by the
bit or by you slamming into his back as he lands.

Most savvy trail horses will walk over anything they can and save the jumping for occasions that actually require it. They will also typically walk *around* obstacles when it makes sense to do so, but be sure that your horse is going where you ask him to go, since you may know something that he doesn't know about the obstacle.

It sounds as though your instincts are already telling you what you need to know: Stay balanced and stay out of the horse's way so he can do his job.

By the way, don't worry about not being a "natural." The best riders I know are not the naturally talented ones but the ones to whom everything came hard. Riders who have to work for every tiny skill may take longer to get to the same place as naturally gifted riders, but they learn patience and perseverance while they're getting there, and once they learn a skill, they *own* it.

Galloping on Trail Ride

Q I have only been riding for two months, taking one lesson a week and having one practice day without a trainer. I had been working on the canter for just two rides when a young girl (she is 12; I am 26) asked if I wanted to go out on the trails with her. I had ridden that particular horse in a lesson before, and I heard that she was a good trail horse, so I agreed, with the stipulation that we would not go any faster than a walk/trot. The problem was that when we got to a particular part of the trail, both the horses took off in a full-out gallop! I was totally unprepared and just did my best to hang on until the horses stopped. Tightening and releasing the reins didn't seem to help and a punishment circle seemed out of the question at those speeds. The girl was very apologetic and said that she always galloped the horses there and it didn't even occur to her that they would do it without asking. She had control of her horse, but my horse had jumped out in front and was just running like crazy.

I know it is not the horses' fault, and that it was a bad situation because of my inexperience, but now I am very nervous about riding out on the trails. How could I have anticipated that my horse was expecting a gallop? What should I do to stop a galloping horse? Do you recommend galloping on a trail ride? The girl I was with said she gallops most of the trail all the time, including crossing railroad tracks and jumping a drainage ditch. To me it seems like a severe safety hazard, even with a helmet on (which I always wear). Am I just a chicken? Will I always be so scared?

A   I think you are very brave. That experience would have frightened *any-one*. It sounds to me as though you kept your head and were very sensible, and you have clearly given the episode a lot of intelligent thought. Well done!

In answer to your questions:

How could I have anticipated that my horse was expecting a gallop? You couldn't have. You weren't familiar with the trail, you were only slightly familiar with the horse, you didn't know that the horse always cantered at that point on the trail and would therefore expect to do it again, and you haven't ridden long enough to recognize the position and balance shifts of a horse that is about to move into a gallop.

What should I do to stop a galloping horse? You did very well just to stay on board! As for how to stop a galloping horse, much depends on why the horse is galloping. If he is frightened and doesn't even remember that you are in the saddle, there isn't much you can do until he calms down or becomes tired. If he's galloping for the enjoyment of it, or because he always gallops at a particular point on the trail, then there are things you can do. If you know the trail, you can point the horse up a hill, which will make him easier to stop. If there is a meadow or field where you can make a large circle, you can circle, sit up, and use a pulley rein (one hand holding rein and mane about halfway up the horse's neck, the

Being run away with can be terrifying even for an experienced rider; it's even more frightening for a novice unfamiliar with the horse and the terrain.

other hand taking upward, not down, with the rein and then releasing, taking and releasing, over and over) until the horse responds.

Do you recommend going at a galloping speed on a trail ride? I would recommend this only if the riders are experienced and only if both riders and horses know the trail very, very well. And even then there can be surprises. For a first-time trail rider, *no.* For a rider who has been in lessons for only a few months, *no.* For a rider who isn't familiar with the trail, *no.* And above all, for a rider who has said quite clearly that she only wants to walk and trot, *no!*

Horses that are always galloped at a particular point on a trail will automatically pick up the gallop at that point, just as horses that are always allowed to play in the water at a river crossing will always stop and try to play in the water. It's a habit, and like most horse habits, it's one created by the rider.

Your fellow rider acted very irresponsibly, but you have now learned a very valuable lesson. A child of 12 may indeed be a better or more experienced rider than you, but riding skill is no guarantee of maturity or good sense, and anyone taking a novice rider out on the trail should possess all three. The best company for your first trail rides would be your instructor or another competent adult who can explain what your horse is doing, and why, and what you can do about it.

Am I just a chicken? Will I always be so scared? If that girl knows the trail and her horse, and feels safe galloping, and remembers to walk the first mile out and the last mile back, then perhaps this is okay for her. It is not okay for you. A helmet can protect you from some things but won't save your kneecaps, your ribs, your arms, or your fingers (among other things) if you hit a tree at speed. A galloping horse can go considerably faster than 20 miles an hour, and if you come flying off the horse into a tree, you will sustain quite a lot of damage. A helmet is just a helmet, not an all-body force field! And even with a helmet, you can sustain head injuries if you come off hard enough. I am glad to know that you wear your helmet whenever you ride, but please realize that you were right to be frightened and concerned about your safety.

You are not a chicken. And you will not always be so scared, though I hope you *will* be afraid when fear is an appropriate reaction. When you have become a competent rider, you will be more confident. If you are willing to invest the time and effort it takes to become a truly good rider, eventually you will develop confidence in your own skills. At that point, you will enjoy a gallop in the right circumstances, but you will probably still not want to participate in unplanned gallops on unfamiliar horses down unfamiliar trails.

I'm glad that you want to continue with your riding. Don't be ashamed to go slowly and master each step before you move on to the next one. Tell your instructor that you want a thorough grounding in the basics, that you want to become a *real* rider, and that you don't mind taking the necessary time. Sometimes instructors can take things too fast because they imagine that the student is in a hurry. Good instructors are always happy to hear that a student wants to learn to ride really well.

Riding Down Hills

Q My horse wants to rush down hills when we are out on a ride. Is it because he's not balanced under saddle? What can I do to steady him? He is an Arabian, so is a forward-going horse anyway.

A There can be several different reasons for a horse wanting to rush down a hill. The most common and most basic reason is usually *balance*. It's harder for a horse to balance going down a hill, and twice as hard if the horse is carrying a rider. Some horses go faster and faster until they're running; others try to rebalance themselves by tossing their heads straight up in the air or even bucking.

First, be sure that your saddle fits well and is positioned correctly; if it shifts forward onto his shoulders while he's going down a hill, even a well-balanced horse may start moving faster and faster in an attempt to get away from the pain.

Second, be sure that you know how to ride correctly on hills. When going down a hill without a trail, or if you're on a trail that doesn't involve

A novice rider might think that she would feel "safer" cutting across and down the side of a hill, but a horse with his "engine" off to the side cannot balance well, and could easily topple over and roll down a steep hill like this one.

*Descending a steep hill doesn't have
to be uncomfortable. This horse is
carrying an experienced and well-balanced
rider who has kept her horse's engine directly
behind and underneath him and then freed his
back to allow him to use his engine.*

switchbacks, avoid angling your horse across the face of the hill. Go straight
down. The horse can't balance over his hindquarters, as he needs to do, if they are
off to the side instead of directly behind and under him. If a horse's hindquarters
aren't aligned straight with the rest of its body, going down a hill can cause the
horse to fall over — not a good thing for the horse or for the rider.

Whether you're going up or down a hill, your position is basically the same:
balanced over your feet, weight in your heels, knees bent, hip angle closed slightly
so that you are leaning very slightly forward. Keep your head and eyes up and
looking ahead, not down at your horse's neck.

Give your horse enough rein to help him balance; he needs some freedom
with his head and neck. If you shorten the reins too much and hold too hard,
you'll make it very difficult for him to go downhill at all because you'll be restricting his movement and pulling him off balance.

Don't try to lean backward going down a hill. This won't help your horse; in
fact, it will get in his way because you'll be putting extra weight onto your seat
and his hindquarters at precisely the moment when he needs to have his "engine"
free to work effectively. Just stay balanced over your stirrups.

Begin by finding some small, low hills in your area so that you can practice.
A short slope that only requires five or ten steps will be best. Practice staying in
balance and holding your position; practice allowing your horse to use his hindquarters; practice keeping as even and slow a pace as possible. When your horse
can keep his balance and stay calm going down a short, gentle slope, you can start
practicing in the same way on a longer slope, then on steeper slopes.

One of the most basic things a riding horse must learn is that the rider's leg
means, "step forward with the hind legs; take larger, longer steps please." Many

riders have trouble on hills because they don't dare use their legs, as they are afraid that their horses will interpret any leg pressure as "go fast, horse!" Stay on flat terrain for as long as it takes for you to teach your horse to take *longer* steps, not *faster* steps, when you ask him to. This will help both of you on hills.

If you feel that you need to lean back or stand straight in your stirrups going down a hill, because your own balance is precarious, practice riding in a balanced two-point (half-seat) position, first on flat terrain and then up and down gentle slopes. If you become fearful and push hard against your stirrups, locking your ankles, knees, and hips and forcing your seat far out of the saddle, you'll become a stiff, dead weight that will be hard for your horse to carry in balance.

If you are worried about falling forward, try this: On a downhill slope, stay in your half-seat, keep your head up and look where you are going, but allow your legs to move a tiny bit forward so that your heels are no longer precisely under your hipbones. In this position, if you looked down (but don't look down on the hill; do it only when you're practicing the position on the flat!) you would see your toes. This should make you feel much more secure, without hurting your horse's balance in any way.

Essential Equine Trail Skills

Q I attended your Equitana lectures a few years back and I really enjoyed the way you used a "Top 10" kind of format. I have to give a talk for our local 4-H group and I could sure use your help. There are a lot of kids doing horse projects this year, and we're planning to take them on some trail rides (yes, we'll all have helmets). I'd like a fun way to get the message across that they need to have some good basic training on their horses before they can take them out on the trails. Our trails have great scenery, but they are a little on the rough and hilly side. I'm thinking that if I could give the kids a "Top 10" list of trail skills, they'd be more likely to listen to me and learn them.

A That "Top 10" format is always useful: It keeps the audience's attention, while moving from point to point also keeps the speaker on track. I agree that it would probably be a good way to get and keep the attention of your 4-H kids.

You know your riders and your trails best, so I'm going to suggest that you tweak my list according to your own needs. Don't be shy about changing it! This

Trail Riding Skills Checklist
TOP 10 THINGS TRAIL HORSES
SHOULD DO WHEN ASKED

1. Walk forward.

2. Step backward.

3. Stop and stand.

4. Step away from the rider's leg pressure (if mounted) or from hand pressure (if leading).

5. Turn on the forehand (one step at a time).

6. Turn on the haunches (one step at a time).

7. Walk up a hill (nothing extreme, just a slight slope to demonstrate horse and rider balance).

8. Walk down a hill (again, just enough to demonstrate balance).

9. Walk through water.

10. Go first, last, and in the middle of the group.

While you're practicing those skills, offer extra points to any rider whose horse has also mastered the skill of standing quietly when tied (to the trailer or a picket line) or when held.

NOTE: It's important to be able to ask a trail horse to do all of these things — from the saddle *and* in hand.

---

is just my own list of the "Top 10" things that I would want to see any rider do with any horse before I started down the trail with them.

If you can arrange it, a trail prep day might be a good idea. Can you call a meeting of all the would-be trail riders? It would be ideal if you had access to a field with a bit of a hill in it and some water, though in a pinch you can use a hose to make a puddle or let the water from the hose serve as a very narrow "stream." A trail prep day would be a grand opportunity to get all of the kids and their horses together in one place so that you can spend an afternoon testing the necessary skills, knowledge, and training *before* you ever get to the trailhead.

If your 4-H kids enjoy this prep day, you can plan others and make them much more elaborate. Someday you may even want to do police-horse training with crowds, balloons, umbrellas, and such, but these "Top 10" basic skills make an excellent "starter set" for a trail horse.

When both riders and horses have good trail skills, they can relax and enjoy their day out.

If any of your kids have trouble catching or loading or hauling their horses when prep day comes around, they'll know what they need to work on between that day and the actual trail ride.

By the way, just in case any dogs are coming along, you might want to check to be sure that they are confirmed in the three absolutely essential *canine* trail skills: "come," "heel," and "down-stay."

PART II

Physical and Emotional Issues

FIGURING OUT HORSE AND RIDER SIZE

WHEN YOUR BODY DOESN'T COOPERATE

FACING FEAR

HELPING YOUR HORSE WITH HIS PROBLEMS

THINKING RIGHT ABOUT HORSES

THINKING RIGHT ABOUT YOUR RIDING

CHAPTER 8

Figuring Out Horse and Rider Size

MANY RIDERS ASK whether they are too heavy for their horses, but there is no simple formula and no easy answer to the question.

A horse can carry a heavy beginner rider if that horse is strong, sturdy, and in good condition; if the saddle fits well and distributes the rider's weight over a large area; and if he is ridden at slow gaits, for short distances, and over easy terrain. With a more skilled rider, the same horse could safely work at faster gaits, over longer distances, and over more challenging terrain.

Riders who are caring and conscientious, who keep their horses and themselves as strong and fit as possible, and who are always alert to any sign of discomfort in their horses should relax, enjoy their rides, and not waste emotional energy worrying about their weight on the scales.

Is This Horse Too Small for Me?

Q I am considering purchasing a horse but I am concerned he may be too small for me. The breeder is in another state, so I cannot ride the horse first. I am purchasing out-of-state because I want to buy a Rocky Mountain Horse, and they are hard to come by where I live.

This is a 4-year-old gelding that weighs approximately 850 pounds and is 14 hands. I've ridden Rockies that are 14.3 hands, which seems to be a perfect fit, but three inches can make quite a difference, especially if I'm constantly bunching up my legs to signal. I am an adult woman (riding level is advanced beginner), 5'4" tall, 118 pounds, and my inseam measures 29 inches. I will be riding primarily on the trail, so proper height and comfort is paramount. I will probably choose a Western or Australian saddle (if that makes any difference).

This is my first horse, so I am a bit green regarding all of this. Can you please advise me as to whether this horse will be too small for me?

A According to the breed standard, a Rocky Mountain Horse should be between 14.2 and 16.0 hands. If this horse is only 14 hands and won't grow any taller, that isn't necessarily a problem. If you're primarily interested in trail riding, a 14-hand horse should be quite tall enough for someone of your height, provided that you feel comfortable on him. Many small horses and ponies are excellent weight carriers. Icelandics, Haflingers, and various native ponies (e.g., Shetlands and Fell Ponies) are tough and strong and routinely carry full-sized adults.

Also, although it's quite true that many small horses stay small, this horse is young, and it will be two or three years before he is fully grown. There's no guarantee, but it's quite likely that he could add another inch to his height by the time he is seven.

Barrel size and stride length are much more important than height. Ask the horse's owners, and the vet, whether the horse has an average or a wide barrel. If the answer is "No, he's actually quite narrow," then this probably isn't the horse for you. If they say, "Yes, he's exceptionally wide," then I would keep him on your list of "possibles."

That said, you are left with two important questions. Even if the horse is up to weight and your vet believes him to be sound and well suited for your riding plans, you still need to know how you will feel riding him! The first question isn't

The fit between horse and rider depends much less on height than on the relation between the horse's barrel and the rider's legs.

how tall he is, but whether his barrel will fit your leg comfortably so that you'll feel secure and be able to ride with relaxed, open hips. The second question is whether this is a horse you will *enjoy*.

I strongly suggest that you go out and visit this horse, try him, and make your final decision based on your impressions. Compare the cost of a couple of days and a few hundred dollars to the amount of money you'll spend buying the horse, shipping the horse, and maintaining the horse for all the years you plan to own him. The visit cost is trivial, but the visit is important. Matching a horse and rider is like matching a couple — there needs to be a connection, a spark, or at least the clear possibility of developing both! Even a detailed description and an exhaustive list of on-paper qualities won't make up for that in-person, face-to-face meeting.

Videos and photos can help you cross certain horses off your list, but they don't tell you everything. They can help you narrow your choices down to the horse or horses that you are seriously considering, at which point you need to get on an airplane or a bus. Bottom line: You *do* need to sit on this horse. Obviously you won't know instantly if the two of you will be best friends forever, but you will, very quickly, get a "feel" for whether you want to take the horse home.

If this horse is wonderful and you buy him, the trip will have been a good investment. If you don't buy him, it will have been an even better investment. If he's *not* wonderful, or wonderful for someone else but just not right for you, you'll want to have your money available and your stall empty when the right horse comes along.

"Outgrowing" a Horse

Q My horse is 14.3 hands, and I'm 5'4." I'm average weight for my height, and my horse is a 12-year-old Arabian, so she isn't going to grow any taller. I'm an experienced rider, and I love her *soooo* much. My mom says we're going to sell her and buy a new horse to work on for the shows next summer because I'm outgrowing her. Is my horse too small for me, and how do you know when a horse is too small for you?

A The short answer is this: You know when a horse is too small for you when he's no longer able to carry you comfortably and easily. The longer answer is more complicated, of course. When the horse's physical comfort isn't the real issue, the term "too small" means different things to different people.

I'd say that beyond the question of the horse's comfort, there are certain indications that a rider may be outgrowing a horse. For example, if you ride over jumps and you've grown so much that your feet are knocking over the jumps even though your horse is clearing them nicely, you're probably too *tall* for the horse, though not necessarily too *heavy*.

If your form of competition doesn't involve jumping, and your horse is comfortable carrying you, then the question is one of show-ring aesthetics, and for advice on that subject, you should probably consult a judge in your particular discipline.

Some show riders consider that a horse is "too small" for them if their legs go more than halfway down the horse's sides — they feel that they need to look like a peanut on an elephant, for whatever reason! Others, less extreme, have been told by their trainers that they don't stand a chance of winning in certain forms of competition if their boot heels are any lower than the level of the horse's belly. None of this, of course, has anything to do with the horse's actual ability to carry the rider — it's all to do with achieving a particular look in the show ring.

In many styles of riding and forms of competition, there are riders taller and heavier than you who ride and compete successfully on horses no larger than your mare. Look at most forms of Western competition, at endurance riding, and competitive trail riding, and then look at what you do with your horse and ask yourself these questions:

▶ Is my horse comfortable carrying me? In other words, does she stride out well, lifting and rounding her back, and showing that she is cheerful and not in any discomfort?

- If I really enjoy competitions and want to continue competing or do even more competing, is there some reason that I won't be able to continue to do well in competition with this particular horse?
- Do I want to continue to ride and compete with my horse, or do I want another horse?

When you know the answers, have a chat with your trainer. In most cases, if a child is outgrowing a horse, the trainer will notice before the child does and will have a talk with the child's parents and find out whether it would be appropriate to begin looking for another horse. Sometimes it is *not* appropriate, because of finances or simply because the child loves that horse and wants to keep it.

If your trainer or instructor agrees with your mother that you are outgrowing the horse, ask for specific reasons. Those reasons may have nothing to do with your height or weight. Perhaps the adults in your life think that you are ready to take on the training of a less experienced horse, or perhaps they would like to see you competing at a higher level and don't feel that this mare can take you there. Again, talk to your trainer or instructor, find out what is going on, and then discuss it with your mother. If possible, bring everyone together for a discussion so there will be no chance of misunderstandings. If there is some question about whether your horse can handle the physical demands of competition, you may want to consult your veterinarian as well.

Knocking over jump rails with your own feet would
indicate that you've outgrown your horse.

Finding the Right Size Horse

Q I am interested in guidelines for making a good match size-wise between horse and rider. I am 5'3" with not very long legs. I seem to fit well on horses 14.2 to 15.2 hands. On taller horses, I feel perched, with not enough leg in the right place to feel secure. I'm considering leasing a 13.2 pony. His gaits, disposition, and energy level are exactly what I am looking for. He is pretty sturdy; should I be concerned that I will run him into the ground as an adult rider? I'm 120 pounds and plan on mostly trail riding.

A Trust your knowledge and feelings, because you are right on target. Horse/rider size matches depend much less on height than on the relation between the horse's barrel and the rider's leg. You may be entirely comfortable on a very tall horse with a small, narrow barrel or entirely uncomfortable on a much shorter horse with an extremely wide, round barrel. Heavy riders often imagine that they need tall horses, either to fit their leg or to carry their weight, when in fact they need strong, sturdy, weight-carrying animals, which usually are *not* tall.

As for fitting the leg, much depends on the conformation of both the horse and the rider. A rider with short round legs on a very wide horse will be unable to sit correctly and use her legs correctly; a rider with long, thin legs on a very narrow horse may feel that her feet are dangling far too low under the horse's belly. Look at upper-level dressage competitions, look at the Spanish Riding School, look at the reiners and cutters at Quarter Horse Congress and at World. You'll see many riders with their feet well below the horse's belly — it's actually an advantage in terms of rider balance. If your legs only reach partway down your horse's sides, you may be riding just the top half of the horse, and as you've noticed, this puts your leg into an ineffective position and makes you feel perched and insecure. This isn't much fun, especially on long trail rides.

A sturdy, well-built pony of 13.2 shouldn't have any trouble carrying you, even on long rides, if you are a balanced and considerate rider. And since you are considering a lease, not a purchase, there's every reason to give the pony a try.

If this particular pony doesn't work out for you, there are many small Quarter Horses that are lovely for trail riding and many large ponies that are equally sturdy and smooth. Connemaras are one possibility; Haflingers, Welsh Ponies, and Welsh crosses make nice walk-trot-canter horses; Icelandic Horses and Peruvian Pasos might appeal if you are interested in a gaited horse.

Or you may meet a taller horse with a narrow barrel, find that your leg fits him perfectly, and fall in love. Focus on barrel size instead of height and try as many horses as you possibly can. Unless a horse is obviously too tall or too small for you, don't make any assumptions until you've actually had a chance to sit on his back.

Horse-to-Rider Size

Q Recently my trainer started suggesting that my horse is too small for me. She said, "You're short, but he's tiny." Simon is a small Thoroughbred, 15.2, and I am about 116 pounds and 5'1." Of course, this upset me no end. I don't want to look stupid on him. I have no intention of changing horses, but I board at a sale barn where they are always trying to convince me that I need a new horse. First it was his long pasterns, then it was how he goes, and now he's too small for me. Should I be concerned?

A There are many ways to look stupid on a horse, but this isn't one of them. A 15.2 Thoroughbred is not *tiny*, and it sounds as though you could ride a much smaller horse and look just fine. What's more important is that you are certainly not too big — in any dimension, height or weight — for any sound horse of 15.2 or 14.2, or, for that matter, for a sturdy pony of 13.2.

Your trainer may have been spending too much time at competitions where tiny riders perch on top of huge horses, and she may think of that as the "correct" look. If so, she is very wrong. Some people don't want to ride any horse unless it's so tall that they can't see over its back when they're standing next to it, which is just silly.

What matters most to horse and rider fit is not the height or weight of either one, but the relationship of the rider's leg to the horse's barrel. It's not complicated. Can you put your leg against your horse, at the girth and behind the girth, and apply pressure from your calf? Does the horse feel the pressure on the lower part of his barrel, below the widest part of his ribs? If so, you're just fine.

If a horse is too large for you, and your legs are in contact with the top of his barrel instead of the bottom, you'll find it harder to give signals and the horse will find it harder to understand them. In this situation, you'll find that you need to use cues instead of aids, because your physical position won't permit you to apply correct leg aids. If you ride a too-large horse, you can't *help* him, you can only *signal* him.

The key words in your question are "sale barn." The staff at a sale barn is likely to push, almost automatically, for every rider to change horses as often as possible. They make their money from sales, not from riders who enjoy and keep one horse for many years. For a sale barn, the ideal rider sees her horse as a piece of sports equipment and is perpetually in search of the newest, latest, most fashionable piece of equipment. Pasterns, way of going, size — next it will be your horse's color or markings or the thickness of his mane or tail! Don't take any of this seriously. If you are comfortable on your horse, and he is comfortable with you on board, that's all that matters.

FYI: Pound for pound, inch for inch, and bounce for bounce, ponies consistently outjump horses, and they can carry much more weight in proportion to their size, over much greater distances. "Big and tall" doesn't mean "extra-strong and

A horse that carries himself inverted — head and neck high, back low — may be finding it difficult to carry his rider comfortably.

Instead of looking for a taller horse, a heavy rider in search of a weight-carrying mount should look for a solid, sturdy animal with good bone.

athletic and able to carry more weight," it just means "big and tall." Larger, taller horses are actually less likely to be weight-carriers and less likely to stay sound.

When people tell you why you need to get rid of your horse and buy another one, just smile, say "Thank you for sharing," and carry on enjoying your horse.

Can My Horse Carry My Weight?

Q Please tell me how much weight a horse can carry. I have heard three different ways to figure this, and they all get different results. I need to know if I am crazy for not getting on my horse, which I have owned for almost three years. My husband and my best friend tell me "Go ahead," but I just don't know.

I have been on a diet my entire life and I walk for exercise every day, but I am still very heavy (over 250 pounds). I bought my Quarter Horse/Morgan cross as a 2-year-old and turned him over to my best friend, who is a trainer with her own barn. She started Dandy under saddle when he was almost four, and he is so good that she uses him in lessons. He does everything she asks and he just loves everybody. I want to ride my horse so much!

Before I bought Dandy, my husband took me to a riding stable as a special surprise, but they had a rule that riders could weigh no more than 185 pounds. If I weighed 185 pounds, I would be dancing in the streets! Of course, we couldn't go riding that day, and I felt so humiliated.

I am pretty fit and solid. I walk four miles every morning. I also practice tai chi; I enjoy it a lot and feel very balanced now. But at my weight, I just don't think I have the right to get on a horse.

My trainer says that I won't hurt Dandy if I ride him briefly every other day, because he is mature enough and built like a tank. He is 15 hands. Riding for 15 minutes every other day would mean the whole world to me, even if we just walked. But I keep thinking about how horses suffer when they have to carry heavy riders, and I can't make myself get on Dandy. What should I do?

A There are several ways to calculate — crudely — the amount of weight a horse can carry. Most commercial stables base their rider weight restrictions on the idea that an average horse can safely carry up to 20 percent of its own weight. If the average horse weighs 1,000 pounds, he could theoretically carry up to 200 pounds (typically 20 pounds of tack and 180 pounds of rider). But there are problems with that formula, and with the "measure the horse's bone" formula, and with any formula that's supposed to give easy answers to difficult questions.

First, there's no such thing as an "average" horse. There are individual 1,200-pound horses that couldn't possibly carry as much as 200 pounds, and there are individual 850-pound horses that routinely and easily carry 250 pounds or more. Second, the rider's skill level must be taken into account, as a horse may have difficulty carrying a light but unbalanced or inconsiderate rider, but could comfortably carry a much heavier rider who is balanced and competent. Third, there are other variables that every rider, whether light or heavy, should consider at all times, including saddle fit and proper hoof care, fitness and conditioning, weather conditions, and terrain.

A horse designed to carry weight needs to have a strong, sturdy body, good bone (in terms of both circumference and density), legs set on well to provide support, a short, strong back, a wide loin, and a deep body. *This* is the type of horse that's usually described as "built like a tank." If that describes Dandy, then listen to your husband and your trainer and go out and ride your horse. Limit yourself to short, slow rides on good footing until you and your trainer are certain that Dandy is comfortable carrying you. As long as he shows no signs of discomfort or fatigue, believe that he's fine. If he begins to hollow his back or take short steps or duck sideways when you lead him to the mounting block, believe that he's getting sore. He won't lie to you.

Here are three more things to think about.

First: Riding horses can carry their own weight, the weight of the rider, and the weight of the tack. But there's more to this than simple addition. Two riders with different abilities and skill levels may weigh the same amount, but a horse might find it easy to carry one and difficult to carry the other. Rider ability, fitness, balance, coordination, and attentiveness to the horse are all very important.

Second: Tack comes in all sorts of sizes, materials, and weights, but again, there's more to the picture than simple addition. A horse carrying a 265-pound cowboy and a 35-pound saddle is carrying 300 pounds. A horse carrying that same cowboy with a 15-pound synthetic saddle would be carrying only 280 pounds, but as this isn't a math question, what we want to know is *how comfortable is the horse?* The lightest saddle may not be the best-fitting saddle, so beware of thinking only in terms of numbers of pounds! If the heavier saddle distributes the rider's weight more effectively and doesn't interfere with the horse's spine or shoulders, the rider should use the heavier saddle.

Heavy riders can ride well and can participate fully in active equestrian activities.

Third: If a horse is carrying too much fat on his *own* body, he's carrying extra weight all the time. *Be careful not to let Dandy become overweight.* Old-style Quarter Horses and old-style Morgans both tend to gain weight easily, and since Dandy is a "tank," he may have gotten the easy-keeper gene from both sides of his family. Carrying an additional 300 pounds at a walk for 15 minutes out of 48 hours is not likely to damage a sturdy, well-built horse. But carrying an extra 200 or 300 pounds on his *own* body, day in and day out, *will* cause damage.

I think that you should take your trainer's advice. You trusted her to keep and train Dandy for you; now trust her when she says that he's ready for you to ride for short periods. Begin by taking the precautions you've described — they're sensible and they'll make you feel better. Look after your horse, ride him sensibly, pay attention to his reactions, and I think he will remain sound and happy and look after *you.*

One more thing: If you're walking four miles every day *and* doing tai chi, I can promise you that a lot of readers are saying to themselves, "Gosh, I wish I were that fit!" In fact, I'm saying it to myself right now.

How Heavy Is Too Heavy to Ride?

Q I have a question that has been stopping me from taking riding lessons for many years. I am hoping you can help me to understand better about riders and horses and weights.

I have a 12-year-old Paint mare that weighs about 1,200 to 1,300 pounds. She is trained Western and English. I have been on a horse only twice in my life, though it has been my heart's desire to ride since I was a young girl. My problem is I am a large woman weighing 260 pounds. My father always told me that I would kill a horse if I tried to ride one, as I was a large child as well, thus my fear of getting on a horse. I am brought to tears worrying I might hurt my horse with my weight and inexperience. I truly wish to ride but do not know how to tell what size horse would be good for me. Please tell me what I should look for before getting on a horse's back and doing harm (which I will avoid until I know what I am doing). This is a lifelong dream that is finally attainable financially. Can you help?

A Learning to ride is the heart's desire of many, many people, and there's no reason in the world that you shouldn't follow your heart if you're able to do so. I'm sorry that your father told you such stories — in addition to being unkind, he was also quite wrong. If your weight is the only thing keeping you from learning to ride, then please start looking for a good riding instructor! If you are fit and have no other major health problems, I can't think of any reason why you shouldn't start right now.

Don't worry about hurting horses because of your weight and inexperience. The fact that you are worrying about this shows your good heart and makes it clear that you will be a rider who is always attentive to her mount's comfort.

That said, I suggest that you not try to ride your own horse until you have an instructor to advise you. If your mare is very fit and strong and suitable for a beginner, your instructor may choose to use her in your lessons. It's also possible that before giving you lessons on your own mare, your instructor may prefer to use a school horse until you have mastered the basics of riding.

Inexperienced riders *can* hurt horses, but this is unlikely to happen in a good riding program. A good instructor will carefully match horses and riders, select appropriate tack, and not encourage or permit any behaviors (human or equine) that would put horses (or their riders) at unnecessary risk. Too-heavy riders can also hurt horses, but again, a good instructor will select the horse and tack carefully and choose exercises that provide maximum benefit to the rider while imposing minimum impact on the horse.

Speaking of exercises, there's so much more to riding than the rider's weight. Balance, coordination, flexibility, strength, and overall fitness are all-important. A good, competent, balanced rider who controls her own body easily and well makes the ride easier and more pleasant for the horse, regardless of her weight. A light-weight rider who is weak and unbalanced makes the horse's job much harder. From the horse's point of view, the worst of both worlds would be a very heavy rider who is weak and unbalanced, so on to the *real* question. How is your fitness level?

If you want to learn to ride, it's most important that you achieve as much fitness and coordination as possible. For the sake of the horse's comfort, your own safety, and your ability to make meaningful progress, you need to be reasonably fit and strong before you arrive at the stables for that first lesson. If you're already fit and strong, good for you — start calling instructors! If you are unfit, then you need to develop your strength, flexibility, and endurance, a process that may or may not involve losing weight. Fitness and coordination should be your primary goals. The fitter you are and the stronger and more flexible and coordinated, the better off your horse will be.

You'll do best if you begin to think in terms of your fitness level rather than your weight. With the right horse and a good instructor, many heavy riders learn to ride not just adequately but *well*. Weight in itself is usually not a severe handicap. Given the choice between a fit, heavy rider and an unfit rider of normal weight, many instructors would prefer the heavier rider because what matters most is your control over your body, not your precise weight.

There are many ways to achieve a better level of fitness, and one of the easiest and best is also very inexpensive: walking. All you need is a pair of good walking shoes and somewhere to walk. I also strongly suggest a notebook in which to track

Many old-style Quarter Horses are wonderful weight-carriers, and
some parade horses carry ornate tack that weighs 200 pounds or more.

your daily activities and your progress! In general, anything that helps you develop strength in your abdominals, your back, and your legs will do wonders for your riding. Once you've begun taking lessons, don't give up your fitness program. You may need to change it a little, however. There will come a point at which you'll find that walking, even several miles each day, is no longer enough, and you'll want to begin doing other sorts of exercise that will help your balance and coordination.

While you are working to become more fit, you can benefit from handling your horse on the ground. Ground work is not a substitute for riding, but it is a good way to learn to know your horse and begin building a relationship with her. Any good instructor can help you learn basic horse-handling skills. If you find a good dressage instructor, you will be able to learn correct longeing, which is excellent for building fitness in your horse and communication between you and your horse. Just don't try this on your own and don't attempt to learn longeing from anyone who believes that it consists of running a horse in circles to exhaust it before you ride. That isn't longeing, and it's a fast way to cripple a horse.

Also, why not take your horse for regular walks on a lead rope? This is a wonderful way to build a stronger bond between you while helping you both become fitter. By the time you can walk briskly next to a fit horse that is striding out at the walk (not just ambling slowly), you'll be well on your way to being fit enough to ride. Since your ultimate goal is not just to learn to ride but to ride your own horse, the best thing you can do for *her* fitness is to see that she gets as much turnout as possible. Turnout 24/7 is ideal, but even half a day would help. A normal horse turned out full-time will typically walk 20 miles in a 24-hour period.

If you are primarily interested in riding as a way to enjoy the scenery and your mare's company, you may be very surprised to discover how quickly you will learn to enjoy spending casual time on horseback. If you have more ambitious plans for your riding, and want to become more seriously involved in one or more equestrian activities, the process of learning will be a much longer one, and your weight may make it necessary for you to work a little bit harder to acquire the skills, but you *can* do it.

One warning: Not all riding instructors are equipped to teach heavy riders. Some don't have suitable horses; some don't have the necessary experience to understand the specific problems involved. There are even some whose attitudes, sad to say, are rather like that of your father. Talk to instructors before you visit them and explain your situation. When you have a short list of "possibles," watch them teach a lesson or two before you sign up to become a student. Somewhere out there, you'll find an instructor who has appropriate school horses, experience, a sympathetic attitude, and a strong desire to help you become a good rider. You deserve a *good* instructor — don't settle for anything less.

When you begin looking for a saddle for your mare, focus on saddle *fit*, not saddle weight. A rider preoccupied with her own weight is likely to look for the lightest possible tack. Don't do this. You need a saddle that fits both of you well. It won't matter whether the saddle weighs 17 pounds or 35 pounds, provided that it distributes your weight effectively and allows your horse to move comfortably. Ask your instructor to help you with saddle selection and fitting.

Now a few thoughts on horses and their weight-carrying abilities. As with riders, fitness and conformation matter much more than height and weight. If your mare is built like an old-style "bulldog" Quarter Horse, solid and chunky and low to the ground, with a short, strong back and a lot of bone, then she should easily be able to carry you when she is fit. Here are some other thoughts to encourage you.

- ▸ When the U.S. government was breeding horses for the cavalry, they tested the horses — Thoroughbreds, Morgans, and Thoroughbred-Morgan crosses, for the most part — on rides that covered 300 miles in five days. Each horse carried a rider and tack totaling 280 pounds.
- ▸ Icelandic Horses are small, extremely sturdy animals standing under 14 hands. They routinely carry large men over miles of rough ground. One horse tour facility I've heard about has a rider weight limit of 280 pounds.
- ▸ The Palomino Patrol of San Antonio, Texas, outfits each horse with a saddle plus tapaderos, bridle, breast collar, serapes, and hip drops, for a total weight of about 200 pounds. Add a rider, and many of those horses are carrying 350-plus pounds. A conditioned, sturdily built horse, carrying a well-fitting saddle and a competent rider, can pack a lot of weight for a short time without becoming injured or breaking down.

If you want to learn to ride, don't let the scales stop you. If you're not *fit* enough to ride, get fit first, but don't regard your fitness program as a punishment! See it for what it is: preparatory work that will enable you to learn to ride and that will make your riding lessons easier on the horse and more fun for you.

CHAPTER 9

When Your Body Doesn't Cooperate

FOR MANY RIDERS, the title of this chapter will evoke an image of at least one stiff or sore body part. Many of us have physical conditions, old injuries, or conformation flaws that keep us from attaining the ideal position and enjoying perfect comfort in the saddle. But many riders are far too *accepting* of pain. There are often ways to help painful, uncooperative body parts become less painful and more cooperative.

Never give up! Riding is a joy and should continue to be a joy even if we need to make a point of finding tack, equipment, and even horses that can allow us to go on enjoying the sport that we love.

Painful Ankles

Q I have problems with my ankles when I ride. So far, I've found no explanation except that my ankles are very weak. I don't think it is my saddle,
because I have the same problem in every saddle I've tried. Is there a reason for this
besides weak ankles? I ride Western; could that be the problem? After about ten
minutes of riding my ankles really start hurting, which puts a damper on the ride!

A Weak ankles can hurt if you're putting a lot of stress on them. You probably can't eliminate ankle stress entirely, but there are several things you
can do to minimize it.

First, check your stirrup length! If you're riding Western, you should be able
to slide your boots into the stirrups comfortably and ride with your feet almost
level, keeping the heel (of your foot, not your boot) slightly lower than the rest
of your foot. If your leathers are too short, and your heels are forced very far
down, your ankles will be sore. Instead of pushing most of your weight into your
lower legs and heels, allow your seat bones and thighs to share the burden. This
will take some pressure off your ankles. For
most riders, however, the most common
cause of sore ankles is *twisting* them.

One of the most helpful gadgets for
any rider with sore ankles is a simple,
inexpensive item that allows the
stirrups to hang straight.

One problem with Western saddles is
that the fenders hang parallel to the horse
and so, of course, do the stirrups. Preparing a new Western saddle for riding has
traditionally involved soaking the fenders
in water, twisting them until the stirrups
are perpendicular to the saddle, and putting a broomstick through the stirrups to
hold them in position while the fenders dry.
In theory, this lets your feet find and pick
up your stirrups easily. In practice, it never
works quite perfectly, and it's not particularly good for the saddle, either.

Consequently, to find and keep their
stirrups, riders tend to cock their ankles
and point their toes in toward the horse's

sides. Because most people's feet naturally point slightly *away* from the horse's sides, this stresses the ankles during mounting and riding. Fortunately there is a solution.

There are several useful gadgets on the market that fit between your fenders/stirrup leathers and your stirrups so that the fenders lie flat while the stirrups hang perpendicular to the fenders. These inexpensive gadgets are readily available through tack catalogs, and once you've installed them they can remain on your saddle forever. Try a pair — they may be just what your ankles need.

Sore Knees

Q How can I prevent my knees from hurting while trail riding? I am 50 years old and started riding on a regular basis again five years ago. We mostly trail ride, always with Western saddles. After several hours, my knees start to ache. Getting off and resting helps, but the pain soon comes back and it cuts our rides short.

A Sore knees definitely take the fun out of riding. There are ways to minimize knee pain or even avoid it altogether. To determine the likely cause of your knee pain, let's look at your saddle, stirrup leathers, and stirrups, as well as your position in the saddle.

Does your saddle fit you? Your body should be comfortably aligned, with your shoulders over your hips and your hips over your heels, and your knees bent. If your saddle is too small, you can't stay balanced; instead, you'll find yourself sitting against or on the cantle, behind your leg instead of balanced over it. In this position, anything you do with your knees takes more effort and puts extra stress on the joints.

If your saddle fits you, consider the length of your stirrup leathers. When you sit in your saddle with your feet out of the stirrups, your weight on your seat bones and thighs, and your legs hanging relaxed with toes pointing down, the stirrup treads should be right at the level of your anklebones. When your feet are *in* the stirrups, your toes will be up, your heels will be down (but not pushed down forcibly), and your knees will be bent. At their highest, the stirrup treads could be just barely above your anklebones; at their lowest, they could be just barely below.

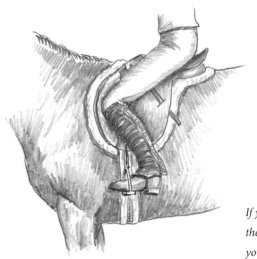

If your stirrup leathers are too short, they will create extra pressure on all of your leg joints: ankles, knees, and hips.

When your stirrup leathers are too short, there is too much bend at the knee, resulting in too much pressure on the knee joint. Your body wants to straighten the knees to avoid the pain.

When your stirrup leathers are too long, you have a different kind of knee stress. Your toes point down instead of up, your ankles stiffen, your hips lock, and your knees are straight. There is no flexing, just concussion. That's hard on the knees too.

Adjusting stirrup leathers on an English saddle is easy. If you don't have enough holes in the leathers, you can make more with a hole-punch, or you can purchase stirrup leathers with "half holes" — that is, twice as many holes, much closer together, for maximum customization of stirrup leather length. On a Western saddle, you have the option of adding holes with a hole-punch, but it's a little trickier.

With Western saddles there's another issue: the fenders. On both English and Western saddles, the default position for stirrups is hanging flat against the horse's sides. When we ride, we turn those stirrups so that our feet point forward, which means twisting the leathers. With an English saddle this is relatively simple if the leathers are pliable. But with a Western saddle, fenders often get in the way. The old methods of twisting the fenders are generally temporary and unsatisfactory.

These days, most Western tack catalogs offer various gadgets (Stirrup Straights and Fender Benders are two popular brands) to hold stirrups in the correct position and take the strain off the rider's ankles and knees. Try these gadgets — you may be surprised to discover just how much strain you were putting on your knees by twisting to pick up your stirrups and keep them in position.

This can also be a problem for riders who use English saddles. In this case, the solution is to purchase a pair of stirrups with the eyes — the part that holds the stirrup leathers — turned 90 degrees. Most major English tack catalogs carry these, and they can make a world of difference to the rider's comfort.

Now take a look at the size and design of the stirrups themselves. Most riders know that stirrups should be larger than the width of the rider's boots. If your stirrups are a little bit too snug (this is dangerous anyway, as you might get hung up in them in case of a fall), you'll tend to tense your feet instead of relaxing them. This may sound trivial, but it isn't. If your feet are tense, your ankles won't flex, and if your ankles don't flex, more strain is placed on your knees. You should be able to relax your feet and spread your toes. When your foot is solidly in the stirrup, with weight on it, there should still be room on *both* sides of your foot for a pencil between the side of your boot sole and the side of the stirrup.

The size of the stirrup tread also matters. The wider the platform for your foot the better, especially if you're going for long rides over varied terrain. Padding is also good — if you use ordinary English stirrups, put rubber pads in them. If you have Western stirrups, be sure that the tread is flat and wide. There are pads for Western stirrups, too (they wrap around the tread).

Endurance riders know a great deal about stirrups. Good endurance riders are experts on the subject of knee pain and how to avoid it by minimizing concussion. You'll find many stirrups featured in catalogs and on Web sites that cater to endurance riders.

On the subject of concussion: Use your weight correctly. It should be distributed between your seat bones and thighs, with some (but not all) of it on the stirrups. Putting too much pressure on your stirrups can cause problems. Your hips, knees, and ankles all flex when you ride and serve to absorb the shock. Keep all three sets of shock absorbers as flexible and strong as possible, so that they can continue to share the job. If you have stiff ankles and tight hips, your knees try to do the work of all three joints, and eventually that extra stress and strain causes pain and damage. If you feel that your knees are working overtime and your ankles and hips are not working very well, do exercises *off* the horse to help regain flexibility in the other joints.

There are some other things you can do to reduce the stress on your knees. Buy or build a tall, wide mounting block and teach your horse to stand quietly while you mount and dismount. When you dismount away from the mounting block, always remove both feet from the stirrups, then slide down and *bend your knees as you land.*

Warm up before you begin your ride. Lead your horse around the arena once or twice, do some bending and stretching, and generally ensure that your ankles and knees and hips will be flexing from your very first moment in the saddle.

During your rides, take breaks by dropping your stirrups and doing some exercises such as ankle circles in both directions. If you feel any part of your body becoming stiff or sore, whether it's your shoulders, hips, knees, or ankles, dismount, take a break, and do some gentle, range-of-motion stretching exercises.

Collapsing Chest

Q I have a problem that is mentally and physically blocking my efforts to ride dressage on a very sensitive young horse (I was okay in hunt seat). At the age of 40, I am not sure how to effect a real change in my posture, one that can be held without my constantly thinking about it. My chest collapses forward, and it seems that without a constantly nagging voice to correct me every time it "goes," it just goes! Also, trying to breathe in the correct position is an effort. I feel as if my breathing becomes labored.

In theory, I know the correct seat and the importance of staying upright and in balance, and I do work on this both off and on the horse. I've had Rolfing sessions to correct crookedness and go to a gym to increase strength and tone, but this chest of mine is starting to depress me. I'm of average height, weight, and build, and not "overly endowed," so cannot blame gravity for this problem!

A You are by no means the only person with this problem. It's very, very common. You can certainly change your posture at 40, or at 50, or at 60. It's one of those changes that you'll find easier to make now, while you're still more flexible, but you'll be able to make it later too. If you are willing to work at it, the only absolute requirement is a pulse.

As for holding a position without constantly thinking about it, that's another story. At first, you *will* have to think about it constantly. That's how we make new habits to overlie the ones we already have. At first, your "corrected" posture will feel "wrong," which is how your body interprets "unfamiliar." That's why you need to think about it. You'll have to remind yourself (yes, constantly) that the new posture is the *correct* one, and you'll need to keep readjusting yourself as your body tries to return to its comfort level and assume the familiar (which your body interprets as "right") posture.

That's the bad news. The good news is that if you can really *think* about changing for even a month or so, you'll have to do less and less conscious thinking after that, because you'll be on your way to a new habit. This is how all of us learn something new.

Be patient with yourself, because it's much harder to learn something that we think we already know how to do. In other words, if you got your first toothbrush tomorrow and were taught how to brush your teeth, you

Stretch your upper body tall, relax your belly, and breathe slowly and deeply.

would learn it easily and quickly. If, however, your dentist told you to brush your teeth in a completely different way from the way you've done it for years, you would find it much more difficult to change an established pattern. That's the problem you're facing with your posture and breathing.

The Rolfing may help and so may the workouts at the gym (do lots of bench presses!), because you need to stretch the tight muscles across the front of your chest and tone the loose muscles across the top of your back.

I suggest that you find someone qualified to teach the Alexander Technique. This is probably the single most valuable tool at your disposal. It will help you readjust the "building blocks" of your body, balance your torso, normalize the tension in the various muscle groups, and *breathe*. I also recommend buying Sally Swift's *Centered Riding,* and putting what you read into practice. If you get the chance to work with a good Centered Riding instructor, take it.

As for things you can do right this minute, I can offer three suggestions.

1. Sit (in a chair or on your horse) and put one hand on your chest, the other on your belly. Inhale. Ask yourself which hand moved more. If you typically sit with a collapsed chest, the hand on your chest will move more, because you're using only the topmost part of your lungs. Stretch your upper body tall, relax your belly, and breathe slowly and deeply. When *both* hands lift, you'll know that you're breathing more correctly. When your lower hand lifts first, you'll know that you are using your lungs properly.

2. Because a collapsed chest goes along with a slumped back and rounded shoulders, you can use a riding crop when you're *on* the horse to remind yourself to sit straight. (No, not by hitting yourself when you slump!) Push your crop down the back of your breeches. When you sit straight, the crop will just touch the back of your shirt between your shoulder blades. When you slump, you won't feel it. You won't want to do this forever, but for a few weeks it can be helpful because those first few weeks are the hardest. Your body wants to stay slumped, because that feels more "natural" and "comfortable," and you need a constant reminder to help your body learn the new position.

3. Use visual aids to help you stay on track. If you're in a dressage arena, use the letters, and make a conscious attempt to check and fix your posture, your breathing, or both at each letter. If you're in a field, use fence posts, trees, rocks — anything at all — to serve as visual reminders to check your balance and position.

Swinging Legs and Stirrups

Q   I have been riding dressage for about a year now, and I love it, but I have a problem with my stirrups. I know that they should be long, but sometimes it's hard for me to keep any weight in them, and they start to swing around. I can make my legs stay pretty quiet at the posting trot, but when I do sitting trot or canter my legs swing. I think it is because I put some weight on my thighs instead of just in my stirrups. If I put them up a couple of holes they are more comfortable, but then my instructor says I look like a hunter rider with my bent knees.

When I ask her how I can keep them long and still have some weight in them, she says, "That's how it has to be if you're going to ride dressage." I feel as if I just can't do it right. Can you give me some ideas to discuss with my instructor? She is a good rider, and I think she gets annoyed with me for being so slow to learn.

A   First of all, let's talk about stirrup length. When you take your feet out of the stirrups and just let your legs hang, where do the stirrup treads touch you? If they are just at your anklebone or *just* underneath it, fine. If your stirrups touch your ankle or foot below that point, they are too long, and they are responsible for many of your riding problems.

Second, let's talk about stirrup positioning. When you drop your stirrups, how difficult is it for you to pick them up again? Can you just lift your toes and slip them into the stirrups, or do you have to move your *legs* forward? This matters! If your feet are swinging forward, there are two probable reasons: Either your stirrups are hung too far forward (as they are on many saddles), or you may be sitting on your backside instead of your seat bones. If your stirrups are correctly positioned and at a good length, then you'll find it easy to put some weight into them and keep them where they belong, underneath your center of gravity.

Let's assume that you've raised your stirrups to a functional length and that you're sitting on your seat bones. Now think about stretching up with your upper body (from your rib cage up) and stretching down with the rest of your body, starting with your seat. Your "seat" isn't just your seat bones, it's everything from your lowest ribs down to your knees. Stretching doesn't mean *tensing,* it means deliberately relaxing and allowing your tight, shortened muscles to lengthen.

When you feel your legs lengthening, take your feet out of the stirrups and do little ankle circles. When your ankles feel flexible and relaxed, pick up your stirrups, adjust them, and then rise into a two-point position for a moment. While

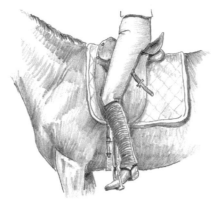

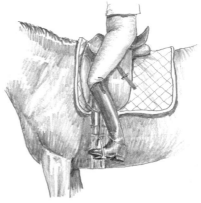

Don't try to create an "instant dressage leg" by dropping your stirrups so much that you have to fish for them with low toes.

Good dressage riding requires a balanced, flexible rider. Your heels should always be the lowest part of your body, and you should always have a bend at your knee.

you're there, take a deep breath, exhale slowly through your mouth, and, while you're exhaling, let your thighs, knees, and ankles relax. You'll feel the weight go down into your heels. Now let your body sink back into your saddle, keeping your knees and ankles relaxed. You'll be able to feel that your heels are still down, your calves are still gently stretched, and you still have weight in the stirrups.

You *cannot* achieve this effect by shoving your heels down — that creates tense, tight ankles and knees, and pops you up out of your saddle. You also can't achieve it if your stirrups are too long, because you'll have to drop your toes to find the stirrups, which tightens your calf muscles instead of allowing them to stretch.

Don't worry about using your thighs actively at this stage in your riding. Your seat includes your thighs, which share your weight with your seat bones. Your legs should be in contact with the horse all the way down, but your legs need to stay relaxed; you're not trying to achieve a tense, forceful gripping of the saddle, but the kind of grip that lets a damp dishtowel cling to the side of a sink. It follows the contours of the sink and stays close, but *not* because it's making an effort.

Why don't you show this answer to your instructor and ask her to help you determine whether your saddle is suitable? If it is, ask her to help you with the exercises I've suggested. She needs to know what you are trying to do and why. And don't worry that she thinks you're too slow — you've said that she's a good instructor, so if she *is* annoyed, she's probably annoyed with herself for being unable to help you more effectively.

Strengthening Rider's Legs

Q I am just returning to riding after a 10-year absence. I own a 7-year-old Anglo-Trakehner gelding that I hope can be my hunter/jumper and, perhaps in the near future, a dressage partner. I took riding lessons from the time I was about seven years old until I was about nineteen. I am working with a wonderful trainer/coach who will be helping us every step of the way.

My lower legs are very out of shape for riding, although I realize that the more riding I do, the stronger they will become. My balance is all right, but my lower legs are quite ineffective, and I have an awful habit of turning my toes out so that I have "wings" in my stirrups. I think I do this to compensate for the lack of strength in my lower leg and seat, and I hope that my toe turnout will be minimized as I build strength in lower leg and seat.

My trainer places my lower leg and foot in the appropriate position, but for the life of me I can't maintain it. As soon as my horse gains any impulsion, my lower leg flops around and my toes stick back out. It is worst at the posting trot. Can you suggest some exercises that I can do when I'm not riding, as well as some pointers that can help me while riding?

A Don't worry, this problem is both common and easy to fix. Time and mileage solve a lot of problems. So do off-the-horse exercises aimed at developing leg strength and stretch. Walking is ideal, and it's cheap and usually convenient. Bicycling is also good; so is skiing.

First, determine whether you truly need to *change* your leg position or whether all you need is to become stronger and steadier. Which parts of your leg are in contact with the saddle? As long as your inner thigh and inner calf are resting against the saddle, your feet will not be in a horrible position. They may not be rigorously parallel to your horse's sides, but very few riders are built in such a way to make that particular position natural!

Why do instructors fuss about feet turning out? Because turned-out feet indicate that the rider is rolling the back of her leg onto the saddle, taking the inner thigh, knee, and calf *off* the saddle and horse. This makes it impossible for the rider to sit in balance and ride with good control over her own body.

Look at the part of your legs that rest against the horse to determine whether you need to change your leg position. You can't spend your entire ride looking

Time spent in a two-point position (half-seat) is time invested in your leg position and overall security in the saddle.

down at your legs, so here's another way to check on your riding, even if you have no mirror and no instructor to tell you what you're doing. Before each ride, clean your boots. After each ride, "read" your boots! They will have picked up some sweat and dirt from your horse's sides: *Where is that dirt?* If it's on the inside of the calf, hurrah, your legs are in a lovely position. If the dirt is partly on the inside of the calf and partly on the back seam of the boot, you are turning your legs out and using part of the back of your leg against the horse and you need to make an adjustment. If the dirt patch covers the back seam of your boot . . . well, you're using the back of your leg instead of the inside, and let's just say that you need to make a more dramatic adjustment.

If you do find that you need to make an adjustment, rotate your *whole* leg inward, very slightly, from the hip. If you move only your feet or only your lower leg to correct your position, you will strain and eventually damage your knees. Your ankles, knees, and hips all serve as shock absorbers when you ride, and if you make your ankles stiff by twisting your feet inward, the knees take much more strain than they should, and you'll pay for it later.

Your two-point position is your best friend; spend as much of every ride as possible in this position. At the very least, spend five minutes at the beginning and end of each ride in two-point, at both walk and trot. Be sure that your stirrups are adjusted correctly. When they are, you can balance over your feet, grab some mane, and let the horse walk around the arena while you make a deliberate, conscious effort to allow your legs to relax around the horse. If you aren't "grabbing" with thighs, knees, or calves, you will feel your thighs relax into close, supportive contact with your saddle. Your calves will stretch slightly and you will feel your lower legs lengthen as some (but not all!) of your weight drops into your heels. At this point, your improved position and balance will make you feel safe and secure. If you wobble madly, take a deep breath and let it out slowly while you relax your thighs and knees and feel your legs lengthen and your heels drop. Now just keep that feeling as you go around the ring. When you post the trot, relax your knees and let your heels drop as the horse bounces you up, then keep your lower legs in that position as you touch down behind the pommel.

Don't try to do too much at once, and do realize that the correct position will feel awkward and wrong at first. The wrong position will feel right because it's familiar, but don't let yourself return to it. Your job is to make the correct position more familiar so that it will begin to feel right, and then to make it so familiar that any other position will feel wrong.

Why Don't My Toes Point Forward?

Q My feet point out to the sides. I know better than to twist my feet in, but I'd really like to know why my feet don't hang straight the way some other riders' feet do and also what I can do to make my toes point forward. I've always been told in lessons and in judges' comments: "Your toes are pointing out," or "Don't point your toes out." But I never heard anyone say exactly why this is bad, except it doesn't look good. And nobody ever explained how it works or what to do about it. I know not to twist my ankles, because you have said that this will eventually damage the rider's knees.

A You're right about not twisting your ankles! Everyone has unique personal conformation, and some people "toe out" or "toe in" according to how their hips are formed, how tight their muscles and tendons are, how straight (or not) their leg bones are, and — surprise, surprise — on how they walk, sit, and move during the 23 hours each day that they are *not* riding a horse. On horseback, it's not really essential that your toes point straight forward. Yes, it creates a pleasing picture, but at what cost?

If your toes point out to the sides because your entire leg is rolled out away from the horse, you have a problem.

If your inner thighs and calves are lying softly against your horse and your toes point out slightly, you don't have a problem.

The only reason to worry about toes that point out is *function*. If your toes are pointing out because you have rolled your legs away from the saddle, you've lost the inside-leg contact that is essential to good riding and instead are riding off the back of your leg.

Glance down at your legs when you're sitting comfortably in the saddle: Never mind your toes, just look at thighs and knees, and feel your calves against the horse. If your inner thighs are resting comfortably against the saddle, your knees are pointing forward, and you can feel the inside (not the backs) of your calves against the horse's sides, then your foot position and angle aren't cause for concern — whether your toes point straight ahead or out at whatever their natural angle may be.

If, when you glance down, you can see your saddle and the inside of your thighs and knees and you can feel the *backs* of your calves against the horse's sides, you need to turn your legs in against the horse, but not because your feet are sticking out. You need to turn your legs in so that you can have effective legs. The way to do it, though, is to turn them from the hip, which means rotating your thighs from the hip.

Did you ever take ballet? Riding "turn-in" is exactly the opposite of ballet turnout. You may find that you are stiff in the hips, have tight hip adductors, and need to do stretching exercises on or off the horse to get your legs ready to "assume the position." Do it — it's worth it. When your legs are draped on the saddle and your contact is inner thigh, inner knee, and inner calf, you'll find that (as if by magic!) your toes point as forward as they can without stressing your ankles, knees, or hips.

Bracing in the Saddle

Q My problem is that I brace in the saddle. Every instructor I have tells me this, and I know I am doing it but don't know how to stop. I don't think I do this when I am riding for fun (maybe I do to some extent, but not as much as in lessons), but when someone is watching me and critiquing my riding I get all tense. Help!

A The only way to stop any bad habit is to start by figuring out *why* you're doing it and then try to eliminate the cause of the habit. Just saying, "don't brace" isn't going to help you at all. Based on the fact that this is something you do more when someone is watching, here are a couple of suggestions.

First, explain to your instructor that you become tense in the saddle and need to relax. Tell her that you become nervous when she is watching you and that you would appreciate anything she can do to help you feel more at ease.

Then ask yourself why you feel nervous when someone critiques you. If your instructor tells you that your heels are too high or that you are gripping with your knees, she doesn't mean "You're a bad person!" She just means that your heels are too high or that you are gripping with your knees. She's critiquing your position, not you, and she's doing it to help you improve and become a better rider. It's hard work learning to ride — you know it and so does she. If you can relax and not take position critiques personally, you'll learn faster and more easily.

Two of the most common causes of tension-induced bracing are breathing and tack, so the first thing you need to do to relax is to *breathe!* You are probably holding your breath a lot of the time, without even noticing it. Most people who brace in the saddle tend to do this — in fact, it's very difficult to maintain enough tension to brace yourself *without* holding your breath.

When you do breathe, you are probably breathing too quickly and shallowly, which also creates tension. When you become tense, your horse becomes tense, too, and then you become even more tense. When you breathe deeply and relax, your horse will relax under you, which will make it easier for *you* to stay relaxed. You can't make the tension go away so that you can breathe better, but you *can* breathe better and make the tension go away!

Practice deep, slow, regular breathing when you're riding on your own. Breathe in through your nose, completely filling your lungs. Then breathe slowly out through your mouth and let your entire body relax as you exhale. Then try to breathe that way *all* the time when you ride (and when you aren't riding too). Singing while you ride will help you breathe better — try it!

Ask your instructor to help you go back a few steps in your riding. Tell her that you know you need to relax and that you want her to help you incorporate the breathing exercises into your lessons. It will be much easier to do this if you spend the next few lessons working on things you already know so that you'll be comfortable focusing on your breathing and relaxation.

Spend some time every day just walking around the arena on your horse, breathing deeply and alternating between your three-point (full-seat) and your two-point (half-seat) positions. It's a wonderful exercise to improve your balance and help you check your leg position. When you can do it easily, and you have no difficulty staying in your two-point with long legs, relaxed knees, flexible ankles, and your weight dropped (not pushed!) into your heels, you'll be well on your way to a lifetime of not bracing.

If you have any doubts, just get into your two-point and hold your breath on purpose for a moment: instant stiffness, instant tension! Then breathe deeply and relax. You'll feel your legs get longer while your hips, knees, and ankles go back to doing their job as shock absorbers. If bracing is a habit, you'll keep doing it unless you're deliberately doing something else, like breathing and stretching. This exercise will teach you exactly what a stiff, braced position feels like, what a relaxed, correct position feels like, and how you can get from one to the other.

The other important thing to do is to *check your tack!* Ask your instructor to help you check the position of your saddle on the horse and the position of the stirrup bars on the saddle. Sometimes riders brace because they can't sit correctly in a particular saddle.

When you breathe deeply and relax, your horse will relax under you, which will make it easier for you to stay relaxed.

Put your saddle on the horse and look at it. When the saddle is in position, the middle of the seat should be its lowest point. If the saddle is too far back, the lowest point will be the pommel, which forces you to push yourself back. If the saddle is too far forward, the lowest point will be the cantle, and you'll be trying to pull yourself forward. You can't relax in either position.

When the saddle is adjusted so that the lowest point is just where you will be sitting, sit in the saddle and leave the stirrups dangling. Adjust them so that when they dangle, the stirrup tread hits you on the anklebone. Then just lift your toes. It should be easy for you to put them into the stirrups. If you are sitting correctly and the stirrups are adjusted to the right length, but they hang down in front of your legs so that you have to put your foot and leg *forward* to find your stirrup, then it's quite likely the stirrup bars are positioned too far forward.

Try taking the stirrups off the saddle and doing some walk-work in your lesson. If you feel much more comfortable, this can be another sign that the stirrup-bar positioning may be wrong. When your stirrups are hanging too far in front of you, you are likely to end up waterskiing — pushing your feet forward, stiffening your knees, and hanging on the reins. This doesn't do you or the horse any good.

If stirrup-bar placement is a problem, try other saddles. Try as many different saddles as you can — the right saddle can make an enormous difference to your riding comfort, and that can make an enormous difference to your tension level.

Too Much Ballet Turnout on Horseback

Q My toes naturally point outward like a ballet dancer's. I took classical ballet lessons for nine years, which accentuates this effect. When I point my toes forward, my knee turns inward slightly. When I point my knees forward, my toes go out at a slight angle. This creates a problem when I ride, because my toes tend to turn out more than they should.

I have a problem keeping my leg against the horse when I jump higher than 3 feet. I feel comfortable at 2'6" and 2'9", but when I go higher, I get popped out of the saddle and my leg swings and comes away from the horse slightly. My background is in hunter/jumper work, and I go up to 3'3" jumps in my lessons. I take lessons twice a week on school horses: one flat class (group) and one jumping class (private). In spite of these problems, I feel pretty confident until the jumps are three feet or higher.

In general, I find that I can maintain a better leg position when I ride without stirrups or even bareback. The problem appears when I use stirrups. How can I deal with this? Are there exercises or special stirrups that might help?

A I know exactly what you mean; many of us took those ballet classes! Some (not many) people's conformation allows them to ride with their toes pointing straight forward because that's the way their legs hang naturally. It's a gift, and they are lucky, but you shouldn't try to imitate them unless your conformation matches theirs. If your feet turn out slightly, you have something in common with most riders. It's *normal* for your feet to turn out a little. Some people have feet that turn out more than a little, and they can still ride effectively.

Your years of practicing ballet turnout don't have to interfere with good riding. You'll just have to learn a new position in the saddle. You'll like learning it, because it won't hurt or cause leg cramps, and you won't have sore knees or ankles during or after your ride. You won't have to slide off your horse at the end of a lesson and stand there holding the saddle and hoping that your legs will stop hurting so that you can walk back to the stalls.

Your foot position in the saddle is linked to your leg position. Don't try to change *just* your foot position! You won't succeed in making yourself a better or more stylish rider, but you *will* damage your ankles and knees, probably permanently. I see a lot of this, sometimes, sadly, in very young riders. Sometimes instructors are trying to achieve a uniform appearance among their students and don't take individual differences into account; they teach their students to grip with their knees and twist their ankles to bring their feet into a specific position. *This is not a good idea.*

Sit in the deepest part of the saddle, just behind the pommel, so that you feel your weight on both seat bones evenly. Let your legs hang naturally. Adjust your stirrups so that the treads hit you just at or very slightly above the anklebone. Then pick up your stirrups, which you should be able to do just by lifting your toes.

With the stirrups straight across under the balls of your feet, have someone on the ground tell you whether your stirrup leathers are vertical. If they aren't, your saddle may be adjusted too far forward on the horse or the stirrup bars may be placed too far forward on the saddle. This makes it virtually impossible for you to sit well or to use your legs correctly because your seat will always be behind your legs instead of directly over them. Based on your observation that your leg position is better without stirrups than with them, I suspect that your stirrup leathers may *not* be vertical. That's typical of riders whose saddles have poorly positioned stirrup bars.

If your leathers *are* vertical, that's great. There are some special stirrups that may help make you more comfortable, but avoid old-fashioned offset stirrups that are designed to lock your feet and ankles into one position. To maximize the mobility and flexibility of your feet and ankles, use good-quality stirrups with jointed, flexible sides and treads that adapt to your feet.

One of the best exercises is also one of the most basic: As soon as you've warmed up and are ready to stretch, spend some time in your two-point position. Keep your hip angle slightly closed, your body just out of the saddle, and your legs under you with your knees relaxed so that your weight can flow down into your heels. Hold the position as long as you can hold it *correctly.*

Pay attention to what your body is doing. If your lower legs start to move around, that means that you have begun to pinch with your knees, which are now acting as pivot points. When that happens, your lower legs begin to swing, and you'll eventually lose a stirrup, so as soon as you feel at all insecure, take a deep breath, then exhale while you relax your knees and let your legs grow very long with low heels.

Go around the arena and use posts, dressage letters, spots on the wall, or anything as markers. Whenever you pass a marker, rise into your two-point and hold it (correctly!) until the next marker. Practice! At a trot, alternate posting six steps and two-pointing for six steps at a time. Concentrate on keeping your legs long, relaxed, and stretched around the horse — no grabbing, no gripping, no tight joints or muscles, no pivot points. You'll ride better and more effectively, you'll experience less fatigue, and your horse will be happier.

The only correct way to rotate your legs inward is to rotate the whole leg *from the hip*. At a standstill, with your stirrups adjusted correctly, stand in two-point for a moment, put your reins in your left hand, and with your right hand, reach *behind* your right thigh and grab your thigh muscle— the big one that lies on the inside and back of your leg. Pull it to the back and let your leg slide into place against the saddle while you remain in your two-point. Then change the reins over to your right hand, reach back with your left hand, and pull your left thigh muscle back behind the leg, and let *that* leg slide into place against the saddle. Then, very carefully, come back to a three-point position. Now your legs should be exactly where you want them, in full contact with your saddle through the inner thigh, inner knee, and inner calf.

Try to keep them in place as you ask your horse to walk on. But be careful — when you ask him to walk, give a brief *inward* squeeze with both calves and immediately relax your legs again. Don't use the back of your calf or your heel. This is part of the new way you need to learn to ride. Warning: You'll find it impossible to keep your legs in this position when you trot, at least at first. But keep trying, even if you get just a few steps at a time. It's hard to change old habits — don't get frustrated if it takes time.

When the new position begins to feel natural, you're on your way. And when you're comfortable and correct over low jumps, you'll find it easier to jump the

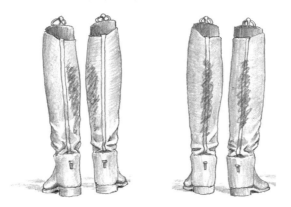

Boot reading: The rider on the left uses her inner leg and turns her leg out slightly; the other turns her leg so far out that the back of her leg is on the horse.

larger fences. When the jumps get to three feet, you might want to shorten your stirrups another hole, and then do a few days of two-point exercises to accustom your muscles to the demands of this new position.

Rider with Painful Stitch

Q My 16-year-old daughter is an accomplished hunter/jumper rider. But often when she's riding, even on just a light hack, she gets a stitch in her side. Most of the things I've read about stitches refer to runners and say that one should avoid eating just before exercise. But my daughter *never* eats before riding (in fact, it's all we can do to get her to eat at shows at all). Obviously the intense pain of a stitch affects her riding. Do you have any suggestions or advice?

A The idea of not eating before exercise is based on the idea that it's better not to need the blood supply for two different systems at once. If the blood is being used by the digestive system, it's not free to be used by the muscles; if the muscles are put into work and the blood goes to the muscles, digestion may not be as smooth and efficient as it should be.

This does make sense, for humans and for horses, and it's one reason why it's not a good idea for either a human or a horse to eat a large meal just before doing something physically demanding. I see many riders like your daughter, who become so tense and excited at competitions that they don't want to eat or drink at all. This isn't good either; they simply don't realize that by starving and becoming dehydrated, they are hurting their bodies *and* their chances of doing well in competition.

If you can convince your daughter to eat at regular intervals during the day, she'll have a better time at shows. I'm not talking about forcing her to sit down for a four-course meal or even a typical horse-show "greaseburger," but she needs to keep her blood sugar at a level that will let her function correctly. Don't feed her sugary foods; cookies and soft drinks are worse than no food at all. Encourage her to have a glass of milk, a banana, a couple of chicken wings, a slice of cheese — anything that will keep her body and brain nourished.

I'm sure that your daughter would be horrified if someone told her to starve her horse or deprive him of water at a show. She probably keeps a full hay net in front of her horse whenever he's not in the show ring, takes him out for a bite of grass whenever there's a break, keeps a full bucket of water in front of him, and encourages him to drink. She needs to realize that she and her horse are a team, and that they both need to be mentally alert and physically able to deal with the demands of competition. She needs to take herself seriously as an athlete and treat herself as well as she treats her horse.

As soon as possible, use one hand to put direct pressure on the painful spot. This will stop a stitch quickly.

As for the stitch in her side, I sympathize; those are indeed extremely painful and distracting. In the long term, staying well hydrated will always help. (Take mineral water along if she doesn't like tap water, but keep her drinking all day!) Warming up her muscles before the ride will always help. In the short term — that is, when she's already on the horse — one of the best ways to avoid getting a stitch is to practice deep breathing at all times. Anxious riders often hold their breath, or do very shallow breathing, and don't realize they are simultaneously holding their muscles locked in one position. It's the tight holding of the muscles that typically brings on the stitch.

In the immediate term — at the moment she experiences the stitch — she should put her reins in one hand and use her other hand to apply direct pressure to the stitch. Ten or twenty seconds of direct pressure will usually stop a developing stitch. If she gets stitches often, she probably recognizes the signs that she's just about to cramp; *that* is the best possible moment to apply the direct pressure, because even four or five seconds of pressure can head off a stitch before it gets started. She should also let that "Oh-oh, stitch coming" feeling remind her to *breathe* slowly and deeply, all the way to the bottom of her lungs.

If your daughter can (a) make deep breathing her default way of breathing, (b) warm up her own muscles before she gets on her horse, and (c) stay hydrated and keep her blood sugar up at competitions, she may find that she won't need to use the direct pressure very often, either at shows or at home.

Riding with a Bad Back

Q I love to ride and have had horses all my life. I've always owned Quarter Horses, and I love them. But now my back has gotten bad and even a short trail ride leaves me in so much pain that I wonder if I ought to own horses at all. My husband says I should just sell them and forget about riding, but I don't want to give them up. But even getting onto a horse's back hurts so much some days that I'm about in tears.

A I can suggest quite a few things, *none* of which involve giving up horses. First, see your doctor and find out what is wrong with your back. If he says, "do exercises," you'll feel better knowing that it isn't a surgical problem! And if there *is* a major problem, you should find out as soon as possible.

Many people have bad backs for one reason or another — most of us spend far too many hours each day at a desk, and most of us sit sloppily and with horrible posture. I'm guilty of that, I know! We sit badly in our cars, at the table, in front of the TV; then we wonder why we can't sit correctly on our horses!

Your spine is a wonderful structure, but it shouldn't be asked to do its own job *plus* the job of your back muscles *plus* the job of your abdominal muscles. Anything you can do to develop and strengthen your back muscles and your abdominals will help your overall comfort, your posture, your riding comfort, and the durability of your spine. Stretching will also help, but always warm up first!

Now, on to the horsy part of the suggestions.

Use a mounting block. This wonderful invention is not for weaklings, geriatric cases, and sissies, but for riders who value their own backs, their horses' backs, and their saddles. Mounting from the ground can damage all three. Do yourself, your saddle, and your horse a favor and use a mounting block. If you have a sore back, tight hips, arthritis, or any number of other painful conditions, you can buy or build a mounting block with steps that take you all the way up to stirrup height so that you simply stand next to the horse and slide on and off. Horses can be trained to stand next to the block for dismounting as well.

Get a comfortable saddle that fits you. Too many riders, especially those in English saddles, sit in too-small saddles that do not fit them. You can't be comfortable if you are in the wrong saddle or if your good old saddle has developed a warped or twisted tree (from years of mounting from the ground?) and makes you sit unevenly.

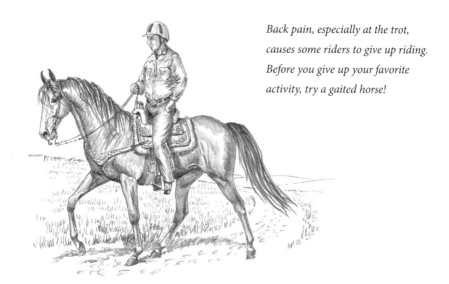

Back pain, especially at the trot, causes some riders to give up riding. Before you give up your favorite activity, try a gaited horse!

Get a comfortable horse. I've seen riders unnecessarily give up riding because trotting was just too painful. Trotting does not have to be part of your ride. If you would like to enjoy trail rides until the end of time, gaited horses can be absolutely wonderful for riders with bad backs. Before you hang up your saddle and bridle, try out some of the breeds that are famous for their smooth, easy-riding gaits: Tennessee Walking Horses, Missouri Fox Trotters, Peruvian Pasos, Paso Finos, and Icelandic Horses, for example. Some are tall and long strided; some are small and short strided, so you'll have a variety of options. Decide which breeds you prefer, and which gaits you find most comfortable, and you'll be able to enjoy your riding again.

There's even a bonus in it for you: Riding will strengthen your back muscles even if you never trot. The best exercises for the back involve hundreds of thousands of repetitions of tiny muscle movements, *not* a few big efforts. The trouble is, doing those thousands of repetitions is dead boring, unless you can simply get on a smooth-moving, comfortable horse and walk or gait down the trail for half an hour, turn around, and come back. That's all it will take — your muscles will make those hundreds of thousands of tiny movements in response to your horse's movements, without any conscious effort on your part. Your job will just be to sit up straight and enjoy the scenery while your back becomes steadily stronger.

CHAPTER 10

Facing Fear

FEAR IS A UNIVERSAL ISSUE FOR RIDERS, but each frightened rider feels utterly alone. Physical fear often makes good sense — it can be nature's way of saying "You're about to get into trouble; stop doing what you're doing!" A rider can lose confidence for many reasons, but most rider fear is based on the belief (often absolutely accurate) that the rider is not in control of the horse or of the situation or of herself. It's true that certain risks are simply inherent to the sport of riding, but it *is* possible for riders to "stack the deck" in favor of their own confidence and safety. The easiest way to lose fear is to build confidence; the easiest way to build confidence is to become a competent, knowledgeable rider.

Afraid to Ride

Q I have started riding again after about 20 years off. The kids are all gone, and I wanted something to do that I loved, so, with the help of a supposedly knowledgeable friend, I bought a horse. Unfortunately, during one of our rides the horse bolted, I came off, was knocked out, and suffered a fractured wrist and six months of downtime.

I sold that horse and now own a 7-year-old Quarter Horse. He is very kind and nice to be around and has never given me any problems. I have started riding again with an instructor who is very good, but I can't get this accident out of my mind. Every time I ride I have to tell myself to relax. If this horse spooked, I would freak. I am very nervous. Why would I want to keep doing this to myself? I think sometimes I am a bit crazy, but I have this desire to go through this until I am relaxed. I am 55 years old. I do stay in pretty good shape, but every time I ride, I am terrified.

Should I try another hobby? This one is very costly. I sometimes wonder if it is worth it at my age. I work full-time so I can usually ride only a couple of times a week. Do you think I am throwing my money away? Don't worry about hurting my feelings. After living this long, solid, honest advice is greatly appreciated.

A I'm afraid this is one of those questions that only *you* can answer. I would say that as long as riding gives you pleasure, then you're not throwing your money away. If riding makes you tense and miserable, and you find yourself becoming anxious and upset hours before your lesson, then perhaps you are throwing your money away. Your age isn't important and neither is the number of days a week that you can ride. There are people in their 80s who ride once or twice a week and love it. There are people in their 20s who are so nervous and frightened that they throw up before every ride. Everyone is different; every situation is different. What matters is whether this is something that you want to do.

If it is, maybe you should ask yourself *why* you want to do it. If it's just that you feel you need a hobby — any hobby — you could easily find something safer, more predictable, and more affordable. If you love being around horses, you can accomplish that without riding. But if it's the *riding* you love and want to do, then there's really no substitute. That is why you have to figure out exactly what it is about riding that appeals to you.

Let's assume that you really love riding or *would* love it if you could only relax. It's perfectly natural for you to feel nervous — after 20 years away from riding, you came back to it and promptly had a crash and an injury, so you know what can happen.

Relaxation in a riding lesson is partly a matter of trusting the horse, partly a matter of trusting the instructor, and partly a matter of trusting yourself. It sounds as though you have a nice horse and a nice instructor and, since you're in good shape, you actually have quite a lot going for you.

Don't put yourself on a fixed schedule — that's not conducive to either relaxation or skills acquisition.

If you decide to continue riding, I'll suggest two things, both of which will involve your instructor.

First, I think that you should go back to square one and have your instructor work with you exactly as she would if you had never been on a horse before. Begin at the very beginning and master each skill before you move on to the next one. This will help you gain confidence by ensuring that you feel competent every step of the way. Fear is a perfectly sensible emotion when you know that you're not really in control of your own body, of the horse, or of the situation. Adults, especially, need to feel that they have some control. Re-learning and *practicing* everything from the ground up, one skill at a time, building-block style, will let you achieve and feel that control.

It's also a good idea for other reasons. A lot has changed in the 20 years since you last rode: horses, riding style, teaching methods, tack, clothing. Most of all, *you* have changed. When you were younger you had a different body and a different outlook. Now you need to act as if you were learning it all for the first time, because in some ways, that's exactly what is happening.

Starting over will also help you build a good relationship with your horse and will reveal any holes in his training. That's all good, because you'll discover those holes in a relaxed, quiet way and be able to fill them safely.

You must have your instructor's enthusiastic participation in this project. Talk to her about what you want to do and why. You may find that she had already thought of this but didn't want to suggest it because she was afraid you might find it insulting. Instructors sometimes feel obligated to give you the lessons that they think you want instead of the ones they think you need. It takes a very secure, strong-minded instructor to propose a complete start-over to an adult rider.

Second, you would benefit from some relaxation exercises — meditation and visualization are great, and if your instructor can help you learn some of these exercises on horseback, that would be ideal. On *and* off the horse, you can practice the most basic form of relaxation and meditation: deep breathing. It's a great way to calm yourself and your horse.

Your question makes it clear that you like your horse and you like your instructor, but it's not clear that you like riding. Think about this. If you decide that it isn't something you enjoy, there's no shame in saying, "Okay, riding's not for me." If you enjoy riding, and your fear is the only thing that's getting in your way, try the above suggestions for a few months. Don't put yourself on a fixed schedule — that's not conducive to either relaxation or skills acquisition. Let your instructor know that you aren't expecting her to "cure" you in a fixed number of lessons. Tell her that you're willing to take as long as it takes and that you want to learn to feel comfortable and competent on a horse.

Ask yourself what you want from riding. Some people welcome the adrenaline rush of fear — it makes them feel alive and energized. Other people already feel alive and don't enjoy experiencing fear. Figure out what you like about riding and what you want from riding and have a talk with your instructor. If you decide to start all over from the beginning, take the project seriously but *enjoy* it. Remember, *we do this for fun.*

Afraid of Horses

Q I just started riding again after a 10-year "vacation." I have two Quarter Horse geldings, both around 15 years old. I guess what I need is more along the lines of encouragement than technique. I'll just tell you: *I am scared to death!* Please help! I finally broke my fear down into two categories (you can tell I have thought about this a lot).

Category one is what the horse may do while I am on the ground. I fear getting a surprise kick or getting caught up between the two horses. Category two is what the horse may do while I am riding him. I'm not afraid of him bucking as long as I don't fall off and get stepped on or caught in the stirrups — so yeah, I guess I am afraid of being bucked! I am extremely afraid of him rearing up and falling back on me. I keep telling myself to just give it time. I try to spend a lot of time around the horses to get the "feel" of it again. But I am not comfortable. Can you give me any advice, encouragement, or miracle cures?

A You don't mention your age, but if you've had 10 years away from riding, I'm going to guess that you are probably at least in your 30s. In any case, whether you are 30 or 60, the issues and answers are the same.

As we get older, we all reach the point of realizing that we are *not* immortal, that we *can* be hurt or even killed, and that we don't have all the time in the world to do all of the things we want to do. If we reach this point while we are actively involved in riding, we can usually work through it by getting some help and advice, by being more responsible about our safety precautions, and sometimes by changing our goals a little. It's much more difficult when we come to this realization during a period of years when we are not riding, because when we finally come back to riding, we remember feeling safe and happy and secure and having *fun,* but now all we know is that we feel afraid.

At some point during your time away from horses and riding, you grew up. Now you want to be around horses again and ride, but your priorities and your fears are different. You are very wise to want to do something about the situation instead of just trying to ignore it or pretending that nothing has changed.

I like your two categories. You're afraid of what a horse might do on the ground and of what a horse might do under saddle. That covers just about all possibilities, doesn't it? I understand that you need encouragement, and I think there's a good case to be made for developing some technique as well.

Before I get to that, however, let me ask you this: Are you sure that you truly *want* to ride? Sometimes people change or their wishes change or their bodies change, and what they really wanted when they were, say, 15 or 20 is not what they want when they are 30 or 40. You may really want to have horses and enjoy riding — or you may not. Before you embark on a big project aimed at getting back into the saddle, take some quiet time and think about who you are now and what you want. You may find that you don't want to ride anymore or that you don't want to own horses. If that's the case, then the real question may not be "How can I stop being afraid of horses so that I can ride them?" but rather "If riding horses just isn't something I care to do anymore, what *do* I want to do? What would I enjoy doing?" Those questions, or rather the answers, may take you in a different direction.

As long as you own horses, you have an obligation to see that their needs are met, by you or by someone else. But don't beat yourself up if the real problem is that you think you *ought* to spend time with horses and you *ought* to ride because you *should* enjoy horses and riding. Some people do; some people don't. Some people do, and later in their lives, they don't. Don't push yourself to get better at something that you don't really want to do at all — instead, look for something that you want to do and that you can enjoy.

Looking after horses well, and riding well, requires a big investment in time and effort, not to mention money. If it's something you love, the investment is worth it; if it's something you no longer enjoy, it is not. Do you bounce out of bed every morning feeling happy because you own two horses? Or do you lie there wishing that you didn't have to handle and ride them and finding reasons why you just "don't have time," day after day? After thinking about this, you may decide that you want to ride more than anything. You may decide that you don't, but you'll have a go anyway. You don't have to make a final decision right now, but do realize that there's nothing wrong with saying, "I've thought about it, and this isn't what I want to do."

If you do decide to keep riding, just giving it time isn't going to work. You need to spend time in the saddle, but *safely* and not necessarily on your own horses. Keep the goal in mind: You want to be back in the saddle, feeling confident and having fun. Intelligent adults can't feel confident unless they feel competent, and right now you don't feel competent, so let's begin with that.

Simple round-pen work can help you learn to read your horse's body language
and to use your own body language to communicate with your horse.

I suggest (no surprise to you, I'm sure) that you start by taking lessons. Find a good instructor who works well with adult beginners. The way for you to get your confidence back safely is for you to start over again from the ground up, with an instructor who understands what it's like to be in your position. Don't let anyone talk you out of taking lessons — it's the best and safest way to get you where you want to go. If you ride stock seat and the best instructor in your area teaches hunt seat, go to that instructor. Don't worry, you won't have to ride in that style forever; what matters most right now is the quality of the instructor.

Basic horsemanship — horse handling, horse care, and riding skills — is the same no matter what the saddle looks like, and sometimes it's actually easier to start over again with lessons if you learn a different style of riding. You may want to begin the search process by looking through the instructor listings at the Web site for the American Riding Instructor Association. Finding a certified instructor doesn't guarantee you a personality "match," but at least you'll know this is someone whose knowledge, teaching skills, and safety practices have been professionally evaluated.

Take your first 10 or 20 or 30 lessons on the instructors' horses, not on your own. You need to build your own confidence first, and be able to think about yourself and what you are doing, without worrying about what your horses might do. Tell your instructor about your horses and ask whether she is willing to evaluate them and then school them for you while you watch. Even a few sessions with each will be enough for a good instructor to know whether you have any business riding those horses any time soon.

If your instructor has good round-pen skills, ask for a demonstration and, if possible, a few lessons. Round-pen work is something you can do with your own horses to develop your confidence in your ability to read your horses' body language, and to make yourself clear to them. It's an important adjunct to your riding lessons.

Do some excercise off the horse that will build up your own strength, balance, and coordination. Swim, dance, skate, jog, or walk, but do *something* active that you enjoy. Yoga and tai chi are wonderful for your riding and will help you with the fear by teaching you to breathe properly. A cheap and extremely effective exercise program is walking and practicing deep breathing at the same time. The more balanced, coordinated, and strong you feel, the more confidence you will have in your own body and the easier it will be for you to feel confident and relaxed on a horse.

Don't try to talk yourself out of being afraid. Bucking is dangerous, and having a horse fall over backward on you can be fatal — it's sensible to be afraid. Avoid the fear by taking your first set of lessons on your instructor's quietest horses, the ones that are more likely to fall asleep than over backward and that would never even consider wasting any energy on bucking. Then work on your physical skills, on and off the horse, and ask your instructor at each lesson to talk you through some "What would you do *if . . . ?*" situations.

Start over again from the ground up, with an instructor who understands what it is like to be in your position.

If you have no idea what you would do if your horse reared, a rear will be much more frightening. Learn what's involved in a rear, what leads up to a rear, how to prevent one, and what to do in case the horse does rear. If you understand what the rider's best position and responses would be, and you practice that position and those responses (even on a horse that is standing half-asleep in the center of the ring), you'll have something to do if that situation should ever arise. Plus, if you know which *rider* behaviors and actions are most likely to provoke a rear, you will find the situation much easier to avoid.

Bucking and rearing are usually signs of great discomfort or complete confusion and frustration on the horse's part. They are also usually caused by the rider, one way or another. The best way to avoid having to deal with a bucking or rearing horse is to learn how to be a competent, kind, and considerate rider and to know what you should do just in case. It's a bit like practicing a fire drill; if you know exactly what you would do, and in what sequence, you can worry less.

Ask your instructor to teach you emergency dismounts. Even if you never have an occasion to perform one in the real world, it's very helpful to know how to get off a moving horse without getting hung up in the stirrups. We all come off sooner or later, so it's good to learn how to come off in a way that doesn't cause damage — even to your pride. Arena dirt may make for a soft landing, but it tastes terrible. Learn how to get it on your boots instead of your helmet.

You can enjoy riding for the rest of your life if you're willing to take the time to get over your fear by becoming a competent rider with confidence in your own abilities both on and off the horse. At the same time, develop a set of realistic goals for yourself so that you can have the mental satisfaction of working on them and meeting them.

One final note: no matter what sort of lessons you take, and no matter what sort of riding you decide to do, get a helmet that meets or exceeds the current ASTM/SEI standards and wear it *every* time you ride, even if you think you're "just getting on for five minutes." There are no miracle cures for brain injuries.

Help, I Am a "Fraidy Cat"!

Q I used to ride horses once in a while at those rent-a-horse ranches. One day when I was 13, I got the ride of my life on what I thought was a trail horse. After losing the reins and total control, I decided to bail. As I jumped off, my foot slipped through the stirrup. He dragged me for about half a mile. (This camp provided no helmets and never told us to wear heels, and I didn't know better.)

It took me 14 years to even go in a pen with a horse, let alone touch one. Now I own two mares, ages 16 and 23. I am sure both are great riding horses, but as I am now 30 years old and not as agile as I used to be, I am petrified of falling. I don't want to go fast on my horses. I prefer walking on the trails, not galloping or any of that. Maybe in the future.

My question is, what are the chances of serious injuries when being dumped from my horse and what can I do to prevent them? Are disabling injuries common, or do we just hear about them more because of their severity? I am sure you can't answer my question 100 percent, but I was just wondering. Also, what is the best helmet to wear?

A I don't think that you're a "fraidy cat," I think you're sensible: You had a terrifying experience. Losing control, falling, getting hung up in the stirrup, and being dragged would be enough to make anyone think twice about ever getting on a horse again.

It's *always* possible to become injured in a fall from a horse. A fall from any height, even a couple of feet, can cause severe injury, and when you're on a horse, the distance between your head and the ground is more like eight feet. It's possible to take precautions by being sensible, learning to ride competently, being extremely aware of the horse and your surroundings at all times, and of course by using appropriate safety equipment, but there's always a risk. The only way to avoid the risk is to stay off horses entirely, but as you've found, that can become frustrating after a while.

I recommend that you take a three-pronged approach to your return to riding.

First, make yourself as fit, strong, and supple as you can *before* you get in the saddle. Whether you go to a gym, take an exercise class, or just take long walks every day, work on your physical fitness. Fit riders get into much less trouble and are better equipped to cope when they do get into trouble.

Second, as soon as you feel that your fitness level is increasing, start taking riding lessons. Find an instructor who is gentle with horses and humans and who deals well with nervous adult riders. A good instructor can help you both on and off the horse by teaching you breathing exercises, relaxation techniques, and visualization exercises. Start looking now so that you'll know whom to call when you're ready to schedule lessons.

In an ideal world, your instructor would have good school horses for your lessons; if that's not the case, ask the instructor to begin by giving your *horses* lessons while you watch. That way, when the horses are ready for you and you are ready for them, you'll be able to take lessons on your own horses, and everything will be under the instructor's supervision.

Third, ask your instructor to teach you how to perform an emergency dismount (otherwise known as bailing out) in case you're ever in a situation where you've lost control of your horse and he's heading in a direction you'd prefer not to go (onto the highway, for example). You might also find it worthwhile to talk to a gymnastics or martial arts instructor about taking a couple of lessons in falling. There are a lot of different ways to fall, and some are much less dangerous than others. Once you know how to fall, it doesn't mean you have to do it all the time to stay in practice, it just means that *if* you start to fall, you'll know what to do, and you'll be much less likely to panic, freeze, and fall badly.

The only way to avoid the risk is to stay off horses entirely, but as you've found, that can become frustrating after a while.

As for helmets, you have a lot of options. As long as it's new and meets or exceeds the current ASTM/SEI standards for equestrian helmets, the brand won't matter. Helmet *fit* does matter. Visit tack shops and try on helmets until you find one that fits your head well and is comfortable when it's properly adjusted and the harness securely fastened. The best helmet is the helmet you'll actually wear, so find one that's comfortable.

You are wise to be thinking about riding in a helmet even though you have no plans to gallop down the trails. Most falls occur at a walk or a standstill, but many riders aren't aware that this is the case.

It may take a long time to build your confidence again, and that's fine. The plan is for you to become comfortable with the horses and eventually *on* the horses, but that might mean spending several weeks just mounting and then immediately dismounting while your instructor holds the horse, followed by several weeks of mounting, sitting for a minute or two, then dismounting, and so forth. It's not easy to deal with a loss of confidence, especially after so much time away from horses. Give yourself permission to go as slowly as you need and take as much time as you need.

Rider Confidence Loss — Whose Fault?

Q My best friend Joy and I (we are 15 years old) have been riding for two years. I was leasing a horse that was rather stubborn, but we were starting to build a relationship. At one of our weekly lessons, Joy was riding an 11-year-old Saddlebred mare that our trainer had owned for several months. The horse had been abused, but our trainer had ridden her many times and even had an 11-year-old girl on the horse and everything went fine.

I had a pretty good lesson, but Joy didn't at all. The horse refused to do what she asked, so the instructor, to prevent further frustration, told us to go outside to cool the horses down. She stayed in the barn with a new student while we walked into the front field to cool the horses out. Things were fine until Joy's horse wouldn't turn. She kicked her and kicked her, and then the horse suddenly reared and flipped back on top of her. Nothing was broken, but Joy had a badly bruised ankle.

It's been a few months, but Joy hasn't been riding since. She told me that she didn't want to ride because she didn't want to see the horse, but that horse isn't at the barn anymore. Joy wasn't a great rider, but it was the one time a week that I could see her and talk to her. Since the accident, I have hardly talked to her because our schedules conflict so much.

I know our trainer shouldn't have left us unattended, but everyone makes mistakes. Joy tells me that she wants to ride, but that she doesn't know if she can get back up on another horse. Recently she said that she has enough courage to come back, but that she doesn't want to face our trainer again. I don't understand why. Is there anything I can do to help her gain her confidence again enough to come back to riding?

A I'm sorry to hear about Joy's accident and loss of confidence. I do understand that you'd like to see your friend, and that riding was a good way for the two of you to get together, but I'm not sure that you can, or should, convince your friend to come back and ride again at this particular stable.

I'm concerned about the subtext of your story. As an instructor and as someone concerned with the ethics and practices of instruction, I find it disturbing that the instructor put your friend on a horse with known problems. A rider with two years of weekly group lessons has very little experience and should be taught on reliable, steady horses.

I also find it disturbing that your friend was unable to get the horse to do what she wanted *in a lesson* and was apparently given no help by the instructor. Sending a frustrated rider outside may get the problem out of the instructor's sight, but it doesn't even *begin* to address the real issues of communication and control. It would have been much more sensible and ethical for the instructor to teach your friend how to handle the horse, or, if this wasn't possible because of your

A rider who kicks the horse and jerks the reins is likely to provoke a buck or a rear.

friend's inexperience and the horse's individual problems, to put your friend on a different horse.

I'm also concerned that when the horse wouldn't turn, your friend "kicked her and kicked her." I'll bet that she was also pulling the reins. This is not the way to ask a horse to turn, but it's a pretty reliable formula for causing a horse to rear or fall over. Why would your friend do something so painful to the horse and so dangerous for both horse and rider? It was the wrong thing to do, and it says a great deal about the quality of the instruction your friend has been getting.

Riding is risky, and there is no reason to make it more so. Unavoidable accidents are one thing; setting up situations that make accidents likely is quite another!

Even though two years is not a long time, a rider who had taken two years of weekly lessons with a good instructor would not have done such a thing. And a novice rider shouldn't have been on her own in this situation — if the instructor had been there to say "Loosen the reins and send the horse forward," the situation would have been much safer. When a horse and rider have been unable to communicate and cooperate in a supervised lesson, it is absolutely inappropriate to send that horse and rider out of the arena and out of the instructor's sight.

I think that your friend had a big scare and a painful fall, which can be hard to deal with even under ideal circumstances (quiet school horse, well-taught rider, good instructor). Under the circumstances, your friend was lucky to escape with just a bruised ankle. I know that it would be lovely for you to ride together again, but I strongly advise that you find another barn where the quality of instruction is better. You're right; everybody *does* make mistakes. But a good instructor wouldn't have made this particular mistake. Riding is risky, and there is no reason to make it more so. Unavoidable accidents are one thing; setting up situations that make accidents likely is quite another!

Your friend sounds very sensible. She didn't want to get back on that horse and she doesn't want to deal with that instructor. I agree with both decisions. If you can find a better-run barn and some good instruction, preferably from an ARIA-certified instructor (to achieve certification, these instructors must prove their knowledge, teaching ability, and safety orientation), I'll bet you can get your friend to come out and ride with you again.

If not, perhaps there is something else the two of you could do together. I know what it's like when friends have schedules that make it difficult for them to get together. I'd like to be able to tell you that you will find more time to spend together when you get older, but I have friends whom I see once a month for coffee because that hour or two is all the schedule overlap we can manage! You have my sympathy.

Dealing with Loss of Confidence

Q I am a very experienced rider who has suffered a gradual attrition of confidence in a way that I do not myself quite understand. I am 38 years old and have evented through Training Level. At various points in my life I have considered myself quite a brave rider, catch-riding horses at a cross-country schooling day, riding "anything" as a working student, or taking lessons and competing in a foreign country where it took an effort to puzzle out the instruction.

Nearly two years ago, I sustained a fairly frightening neck injury in a freak fall while hacking at a walk on my young but normally exceptionally quiet mare. She had a particularly hard-to-stick buck that she only did under extreme conditions of high energy. I learned to longe her on cold days and subsequently was only bucked off when she was on a walk-only regime following injury. But I never had the feeling that I could ride through one of her bucking sessions.

With the same mare, I ran into a problem of being mutually overfaced during training and wound up with a serious stopping problem, which made me feel powerless and frustrated. That down period, however, followed a wonderful period of successes far beyond what I had dreamed I might accomplish.

I stuck it out, dropping back levels, and toward the end of my association with her we were still out there competing and had completed a Training Level event, albeit with a number of faults cross-country. I then had to sell her and move back to the United States.

During my time with this mare, I occasionally felt some fear, but on balance I was still participating and enjoying myself. A little over a year ago, I began to search for a new horse, this time looking for one a little less green and with a very honest attitude. On a limited budget, though, I found mostly very old, green, or "experienced rider only" types. I eventually found a fairly green off-the-track Thoroughbred with an exceedingly honest attitude.

He has silly days when the mountain lions are hiding in every corner, and on those days it takes a great deal of persistence to get him to settle. I have never fallen off of him, but he has quite a big spook, and my confidence has spiraled further and further, to where I am doing less and less with him.

When it became apparent that I was having some issues with him, I started a regular program of both dressage and jumping lessons, and I found a jumping trainer to work with him from the saddle on a weekly basis. Still, on a bad day, very minor reactions on his part can reduce me to an ineffective quivering mass, and I find *myself* spooking at things that the poor horse never noticed. On a good day, we can do very nice work, and we had excellent results in our first schooling show together. Nevertheless, I am not having fun and the horse is not working at anything like his potential. I have finally decided to sell him, as he will be a lovely horse with someone who is not disconcerted by his occasional silly (but within normal range) behavior. He's by far the nicest horse I have ever owned.

I am puzzled by my loss of confidence and wonder how I can get back to a level of performance that I enjoy without constantly having to bully myself into riding. While I am brave enough to get on a strange horse and ride it, I have not been truly comfortable, and I feel I have lost all confidence in my ability to handle any sort of trouble.

How do I regain the feeling that I am not going to lose control over a spook, or buck, or scooting-off incident? How do I find a horse that will challenge me at an acceptable level but reward persistence on my part with reasonably steady behavior? I think that people who see me ride, or who have known me for years, are puzzled by what amounts to a gross regression in riding ability that is entirely driven by my attitude and not my physical ability.

My ego, which not too long ago aspired to upper-level eventing, is fairly seriously dented, and I am worried that my ability to accept the risks inherent in riding has become severely compromised. I am afraid I will become bored and even a little embarrassed if I buy a "schoolmaster," but I am clearly having problems dealing with a moderate challenge to my sense of control. Can I get over this and be a competitive rider on "real" horses again? What is the best way to get there? How can I find a horse that will give me confidence?

A   As you already know, there are no simple answers to your questions. You certainly have my sympathy, and perhaps I can offer some thoughts that will help you with your process of self-examination.

Even a quiet, kind, reliable horse can have days when he sees mountain lions
everywhere; even an accomplished rider can find herself airborne.

First, I think that you are right to sell your present horse. He is not enhancing your life, and you are not enjoying him. You deserve a horse you can enjoy; he deserves an owner who can enjoy him. This is a wise move on your part, but please be clear in your mind about the real reason for the sale.

It makes very little sense — and from the horse's point of view, it makes none at all — to get rid of a horse because you aren't using all of his potential. What potential do you mean? The horse's performance potential and competitive potential mean nothing to him. Ambition is not an equine quality, so let's put that notion aside for the moment.

What other sorts of potential does a horse have? What about his potential for friendship? What about his, and your, potential for real companionship? What about your potential as a team and his potential for joyous involvement in the activities you share: hacking, jumping, and schooling? In the long term, *that* is the potential that should concern you, and that's the potential you need to reach for.

If your only interest were competition, you wouldn't be asking these questions; you would be keeping, and riding, this horse. He has great competitive potential, and you said he's a nice horse. I think that before you begin shopping for a different horse, you need to look into yourself and figure out what you want.

You have a lot of experience, and your goals until now have been primarily competitive, with the plan that you would work your way up through the levels of eventing. As part of this experience, you've sustained falls and injuries and you've developed fear. There is nothing wrong with this and nothing wrong with you. Ask yourself what it is that you enjoy about competition. At this point, it's probably clear to you that the thrill of the adrenaline rush is no longer a big factor in your life. You may simply have outgrown the roller-coaster fixation and not be looking for speed and scares and an increased heart rate.

Is it possible that you may be less interested than previously in pushing yourself to the limit in competition? Yes, there are riders who stay fiercely competitive until the day they hang up their spurs, but not everyone has the same riding goals throughout life. The competition-focused life doesn't suit every rider, and of the riders who enjoy it, not all of them enjoy it forever. There are many different ways to appreciate horses and enjoy riding.

Ask yourself these questions: If someone were to tell you that you could no longer compete under *any* circumstances, would you be angry? Frustrated? Relieved? Would you immediately think of giving up riding or would you want to find other ways to enjoy your time with horses? Do you feel that you "should" compete, that you "ought to" be ambitious? Do you feel that you are somehow "giving up" and "selling yourself short" by not following the plan you developed when you were much younger and less experienced?

There's much to be said for consistency of purpose, but not when it gets in the way of personal growth and change. The ambitions that suited you when you were 18 or 20 may no longer be relevant now. Don't try to hold on to them just because they were yours for a long time. It's perfectly logical for you to have new and different ambitions and interests. Don't push yourself to perform when you aren't enjoying the sport. If you still love eventing, pursue it to the limit, but if you *don't,* for heaven's sake, don't continue in the face of your own fear, frustration, and lack of enjoyment.

When you loved the sport, what did you find most appealing and most compelling? Was it the communication and precision of the dressage phase? Was it the courage and speed of a brave horse going cross-country and jumping boldly over unfamiliar fences? Was it the knowledge that you had prepared and conditioned your horse so well that the final show-jumping phase presented no problems for either of you? *Each of these sensations can be found elsewhere.* Dressage is entirely worth pursuing as a sport and an art of its own; hunting provides the scenery and spontaneity of a cross-country run; and there are many forms of long-distance and endurance riding that test your ability to prepare and condition your horse and yourself.

You've been badly injured and you probably had one of those life-changing visions of yourself in a wheelchair — a reaction that is entirely normal after that sort of a fall. I'm sure that you've had falls before, but consider this: At 38, you don't bounce as easily or recover as quickly from injuries and you probably have a much stronger sense of your own mortality. A fall or an injury that a 12-year-old might brag about can cause long-term nightmares for an adult, just because the adult knows more about life, death, serious injury, and the ease with which we can cross the lines that separate them.

It's quite possible that you would have handled both fall and injury with comparative ease if you'd been on an unfamiliar horse or one known to be difficult or spooky — what made this so bad for you is that it happened on a quiet horse you trusted. This should have taught you a very important lesson, however: No matter how much you trust a horse's character and intentions, you must never forget that *a horse is a horse*. Trust your horse, but always remember that he has a full set of built-in, hard-wired, fully automated horse reactions, including sudden jumps, bucks, and leaps that can unseat a rider.

There are many different ways to appreciate horses and enjoy riding.

Let's look at the physical fear. There are things you can do to reestablish your sense of control, at least over your own body's balance and breathing and emotions.

One of the most useful things you can do is increase your confidence in your own physical ability and reactions. Do exercises to promote strength and flexibility. Take a good class in yoga or tai chi to help you with stretching and breathing, and physical and emotional balance; take a Pilates class to help develop your core strength and overall flexibility; take a martial arts course for self-confidence and for the ability to deal with falls.

I think that your best way to come to terms with all this would be to follow through with your plan to sell your horse. Then try some of the things I've suggested to increase your physical and emotional control over yourself and take the time you need to figure out what it is you like best about riding and what it is that you most want to do. If you don't ride for six months or a year or two years, don't worry; you can always go back to it when you're in a condition to enjoy it more. My fear for you right now is that if you continue to ride without enjoying it, something will happen to make you give up horses and riding entirely.

Taking some time out to work on your confidence doesn't mean giving up or quitting; it means that you're acting to improve your life. Take steps that will let you come back to riding, *if you find that you want to,* with renewed confidence and enjoyment. If you find that you don't want to, then don't, but don't think that this makes you a failure. It doesn't. Times change, people change, priorities and perceptions change, and we don't necessarily always want, or do, what we once wanted or did.

When and if you come back to riding, I suggest starting over again with a really good instructor, on a reliable school horse, and trying something other than eventing at least for a few months. If you take dressage or hunt seat or stock seat lessons, you'll be able to focus on riding and learning, without feeling that you ought to know everything already or that you are somehow failing because you aren't performing at a certain level. Spending some time studying another discipline may help you return to riding without carrying the heavy baggage of your own expectations and associations.

Restoring Rider Confidence

Q I am 18 years old, and my problem is that I have lost all confidence in riding and sometimes being around horses. I quit riding because my instructor was intimidating me. Every time I tried to ask him a question, he would just scream at me for doing it wrong. He would never tell me exactly what I was doing wrong or how to change what I was doing. He also sometimes forced me into jumping higher than I wanted to. He would taunt me if I didn't jump like the others (who were much more experienced than I was). He was purely the instructor from hell.

I didn't take lessons after that. Almost a year later, I test-rode a Quarter Horse mare. I thought the ride went well, but apparently the owner of the stable didn't think so because she said I couldn't ride her again, even though she had never seen me ride!

I went another year without riding and then I tried out a Quarter Horse gelding. Everything was fine until I dropped my stirrup. I leaned a bit to pick it up but at the same time a dog was chasing the horse and this girl, clearing a jump, flashed right before our eyes. I think my horse got kind of confused because he bucked me off. It really hurt mentally and physically, but I realized that if I didn't get back on, I would lose my confidence altogether.

The last time I rode was a month after that incident. I rode my friend's Thoroughbred mare, and Murphy's Law prevailed. We were cantering, and I dropped my stirrup. I leaned forward to pick it up because I couldn't find it, and BOOM! She took off! Everything became a blur after that. I tried to pull her into a circle because I read somewhere that some horses calm down if you pull them into a circle. Well, this one just went faster. The whole time, my friend was yelling "Sit back, sit back!" But I was literally paralyzed with fear and eventually I was thrown off. And that *hurt*.

I have no confidence anymore in riding. I don't even like to jump because it scares me. I want to own my own horse one day, but right now I doubt that that will ever happen. Somehow, I have some kind of a guilty conscience every time I ride. It's like I know I'm going to fall or do something stupid. I would like to part-board a horse this summer — *successfully!* What should I do?

A You must love horses and riding very much to want to ride in spite of all the events you've described. Will it comfort you if I tell you there are many, many riders in your situation?

Don't be in a hurry to arrange a lease. First you need at least six months to a year

Now you need to begin again and learn correct riding with an emphasis on safety.

of weekly lessons with a good instructor. You've been pushed too fast and too far, overfaced, and put into one dangerous situation after another. Now you need to begin again and learn correct riding with an emphasis on safety.

First, call the American Riding Instructor Association (ARIA) and ask whether there is a certified instructor in your area who teaches what you want to learn. This doesn't guarantee that you'll find the perfect instructor, but at least you'll know that the instructor has good basic knowledge, proven teaching skills, and a strong emphasis on safety.

Second, go to local schooling shows and look for riders who seem comfortable, competent, calm, and cheerful, and whose horses seem comfortable, competent, calm, and cheerful. Then find out who is teaching those riders, and try to arrange a trial lesson with that person.

Third, visit local stables and ask who teaches there, and then arrange to watch a lesson or two with each instructor. When you find yourself watching a lesson and wishing that *you* were the student, because the instructor is so clear and sensible and kind that you know you would learn and not be overfaced, ask to take a trial lesson.

Learning should be fun. If it isn't, then you've got the wrong instructor. A good instructor will not scream at you or ridicule you or force you to try things that are beyond your skill level. It may take several months to find the right instructor for you, but it's worth it, so take the time. Once you've taken lessons for several months, you can ask your instructor for advice about leasing or part-leasing a horse, and she'll be able to tell you when that would be appropriate and help you find a suitable horse.

CHAPTER 11

Helping Your Horse with His Problems

EVERY HORSE, LIKE EVERY RIDER, has certain problems and limitations. Age, injury, illness, fitness level, and emotional baggage affect both horses and humans. It's up to the rider to determine what a horse needs: training, retraining, a change of tack, or, perhaps, a change of rider.

Many problems are not caused by the horse being "naughty," but are the consequences of riders making unwarranted assumptions about their horses' level of understanding, training, or experience. Never assume that a horse should know certain things! Instead, take the time to find out exactly what that horse actually does and doesn't know.

Horse Too Sensitive to the Leg

Q My new horse Farley, a 7-year-old Arab gelding, must have been very well trained, because he reacts so strongly to my leg aids! If I just touch him with my leg, he takes off; if I accidentally touch him when I don't mean to, he runs faster; and then if I pull on him to slow him down, he bucks. Is there some way I can make him less sensitive to the leg? I ride hunt seat.

A From your description, I suspect that Farley is not, in fact, very highly trained, and that he is not at all trained to the leg. His reaction to your leg aids sounds like that of a nervous, barely trained animal that expects something unpleasant to follow the leg signal.

I'm going to make a guess here — was Farley perhaps shown in Park classes? That might explain his reaction. If he's been trained to expect *no* lower-leg contact from his rider and you have been trained to keep your lower leg on the horse at all times, you have a great formula for mutual misunderstanding.

You are going to need to treat Farley as if he were completely green and completely ignorant, which in hunt seat terms, he probably is. You don't have to deal with any of the major green horse issues: He already accepts a rider, knows how to steer, performs all three gaits, stops, starts, and turns. What he does *not* know how to do is (a) accept leg contact without getting agitated or upset and (b) interpret leg signals and respond correctly within your style of riding. He does seem to know that you expect *something* of him, however, and he is trying to figure it out. This is a good attitude, and you can work with it.

My first suggestion is that you go back to square one. Beginning with work on the longe line, teach Farley verbal commands for the gaits and for moving out at each gait. He needs to learn to listen to your voice and obey it, so you can use the voice as a bridge for your under-saddle work. It's a simple progression: Use voice while he is on the longe, then voice coupled with very light leg aids when he is under saddle, then eventually make the voice softer and finally disappear altogether. By that time he'll have learned the leg aids. (If you have a good instructor, ask for some help with this and take a lesson or two on a longe line. That would be an excellent way to teach Farley to relax when your legs are touching him.)

Be aware of what you are doing with your legs. Lessons with a good instructor would be very helpful to you and your horse, because the instructor can tell you when you are beginning to hold your breath and grip with your legs, and she can remind you to sit up, breathe deeply, and relax so that your horse can relax too. You need someone on the ground who can watch you and remind you that your legs should rest gently against the horse — not gripping, but just "breathing" with him — and that using a leg aid is a matter of increasing pressure for a moment, then relaxing the leg again.

If you try to grip, you will be tense, and your tension will make Farley tense. If you kick, or use too strong a pressure, or hold the pressure for too long, this too will make him tense and nervous. That's what's bothering him right now — he knows that you want *something* from him, but he doesn't understand what it is, and he thinks that your legs just touching him means that you want some sort of response. Because he can't figure out what it is, he's confused and frightened, and everything escalates from there.

The bucking is a symptom of an escalating communication problem between you and your horse. When he responds to your "speed up!" signals (leaning forward and gripping with the legs) by speeding up and you then pull hard on his mouth, the message he receives is "When I ask you to do something and you obey, I will hurt you!" Again, a good instructor will be able to help you learn to give clear, consistent messages to your horse.

While you're becoming more aware of what you're doing with your legs, learn to be aware of your breathing too. If you hold your breath, your legs will grip. If you can keep breathing slowly and deeply, your legs will stay relaxed on Farley's sides, and he'll be able to learn the lesson much more quickly.

Be patient. Remember, he already knows his job; it's just that you want him to do an entirely different job. He's quite capable of learning it and enjoying it, but you must be very clear, very consistent, and very kind, and give him — and yourself — time.

Retraining an Ex-Racehorse

Q Do you have any exercises for retraining ex-racehorses? My horse, Turning Tide, has a slightly hard mouth. We've just finished several weeks of longeing and are starting to ride.

A If you're just beginning to ride an ex-racehorse, you will have to teach him many things from the very beginning. He won't be able to handle a lot of ridden work at first, so ride him for brief periods and don't try to do *any* sitting trot. His back needs to develop in a whole new way to carry a sitting rider or any rider that stays on him longer than twenty minutes or so.

Ex-racehorses can make wonderful riding horses, but you have to keep two things in mind at all times:

1. Horses off the track don't know much about the kind of riding you want to do and must be taught, slowly and systematically and kindly.
2. Horses off the track are much more fit than any green horse just up from pasture would ever be, but it is not the kind of fitness that allows you to sit on their backs and work them for hours at a time. Your horse is probably quick, sensitive, and energetic, but not necessarily responsive in the way that you would like, because he hasn't yet been taught a new way to move and to channel his energy.

At the racetrack, horses learn that contact means *Go!* Remember this, because the first time Turning Tide starts to go a little faster than you like, you might curl up and hold the reins tightly, and he will probably take off with you. He won't be running away; he'll just be doing exactly what he was trained to do. Instead of curling up and hanging on the rein, make yourself sit up very tall, take a deep breath, and relax your contact, making the reins longer instead of shorter.

His mouth isn't literally "hard"; that's just an expression that riders and trainers use to describe a horse that doesn't respond the way they want him to. His mouth *is* uneducated, and you will have to educate it. To do this, use the reins as little as possible. Teach Turning Tide that he can trust you not to pull on him but that you won't throw the reins away either — you'll just stay softly at the other end of them, holding hands with his mouth.

Focus on teaching him to respond to your legs, which he won't understand at first. He is completely green when it comes to the kind of leg and seat and rein aids you'll be using. He isn't used to feeling anyone's legs low on his sides, and he has no clue what you want him to do when you apply pressure with one or both of your legs. Ask your instructor to help you teach him what the aids mean. As he learns to understand what you want from him and what your signals mean, you'll find that his mouth will magically become "soft" again.

You'll be better off if you work him in places and in ways that don't remind him of the racetrack. A different saddle, bridle, and bit will help, as will a different environment. Keep the atmosphere pleasant, calm, and quiet, keep him in an

A racehorse's training teaches him that increased pressure on the reins and a forward-leaning rider mean, "Let's gallop!"

enclosed arena if you can find one, and work on straight lines, large circles (20 meters at least), and large, sweeping turns. At first, do all of your ridden work at the walk because he will stay calm and learn more, and you'll be able to teach him the things that he'll need to know at faster gaits. After a month or so, when he is happy and comfortable and moves easily from a straight line to a circle and back again at the walk, move up to a slow trot with a lot of walk-trot transitions.

If you prepare him well at the walk, the trot won't be a problem because he'll be calm and balanced when you begin trot work. Then you'll be able to use under-saddle trot work to strengthen his back and legs and make him more responsive to your aids. And if you prepare him well at walk *and* at trot, canter won't be a problem either. By the time you canter, he'll understand exactly what you want from him in terms of speed and balance, and he'll be able to do what you ask without getting excited or upset. Take all the time you need at the walk, and if you find that you have an excited, agitated horse when you begin trot work, go back to the walk for a while. Take as much time as you need at each stage.

Nervous Horse or Brat?

Q My trainer says my horse is a brat, but I think Callie (my horse) is just nervous because the more my trainer punishes her, the worse she gets. Wouldn't she get better if she were just being bratty? That makes sense to me, but my trainer says Callie is just stubborn and trying to push the limits. She never does anything very bad as far as I can tell, and she's okay when I ride her except for worrying about dark places. And even then she's usually okay if I back off some and let her stand and look at the dark place.

My trainer says I'm letting Callie get away with stuff, but I don't think so. I like to look into dark places so my eyes can adjust before I go there, so why isn't this okay for my horse? After I let her look in the dark places, she always goes there when I ask her to. My trainer is really good with show horses, but I'm not interested in shows, just riding for fun and some trail riding. Mostly I just like to be with my horse.

A From your description, I'd say that you're right. Nervousness in horses doesn't always take the same form — some horses tremble and sweat, some get pushy and aggressive, and some, especially the quiet, more timid personalities, tend to get quiet and go a little numb. This last is often confused with being stubborn.

It sounds to me as though you are a very suitable rider for Callie, because you know when to back off and leave her a little breathing space so she can calm down and you can avoid a fight. Your trainer, however, sounds like a more aggressive personality who doesn't always recognize when backing off is the right thing to do.

Part of becoming a real rider, as opposed to just a passenger, is developing "feel." This means learning to *listen* to the horse, learning to understand what the horse needs at a particular moment, and learning to respond appropriately. The appropriate response, with any horse, will differ according to the situation and the horse's needs at that moment. Sometimes the right thing to do is push a little, and sometimes the right thing to do is back off. It sounds to me as though you are already developing into a real rider.

Horses are extremely sensitive to the moods and emotional states of their riders. A calm and loving rider can help a horse relax, while an angry and aggressive rider often makes a nervous horse so nervous that it just can't cope and will either explode or "tune out," depending on its personality. None of this is magical — horses are herd animals, and their survival can depend on their sensitivity to the emotions and moods of those close to them. The horse reads the rider through the aids, posture, breathing, heart rate, involuntary movements, and other signals.

Part of the difference between you and your trainer may be that you have more "feel," or it may be that you are less tense than she is. This could be just a basic personality difference, made worse by the difference between your interests and goals. It's sometimes hard for a high-powered, show-oriented trainer to know how to work with a horse and rider who just want to learn quietly and enjoy each other in the pasture or out on the trails.

I suspect that your trainer — probably not on purpose — intimidates Callie, who then becomes nervous and "tunes out," which makes your instructor angry, so she pushes Callie harder instead of letting her relax and starting again. Try to have a quiet talk with your trainer. Let her know that you are worried about the communication problems between her and your horse, and between her and *you*. Tell her about your riding goals and what you want from Callie. If your trainer is strictly show-oriented, as you say, and is used to dealing with high-energy, extroverted show horses, she may just not know how to deal with a more introverted, nervous horse like Callie. But whatever the reason for the problem, it's something you need to iron out before your horse gets really frightened, your trainer gets really angry, or *you* end up having to do something to your horse that you don't want to do.

If you find yourself looking for a different trainer, someone who is more sensitive to your horse, don't leave your current trainer in an angry mood. If her style doesn't work for you and Callie, then leave, but handle it in a friendly way. You may even find that your trainer will be relieved. She is probably doing her best to help you, according to her own training and experience and expectations, in which case she is almost certainly as frustrated as you are by the way things are going. She might even be happy to recommend someone else who could work with you and Callie.

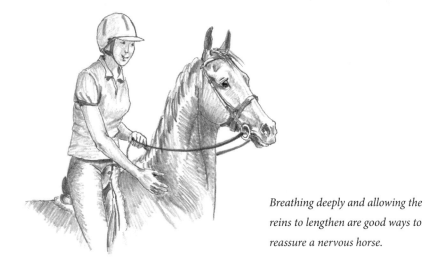

Breathing deeply and allowing the reins to lengthen are good ways to reassure a nervous horse.

My Horses' Mouths Can't Tolerate Bits

Q Both of my horses have physical problems with their mouths, and I need to begin riding them without bits. I have owned my sweet, pretty, gray mare, Snowdrift, for 11 years. Three years ago, tumors began appearing, at first just under her tail, but now there are two on, and one *inside,* her mouth. I can only ride her in a halter now, because a bit makes her cranky and distracted. Since she has never objected to her bit before, I am sure that it is rubbing on the melanoma, and my vet agrees.

My other horse is Sam, a gelding I rescued a year ago when he was 400 pounds underweight and very weak. Now he is a different animal, very shiny and healthy and beautiful. You hear about starved horses turning into monsters when they finally get enough food, but Sam has been a complete sweetheart from the very first day. My vet says that I can begin riding him, but that I should probably not try to use a bit because part of his tongue is missing and the rest of it has terrible scars on it, probably from a wire bit (we found this out when we floated his teeth after I brought him home).

So, nothing in my bit collection works for either one of my horses! I do mainly trail riding and some dressage (not very well) and a little bit of jumping. I don't go to shows.

I really enjoyed the way Snowdrift and I could communicate through the reins, and I will miss that if I have to use a hackamore, but of course I want to do what's right for her. I don't know what kind of training Sam had, if any, but I was planning to train him English, just like Snowdrift, and I was hoping that we could eventually have the same kind of communication.

Various people have suggested trying a bosal, a mechanical hackamore, or a rope halter, or using a rubber bit because that would be soft. Since I like dressage and jumping, I don't think that a bosal or a mechanical hackamore or a rope halter would be right. A rubber bit is still a bit, but would the rubber be soft enough that it wouldn't bother my horses? If not, what kind of hackamore would be best for English riding? I don't want to use anything severe. Also, is there a hackamore that would let me ride "on contact," even if it's just contact with the horse's nose? I'm 49, and I don't know if I could learn to ride *off* contact at this point. Can you suggest something that lets me use the reins to communicate without involving my horses' mouths? Neither Snowdrift nor Sam needs a bridle that provides strong "brakes."

A You are right: As long as you have these two horses, your bits are likely to remain unused. Don't worry; there are some very good alternatives.

I wouldn't recommend a rubber bit, even a soft one, for any horse with an injured tongue or a melanoma in its mouth. I think that you are right to be looking for a bridle that doesn't involve a bit at all. Some riders believe that a rubber bit is milder, perhaps because it seems logical that a thick piece of soft material would be more comfortable than a thinner piece of hard material, but even for a horse with no mouth problems, a rubber bit can be a source of discomfort and annoyance. Unless a horse has very loose and flexible lips, he's likely to have problems closing his mouth around a rubber bit and consequently is likely to develop a dry mouth.

If you want to continue to ride on contact, there's really only one form of hackamore that would work well, and that's something variously called a hackamore noseband, an English jumping hackamore, or a jumping hackamore noseband. As the name suggests, it's basically a noseband made of rope covered with soft leather, with a chinstrap and buckle attached. It has two sets of rings: one set at the ends of the piece of rope for the reins and one set a little higher for the cheekpieces of the bridle. This is *not* a mechanical hackamore, as it creates no leverage whatsoever. It's just a fancier, better-looking, more adjustable, and safer

An English jumping hackamore noseband is an inexpensive and gentle alternative to a bit.

The Bitless Bridle is a more expensive and subtler piece of equipment; in the long run, this may suit some horses best.

version of a pair of reins attached to a halter. This is a useful bridle for starting a horse, so it might suit both Snowdrift and Sam very well.

There is another bridle that might suit you and your horses even better than the hackamore noseband, because it allows you to ride and handle the reins just as you normally do, and permits much more subtle communication. It's called the Bitless Bridle. You can do all the things you enjoy doing — trail riding, dressage, and jumping — with this bridle, without worrying about losing either control or the ability to communicate with your horses.

Changing the bit or the bridle is not always the solution to a horse's or rider's problem, but in this case, both of your horses have physical problems that make any bit annoying, painful, or both. I'm glad that you're concerned with your horses' comfort and with the quality of your communication through the reins. Your horses are lucky to have you for an owner.

My Horse Can't Do What I Want to Do

Q I really like my horse a lot. I have owned him for six years, and he would do anything for me. He likes to jump and so do I. I ride hunt seat, and I have a good instructor who likes my horse. The problem is that I don't think he can do what I want to do now.

The thing is that Doc is a Quarter Horse, and he is kind of on the chunky side (not fat!). He is very honest and a good jumper until the jumps get to be over three feet, and then he starts to quit or run out on me. I've checked his saddle and bit and teeth, and I even had the vet check his feet in case he was getting navicular, like a lot of Quarter Horses. But he is healthy and everything fits fine.

My instructor thinks that he just doesn't like to jump higher than three feet and that we shouldn't make him do it if he doesn't enjoy it. I know he doesn't like it because he puts his ears back and gets mad. He is always good about lower jumps even if I ask him to jump a lot of them at once. Can I make him enjoy jumping bigger jumps? If I can't, then what should I do?

I think that my instructor thinks I should get another horse, but she hasn't come out and said that yet. She likes to let me figure stuff out on my own sometimes. Is there anything I can do to make Doc jump higher? I know I could just jump little jumps with him, but I love jumping and the high jumps are so exciting. I would like to do jumpers someday, but obviously not with Doc.

A   Congratulations: Not only do you have a nice horse, you obviously have a wonderful instructor. Things that you discover on your own are much more powerful than things you are told or that you read. An instructor who lets you figure issues out by yourself, while keeping an eye on you to be sure that you aren't going to get into big trouble, is a great asset.

So far, you've taken all the right steps. You've looked at physical possibilities, you've considered the idea that your horse may simply not enjoy or like jumping higher fences, and you're looking for a solution that will let him be happy while you advance your jumping skills.

It's very likely that your horse will never jump higher, no matter what you do. But one thing that might help is a good book or video on passive stretching. Work through the exercises when your horse is warmed up and relaxed. After a week or two of daily stretching sessions, try adding some higher jumps to your over-fences work, and see whether his attitude has changed.

Old-style, chunky Quarter Horses (the bulldog types) don't usually make very good jumpers. A long, lanky, racing-type Quarter Horse might find higher fences easy, but it's quite possible that Doc is giving you all he's got. It's also possible that even if he does respond well to stretching, he still won't be happy or comfortable over higher jumps. Be prepared to deal with that eventuality.

Your goals and your horse's comfort are coming into conflict. You're facing a difficult decision here, and you have to ask yourself what you truly want. Start with these questions, write down your answers, and discuss them with your instructor.

- What, exactly, are your athletic ambitions?
- What are your objectives for *yourself*? You'd like to ride in jumping competitions — which ones?
- How far and how high do you want to go?
- Is Doc the right horse for your ambitions and objectives?
- Can he do what you want and enjoy doing it?
- Can he stay sound doing it?

Right now, you have two conflicting wishes. You want to jump higher and be competitive. You want to ride Doc. It sounds to me as though you're going to have to choose or compromise.

How much do those goals mean to you? A rider in your position really has only two choices: You can compromise your objectives or you can find another horse that can help you meet those objectives. No horse should ever be forced beyond its abilities. You can't take chances with Doc's health and happiness by asking him for more than he has to give. It's clear that (a) you very much want to go on and become a good jumper rider, and (b) Doc is *not* going to be the horse you ride in the jumper classes.

So how do you deal with the situation? There are many possibilities. If you can afford it, buy a jumper. If you're not quite that rich, buy a horse that has shown some good potential as a jumper and bring him along with your instructor's help. If you can afford to keep two horses, you can continue to enjoy Doc by riding him in ways that he enjoys being ridden, while you make the athletic efforts on your jumping horse.

However, I'm going to assume that you're like most people — you have school, you have chores, you're probably working hard just to have the time and money to maintain *one* horse, and there's probably no way you can afford a second one.

If you can afford a horse and a half, you could part-lease a horse that jumps higher fences more happily than Doc, and continue your jumping lessons over higher fences that way.

Not all horses enjoy jumping large fences and not all horses
can remain sound if they're asked to jump large fences.

If one horse is your maximum, as it is for most riders on a budget, you could part-lease a horse for jumping and find someone to lease or part-lease Doc. He would be ideal for someone beginning to learn to jump. A reliable, steady, willing horse that jumps small fences happily would be just the thing for a rider who was starting jumping lessons, especially if the rider were having lessons with your instructor.

It's possible that somewhere along the line, you might be willing to sell him to the right person. Willing, reliable, good-citizen horses like Doc are always in demand by instructors, by parents with beginning rider children, and by nervous adult beginners. Your instructor probably knows at least five people who would love to own Doc. She may even have a new horse in mind for you to part-lease, lease, or buy.

Good instructors don't always tell their students everything they're thinking, but they are usually planning ahead for what those students will be doing a few months or a year from now. I suggest you go to your instructor and bring the subject up yourself. I'd bet that she's put the whole issue of changing horses squarely in the "figure it out for yourself" category, and is just waiting for you to broach the subject.

CHAPTER 12

Thinking Right about Horses

GOOD RIDERS USE THEIR KNOWLEDGE, skills, and riding technique to deal with horses honestly and fairly. The best riders understand, respect, and appreciate horses, and they constantly strive to build a horse-rider relationship based on mutual trust, understanding, and enjoyment. Horses are not wicked or devious; they are fundamentally generous, trusting, willing, and eager to please. Riders have a responsibility to take care of and look out for their horses in all ways, at all times. It's important to be able to put yourself in your horse's place, imagine what he might be feeling, and always give him the benefit of the doubt.

Horse Is Always Testing the Bit

Q I am 12 years old, and my horse is almost four. He is always testing his bit to see just how much he can get away with. Sometimes he leans on it hard, other times he'll twist his head around and make faces or hang his tongue out one side of his mouth. Sometimes he grinds his teeth on it.

I've tried at least 12 bits in the last year. I know my hands are probably not perfect, but I am very careful not to pull the reins hard unless I need to tell him to turn or stop or remind him to behave.

Every time I put a new bit in his mouth, he carries himself better and seems to respect the bit for the first day or two, but pretty soon he starts pushing and twisting and grinding again. I've tried putting it up where it made three wrinkles (my English trainer's suggestion). I have also tried dropping it below his mouth corners so I could put my finger in between the bit and the corners of his mouth. My Western trainer said to do that because then he would have to carry the bit himself, and he actually closed his mouth when I put the bit low like that. But he still flipped his head and twisted around and got very stiff in his neck, probably because he was angry.

I also tried putting the bit where it just touches the corners of his mouth. He was pretty good at first, but after about 20 minutes he started being bad about his head and neck again. He started dropping his head all the way to the ground, trying to test if I was secure in my saddle or if he could get away with pulling me out of my saddle.

K.C. is half Arabian and half Quarter Horse. My vet says there is nothing wrong with him. My saddle and bridle fit just fine. Both my trainers agree that he is just an ornery horse who has a problem respecting bits. It's not like he is a yearling and doesn't know what bits are for.

Why does he always test the bit, and is there some kind of bit I haven't tried that he wouldn't be testing all the time? My trainer says I should try a Waterford bit. Will that make him stop testing the bit? You say it's not good to close a horse's mouth with a noseband, but if I don't, he just keeps his mouth wide open all the time and twists his head around. It's driving me crazy — help!

A Your horse doesn't sound ornery to me; he sounds uncomfortable and confused. If you're willing to try, I think you can help him become much more comfortable and much less confused, but you're going to need to look at the whole situation differently.

First, when it comes to horses, I don't like the word "ornery," for the same reason I don't like the word "resistant." I've yet to meet a horse that is naturally ornery or resistant, but I've met many hundreds of horses whose owners or trainers use those words to avoid taking responsibility for the way they manage, handle, ride, and train their horses.

Every single time I've been asked to analyze an "ornery" horse, I've found a horse that was in pain, frightened, or confused. The specific problems are many and varied: injury, stiffness, tooth problems, poorly fitted tack, bad footing, incompetent riding, etc. The only common factor was a human blaming the horse instead of trying to figure out what was actually wrong. Horses are reactive, and when I hear about an "ornery" horse, I know that the horse must be *reacting* to something. The next step is figuring out what he's reacting to.

Now let's talk about horses "testing" their bits. The problem isn't that they do this; the problem is in the way riders and trainers interpret what the horses are doing. Testing is a misunderstood concept. If you think that your horse tests a bit to avoid it or to move it so that it doesn't work or to see how much he can "get away with," then you need to think again.

No horse can get away from a bit in his mouth, although an uncomfortable horse may curl his neck inward or hold his head at an odd angle to try to make the pressure and/or pain more bearable. A more uncomfortable horse may push

A horse cannot relax if a bit is fastened so high and so tightly
that it puts constant pressure on his mouth.

against the bit in an attempt to move forward, but that's a typical equine reaction to pain and fear: running away. All of this involves moving the bit around and moving his jaw, tongue, head, and neck around. The horse is testing for a very good reason, but it's for none of the reasons usually suggested by misinformed or misguided riders and trainers.

When a horse fiddles with a new bit, tastes it, and moves his tongue and jaw and head and neck around, he is not trying to get away with anything. He's testing the bit in the same way that you test a new pair of shoes before you buy them. You find out, by moving around in the shoes, whether they're comfortable and if they pinch your toes or rub your heels.

That's what your horse is doing whenever you change his bit. The difference between you and the horse is threefold:

1. Testing a pair of shoes is entirely acceptable, even expected. Yet your horse's testing of the bit is considered grounds for punishment. Why?

2. If you determine that the shoes don't fit, you can explain why. The horse can't give you his impressions in words, so his discomfort is often ignored or labeled "testing" without any thought given to the cause. It's *your* job to find out if the horse can be comfortable in this bit.

3. Finally, if you determine that the shoes are unsuitable, you can take them off. Your horse doesn't have this option — the bit is strapped into his mouth, and he has to deal with it for better or for worse.

That's what "testing the bit" means: The horse is trying to figure out how the bit hangs and balances and how he can carry it with the least amount of discomfort. Some bits, like some shoes, just don't fit and can't be made to fit. Some bits, like some shoes, can be reasonably comfortable if certain adjustments are made. With a good-quality bit that fits the horse's mouth well, this means adjusting the bit to hang a little bit higher or lower and watching the horse's response. When your horse twists around, makes faces, becomes stiff in the neck, continually opens his mouth, or clamps his mouth shut, he's expressing his discomfort in the only way he can; he's not trying to be difficult.

Before we leave the shoe store, I'd like you to consider one more thing. There are important differences between your shoes and your horse's bit. Shoes are designed for comfort, protection, and support. Your horse's bit doesn't protect him from anything or support any part of him. Bits directly affect the very sensitive tissues of the tongue and the bars (the space where the bit rests). They are designed for communication but often are misused for control. The mouthpieces are typically made of metal or hard nylon or rubber, and some of them are not even smooth (e.g., chain-link bits, "triangle" or "knife edge" bits, twisted wire bits).

With all this in mind, be more tolerant of your horse when he tests a new bit. Allow him to experiment with head and neck positions and ways of carrying the bit in his mouth. If the bit is suitable, this testing period will be brief. If the horse is unable to find a way to carry the bit quietly, you can be sure this isn't the right bit for him. If he finds a way to carry it quietly but spends most of his time overbending or twisting his neck or letting his tongue hang out, that should tell you that you need to try another bit.

Know your horse's mouth. Know bit design, construction, and function. Become familiar with bit materials. It's not too much for you to learn. Your horse's comfort and ability to perform depend on you.

As for adjusting the fit, there's no such thing as a "wrinkle rule." Once you've found a suitable bit for a horse, adjust the bit so that it just touches the corners of his mouth and let his reaction, then and under saddle, tell you whether he would be happier with it adjusted a little higher or a little lower. Keep in mind, though, that higher never involves creating multiple wrinkles, and lower never involves dropping the bit so that the horse has to hold it tightly to keep it from banging against his teeth. When you dropped the bit too low, your horse shut his mouth to hold the bit tightly. This made him tense his jaw and poll and neck, and his demeanor showed you that he was very uncomfortable with the situation.

Now for the specific conditions you mentioned in your letter: A horse that seems to be offering more obedient behavior for the first day or two after a change of bit may be doing so for any number of reasons. Sometimes the new bit is so painful that the horse will do anything to avoid rein pressure. Sometimes, though, there is a more subtle reason. The new bit may be just as uncomfortable as the old one, but in a different way.

Perhaps Bit A hurts, creates bruises, and then hurts more. The rider realizes there is a problem and uses Bit B instead. Bit B puts pressure in different spots. The pressure hurts, but not as much as the previous pressure on existing bruises. But in two days there are *new* bruises, and the horse once again experiences painful pressure. This doesn't mean that he didn't respect the first bit, respected the second bit for a day or two, then stopped respecting it. This isn't about respect — it's about pain.

I'm glad you don't pull the reins hard all the time, but you should *never* pull them hard. Even a smooth, gentle bit causes pain and damage if the rider pulls the reins hard. There is no appropriate time to do that, except in an extreme emergency. (Your horse is about to run in front of a train, for example!)

If your horse's mouth is badly bruised or cut, you should probably ride without a bit for several months while his mouth heals. Even then, you might want to continue to ride him without a bit while you work at becoming a more proficient rider. If you use the reins for balance or for "brakes," you're much more likely to hurt your horse's mouth.

Know your horse's mouth. Know bit design, construction, and function. Your horse's comfort and ability to perform depend on you.

Because your horse responded well to the bit just touching the corners of his mouth and didn't show any problems for 20 minutes, I have to wonder what went on during your ride. Did you ask him to hold his head and neck in one position that whole time? For a youngster of his age, it would be difficult to maintain a fixed head and neck position for *two* minutes at a time, never mind 20!

Dropping his head all the way to the ground is something that a horse *needs* to do to stretch his neck, relieve discomfort in his neck and back, and clear his respiratory system. Considerate riders invite the horse to stretch every few minutes and never try to force the horse to "hold a pose" with his head and neck for more than a few minutes at a time. After 20 minutes in one position, your horse was probably desperate to stretch his neck and get his circulation working properly, and he may have been finding it hard to breathe.

Even if you use no bit at all, you can cause your horse discomfort and cramped neck muscles if you insist that he put his head and neck into one position or "shape" and keep them there for long periods. You can test this by riding him without a bit — not with a mechanical hackamore, but with a plain hackamore noseband or a Bitless Bridle. If he still twists his neck, makes faces, and drops his nose to the ground whenever possible, you'll know that there's more going on than just mouth pain, and you'll need to talk with your vet about bringing in someone to help your horse with massage.

I can't think of any reason to try a severe bit like a Waterford on this horse. Some eventers like Waterford bits for horses that get too strong going cross-country, but your horse should just be starting light work under saddle and shouldn't be started over fences for another two years. He is an immature, half-grown youngster just learning to balance himself, let alone carry a rider. He's also just learning about bits.

Furthermore, at his age, he is almost certain to be teething. No bit will be comfortable if a young horse is teething, even if the rider is highly proficient and extremely soft. Your horse is young enough to have a retained cap, and old enough to have wolf teeth coming in, so ask your vet or your equine dentist to take a close look at his teeth.

It sounds to me as though your horse does have some issues, but I don't think that the bit is the real problem. Training and riding are more likely to be causing his behavior. Everyone is assuming that your horse understands the use of the bit, but where, exactly, did he learn this, and who taught him? He is probably doing his best to understand, but he doesn't know what you want.

You and your horse are not an ideal combination right now, as you both need more education and training. You need to learn the correct use of the reins and the rein aids, and you need to achieve a balanced seat so that you can use the reins correctly, which is to say lightly, consistently, and as little as possible. Your horse needs to grow up more and he needs to learn the language of the aids. You can't use *any* bit to communicate with a horse if he has no idea what the bit is for and sees it only as a source of pain. A rider who doesn't know the rein aids cannot teach an untrained horse how to respond to them.

I recommend turning your horse over to a kind, gentle, competent professional trainer, watching the trainer work with your horse, and taking lessons from the same trainer (on an experienced school horse, not on your own horse) for several months. When the trainer puts you and K.C. together again and works with both of you at once, you'll have more fun and he will have learned to understand the whole process of being ridden. If things go on as they are, you aren't going to enjoy riding your horse, and he will be miserable all the time.

Think of this as an investment in both your futures, in your partnership, in his soundness, and in your safety. Also, it will save you a fortune in bits, auxiliary reins, nosebands, and all the other gadgetry that too many riders try to use as substitutes for skill. Horsemanship involves making the horse as comfortable as possible in all situations, so no matter what you are doing, it always involves two-way, calm communication between horse and rider. Learning to identify and use suitable training techniques and suitable equipment is part of your responsibility as a horseman.

Talking to My Horse

Q At one of your clinics you said we should talk to our horses, so I'm trying to do that more because I realized that I don't talk to my horse at all. But all I can think of to say is stuff like "good boy" and "whoa" and "get up." When you rode my instructor's horse, you talked to him all the way around the ring and he really calmed down, so what I want to know is what were you saying to him and will it work with my horse?

A Talking is good because it keeps you breathing and keeps your horse calm as long as your voice is calm. You can say anything you want — recite your favorite poetry, list all the people you know who have birthdays in April, or talk about your plans for painting the house. Singing is also great!

I find that what works best, though, is to talk to the horse about what you want him to do and what *you* are going to do. If you're going around the ring, you can keep up a steady stream of conversation, telling your horse, "Steady the trot, there's the boy, move a little to the outside, that's it, bring your nose a little more to the inside, yes, that's right, now push on a little up the rail, thank you," and so forth. The nice thing about this is that it makes *you* think ahead to where you are going next and it reminds you, right along with your horse, of what exactly you would like him to do at any given moment.

You can also talk to yourself — this is particularly helpful if you're working on your position or your aids, because you can remind yourself of what you need to think about. If you're telling yourself, "Open chest, eyes up" or "Relax knees, long legs" or "Inside shoulder back on turns," it's very effective to say it aloud. So just keep on talking — whatever you're saying, your horse will appreciate it.

Confused about Seesawing the Bit

Q My three-quarter Thoroughbred, one-quarter Arabian is almost four years old. I ride him mostly at the walk, and he is nice and smooth and always obedient. My problem is that I want to work him in trot also, but he isn't very good in trot. He pulls on my hands and wants to lean his head forward.

My instructor has told me that I need to play with my hands a lot, pulling and releasing right hand, left hand, right hand, left hand. This will make him put his head in the right position and not pull on the bit, and then when his muscles develop they'll help him stay in the right position. It does seem to work, but one of my friends with a different instructor says that this is called "seesawing" and that it's bad riding.

When I play with my reins all the time, my horse has a good neck position and a light mouth. When I don't, he pulls and leans, and it's more than the ideal five pounds of contact. But my friend is a really good rider, so I wonder if I'm doing something wrong. Am I? And can you tell me some things I can do to develop my horse if I'm not playing with the bit? I want him to have an active mouth and a pretty neck, but I don't want to do anything wrong.

A Keep in mind that you're working with a very young and immature horse who is still several years away from physical maturity. If you're riding him very lightly and no more than two or three times a week, you may be able to do it without damaging him. You didn't mention his size, but I hope he's a small, compact horse. If he's a tall, leggy horse, then you should take your training even more slowly and start under-saddle work even later.

The horse's mouth should be active, yes, but *quietly* active — you want a gentle mouthing of the bit, showing a relaxed jaw and poll. You can't get this by "playing with the reins." From your horse's point of view, this is not *playing* — it's the rider constantly pulling and hurting his mouth.

Seesawing the reins is never appropriate. It hurts the horse and forces him to tuck his head in toward his chest to get away from the pulling. This won't develop his muscles in any good way. The kind of active mouth that *is* appropriate will come only if the rider's hands are still and quiet, there is only very light tension on the reins, and the horse can move the bit a little by moving his tongue and jaws.

Contact is something the horse, not the rider, has to control. Let your horse tell you how much contact is comfortable and appropriate for him at his stage of training and development. He should be worked quietly, at walk and a little trot, with a long, stretched neck. Your main concern should be with teaching him to respond to your leg aids by stepping well forward from behind; you really shouldn't be worried about his head and neck, except to be sure that they are both comfortable!

Five pounds of contact is certainly *not* the ideal; it's a heavy, painful pressure on your horse's mouth. If you want a specific weight to think about as an ideal, use three ounces. If and when you can work your horse while maintaining a consistent, quiet, steady, three-ounce pressure on the reins, you will both be much happier. Your horse won't be in pain, and you won't feel that riding requires immense biceps.

To develop your horse, take him out for hacks and do a lot of transitions, both between walk and trot and within those gaits (alternating longer and shorter strides). Don't stay out for too long, though — remember, you're riding a baby. And when you work in the arena, 20 minutes at a time is plenty.

In another year, when he is more mature, you can start working him longer and focusing on ring figures, especially on trot circles and trot spirals. This will help him engage his hindquarters, reach under and across with his hind legs, and balance his weight without leaning on the forehand. Walk-halt transitions and good walk-trot and trot-walk transitions will also help him balance and will start to prepare him for half-halts, which in turn will help him shift some weight to his hindquarters.

You really shouldn't be worried about his head and neck, except to be sure that they are both comfortable!

The best advice I can give you is this: Don't be in a hurry! At your horse's age, the best aid to development would be turnout in a hilly pasture with other youngsters. I know that you want to ride your horse, and you can, but be patient. Keep it slow and easy and don't ask for too much too soon. It's not time yet to be thinking about keeping the horse in an outline; he doesn't have the physical development or the understanding to sustain a rider-imposed outline!

It might help you quite a lot if you could take lessons from the same instructor who is teaching your friend. If that instructor doesn't teach at your barn, perhaps you could trailer your horse to the barn where your friend has her lessons. I am worried about your instructor's knowledge and her ability to teach well. Based on what you've said, you are being taught to ride front-to-back, seesawing the bit to put the horse into a false frame. Your friend is right: This is *bad riding*, pure and simple. The long-term results will create a bad rider and a damaged, unsound horse.

Is Seesawing the Bit *Always* Wrong?

Q Sometimes people may mistakenly use the term "seesawing" when all they are doing is *squeezing* each rein to lift the horse's head. That's not really seesawing, is it? If a horse is very heavy in the hands, the rider needs to do *something* to bring his head and neck up into the proper position. I have great success in getting a heavy-headed horse to pick up his head by squeezing the alternate rein to annoy him just until he stops leaning. Is this a bad thing to do, and if so, why?

A   I'm glad you asked this, because it gives me the chance to clarify a very important point. "Squeezing" the reins with alternating hands to make the horse tuck his head toward his chest is a somewhat less obvious (to spectators, perhaps, but not to the horse) version of seesawing the reins, but it's still not correct and it doesn't teach the horse or the rider anything useful.

The way to pick up a heavy-headed horse's front end is *not* to back him off the bit and force his head down with the reins; it's to engage his hind end and let him stretch his topline. As his hind end steps under and his back lifts, his neck and head will find their proper position. This is not a single, fixed position! What is "proper" will vary according to the horse's conformation, development, and stage of training.

It's not up to the rider to try to decide what's correct for the horse or to try to force the horse into an artificial frame. Seesawing, "playing with the reins," and "squeezing alternating reins" are all the same thing: an attempt by the rider to put the horse's front end into a particular outline. In the short term, this can put the horse's front end (and *only* the front end) into a "shape" that may fool the uneducated, but it won't fool a horseman and it certainly won't fool the horse! In the long term, it will create a horse that can't move properly and a rider who is in the habit of using hands instead of legs.

The purpose of the reins is to allow the rider to communicate with the horse, gently and clearly and softly, by means of the bit. The bit should never be used to hurt, force, or "annoy" the horse. Pulling the bit isn't annoying, it's painful. If you are in doubt, hang the bridle from your knee so that the bit rests across your bare shinbone and have someone stand behind you and pull the reins back and forth. The pain you feel will be very close to what the horse feels, as the shinbone is the structure that most closely approximates the structure of the bars of the horse's mouth: skin over nerve-rich tissue over bone.

Letting Others Ride My Horse

Q   I have two nieces, nine and ten years old, who have taken some riding lessons and ridden a few other times. Now they want to ride my horse.

He is a very sane Quarter Horse who is not too big (14.3 hands), so I don't worry about him being "too much horse" from that standpoint, but he is in dressage training and is working Second to Third Level. He is *very* forward and has a huge trot. Do you think that the horse would be overtrained for them to ride? Might they get him going more than they could handle by bouncing around and being generally unbalanced?

If so, do you have any explanation that I could give my brother and sister-in-law? They think that I'm being silly to worry. If you think that this would *not* be a problem for my horse, what can I do to make sure that he doesn't inadvertently get socked in the teeth? He is pretty fussy about that and if it goes on too long, he can get angry, which leads to major head flipping.

A   This is an issue for many riders, but it doesn't have to become a problem if you take control right now.

Your brother and sister-in-law are just thinking that it might be nice if their kids could have fun with your horse. They don't have the knowledge or the experience to understand the possible risks to their children, much less the risks to your horse and to you.

You know that your horse will not be particularly happy if you inflict novice riders on him, and since you've gone to some effort to build a meaningful partnership with your horse (that's what dressage is all about, after all), I can't imagine that you would take any chances with his comfort and happiness. I do realize, however, that those are not considerations that are likely to register with non-horsey visitors, even if they are family members. So here are some things you may not have considered but that all have a bearing on your decision.

Insurance and liability issues: Whenever someone else rides your horse, you have a liability issue. Are you carrying the kind of insurance that allows you to do this? Are the children in a confined area, under supervision, and wearing, at the very least, ASTM/SEI approved helmets and proper footgear whenever they are on or near the horses?

Litigation: This is why you need the insurance! I'm sure that your brother and his wife would never want to sue you if their kids got hurt while playing with your horse, but here's the problem: They wouldn't have to. Their insurance company could and would sue you, *with or without their consent,* because even if their own insurance covered the cost of any medical work, the insurance company would, after paying out to the hospital, want to recover that money and would come after you.

Family relationships: These tend not to be the same after an accident happens. It's better to be known in the family as "nasty Aunt Mary who won't let us ride her horse" than to be known as "crazy Aunt Mary who should have known better than to put those babies on that vicious, dangerous animal." And believe me, any horse that a child has fallen off, for any reason, will instantly become, to the rest of the family, "a vicious, dangerous animal."

As for the things you're wondering about: Your horse's training will, of course, deteriorate, along with his soundness, if he is used for "fun rides" by untrained, uneducated riders of *any* age and size. A dressage horse in training is a work in progress and should not be handed over to anyone, child or adult, for random riding.

Furthermore, your nieces will not enjoy trying to hang on to an energetic, well-trained, confused, uncomfortable, and upset dressage horse. That's precisely what they will be doing if you let them ride your horse, and even a short trot could cause them to fall off and become injured.

> *Your horse's training will, of course, deteriorate, along with his soundness, if he is used for "fun rides" by untrained, uneducated riders of any age and size.*

Think of it in driving terms — they're at bumper car stage, not at Maserati stage. You wouldn't lend a youngster your Maserati just because the child (a) was related to you, (b) wanted to drive a Maserati, and (c) had been allowed to sit on Daddy's lap and steer the family car up and down the driveway a few times.

If you feel very strongly that these children need to ride when they come to your house, I suggest that you do three things. First, get all the necessary insurance. Second, buy an "elder statesman" school horse or pony — one that knows it all, is used to putting up with neophytes, and is as patient and as unflappable as a horse can be (and remember, no horse with a pulse is 100 percent unflappable or 100 percent safe). Third, get a good instructor to give the children lessons when they visit and have *that* be their special treat at your house.

You could, of course, offer them the option of being led around on your horse's back for a few minutes, with the horse wearing a halter and lead rope (certainly not a bridle), but most youngsters who have had a few lessons and think they know how to ride are likely to be insulted rather than pleased by such an offer. That's unfortunate, but the bottom line here is that your private horse is not a public or a family commodity. Your private horse in dressage training is not suitable for beginner riders of any kind. Your nieces are unique, irreplaceable children. Keep these things in mind, and just say no. You'll be doing the right thing, and no sane adult will question your actions or your motives.

If it does cause a little frostiness between you and the children's parents, so be it. Refer them to any reliable source of information about riding and children, such as the American Medical Equestrian Association (AMEA) and the United States Pony Clubs (USPC, Inc.), where they will find that you are absolutely right, and that your "No" is in the best interests of their children.

Do Horses Enjoy Being Ridden?

Q I have just started taking riding lessons and am having fun so far, but I am a little worried about the horses. Do they like people jumping on their backs and riding them around? I am a total animal lover and want to make sure that I am not harming the horse. I hope that they enjoy it, but as a new rider I make quite a few mistakes.

Could you shed some light on whether horseback riding goes against a horse's nature? Is there anything I can do to make it more enjoyable for them? I'm sure being a better rider would help!

A You may be new to horseback riding, but you're already thinking like a horsewoman. You ask a very good question. The answer is that horses *can* and *should* enjoy being ridden, but whether they enjoy it or not, and how much they enjoy it, depends for the most part on their riders.

Horseback riding does go against a horse's nature in a way. That's why some people object to the term "natural horsemanship," because there is nothing natural about a horse carrying a rider. Horses aren't properly designed to carry loads, and in nature, the only thing that's going to leap onto a horse's back is a predator that's trying to kill and eat the horse.

Horses have to be taught to accept and carry a rider. One of the lovely things about them is that they are such willing and companionable animals that they can and do learn this easily, provided their trainer makes the experience pleasant for them.

If a horse is trained and developed to be strong, flexible, coordinated, responsive, and easily able to carry a rider, is taught to understand the language of the aids, and is ridden by a considerate rider who makes the horse's physical and mental comfort top priorities, that horse will definitely enjoy being ridden and will typically trot up to meet his rider at the pasture gate. A horse that is forced into submission, ridden with equipment that causes pain, and jerked around by a harsh, ignorant, and thoughtless rider will quickly come to fear and loathe being ridden and will try to keep as much distance between himself and humans as he possibly can.

Being a better rider does help, of course, but your attitude and behavior toward horses are extremely important, so begin there. If you accept that the horse's physical and mental comfort are *your* responsibility, you'll be on your way to becoming the sort of responsible rider that horses appreciate.

If you treat horses kindly and well, handle them gently, talk to them, and avoid fast or sudden movements when you are on them or around them, they will like you. If you encourage horses to do what you want them to do, give them time to respond when you ask them to do something, and praise and reward them for trying, you'll be the kind of rider horses accept and enjoy. Over time, if you have good lessons and you become a technically proficient rider with good riding skills and a sound understanding of physiology, psychology, and balance, you will be able to communicate with horses in a way that is both clear and subtle, and they will enjoy you even more.

Every rider should start with riding lessons to acquire both skills and understanding. One of the nicest things about horses is that they are very forgiving,

Horses appreciate riders who are balanced, quiet, and kind.

and as long as your mistakes come from clumsiness and lack of skill, not from ill will, they are extremely tolerant. A violent and angry rider is far more frightening to a horse than a rider who simply hasn't yet become balanced and coordinated. Relax, focus on learning, and make it a point to be nice to your horses at all times. If you do that, then they will always enjoy your company, even if your current skill level leaves something to be desired. Since you obviously already have a kind heart and a good attitude, I'd say that you're well on your way.

Horse "Feeling His Oats"

Q I'm wavering back and forth on whether I should sell my horse and was wondering whether you might have some insight. I bought this horse (my first), a 6-year-old racing-type Quarter Horse, about a year ago. He was spoiled, had terrible manners, and was barely broke, but he had good conformation and a kind eye, was sound, and in my price range. He spent several weeks with a professional to learn basic manners. I have been riding him for about 10 months, taking lessons twice a month, and things have been going well; he's the first horse I've ever ridden that's lifted his back in response to my aids. We're currently working to achieve a slower canter and doing laid-back short trail rides.

But a month ago, he was paying no attention to me and started to buck and bolt. I came off against the arena wall (no permanent damage, thanks to my helmet and safety stirrups). I later found out that he had been getting grain, which is probably why this happened. But my riding confidence (not too strong to begin with) is way down.

After this happened, a very experienced friend rode him twice and said that although he is a nice horse, she considered him to be a brat and that his misbehaving was not fear (he bucked at the canter with her). I'm now riding again and things are returning to normal, but I'm not sure I will ever completely trust him again (even though that extreme behavior only happened one time, we still have other small problems, like nipping).

My trainer (whom I respect very much) and several friends feel very strongly that it would be a mistake to sell him because he is such a nice horse and he has changed so much for the better since I got him. My experienced friend said that in order to keep him I would have to "change my personality" and be ready to discipline him if he ever behaves like that again. I keep changing my mind about whether to keep him or not. One person suggested that what he needs is to know what it's like to work for a living, and I know someone who could take him to be a pack/dude horse this summer into the mountains (pretty rough country).

What do you think of that option, and do you have any suggestions? I ride purely for pleasure, to relax from the pressures of being a grad student.

A "Feeling his oats" is exactly right — that's where that expression comes from! You had a rather uncomfortable and scary illustration of what can happen when a horse is fed too much for the work he's doing.

Your horse sounds lovely — a real pleasure horse. He doesn't need to be punished, but he *does* need to be fed according to his size and the amount of work he is doing. Overfeeding a horse can create a monster; depending on whether the food is stored or used for energy, you will end up with either a fat horse or one that seems on the edge (or past the edge) of being out of control. Because he is a pleasure horse, and you want to enjoy him quietly (you're not preparing him for a race or a three-day event), he may do very well on hay (or grass), water, and salt.

Here's a story from my own experience. Many years ago, thinking that more was better, I made the mistake of overfeeding one of my own horses. It would have been easy if he had simply gotten fat, but instead he got more and more energetic until he was just about bouncing out of his skin. Under normal conditions, this horse was calm about bicycles, tractors, goats, sheep, and screaming children, but when he was "high" on too much feed, even a falling leaf was enough to provoke a buck or a bolt. Finally, he became aggressive and bit me. It took *all of that* before I figured out what was wrong and put it right. I was very young, and it truly hadn't occurred to me that overfeeding might be the problem, because my horse hadn't gotten fat.

After 10 days on a more appropriate diet, everything was normal again and I had my sweet horse back. Some years later, the owners of my new boarding barn couldn't believe that a big horse like that could stay healthy without a lot of grain, so they tripled the amount I had asked them to feed. My horse once again turned into a fire-breathing dragon with aerial capabilities, but when we straightened out the feed situation, he returned to normal very quickly.

As for your own confidence, I suggest that you drop back a little and spend your next few lessons (and riding time between lessons) working on things you've done before and things that don't make you worry about losing control. Your instructor (who sounds very sensible, by the way!) can suggest lots of exercises that will make your horse more attentive and make you more secure in the saddle. You can't go wrong with walk-trot work and lots and lots of transitions. In fact, if you did only walk and trot and transitions and a little lateral work for the next year, it wouldn't hurt you or the horse at all, and when you went back to cantering, you would both be better balanced and much more secure.

Overfeeding a horse can create a monster, depending on whether the food is stored or used for energy.

As for your friend's comment: Changing your personality is not a reasonable suggestion! You and your horse like each other and enjoy each other's company, and he's improved in the time that you've owned him. You don't need to change anything. Be kind, be clear, be consistent: That's how to deal with *any* horse.

Sending him off to be a packhorse or a dude ranch mount might be fun for him or it might not, but it won't instill a "work ethic" in him — he has no concept of what that means. You may have to remind your "helpful" friends that this is a *horse.* Many people ascribe human motivations to horses, but that's a big mistake. Horse motivations are really quite simple: Horses want to feel safe, they want to be able to move around freely, and they want to eat. When someone tells you that a horse got dirty on purpose to inconvenience the groom or stepped on someone's foot in order to hurt that person, just close your ears. This kind of nonsense is not accurate, it's not useful, and it will get in the way of your work with your horse.

It sounds to me as though it might be beneficial for you to drop back a level in whatever you are doing, work on simple things until you feel strong and confident again, and then go back out and enjoy yourself and your horse. And watch his diet: Now that you know what happens when he's getting the high-octane fuel, keep him on "regular."

Is It Always the Rider?

Q I had the pleasure of taking one of your clinics last year. My Trakehner mare was very difficult during the first half of our lesson, but you wouldn't let me discipline her for pulling on the reins. You explained that she wasn't pulling but pushing and that she was doing this out of discomfort. You gave me exercises to do that made me pay great attention to Talia and taught me to ask her to stretch just before she was about to push on the bit.

I've been doing it ever since, and it still works, but now I don't have to do it nearly as often, maybe every ten minutes instead of every two minutes! But here's what I am really wondering about: You said "Whatever the horse is doing that you don't like, look to yourself for the answer; it's always the rider." But is it really *always* the rider? What if the horse is just being obnoxious, or what if the horse is expecting something because some other rider did it, like Talia was expecting me to jerk the reins even though I don't? Wouldn't that mean that the *horse* is causing the problem, not the rider?

A   Yes, it's always the rider, and here's why. Horses react. Horses respond. When a horse gives you the "wrong" answer to an action or a question, you must ask yourself what you just said to him. If you're unclear or if you're just plain asking the wrong question, you'll get an accurate response to the question you asked, but it probably won't be the answer you *wanted* or *expected* to the question you *thought* you'd asked.

Imagine that you are coaching a small child in arithmetic. The child consistently answers "five" when you say, "What's the sum of two and two?" Before you label the child "mathematically incapable," you videotape a session and discover to your dismay that you've actually been asking, "What's the sum of two and three?" all along. The answer was right, but the question was wrong.

Riders do this to their horses all the time. A rider who wants her horse to canter from a trot leans forward, grabs the reins tightly, and kicks the horse; the horse responds by trotting faster and faster, until the rider finally sits up and pulls hard on the horse's mouth to make him slow down. The rider thinks, "This darned horse just won't canter; I guess I have to kick a lot harder next time!" The rider repeats her performance, kicks harder, and the horse trots still faster and is pulled in even harder.

The rider feels angry because the horse "won't listen" or "refuses to canter." Meanwhile, the horse becomes steadily more upset and confused, because he is responding correctly to body language that says, "Trot faster! Trot faster!" and is then punished, by being hurt in the mouth, for trotting faster.

Only the rider can stop her increasingly harsh behavior and the escalation of fear, pain, and confusion on the horse's part. It doesn't take much: just listening to the horse and being willing to assume that he is responding to the rider's signals to the best of his ability. A good rider always asks, "What did I do?" when she gets a response other than the one she had in mind. If someone describes a horse as "full of evasions" or "full of resistances," ask yourself what the horse is evading or resisting?

As for your example about Talia pushing on the bit although you weren't doing anything to provoke it, I have two thoughts. The first is that while you weren't deliberately causing that behavior, you also weren't doing anything to *prevent* it. When you learned to listen to your mare and offer her the chance to stretch and relax *before* her muscles went into spasm, she had no reason to push and she stopped pushing.

The second point, as you suggested, is that Talia was responding (at least initially) not to what *you* were or weren't doing, but to what her *previous rider* had done. Someone had obviously ridden your mare badly, probably in draw reins, to create those muscle knots and all that nervous anticipation and apprehension. It's the present rider's obligation, however, to clean up after all earlier riders and to make the horse comfortable and confident.

If you assume that it's the rider when it's actually the horse, you won't hurt anything by improving yourself, but if you assume it's the horse when it's *not* the horse, you won't improve and neither will the horse.

CHAPTER 13

Thinking Right about Your Riding

THE WAY RIDERS THINK ABOUT THEMSELVES and their riding affects the way they ride, the progress they make, and the way their horses perceive them. Some riders are cocky and overestimate their own knowledge and skill, but many more constantly underestimate their own abilities, skills, and understanding. They can be terribly self-critical, constantly blaming themselves for all sorts of things that are not their fault or that are not even wrong. This attitude interferes with the learning process. Riders who have a realistic view of themselves, their horses, and the time and effort involved in learning to ride well are much better able to evaluate their own abilities and progress.

Rider Strength

Q My teacher says that riders need to be strong, but I want to be a gentle rider with soft hands. She is trying to get me to take some classes in gymnastics or dance to make me stronger, because when I'm not riding my horse I mostly read or write on the computer.

I never see my teacher pulling or kicking or shoving or doing things that need a lot of strength, so why should I work to get stronger muscles that I won't use when I ride? The last time I asked her this, she said she couldn't explain it so it made sense to me, but she knows she is right. Can you explain it?

A Riders do need to be strong, but not so they can jerk and pull and shove the horse around. Riders need to be strong so they can sit quietly, use only as much strength as they need to at any given time, and make tiny shifts in position and balance that mean something specific and clear to the horse. Riders need strength (and balance and coordination) so they can have good control over their *own* bodies. Only then can they hope to become "soft" riders.

The gymnastics suggestion isn't a bad one. Gymnastics, martial arts, dance, yoga, or anything else that helps you develop strength, balance, breathing, and body control will help you with your riding.

Using your computer is an excellent example of developing your strength and control. It takes much more fine control and strength to type properly on a computer keyboard than it does to pick up a big rock and drop it on the keyboard. (It gets better results, too, unless your ambition is to smash the keyboard.) You probably don't even realize how much strength and coordination you've developed in your hands and arms and shoulders, but without it, you would type slowly and poorly.

"Soft" riding is controlled and precise riding. It takes strength to "talk" to your horse with the twitch of a calf muscle and a slight momentary tension in one finger. The muscles needed for good riding must be in good shape for the rider to make tiny, controlled movements.

There's an old saying, "You have to control yourself before you can control your horse." This is sometimes interpreted to mean "Don't ride if you're having a temper tantrum," and I certainly agree with that, but the real meaning of the saying is somewhat different. If you are fully in control of your own body — if you have the proper mixture of strength, flexibility, and balance — then you will be able to sit correctly, stay out of your horse's way, tell him quietly and clearly what you want, and listen to his response. If you're not really in control of your own body, you'll be sending signals you don't mean to send, the horse will be confused, and there's every chance that you won't be able to understand or even hear his response. That's when people get into fights with their horses.

Riders need strength (and balance and coordination) so they can have good control over their own bodies.

So strength does matter. When you are first learning to ride, unless you're lucky enough to have a truly classical instructor, you're quite likely to get the (wrong) impression that riders need strong hands and strong legs, when it's actually a matter of having *quiet* legs and hands. You will have those only when you have achieved a good seat, and that will happen only when you have strengthened your abdominal muscles so they can be in balance with your back muscles. Most riders think more about their back muscles than their abdominal muscles, but your abdominal muscles move your pelvis. Your back muscles need to be able to relax, release, and allow your abdominals to work. If you try to use your abdominal muscles when your back muscles are tight and stiff, you won't be able to move your pelvis well, and your muscles will be fighting each other instead of cooperating and balancing.

If you start doing some kind of physical training to develop strength and flexibility and coordination and balance, you'll be on your way to becoming the kind of rider who is not only effective but gentle and helpful to the horse.

Finding the Right Horse

Q After taking weekly lessons for almost two years, I took on a half-lease on a sweet older Arabian gelding this fall. I love him dearly, and he is a good learning experience and a good size for me. His owner and I get along well and ride at about the same level. He has wonderful manners and puts up with my learning with and on him, and even though he is in his late teens he still has a lot of get up and go (often more than I wish he did).

I now understand about the costs of owning a horse and I have enough money to meet the expenses. I've learned how to clean a stall, feed, longe, medicate, groom, bring in, turn out, and so on. I have a super vet, a good farrier, and a great teacher, as well as an available stall at a wonderful barn full of riders who are encouraging, not condescending, to a beginner. So how do I figure out what kind of horse to look for?

I'm middle-aged, stocky, timid, riding again after a 20-year gap, not completely balanced, hands not independent yet but getting closer. I'm getting braver and am able to ride through bumps rather than freak out and cry. I'm not yet able to anticipate stuff, but I'm learning to feel and react to what the horse is doing.

My goals involve mostly dressage, some trail riding, and eventually a little bit of jumping. Riding is starting to be *fun,* and I want my own horse partner to bond with. Part of me wants a companion horse for life, but part of me hopes that I will be able to move to a higher-level horse in a few years. Everyone is advising me differently, on everything from how much I should pay, how old the horse should be, to what breed and color he (the consensus is gelding) should be.

I would love to find a warmblood or draft cross, or a calm Morgan or Quarter Horse-Arabian cross, but all I can find in my price range are Thoroughbreds off the track and Quarter Horses.

I am nowhere ready to retrain a racehorse, so I'm thinking about getting a Quarter Horse. I *don't* want a halter Quarter Horse with little feet. A balanced, medium-sized Quarter Horse seemed like a possibility, but a friend's very good trainer told me that Quarter Horses are downhill and unable to extend (at this point I'm thrilled with any sort of rhythmic trot). But friends who are serious riders (adults who event at Preliminary) said that a Quarter Horse is just what I need to start out.

I love the horse I'm leasing, so I am not in a super hurry. I've contacted Internet sources and local papers and have asked the farrier, vet, and other people to be on the lookout for a suitable horse for me. I recently saw a video of a young Quarter Horse that seems sound, nicely put together, and in proportion. He is being shown in Western Pleasure, so his gaits are really slow, but he seems to be stepping under and showed signs of potential for impulsion.

Can a Western Pleasure Quarter Horse learn to carry his head "properly"? This guy appeared to be pretty even on top, though it looked as though he could trip over his lovely nose or I could get ahead and slide off over his ears! He seemed to move quietly and willingly, but carried his head low under both English and Western tack. He did stay in a three-beat canter, which everyone seemed to think was a great thing. Several people besides me thought he looked nice on tape, so I plan to go see him.

A   Let me begin by reminding you that you like your leased horse. Hold that thought, because it may take several months or a year to find *exactly* the horse you want to own, and in the meantime you can go on learning and improving on that good horse. He will save you from the impatience that results in bad decisions — that "Oh, I just *have* to buy a horse *now*" feeling. That leased horse is one of your best friends.

Your other best friend is, or should be, a competent, safety-oriented instructor whom you trust — someone who works with you; knows you, your riding, and how you interact with horses; understands your fears, physical problems, and goals; and can advise you whether you and a particular horse will be a good match.

There's no reason that a good sound horse can't be a companion for life *and* a move-up horse. Horses move up to match their riders' abilities. Unless you're looking for a Grand Prix jumper or dressage prospect for competition, the sound, solid, sane Training Level/trail/cross rail horse you buy today can be a First Level/trail/small jumps horse in a couple of years. Horses aren't fixed in one place in their training. If you continue to learn and make progress, you'll find that you are retraining that horse every year or two. This will continue throughout the horse's life, as long as *you* are making progress with your riding and your understanding of horses and horsemanship. I've seen riders change their riding style, find a really good instructor, and completely transform their horses in a year or two, even when those horses are in their late teens and have less than wonderful conformation.

If you find a pleasant, reasonably well-built, sound, experienced horse for your first mount, you will discover two things. First, it will take you several years to reach your horse's stage of training, and second, once you catch up with his abilities, you and he will be able to move up together.

Again, this presupposes the presence of a good instructor. Many riders make the mistake of buying a horse that is many levels ahead, hoping that the horse's knowledge and experience will somehow create an instant improvement in their riding skills. In fact, unless a rider has constant, competent instruction, her horse's training simply drops back to match the rider's skill level. This is often seen at the upper levels of dressage, where some riders with more money than sense try to buy their way up the levels by purchasing horses that are many levels and years beyond them. With a good teacher and an immense amount of work, the rider may eventually catch up with the horse. But in most cases, the horse drops down through the levels until the frustrated rider sells it, purchases another expensive upper-level horse, and begins the process again.

Color shouldn't matter. In fact, there's an old saying that "a good horse is never a bad color," although color and markings can drive a price very high. Pinto Warmbloods, for example, are presently in great demand, and many horses sell for high prices on the basis of their coloring and not much else. Size shouldn't matter much either. A compact horse would be ideal; look for something like an old-style Morgan or a Quarter Horse or QH cross with a wide barrel.

There's no reason to avoid Quarter Horses — a good QH is a sane, sensible, athletic animal. But look among trail horses and "using" horses, *not* Western Pleasure show horses, for a riding prospect. Many Western Pleasure horses are trained using methods that damage their bodies permanently, and all are started very early, before they are anywhere near maturity. It can be heartbreaking to fall in love with a horse that has been damaged and then discover that he'll never be able to do what you want him to do.

If you find a good Quarter Horse that's been a trail horse or a working ranch horse, you'll have a much better chance of getting the movement, mind, and soundness that you want. Quarter Horses are certainly *not* all "built downhill" or "unable to extend." Watch a reining horse competition to see balanced, uphill horses with the ability to extend and compress on demand. The world is full of athletic Quarter Horses; you just have to look for them in the right places.

Your first horse should already know how to do the things that you plan to do with him.

Try to find a horse that is already doing what you want to do: elementary dressage, trail riding, and small jumps. Someday, you may want to take a green horse, or a horse that's been used for something else, and train it to do what you want to do, but don't try to do that with your first horse. You should be looking for an equine *teacher*, not a student. You need a cheerful, sane, sound, confidence builder that can help you learn and can move on with you in a few years. Don't look for the horse that you think you'll want in five years' time — your ideas and goals may change. Find a horse that you can ride, learn on, and enjoy *now*. It's a good idea for you and your instructor to go and see the horse together, but don't let yourself fall in love until you've had some reassurance that it's likely to work out. Another horse will come along, and you have time.

Don't worry about the conflicting advice you're getting; most riders favor a particular breed, color, gender, or age. If I were looking for a horse for you, I would be looking for a sound, balanced, quiet, and willing gelding between 10 and 16 years old and around 15 hands. I would hope to find one that was already experienced at basic dressage, trails, and small jump courses. Those would be my priorities, and the "pool" of suitable horses would be much larger if I didn't have to restrict myself to a particular breed or color.

You're doing exactly what you should be doing: homework and networking. You'll be ready when the right horse appears. Accept input from everyone, but remember that every rider has unique preferences and that you're buying a horse for yourself, not trying to satisfy your friends. With a good vet, farrier, and above all a good instructor helping you, you'll find the right horse if you're patient. Meanwhile, enjoy your leased horse, learn as much as you can from him, and ride other horses whenever possible (talk to your instructor) and learn from them. Everything you learn about horses and about yourself will help you add to your "want" list, making it easier for you to recognize the right horse when you meet him.

Inconsistent, Sad Rider

Q I am worried that my riding is not improving, although my instructor is very good, nice, and understanding, and my horse has become much more balanced, supple, and cooperative in the last eight months since I started taking lessons. He is so good now, and I couldn't have done it without my instructor. But I am not pleased with myself and I spend a lot of time being angry that

I'm not improving my riding skills more. Some of my rides are bad and others are not so bad, but I don't seem to improve the way I want to.

I often think that I should just sell my horse to a better rider and find some other way to occupy my time. But I love riding, and I want so much to improve. I am 32 and have been riding most of my life, but only riding seriously for the last two years since I discovered first dressage and then my new instructor.

Sometimes I experience one of those magical rides when I think something and he does it and it truly is as if we were one being. On those days, when everything is easy and feels wonderful and I am not stiff or sore after the ride, I can't imagine ever giving up riding! But the next day the magic is gone, and we are back to trying, trying, trying.

I have tried to discuss this with my instructor but she says that this is typical of adults who take up dressage and that she can see the improvement even though I don't feel it. Because she is a very kind person, I worry that she is only being nice. I am grateful for the chance to work with someone who is helping me to overcome my past bad habits and bad posture on a horse, but I can't help thinking that she must be disappointed in me. *I* am disappointed in me! I want more of those moments when I can be happy after my ride instead of being angry with myself, sad about letting my horse down, and a disappointment to my instructor.

A Those "magic" moments when everything is perfect and almost in slow motion are absolutely wonderful — everything is easy, you know exactly what to do, there is time to work without effort or strain, breathing is easy, and you feel glued to the saddle and able to move as your horse moves, easily and softly. Those are the moments that all riders treasure. Those moments are also *rare*.

All riders who have experienced those moments want more of them. That magical feeling lights the way when everything seems to be difficult and uncomfortable and frustrating. But you need to remember that they are *moments*. Even riders who are technically accomplished and very much in tune with their horses' bodies and their own, don't experience that feeling all the time or even during the course of every ride. When they do find those moments, they enjoy them and don't accuse themselves of being inconsistent.

> *Those "magic" moments when everything is perfect and almost in slow motion are absolutely wonderful.*

As you and your horse continue to improve, you'll experience such moments more frequently, but you shouldn't expect to be in that sort of Zen-like state all the time. Be happy when you experience those moments, but don't beat yourself up for not having more of them. All that will do is make you unhappy and tense, which will make your *horse* unhappy and tense, because he reacts to what you do and reflects your posture, degree of relaxation, and emotional state.

I'm sure that your instructor is telling you the truth, not offering you a kind lie. She can't see into your brain and know what you are thinking at any specific moment, but she *can* look at your horse and know exactly how you are riding at any given moment. During the last eight months, he has become, in your words, "more balanced, supple, and cooperative." Just how do you think that happened? Yes, your instructor played a large part, but *you* are the rider and *you* created those changes in your horse.

Because horses react to their riders, you can *know* that your riding has improved. Those magic moments may be rare, but they're not accidental. They occur when you are in that perfect, peaceful state, and your horse reacts and responds accordingly. Tension, stress, pain, discomfort, worries, apprehension — any normal, everyday human feeling can interfere with the creation of such moments. When you experience one of those moments, it means that nothing is interfering. That doesn't mean that you should expect yourself to be perfectly physically relaxed, mentally calm, and emotionally balanced at all times. That's not realistic. But you are able to create those perfect moments because you *have* improved, and you will create more and more of them as you continue to improve. Are you familiar with the four stages of learning to ride (or, really, of learning any new discipline)?

1. Unconscious incompetence. (You don't know how bad you are.)
2. Conscious incompetence. (You begin to realize how bad you are and become highly self-critical.)
3. Conscious competence. (With much practice, effort, and thought, you master the techniques of the discipline and learn to apply them deliberately and appropriately.)
4. Unconscious competence. (Through thoughtful repetition, your mastery of technique becomes second nature.)

The "magic moments" that you've begun to experience don't occur at all during the first stage of learning. They occur rarely (if at all) during the second stage, more often during the third stage, and much more frequently for those who achieve the fourth stage. So don't worry. You will have more of those moments as you and your horse continue to improve together.

These two thoughts may help you become less frustrated and self-blaming:

Quality is never accidental.
You're as good as your best ride.

Make these two sentences into a mantra and repeat it to yourself, over and over, when you catch yourself thinking negatively about your riding and your progress. Ideally, I'd like you to add a third sentence:

It's all good, all the time.

That may sound silly, but it's an excellent idea to have in mind during every ride. Instead of thinking in terms of one ride being "bad" and another one being "not so bad," focus on making all of them good experiences for your horse. If you do this, you'll accomplish much more during your rides and you'll be able to dismount, pat your horse and say, "Thanks for another good ride," and *mean* it.

You're very lucky, actually. You have a good horse and a good instructor and you've discovered that "magic moments" exist. Some riders never experience them at all. It seems clear to me that the three key elements — horse, instructor, and rider — are good, and that you simply need to go on doing just what you are doing, but with a change in the unrealistic expectations and demands you've placed on yourself. Beating yourself up for not experiencing those moments all the time is unkind, unrealistic, and utterly unfair. Riding's a joy, and no matter how caught up we can get in matters of technique, craft, and art, it must always be true that we do it for *fun*. Remember: It's all good, all the time.

Dressage Rider's Potential

Q I've been riding in hunters for three years and dressage for one year. My biggest dream is to ride in Grand Prix dressage. I am not a talented and naturally good rider; I have to work extremely hard and I'm still not very good. I'm incredibly determined, though, and I'd work 10 jobs if I had to in order to pay for riding and lessons every day and a suitable horse, but I am wondering: Is there a limit to how far a rider can go? With practice, determination, and a suitable horse, can any rider get to the Fédération Equestre Internationale (FEI) Dressage levels or does the rider need to be naturally talented?

A   If you take a close look at some of our most famous riders, you'll see that not all of them have bodies that are "designed for riding" and that others are not exceptionally naturally talented riders, just exceptionally *dedicated* ones. What they have in common is a strong interest in learning and the ability to back up their interest with work. Some of them also got to Grand Prix level with horses that were sound and cooperative but not really spectacular movers. If you talk to these riders, it's clear that having to work for everything, all the way to the top, didn't put them off or discourage them or keep them from reaching for their goals.

You've only been studying dressage for one year: Don't worry if you're not very good yet. It takes time, and it's difficult to come to dressage from a hunter background. If you're an eventer, or even a good Western rider, the transition is a lot easier because the position isn't as unfamiliar.

It sounds as though you have the determination to do this. My question is, do you *enjoy* the learning and the practicing? If you do, then there is no limit to your ability to improve. That's the lovely thing about dressage; you can *always* get better, no matter how skilled you are. But it's a lifetime job, so it had better be one that you enjoy for its own sake. You'll have a lot more schooling days than show days, so you need to appreciate and enjoy the routine work.

I don't think that you need daily lessons. You need time between lessons to work on what you learned, and your body needs time to adjust to changes in position and such. What you do need is a good instructor who works well with lower-level riders and can give you the correct basics.

Winning ribbons is fun, but be sure to enjoy schooling as well as showing, because you have many more schooling days than showing days.

The one thing that really can impede any rider's ambitions is choosing the wrong trainer for those crucial first years of training. It's heartbreaking to find out, four or five years into your training, that you need to go back to the beginning and start over. This happens all too often. Just as your first dressage horse shouldn't be a Grand Prix horse, but one that can help take you through the lower levels correctly, your first instructor should be someone whose expertise is in building a solid foundation and getting riders through the lower levels *correctly*.

Once you have a good instructor, give yourself a few more years to get the basics down really well, because those will be the foundation for everything else you will ever do, right up to Grand Prix and beyond. The very best riders and instructors in the world will tell you that the higher you want to go, the better your basics must be. "Advanced work" is all about refining the basics. That's why you will discover, if you stay with dressage, that 90 percent of your work, even in a very advanced lesson, will always focus on the fundamentals. Don't skimp here — it's the foundation for all progress.

If you wish to become a winning international competitor in Grand Prix dressage, a lot depends on your finances. But if you wish to become a good rider at that level and perhaps someday to train a horse to that level, your patience and determination are all that matter. There are many more Grand Prix riders and horses capable of performing a solid Grand Prix test than you'll see at the big competitions. Some riders don't have the money to compete at that level; some know that their horses are not fancy enough movers to be competitive at those levels; some simply aren't interested in competition. But they ride beautifully and take their horses to high levels of training, and there's no reason you couldn't be one of them.

Moving Up a Level in Eventing

Q I'm an event rider who hopes to go very far, maybe even to the Olympics someday. I haven't been eventing for very long, but I think I have a lot of ability for it. My instructor says I have natural talent. Right now I am competing pretty well at Novice Level. In my first event I got eliminated on Stadium because we knocked over a fence and I fell off, then I forgot to jump both parts when I jumped it again, but we were allowed to finish the course anyway. At my second event I placed 15th out of 23, and my instructor said that was good. At the third one I placed 10th out of 14! I was pretty happy about that.

Now my instructor and I are arguing because I want to move up and compete at Training Level. I know my horse can jump the Training Level jumps and do the dressage, because he evented at Preliminary Level before my dad bought him.

I feel like I am wasting time at Novice Level because I have talent, and my horse already knows more than just Training Level. My instructor wants me to spend the next six months doing dressage and gymnastic stuff and then she wants me to compete Novice Level next summer again and possibly go to Training Level at the end of the summer. How can I make her understand that it's time for me to move up? The jumps are not that much higher. We can handle them.

A I'm sure that you do have talent, and it sounds as though you've got a very nice horse. It also seems that you have an excellent instructor who is looking after your best interests whether you like it or not.

There's much more to moving up a level than just having survived a few competitions at your current level. Yes, the horse's ability and experience count for a lot, but if you're a rider with talent and ambition, you want to be more than just a passenger! You need to become the best rider you can be, and that means that you need to "graduate" from each level legitimately and honestly, by mastering all of the skills needed at that level. It's great that your horse already has the skills, the knowledge, and the experience. Now it's time for *you* to acquire those things.

Spending a year, or even two or three years, at one level isn't unusual and doesn't reflect on your innate abilities. Riders who take two lessons a week and compete frequently on different horses will progress more quickly than riders who have a weekly lesson and a single horse on which they compete two or three times during the season. That's reality. But the nice thing about eventing is that what matters is *how well you do what you do,* not how old you are or how long it took you to reach a particular level. Think of the process as "eventing school," with the focus on skills acquisition, not on a lock-step promotion system.

In many school systems, students are promoted from one grade to the next just because "it's time for them to move up." They haven't acquired the skills they need to function at the next grade level, but they keep getting promoted and eventually they graduate from high school with no fundamental skills. They'll be in trouble in the real world, and the fault lies, to a great extent, with the system that passed them from grade to grade just because they were a year older.

Some instructors are ruled by this same concept. They "promote" their riders every year, based merely on the fact that the rider competed at the previous level the previous year. Instructors who do this may be stroking their students' egos, but they aren't doing them any favors. For one thing, they're putting both the riders and their horses at risk. For another, they are letting riders imagine they are competent to do things they are not actually competent to do. It's dangerous and it's irresponsible.

Instructors like to have their riders move up, but good instructors advance their riders only when they are legitimately ready to do so. In the world of horse shows and competitions, not having mastered the skills at one level means that you're likely to be in trouble at the next level — and in eventing, the difficulty and speed increase with each level.

Let's talk about fence height for a moment. Again, even if your horse can handle Training Level jumps, this isn't about your horse, it's about *you*. You need to learn how to ride a Training Level course. At Novice, it's often possible just to point the horse at each fence in the proper numerical order and kick your way over them. At Training, there are more demands in terms of turns, terrain, and combinations; at Preliminary, the course designers begin to get serious.

The height of the jumps is the least of your concerns. Any talented course designer could design a 3'6" course that most Novice eventers could sail around easily. That same designer could put together a 3' course that would stop seasoned

As you move up the levels in eventing, you need to become more of a rider and less of a passenger.

Prelim horses and riders in their tracks. The height of a jump is much less of an issue than the appearance of the jump (inviting or forbidding?), the approach to the jump (level, uphill, or downhill? straight or turning? over grass, over gravel, or through water?), the position of the fence, the landing, and the distance to, and position of, the next jump. As you go up through the levels, all of these factors will come into play.

You might be able to send your horse around a Training Level course and just hang on while he makes all the decisions, which would say a lot about the quality of your horse, but it wouldn't do anything for you. And if you ran up against a difficult course that made it necessary for you to help your horse instead of just being a passenger, you could end up getting hurt or injuring your horse. And once again you wouldn't be learning anything useful.

My advice: Listen to your instructor. Take your time to master the skills. If you want to ride in the Olympics someday, begin by getting a riding education that isn't full of holes. Take the winter and early spring to work on dressage and gymnastics, as your instructor suggested. In the spring you can compete at Novice a time or two and hone your cross-country skills. When your instructor says, "Okay, I'm signing you up for Training Level," you'll know that she thinks you've mastered the skills and that you're truly ready to move up.

If it's any comfort, here's a thought to contemplate this winter while you're schooling: The first few years of *any* discipline are the ones that involve the most effort and the slowest progress. But there's a payoff: The more time and effort you invest in the beginning, the more smoothly and easily you will advance. If you're a solid Training Level rider with a good background at Novice events and you work hard to become an equally solid Preliminary rider, then you won't find it hard to move up to Intermediate and eventually to Advanced. Meanwhile, the riders who thought they didn't need to master the skills at the lower levels will get stuck at Prelim, if they don't get injured or injure their horses, both of which are very likely outcomes.

"Just" a Pleasure Rider

Q My life's ambition has been to become a true horseman. I learned to ride a few years ago, and at age 46, I have my own horse at last. Riding is a complete joy, and my horse is the love of my life.

The barn has always been my "safe place" where I can forget about the annoyances and frustrations of my job and just relax with my beloved horse. But it is getting more and more difficult to relax at the barn, and I don't know if this is my fault or if it is because the atmosphere there has changed.

Sometimes all we do is walk, but I talk to my horse and sing to him and we enjoy each other's company.

When I first came to this barn, I was very excited at the thought of having friends to ride with. The other boarders were mostly older riders like myself who had always wanted to have the chance to ride and possibly own a horse. We were from different backgrounds but very much alike in our love for horses and riding. But in the last year, the others have changed or maybe I have.

I am not very happy right now. My riding continues to improve slowly. I do yoga three nights a week and tai chi daily, and I certainly feel more balanced and much more coordinated! But the other boarders are not with me on this; they think these are unnecessary practices and that the way to get better at riding is to ride. They do not understand why I am happy to go to my exercise classes and then come out to the barn and enjoy a long leisurely ride on my horse. Sometimes all we do is walk, but I talk to my horse and sing to him and we enjoy each other's company.

In the past two years, the other boarders have become very interested in showing. They spend a lot of time discussing the competitions and the judges and looking through catalogs and buying things. At first, they tried to get me to do this with them, but then they began to leave me out. This is okay since I have no interest in showing. Most of them have sold their old horses and bought new horses to be more competitive. I thought it was sort of sad they didn't want to keep their old horses, but it wasn't my business. It didn't occur to me that they might think my keeping my horse would be a problem, but apparently it is!

Recently, two of the women have asked me if I plan to stay at the barn. Apparently I don't fit in now that everyone else is competition-oriented. Another woman asked me if I would like to go to competitions with them this summer and if I was planning to get a new horse. When I said no, she told me that she was sad to see that I was "giving up on myself" and had "low self-esteem." Since then, all three of these riders have commented that I am "just a pleasure rider." I *do* ride for pleasure! Riding and owning a horse has been my lifelong dream, and I am very happy to spend time brushing and riding my horse every day.

Is it so awful to ride for pleasure? Does not wanting to compete make me a second-class rider? I love my horse, I love riding, I try to improve, and I am, or at least I was, happy. Why do people say "pleasure rider" with a sneer? I'm worried that I will be asked to leave the barn because I don't compete.

A You have two different concerns here. One is why the term "pleasure rider" is often used pejoratively, and the other is about the nature of changes at boarding barns.

First, I'm sure you know there is nothing terrible or even slightly bad about riding for pleasure. There is nothing at all wrong with anyone who takes good care of her horse, works to improve her riding skills, and takes pleasure in her horse. There *is* something wrong with anyone who sneers at another rider who takes good care of her horse, works to improve her riding skills, and takes pleasure in her horse.

The term "pleasure rider," like the term "recreational rider," should mean exactly what it means in your case — a rider who enjoys and cares for her horse and rides for the sheer pleasure of riding, not in a quest for ribbons and trophies.

The problem is that the term "pleasure rider" is also sometimes used to refer to those riders who aren't interested in improving their riding skills and who don't consider their horses' comfort — the kind of people who gallop the first mile out and the last mile in. I think "pleasure rider" probably began to take on a pejorative meaning when riders used it as an excuse for not knowing or caring about the effect their riding was having on their horses. Many such riders describe themselves as pleasure riders — as in, "Oh, I've never had lessons; I'm just a pleasure rider," or "I don't worry about all that lead and diagonal stuff; I'm just a pleasure rider."

Riders like that are just bad, ignorant riders and they can be found at any competition! It's not a question of pleasure versus competitive riders, but of good riders versus bad riders. *Good* riders care about their horses' soundness and comfort, not just their performance.

If your interest is in good riding and horsemanship, then riding is likely to be pleasurable for you *and* for your horse, which is as it should be. If you take that attitude into competition, that too can be a pleasure for you and for your horse. I'd like to see *all* riders become actively interested in improving their own skills and increasing their horses' enjoyment of being ridden. There should be no "just" about being a pleasure rider, because everyone should be riding for that kind of pleasure.

The reality, however, is that you may find it practical to say, "I'm working hard to improve my riding, but I don't compete," or "I ride for my own enjoyment and I'm always striving to improve," instead of saying, "I'm a pleasure rider." Defining the term to your fellow boarders probably won't help you much right now, so I'll give you some general advice on dealing with those who sneer.

Ignore them if you can. They're not sneering at you personally; they're sneering at some idea they have about riding for pleasure being inferior to riding in competition. When riders become obsessed with competition, as your friends at the barn seem to have done, they can sometimes forget that competition is *not* the be-all and end-all of riding. Competition is fun for those who enjoy it, but it's by no means the point of riding. They'll have to mature as riders and find out for themselves that at the end of the day, what matters is good horsemanship and good riding, not labels and ribbons. Don't try to force the issue. Right now, they're not ready to understand.

There is nothing at all wrong with anyone who takes good care of her horse, works to improve her riding skills, and takes pleasure in her horse.

I expect the other boarders are just full of themselves right now because they're new to the world of competition and very excited about the fact that they have new horses and they're participating. If they make comments to you about your being "just" a pleasure rider, you can smile and ignore them. If you really want to answer them, you might say, "I think it's very important that riding be pleasurable for both horse and rider. That's why I work so hard to improve my riding and why I take yoga and tai chi classes to improve my balance and coordination and flexibility!" But think before you answer, not just about whether you'll get your message across but about how a "discussion" like this is going to affect *your* enjoyment of that day and that ride.

If you can make your point gently and without becoming agitated and then put the matter behind you and go out and enjoy your ride, good for you. If you know that engaging in a verbal confrontation is going to ruin the evening's ride for you, don't do it! Your first responsibility is to your horse; your second responsibility is to yourself. You're not responsible for educating your fellow boarders, and in any case, how likely is it that they'll listen?

I know that the other boarders' attitude of "we compete, but you're *just* a pleasure rider" sounds as though they think they're better than you, and perhaps they do.

Perhaps, in some ways, *you* also think you are better than they are — certainly you feel that your priorities are better than theirs. (I agree with you.) But nobody is going to convert anybody if there's animosity between you and your fellow boarders. You'll just waste time and energy contradicting one another. Instead, why not try to create an atmosphere in which both sides have some respect for one another?

You have several options when it comes to coping strategies.

1. You can continue to enjoy your horse in the way you've always enjoyed him, ignoring and/or avoiding the other boarders and their attitudes. You'll have to decide whether this is the best way to "ride things out" or whether it's likely to make you and the other boarders feel increasingly estranged from one another.

2. You can confront the other boarders and try to argue the point that "pleasure rider" doesn't mean "bad rider" or "inferior rider who isn't good enough to compete." Again, you'll need to use your good judgment here — is confrontation the answer?

3. You can accept the offer your friend made and accompany the group to one of those summer competitions. I think this would be worth a try. Who knows? You might enjoy it, your horse might enjoy it, and at the end of the day, you might have discovered yet another way for you and your horse to be together. Or you might not enjoy it very much, in which case you could say "No, thank you" the next time you're invited.

Even if you find that you don't like competing, you may find that you enjoy cheering on the others. Either way, you'll show them that you aren't rejecting or disrespecting their choice, you simply prefer other ways of spending time with your horse. Have you considered the possibility that, simply because you haven't jumped on the competition bandwagon with them, your fellow boarders may feel that *you* are rejecting *them* and their values and priorities?

4. You might tell the other boarders how much you feel yoga and tai chi are doing for your riding and invite them to come with you to the next class. If their sneers are directed at the uncaring kind of pleasure rider mentioned above, then they might benefit from a reminder that you are an entirely different sort of pleasure rider. If they understand that *all* of you are trying to improve, they may realize that you have a lot in common with each other.

As for leaving the barn, that seems extreme. If you're really worried that you might be asked to leave, ask the barn owner or manager. If there's a big change in the wind and the barn is going to become a different sort of establishment that is managed and run a new way, then the owner/manager will be able to tell you.

If she says, "Yes, we're going to become a high-power competition barn, with required weekly lessons and shows every weekend," then you might consider taking your horse somewhere quieter and more suited to the sort of riding you enjoy most. But I don't think this is likely to happen. If the owner has been in the boarding-barn business for some time, she will probably be able to reassure you that regardless of the age of the boarders, most boarding barns are periodically swept by one craze or another and that eventually the excitement dies down or a new craze takes over.

It's true that boarding barns sometimes change style and focus, for example, going from "primarily a boarding barn" to "primarily a lesson barn" or going from a hunter orientation to a dressage one. A good barn should have room for all boarders, even if many of the other boarders have started going to a lot of competitions or have changed their style of riding. Whether the conditions and atmosphere at the barn will make some boarders feel out of place is something that only those boarders will be able to determine.

I'm sorry you're getting sneers from the other boarders. People can be very scathing about things they don't do themselves and don't understand. Make sure you don't trivialize their interest in competition either — they're pursuing what *they* enjoy most, just as you are. Right now you're the courteous, tolerant one, so don't change. Let them rise to *your* standard of behavior.

Riding should be a pleasure for horse and rider wherever they are.

In the meantime, just go right on enjoying your rides and improving your skills. Learning to ride well is a lifelong process, and horsemanship has to be your standard as well as your goal. Oh, and go right on talking and singing to your horse! *He* isn't going to sneer, and his opinion should matter most to you. If riding is truly a pleasure for you and your horse, then you're my kind of rider, no matter what kind of riding you do.

Horse Too Fit for Wimpy Me

Q My 13-year-old Quarter Horse-Thoroughbred gelding, Scrabble, is getting so fit and feeling so good that he reacts with glee to things going on around him. I am not a confident rider, and he scares me! I am 55 years old and that many pounds overweight. My seat is quite solid, but rather than developing confidence in my ability when he is "enjoying" himself, I become more apprehensive.

Scrabble has chronic stiffness in his rear end and receives chondroitin sulfate. I ride him two or three times a week. I work Scrabble in hand before I ride, getting him to bend and step under. I also sometimes longe him at a walk, trot, and limited canter. My dressage instructor is only in this area for a few months each year. We have been working on bending and flexing, trying to get him loose in the rear end and lighter in front. Now that we are starting to accomplish that, he is so much fitter and stronger that he scares me.

A It sounds as if you have a common problem. Your horse is fitter than you are, and it's getting hard for you to keep up with him.

Thanks to your in-hand work and longeing, your horse is becoming fitter. That means you're working him correctly, which is good. If he just became tired, you might be grateful in the short run but you'd be damaging your horse in the long run. As it is, you're building him up. Now you need a way to build *your* strength and coordination as well, so that you can keep up with the horse and enjoy your riding.

Even people who have enough time (and horses) to ride six or seven horses a day, six or seven days a week, can't count on riding alone to make them fit enough to ride. If you're only able to ride two or three times a week, you definitely need to do some other things to get riding-fit. You need several kinds of fitness: endurance, strength, and flexibility.

The first thing to work on is aerobic fitness. You can achieve that, nicely and with minimum impact, by walking at a reasonable pace every day. Even 15 minutes will help, and if you can manage 30 to 45 minutes, you'll notice a *big* difference in your riding within a week. Another advantage to aerobic fitness is that you begin to breathe more deeply and slowly, which will help your riding by enabling you to sit tall and go *on* breathing deeply and regularly when you feel nervous, instead of rounding your shoulders forward and taking shallow breaths or holding your breath (either of which will make your horse nervous, tense, and quicker to shy).

The second thing to work on is strength. You need to develop stronger abdominals (which support your back), back muscles (which hold up your spine), shoulders and arms, and legs, especially thigh adductors. Working gently with light weights for even 15 minutes 3 days a week will pay off.

The third thing to work on is flexibility, and here, stretching is the key. The time to stretch is *after* your walk, when you are warmed up, and *before* your strength training, because you can't contract a muscle properly until it's been stretched. Here again, the payoff is all out of proportion to the effort you have to make.

The advantage of working on your own physical fitness is that you can do it every day, not just on riding days. Being more fit will allow you to *ride* for your entire session and not become a passenger from fatigue during the second half. It will also allow you to relax more as you *begin* your ride. Early tension contributes to fatigue later in the ride, so the less tension, the better.

As for Scrabble, I'm sure you're delighted that he's no longer moving cautiously because of discomfort. However, as you've discovered, now that he is feeling comfortable enough to take joy in physical movement (which is the birthright of all horses), he may be a little too active and enthusiastic for your comfort and security.

Check his diet. Many horses are overfed, and a healthy, overfed horse will develop a case of the bounces in no time. The next thing I would do is look at his exercise schedule — is he getting enough turnout? If a horse is healthy, comfortable, well fed, and kept in a stall, it's natural for him to be extremely energetic and expressive during a one-hour ride. If Scrabble could be turned out to play for a few hours before you ride, that would help take the edge off. If turning him out is impossible, put him on the longe line and let him blow off a little steam at a steady trot on the biggest circle possible — much bigger than the standard 20 meters. Walk a big circle of your own inside Scrabble's circle, so that he can trot energetically without hurting himself.

In-hand work is nice, but it's better if you save it until after Scrabble's warm-up, either free-schooling or on the longe. You're basically asking him to stretch and flex, and those are difficult things to do unless his muscles have warmed up. Just like you, he needs to warm up before he stretches.

During your ride, have a plan and ride the plan, but always remain flexible in case one of you has a stiff day or the riding arena is crowded. Decide, for example, that you are going to spend 10 minutes in an active, forward walk, then 10 minutes doing walk-trot transitions on a 20-meter circle, then another minute of walk on a long rein, then leg-yields or trot-canter or walk-canter transitions. Start slow, work hard, then slow again toward the end of the ride, and ask for more flexibility and stretching as you cool down.

Keep Scrabble busy, keep the transitions coming, and tell him "good boy" every single time he does something you like, or comes close to doing something you like. If you keep him busy and reward his prompt responses, he won't have as much time or inclination for those spontaneous expressions of joy.

Horses find it incredibly difficult to entertain two ideas at once, which is why you lose their attention entirely when they spook. Use this trait to your advantage. Keep Scrabble busy responding to your requests, and he will settle down more quickly. If you focus on your horse, he will focus on you, but if you begin thinking about something else and put him on autopilot, he'll be very distractible, because as far as he is concerned, you have hung up the phone, so to speak, or at least put him on hold.

Analyze your position and problems and make yourself a little checklist to recite as you ride. If your trouble spots are your eyes, shoulders, and heels, say "eyes, shoulders, heels" to yourself every minute or two and check your position each time. If you need to push Scrabble into his corners, think of what you would tell your student: "Position your horse, leg-yield into the corner, keep the rhythm, and keep the position as you come out of the corner," and then say it to yourself *and mean it.*

If you get a chance to work with a good visiting instructor, even if she isn't your regular one, go for it! It can help a lot to have someone look at your riding with a fresh eye.

CHAPTER 14

Bits, Reins, and Contact

MANY RIDERS HAVE TAKEN LESSONS for years but worry that they still don't understand the concepts of "contact" or "following hands." Quite often, they feel that they shouldn't bother their instructors with these "stupid" or embarrassingly elementary questions. In fact, no question is stupid and no question is too elementary. Riders have many different learning styles, instructors have many different teaching styles, and it's important to continue to say "I don't understand, could you explain that in a different way?" until you reach that "Aha!" moment of understanding.

Correct Way to Hold Reins

Q I am 45 years old and have returned to riding in the last few months after a very long "pause." I have forgotten a lot, and what I do remember no longer seems correct (my seat apparently tends to be too forward and my hands too low, for instance). My previous instructor was a British ex-cavalry officer who drilled things into us; that I do remember! My present instructor is very patient, kind, and generous with praise.

My question concerns the correct way to hold the reins when riding English using a simple single joint snaffle bit. I was previously taught to hold the snaffle rein beneath my baby finger, not threaded through the baby finger and the fourth finger. I was told that you only threaded the reins when using a double bridle and then the snaffle rein was still beneath the baby finger.

Is one way better than the other? Why do you suppose I was taught what seems to be incorrect?

I have tried threading the reins but I find it very distracting. My instructor is not fussy and says that for now, I may hold the reins the way I was taught, but I want to switch eventually if it is totally wrong.

A Don't worry, there are several different ways to hold reins, whether you're holding a single pair or two pairs. Some ways are better suited to different types of riding and some ways have been in and out of fashion several times over the last few hundred years.

You're using a simple snaffle bridle with one rein in each hand. Wherever the rein enters your hand, under your baby finger or between your baby finger and your ring finger, your hold on the rein at that point is a passive grip. The active grip is where the rein passes between your thumb and forefinger. If the rein enters your hand between the baby finger and ring finger, the passive grip is a little stronger, as is the security of your hold, because your ring finger is stronger than your baby finger. In addition to being stronger, your ring finger is also more independent and better able to give the tiny squeezes and releases that make up so much of your riding dialogue through the reins. You *hold* the rein with your thumb and forefinger and *talk* through the rein with your ring finger. But that said, it's entirely possible, and no less correct, to have the snaffle rein on the out-side of your baby finger. As long as you and your horse are comfortable, and you are able to use your rein aids softly and clearly, there is no need to change.

Riding instructors typically teach beginners that the snaffle rein should enter the hand between the baby finger and ring finger. When more advanced riders are learning how to use a Pelham or a double bridle, or if beginner riders are just learning to use the snaffle but the instructor fully expects them to graduate to the double bridle in time, the instructor may prefer to teach that the snaffle rein (the upper one) should enter the hand under the baby finger so that when the curb rein (the lower one) is added, it can be placed between the baby finger and ring finger. The theory behind this practice is that most riders make fewer unintentional movements with their ring fingers, creating less action on the curb rein. This may be correct in some cases. In my own experience, I've found that riders are often more gentle with their baby fingers simply because those fingers are weaker, so I find the baby finger quite suitable for the curb rein.

Different instructors teach different methods because they teach what they were taught by *their* instructors, who may have learned specific practices for very good reasons and then passed on those practices (but not the reasons) to their own students. For instance, you may be taught one style if your instructor is (or was taught by) a civilian and another style if your instructor is (or was taught by) a cavalry instructor. In the case of the seemingly conflicting ways of holding the reins of a double bridle, there are reasons for the two different styles.

In the cavalry, much riding was done with the curb alone, so the curb rein was placed outside the snaffle rein and held outside the baby finger. This makes sense when you remember that for the cavalry's purposes the reins often needed to be held in one hand, freeing the rider's other hand to hold a weapon. For civilian riding, the snaffle rein was outside the curb rein because the rider kept both hands on the reins and the snaffle, not the curb, was the primary rein.

Your snaffle rein can be held outside or inside your baby finger — either way is correct.

As long as you hold your reins firmly with closed fingers and relaxed arms, it doesn't really matter whether your baby fingers are on the outside or the inside of the rein — it's more useful to be concerned with the position of your hands in front of you.

If you look down at your own hands holding the reins, you should see your thumb joints bent upward like little rooftops. Your thumbnails should point slightly inward — not directly toward one another, but angled, so that your left thumbnail is pointing at the base of your horse's right ear and your right thumbnail is pointing at the base of your horse's left ear. The reins should come out between your thumbs and forefingers, which is why that bend in your thumb is all-important. Practice holding the reins with your thumb bent and then with your thumb flat and you'll quickly see why the bend matters.

With the rein firmly held between the ball of your thumb and your forefinger, your hand and forearm can extend softly, your wrists can relax, and you can tighten and relax your fingers to send quiet signals to your horse. With flat thumbs, your hand, forearm, wrist, and fingers all become stiff, and you can no longer achieve quiet communication with the horse's mouth through subtle movements of your fingers.

Here is an easy way of picking up the reins so that the reins and your hands will be in the correct position instantly with no deliberate, slow process of "threading" required. With practice, picking up your reins in this way will become easy and smooth, and you will be able to do it without looking, and indeed without thinking about it at all.

1. With the reins hanging loose on your horse's neck, reach down with both hands open, palms down, fingers pointed toward your horse's neck, and your extended thumbs just touching one another.
2. Place your thumbs on either side of the buckle connecting the reins and pick up the reins between your thumbs and forefingers.
3. Leaving your baby fingers open and pointing, close the rest of your fingers around the reins.
4. Rotate your closed hands outward so that your thumbs are on top and your thumbnails angle toward each other, pointing at the horse's opposite ears.
5. Close your baby fingers, which you will find to be (surprise!) on the *outside* of the reins.
6. Congratulations! Your reins are positioned correctly in your closed hands, your hands are positioned correctly, and the reins are entering your hands between baby fingers and ring fingers, exiting between thumb and forefinger.

Once this becomes easy and comfortable, you can practice shortening the reins. If the reins between your hands and the horse's mouth are hanging in festoons, don't worry. Just rotate your hands inward so that your thumbs touch, then relax your thumb-hold slightly and separate your hands, letting them slide away from the buckle, away from each other, along the reins. When you've taken up enough rein, bend your thumbs again and tighten your hands to confirm your grip, then rotate your hands again so that your thumbs are uppermost and your thumbnails are pointing toward one another. This will bring your upper arms back into their correct default position, hanging softly at your sides with elbows bent, and it works equally well whether the reins are inside or outside your baby fingers.

Acceptance of Contact

Q I own a dressage horse in training. My trainer works with the horse three days each week, and I ride him the other four days. Right now our objective is to make the horse accept contact, but this is strangely difficult. Could you suggest some methods that would help us solve this problem? We have tried riding in side reins, also in draw reins for one week, but the results were not impressive. I understand that dressage is difficult and that horses in training often resist the bit, but we have only a few months before our competition season begins, and we must solve this problem soon.

A There is no way to *make* a horse accept contact. That's not how contact works and it's not how dressage works. Any resistance and problems you and your trainer are experiencing with your horse are, I suspect, all based on this profound misconception.

Dressage is only difficult for the horse when the training is incorrect and the horse is unprepared. You mention that horses in training often resist the bit — again, this is true only when the training is incorrect. Finally, you are trying to train on a timetable with gadgets (side reins and draw reins) to speed up the process of training, whereas a more useful resource would be a chart on which you could record your horse's progressive increases in understanding, strength, and flexibility. Those attributes are what will eventually bring him through the process of skills acquisition. Side reins, draw reins, and timetables won't help.

Here's something you should keep in mind at all times: Contact is communication. At first the bit and reins are the links between the horse's mouth and the rider's hands. As both horse and rider develop, the reins gradually become a link between the horse's mind and the rider's mind, but this requires time and calm, correct practice. If you think of contact as communication, and "on the bit" being analogous to "on the phone," you'll understand why the quality of the connection is all-important, and why we can't force or improve communication by screaming down the line at our end.

The bit and reins are only one form of communication between horse and rider. They are the "last and least" part of the overall, all-body communication that we describe as "the circle of the aids." When the rider has learned to sit well and to "listen" as well as "talk" with seat, legs, and shifts of weight and posture, then the rein contact can be refined until riding becomes the dialogue it was meant to be.

"Last and least" doesn't mean "unimportant" — it's just that everything else needs to come first. Contact through the reins closes the circle of the aids and makes the horse-rider communication loop even easier and clearer.

Contact isn't something the horse should "accept," it's something he should offer, seek out, and be happy to have the *rider* accept. The horse that is taught slowly and carefully to use his belly muscles, lift his back, and engage his hind end will naturally reach forward into the rider's hand. It's the rider's responsibility to see that this happens and to provide soft, "live" communication through the rein to reassure the horse that he has done well and that completing the connection was exactly the right thing to do.

Good contact is light and alive; the rider is holding hands with the horse's mouth.

Contact can't be forced. The horse can learn to seek contact with a trusted rider, but if force and leverage are used, he will either lean on the bit in a desperate attempt to run away from the pain or he will learn to curl his neck into an overbent position in an attempt to stay behind the bit at all times, regardless of the rider's actions.

It may well be possible to push and pull your horse into a "shape" or "frame" during the next few months, but I strongly advise against it. From the sound of things, you would do much better to throw away your timetable and focus on real dressage by following a logical progression of skills acquisition and deepening understanding on the horse's part and on yours. If you must think in terms of competition and you can't put your ambition aside entirely, at least push it back a year and allow your horse more time to develop.

If you are truly ambitious, you'll see the value in the kind of proper preparation that will enable your horse to progress through the lower levels at least. Good judges are not fooled by false frames, and the sort of work you are doing now will take you nowhere. Progress is not possible when someone uses leverage to create a false frame for a horse — your horse is likely to become too unsound to continue in his training, or too unhappy and confused to accept more training. Eventually, the only way to make any progress at all will be to start over from the ground up! That will take much more time and effort, and offer less reliable results, than taking the time to do things right in the first place and keeping your horse sound and happy all through his training.

If you find that you are interested in training your horse correctly, you will need help, and it sounds as though you will need to look for another trainer. Visit every establishment you can and try to locate someone whose horses are sound, happy, and progressing at a rate of speed that doesn't endanger their bodies or minds.

Change Bit for More Control?

Q I have a 9-year-old Thoroughbred that I use for jumper classes. We take lessons twice a week (one flat, one jumping). When we ride on the flat I use a Dr. Bristol snaffle bit and when I ride over fences I use a Pelham. My problem is that my horse still gets strong sometimes over fences. My trainer says he will improve if we continue doing slow work over fences, but in jumper classes we need to go faster sometimes. I wonder if a stronger bit like a gag or something similar wouldn't be a better choice for us. My trainer doesn't think so, but I feel that I need the control. Do you have any suggestions?

A I have to agree with your instructor. You're already using strong bits on your horse: a Dr. Bristol is a very strong snaffle, and the lower rein on the Pelham gives you leverage through the use of the curb. Escalating the severity of the equipment won't work in the long term.

With one lesson on the flat and one lesson over jumps each week, you're not likely to fall into bad habits between lessons. Take advantage of this. Take a few months off from jumping and focus on your flatwork. A few months of concentrated flatwork and seat development will help you a great deal. If you were riding with me, I'd have you use a very mild snaffle such as a French-link.

When your horse has become more balanced, obedient, and maneuverable, when he can lengthen and shorten his stride easily and smoothly at all three gaits, when he can perform smooth, prompt transitions between and within the gaits, and when he can stop easily from any gait and stand on a loose rein (all of this using a gentle bit, not a Dr. Bristol), you can begin working over jumps again. When you do, you'll find that you and the horse are both amazingly improved.

Your money will be better invested in lessons than in hardware.

When you start jumping again, ask your instructor to set up gymnastic lines for you. When you can navigate these easily and smoothly, begin working over individual fences, short lines of related fences, and small courses, keeping all the jumps low. Then make the courses more tricky and complicated, but continue to keep the jumps low. When *those* courses become easy, you can begin to raise the jumps *or* increase your speed, but don't do both at once.

Your instructor is right about the benefits of slow work over fences. Your horse needs control, accuracy, and power, not speed — not yet, anyway. You can develop control, accuracy, and power by making the courses more demanding in terms of distances and turns and complexity *before* increasing the height. By the time you're asking for real speed, you and your horse should have a very strong partnership based on mutual trust, and you should have a clear understanding of what it takes to lengthen and shorten your horse's stride and to increase and decrease his speed.

If your horse works smoothly and easily on the flat and over fences at home in a simple snaffle, you can save the Pelham for use at competitions, foxhunting, or other venues where he is likely to become excited and quick.

A gag bit is very strong and it isn't a brake — its purpose is to make a horse lift its head. A gag puts pressure on a horse's mouth *and* on his poll, and as long as there is any rider contact with the gag rein, the horse will experience that pressure. Gags are generally used only on horses that tend to drop their heads and necks low and fall on their forehands, and they're used *only* when those horses are being ridden at high speeds over jumps and uneven terrain.

Here are some suggestions you can use throughout your riding life.

Don't use any equipment you don't need or don't fully understand. The more you learn and the better you ride, the less often you will think in terms of equipment changes. When you *do* change something, it will be because you are replacing a severe or ill-fitting piece of equipment with something more gentle or better fitting.

Solve training problems with training, so your horse understands and can give you what you want. To correct problems of strength and balance, use good flatwork and gymnastics to help the horse become stronger and more balanced. And when you find an instructor who understands these things, stay with that instructor. Your money will be better invested in lessons than in hardware.

You're very lucky to have an instructor who doesn't reach for equipment to "solve" every problem. Work with your instructor, be patient, take your time, focus on flatwork and gymnastic jumping for maximum precision, flexibility, and control, and you'll be ready to have a great time jumping at competitions next spring. You may even find that you'll be able to do it all on light contact in a snaffle.

Bit Pressure and Western Bits

Q I've always ridden English, but I've just moved to Arizona and am starting to ride Western because that's pretty much all I can find. I'm used to riding hunters on light contact and am having a hard time adjusting to the reins always hanging loose on a Western bridle. I've heard many different explanations about how bits work, and I'm pretty sure that however they work, it's not supposed to look the way it does in the movies. Is it true that Western horses work without any pressure from the bit?

A   That's a really interesting question. In English riding there should be constant *contact,* not constant heavy *pressure.* Technically there is some degree of pressure in any contact, but the sort of light, elastic contact that characterizes good English riding should not make either you or your horse think in terms of pressure. With a snaffle bit, which works off direct pressure, a very light feel at your end of the reins means a very light feel at your horse's end of the reins.

Western curb bits are much more complicated. They work by leverage, affecting the bars and tongue as well as the chin groove, poll, and sometimes the roof of the horse's mouth. How these bits work depends on many things, including their design; Western curbs vary widely as to shape, weight, and balance. The horse *does* work off pressure in the mouth, but the pressure isn't caused by fingers moving at the end of a lightly stretched rein as it is in English riding.

In Western riding, as in English riding, the movement of the bit in the horse's mouth tells the well-trained horse what the rider wants. The difference is that in Western riding, the bit can be moved at the end of a loopy rein just by the rider's moving his or her rein hand. The mouthpiece of the bit moves in various ways to create pressure. It may move up, down, forward, back, or in some combination of directions. Some bits, through their weight and design, have a strong effect on a horse's head carriage, as the horse must carry his head in a certain way in order to avoid putting bit pressure on the roof of his mouth, for example.

A good sliding stop involves no rein pressure.

In Western riding, as in English riding, the movement of the bit in the horse's mouth tells the well-trained horse what the rider wants.

Some Western bits exert no active pressure on the horse's mouth until the rider lifts or drops his rein hand or takes the rein hand to one side or the other. Other bits, especially the ones with long, swept-back shanks, put some pressure on the horse's mouth even when both reins are hanging loose.

Many Western horses are trained to stay behind the bit at all times, and trying to convince a good Western horse to go up to the bit and seek direct contact with the rider's hand would be uncomfortable and confusing for the horse.

The most important thing for you to remember right now is that good Western riding, like good English riding, emphasizes legs and seat and balance before reins and bit. Your horse should go, stop, and turn because of what you tell him with your body, not because of what you do with your hands. At the very least, he should do all of those things with just a whisper from the reins.

You're right about Western movies; rent a couple of videotapes of the National Reining Championships instead. Look at how much a horse and rider can do — including spins, gallops, and sliding stops — with no pulling from the rider and no tension in the neck, crossing of the jaw, or opening of the mouth from the horse. It's especially impressive when you consider that these horses wear no nosebands, so there is no way to hide a strong pull or a wide-open mouth.

I think you'll be pleasantly surprised by the options available to you in Western riding. A good reining horse-and-rider combination epitomizes finesse. Keep your eyes open for exhibitions of vaquero-style work or "doma vaquera" competition. It takes an incredibly sophisticated, well-educated horse to carry a spade bit and an incredibly balanced, well-educated rider with a delicate, sensitive hand to ride that horse.

Asking My Horse to Stretch Forward and Down

Q I have a question about the movement in dressage tests where the rider puts the horse on a 20-meter circle at the trot and the horse is supposed to take the reins and stretch his head down toward the ground.

My horse is very nice and kind, but he is not very talented for dressage (according to my instructor and everyone else who sees him), and we have not yet been able to do this "stretchy, chewy" movement (that's what my instructor calls it). Either I forget to release the reins and he just trots in a circle with no change, or I drop the reins and he pops his head straight up in the air instead of stretching down. He also pops it up when I try to pick up the reins again. My instructor says that in the beginning I should just release with my elbows, but my arms are short and I think he needs more rein than just what I can give him by locking my elbows open. I need to learn to do this movement, but no matter how soon I give him the reins, he never reaches down the way he is supposed to.

A   Putting aside the question of your horse's innate talent for dressage, let's focus on what this particular movement is, what it's for, what it means, and how you can improve the way you and your horse do it.

This is not a complicated movement, although many riders make it more complicated than it is. It's simply a matter of riding a 20-meter circle at a posting trot, something you've done hundreds, if not thousands, of times. The only difference between an ordinary 20-meter trot circle and this movement is that the horse is supposed to stretch his head and neck downward as you allow him the rein to do so, then bring his head and neck back up as you take back the rein. If you read the description of the movement directly from the test, you'll see that what you are asked to do is "Circle right (or left) 20m, rising trot, allowing the horse to stretch forward and downward."

The trick to mastering this movement is to realize that the movement is not a trick and doesn't involve a cue. The key word is "allowing." Your horse should already be working from behind, tightening his belly muscles, and stretching his topline. He stretches his head and neck on the circle not because you give him a special signal to reach forward and down, but because he is glad to have the chance to reach forward and down whenever he's allowed to do so. Performing the movement simply means that while riding your horse in a balanced, rhythmic, energetic, forward circle, on soft, stretchy contact, you *allow* him to stretch forward and down. This is something that he should always be ready and happy to do, at any gait, because (a) he should be in a position to stretch easily and (b) the stretch should feel pleasant. When you shorten your reins and he brings his head and neck back up at the end of the movement, he should be happy to do that, too, because he's just had a lovely stretch and he should feel good.

This circle is essentially the same as any other correctly ridden circle, only this time you invite and allow your horse to initiate the stretch. It's not about *making* him stretch. This isn't a circus trick — it's an important moment for horse and rider. The purpose of every dressage test is to allow the judge to evaluate the quality of your horse's training and the effectiveness of your riding. Your scores and the judge's comments help you to know how accurate your own perceptions are and assist you in deciding whether you should continue at the same level and polish your performance, whether you should move up and tackle a more difficult series of movements, or whether you might need to drop back for a little while to fill in the gaps. Without the judge's comments, many of us would remain blissfully unaware of the flaws in our horses' training and in our own riding.

The specific purpose of this movement is to verify two things: First, is the horse not just accepting the bit but actively seeking to maintain the contact with the rider's hand? Second, is the horse sufficiently balanced to stretch his topline and follow the bit as far as the rider will let him go — even, perhaps, as far as the ground — while maintaining the contact *and* his energy and balance and rhythm?

If the answers are yes, good! You're working correctly and heading in the right direction. If the answer to either of these questions is no, then you've discovered a fundamental gap in your training and you'll need to go back and fill it before you can hope to work at this level or move up.

The horse will find it easier to reach forward and down into the stretch if the rider's position does not change.

If you take a dressage test apart into a series of individual movements and components, you'll find there's nothing exotic or esoteric about any of them. They're training exercises: circles, straight lines, bends and turns, regular rhythmic gaits, balanced transitions, square halts. These are all things that you should be practicing and improving and refining all the time, whether you're "doing dressage" or "just riding around."

To practice this particular movement, begin by practicing a lot of *good* circles (remember, quality always counts) at the posting trot. When you are sure that both you and the horse are balanced, that your horse's trot rhythm is absolutely clear, that his tempo is neither too fast nor too slow, and that he has looked for, and found, a soft, steady contact with your hands, you can move ahead.

When you are ready to begin the movement, don't change *anything*. Continue to ride your horse forward with energy, keeping the rhythm and tempo and contact just as they were, and then very slowly allow half an inch or an inch (no more!) of the reins to slide through your fingers. Keep looking where you are going, and *feel* what your horse is doing. If you drop *your* head to see whether your horse is dropping *his* head, you'll make your seat and legs ineffective and you'll drop the contact, at which point the horse will feel lost and his head and neck will pop up.

Remember to allow the reins to slip *slowly* through your fingers. The idea is not to throw the reins on the horse's neck and tell him, "There's where the bit went, go fetch!" He's not a dog and he won't understand that. He'll just know that you were holding hands with his mouth and then you suddenly dropped him on his own. This startled him a little, then he started to worry and lost his balance, so he threw his head up to regain it.

By letting the reins slide through your fingers slowly, you never actually lose contact. The horse feels the contact becoming too light for comfort, so he reaches for the bit. You let the reins slip a little more and he continues to reach, but all the time he should remain balanced and rhythmic with no change of tempo. That way, as he reaches, he'll stretch his entire topline. If you just drop the reins so that he has to dive for the bit, he'll either lift his head in surprise, or he will drop his neck and his withers and you'll suddenly feel that you're going downhill on a not-very-balanced horse.

When you bring him back up at the end of the circle, keep the same position and remember the same priorities: Stay balanced so that he can continue to be balanced, continue to post (your energy and the forward movement of your hips should remain unchanged), and as you touch down just behind the pommel, use your legs lightly and close your fingers tightly on the reins for just an instant. The next time you touch down behind the pommel, do the same thing again.

Your posture is telling your horse, "Keep the same balance and rhythm and tempo, please" while your legs are saying, "A little more forward, please" and then relaxing to say, "Yes, that's right, thank you." At almost the same time, your hands close to say, "Bring your neck up and your head in just a little," and then relax to say, "That's it, thank you." When you do it this way, there is no loss of energy, your horse doesn't fall on his forehand or drop his back, and you don't change position and therefore cause him to change position. Instead, you're communicating with him every step of the way.

This wonderful gymnastic exercise is essential for any dressage horse, because it's one of the basic, elementary training exercises that are used all the way to Fédération Equestre Internationale (FEI) Level and beyond. The more you do it, and the better you do it, the easier it will become and the more stretch you will get.

I know what your instructor means by telling you to use just your elbows. At first, the horse (especially if somewhat stiff and unaccustomed to this exercise) will be able to reach/stretch comfortably only briefly and for only a few inches. If your horse is very stiff, two inches of rein may be all he can reach for while maintaining the contact, so if this is the case, don't ask him to reach as far as he can and then drop him by suddenly throwing the reins away. If you do, your horse will never gain the confidence he needs to relax and reach forward. In the early stages with a stiff horse, you may never need to change your grip on the reins — most people can give a horse another two inches of rein just by moving their arms forward and/or opening their elbows.

This also makes your life easier when it's time to bring the horse back up, because you won't need to shorten your reins. Bending your elbows a little more and/or bringing them back toward your body will be all you need to do. However, you may as well begin practicing lengthening and shortening your reins quietly, because as soon as your horse has been gymnasticized enough to stretch more effectively, you'll need those skills.

CHAPTER 15

Whips and Spurs and How to Use Them

WHIPS AND SPURS ARE ARTIFICIAL AIDS that are meant to reinforce the natural aids and enable the rider to give the horse soft, clear, and precise signals. Whips should not be used to inflict punishment; used correctly, they help the horse learn the correct responses to the rider's light leg aids. Spurs should not be used to demand speed; used correctly, they can make the rider's light leg aids more precise. Riders who have achieved a balanced seat and good control over their own legs should not be afraid to wear spurs.

How to Use a Whip

Q I try to use natural aids in riding as I'm very much against being unkind to horses in any way, but I know it's sometimes necessary to use a crop to reinforce these aids. I've seen conflicting use of the crop/whip/bat on horses and wonder if it's just a matter of different styles of usage in the different disciplines of riding. Is it true that all artificial aids should only be used to reinforce the natural aids?

When I first began to ride I took lessons in a small arena and mostly rode out on park trails. My instructor always had me hit the horses on the shoulder with the crop. What message does being hit on the shoulder convey to the horse?

Now I'm riding hunter/jumpers, and we use a bat behind the leg to reinforce the leg on most of the school horses. There are some particularly stubborn horses, however, on which we have to use a long dressage whip (on their rumps), as tapping them behind the leg makes no impression. As this doesn't reinforce a natural aid, is it really teaching the horse anything other than pain means "move"?

A Whips can be very useful when you're training a horse to listen to the leg. Correct use of the whip can teach a horse to respond to very light, subtle leg pressure, and once the horse has learned, the whip is something you will use only if he seems to be forgetting the lesson. The point of using a whip to reinforce the leg is that (a) it allows you to use a lighter leg aid, instead of resorting to constant pressure or kicking, and (b) it allows you to teach the horse to respond to that aid without having to put your leg out of position to make your point.

The artificial aids must be used only to reinforce the natural aids. Your aim is always to use the least amount of pressure to elicit the most response, and a sharp smack with the whip behind the leg is an excellent (and much less annoying and painful) alternative to constant kicking, pushing, and pumping. Whips are for clarification, reinforcement, and discipline — *never* for punishment.

If you use a whip not to reinforce your leg but as an *alternative* to your leg, you'd better have a very good reason — paralysis or amputation, for instance! Some riders with polio or missing/damaged limbs have taught their horses to respond to whip signals, because for these riders, giving leg signals is simply not an option. In this case, the artificial aid replaces the natural aid. But if both of your legs are present and in good working order, your whip should be used only to reinforce the leg (natural) aid.

The sequence is as follows.

1. Apply the aid that you want the horse to respond to: a slight squeeze.
2. Relax your leg and wait a moment, to give the horse a chance to respond.
3. If he doesn't respond, repeat the same light squeeze and follow it *instantly* with a single sharp smack (not a soft, annoying tap) of the whip behind your leg.
4. If necessary, repeat the entire sequence until the horse moves forward energetically from your light leg aid (the slight squeeze).

Most horses can learn this lesson in one brief session, although they may need to be reminded regularly so that they can repeat the desired response until it becomes a habit. Once that happens, you will rarely need the whip.

Because the whip is being used to reinforce the leg, it should be applied behind the leg, where it actually encourages the horse to move forward. Hitting the horse on the shoulder does not send him forward, nor does it enforce any aid that you would ever give with your leg or seat. (I can think of *one* situation where you might use a whip on a horse's shoulder. When you're riding a cross-country course and you know where all the jumps are but your horse does not, a light tap, not a stinging smack, on the shoulder with a short whip can be a useful "wake up, be alert, fence coming up" signal to a horse that's cantering or galloping along with no idea there's a big jump just around the next turn.)

A horse that is ridden by rid- ers who have swinging, bouncing, or kicking legs, and/or by riders who constantly tap-tap-tap his sides with the whip, will sooner or later learn to ignore what he perceives as meaningless, random bumping. This often happens with overworked school horses used for group les- sons. In such cases, using a whip on the horse's rump may be the only short-term way to indicate to the horse that you actually want it to respond. (In the long term, retrain- ing the horse would be a good idea.)

This rider can easily take both reins in her left hand and use her whip behind her leg.

When Can I Start Wearing Spurs?

Q I have been taking riding lessons (English style, what my instructor calls basic balanced seat) for almost a year. When I arrived for my first lesson, I wanted to be sure that I had all the right clothes and equipment, so I was wearing boots and breeches and a riding vest and helmet and gloves and spurs, and carrying a riding crop. My instructor made me take off the spurs and put the crop away; she said I wouldn't need those for a long time yet. About a month ago, I got the okay to use the crop. She is very picky about how and when I use it, and she still won't let me wear my spurs! She says that she'll tell me when I'm ready. When I ask her why I'm not ready after almost a whole year, she just smiles. She's not the chatty type, but this is frustrating! Can you explain why I can't have my spurs?

A Here's what "She's ready to use spurs" means to me, when I hear it from a good instructor. First, it means that the rider's balance and position are reliably good; second, that the rider is adept at using quiet, simple, brief leg aids. A rider who is ready to use spurs doesn't kick or swing her legs and doesn't dig into the horse's sides with her heels. She keeps her lower leg in place and just lifts her toes slightly so that her calf muscles tighten against the horse for a second before she relaxes her leg again. She has good control over her legs and can bring each leg back a few inches and use it lightly, just for a fraction of a second, without becoming unbalanced or moving out of position. It means that the rider can deliver a very brief nudge — not a kick or a severe prod, and not prolonged pressure — to the exact spot on the horse's side that she intends to nudge.

When a rider can do all of those things easily and well, time after time, she may be ready to wear spurs. There are two more criteria, though: The instructor must be certain that this rider does *not* clamp the backs of her legs into her horse's sides when she is startled. I'm sure you can imagine the consequences if a rider were to do that while wearing spurs. The instructor must also be certain that the rider *never* takes her temper out on the horse.

Being "ready to wear spurs" means having achieved a combination of proven abilities and skills, understanding, and behavior patterns; when a rider is balanced, adept, aware, considerate, and emotionally mature, then she is ready to wear spurs. After all, the purpose of a spur is to refine the rider's leg aids, so that she can speak more clearly (not more loudly!) to the horse.

I realize that some instructors are not very chatty, but you might get more detailed answers from your instructor if you tried asking some different questions, such as "What must I be able to do, and what skills and habits must I have, before I will be ready to wear spurs?"

Does a Whip Equal Abuse?

Q Could you explain how to handle a situation you feel constitutes "horse abuse"? I ask because I've recently been called a "horse abuser," and it has just about torn out my heart.

My horse is healthy, happy, and kept at a nice place. The problems began when I started bringing him back after an injury he sustained in the pasture. I train in a discipline different from most of the people at my barn, and some of them see my and my trainer's methods as, to put it mildly, incorrect. Specifically, I use a whip while I ride, not to beat my horse but to reinforce my leg and to ask him to step a bit more with his hind end. But I was told that because I use a whip instead of kick, Kick, KICKING to make him trot, I'm a horse abuser. In my heart I know I'm not, but it hurts so much I don't even want to go to the barn anymore.

I've always thought that anything can be either a weapon or a tool; the only difference is how you use it. For example, if you use a cotton lead rope to beat a horse, it's a weapon, but if you're just leading the horse around, obviously it's a tool. That goes for specific equipment too. Skilled and tactful trainers can use specialized equipment to improve a horse's way of going, but that same equipment can do great harm in the hands of someone less skilled.

Of course, everyone, regardless of their skill level, makes mistakes or is just plain wrong sometimes, but carelessly throwing around the term "horse abuser" seems like one of the biggest mistakes of all. It's one thing to willfully and maliciously mistreat or neglect a horse, and it's another to do something foolish out of ignorance. But just because someone is not doing things "your way" is not reason enough to use such strong language.

I do appreciate that someone would care enough about my horse that they would have the courage to speak out against what they honestly think is a dangerous or harmful practice. In fact, I hope that other riders will help and correct me when they see me doing something that could hurt my horse, or ask me about it if they see me doing something they don't understand.

A I see only two forms of real abuse described in your story. One is the verbal abuse perpetrated by the person who called you a horse abuser; the other is the all-too-real abuse being perpetrated on a horse being "trained" by the kick-Kick-KICK method.

The use of a whip does not, per se, constitute abuse, provided that it's used correctly as a training aid and not as a means of punishing or pestering the horse. The point of the whip is not to teach the horse to respond to the whip, it's to teach the horse to respond to the rider's *leg*. If you want to be absolutely certain that your use of the whip is correct, ask yourself these questions:

- Do I *ever* use the whip to hit my horse in anger? (Hint: the answer should be no.)
- When I want my horse to move forward with more energy, do I ask him with my legs?
- If he responds promptly and correctly, do I thank him?
- If he doesn't respond promptly and correctly, do I repeat the same gentle "ask" and reinforce it with *one* sharp smack of the whip behind my leg?
- When he responds to that by moving forward, do I thank him instantly?
- The *next* time I use my light leg aid, does my horse respond quickly and with energy?

If your answer is yes to the last five questions, good; you can relax. Your use of the leg aid is correct, your use of the whip is correct, your horse understands what you want, and your training is effective.

That said, you must be honest with yourself. If you use the whip every time you use your leg, without giving your horse a chance to respond to the leg alone, you're not using the whip correctly. If you ask for forward movement by using the whip on an area that doesn't correspond to forward movement (on the horse's shoulder, for instance), you're not using the whip correctly. If you use the whip repeatedly, you're not using it correctly, whether you're using it so gently that it tickles and annoys your horse or whether you're beating him like a dusty carpet. And finally, if you find that you need to use the whip *more* often during each successive ride, something is wrong. As your horse's training and rehabilitation progress and his muscles, responses, and habits become strong again, you should be using it less and less.

It sounds as though you are using the whip exactly as you should: to reinforce your leg. Riders who use the whip correctly are actually much kinder to

A rider who pumps her hips, flaps her reins, and kicks constantly
cannot teach her horse; she can only hurt and annoy him.

their horses than riders who insist that they could "never use anything as unkind as a whip" but who think nothing of squeezing their horses constantly with their legs or kicking them repeatedly with their boot heels to get them to move forward. This sort of thinking is based on a fundamental lack of understanding of horses, training, and riding.

The horse needs to learn that he should reach forward with more energy in response to a brief, light pressure from the rider's leg. In the early stages, when the horse is first learning what the rider wants, the whip may be used more often. It is *not* appropriate to use more leg pressure or hold the pressure longer. The whole point of teaching the horse to respond to the leg is to be able to offer a quiet, gentle signal and to have him respond immediately and energetically. Once the horse develops the habit of responding to a light leg aid with enthusiasm, energy, and a more active use of the hind leg on that side, you may need the whip only as an occasional reminder.

You're quite right that misuse can turn an ordinary tool into a weapon. Beating a horse with a lead rope is obvious abuse; leading the horse and jerking on the rope every two steps is less obvious. An even more subtle form of abuse is leading the horse with such a tight grip on the lead rope that he can't walk comfortably or with a normal stride. This sort of misuse/abuse is very common, even with riders who would never deliberately harm their horses.

Deliberate abuse is a bad thing, as is ignorant abuse. A too-high bit, a too-tight noseband, a too-tight girth, an inappropriate bit, a saddle that doesn't fit or is placed too far forward — all of these are painful for the horse. But it's easy and very common for someone to say, "She uses a whip (or spurs), therefore she is abusive; I don't, therefore I am not abusive."

The whip is an aid that the horse understands very readily. One smart smack with a whip, administered correctly, won't damage or frighten the horse. It doesn't even have to cause any pain; most horses will respond to the *sound* of a sharply applied whip, and if your horse already understands the whip use, you can smack the side of your own boot. If you're using a dressage whip (best for training because it's long enough for you to use correctly without getting out of position or moving your arm), a whack on your own boot will be accompanied by a slight tickle of the whip's end on the horse's croup or hip — useless on its own but effective when accompanied by the sound of whip on boot.

The important thing to remember is that even if you do smack the horse with the whip, it's not going to cause great pain or lasting damage, unlike constant squeezing and kicking, which first desensitize the horse to the leg and then cause physical damage to his body. "Desensitizing" doesn't mean that the horse no longer *feels* the kicks, it means that he no longer responds to them because he has received so many meaningless kicks that he has learned to accept them without reacting. Such horses, unless they are lucky enough to be sold to a better rider, are doomed to a lifetime of abuse.

Sadly, there are many riders who justify this practice because they have no experience with or knowledge of horsemanship and imagine that the purpose of a whip is to cause pain and injury to the horse. They truly believe that constantly kicking the horse as they ride, and kicking very hard when they want to go faster, isn't abusive, and, sadly, they truly believe that constant kicking is somehow preferable to teaching the horse to respond to a light leg aid.

In response to the comments you received, consider the source. If an ignorant person accuses you of abusing your horse, you shouldn't take it seriously. You won't hear these things from people who know horses and riding, who are educated, and who have good manners. Unfortunately, the less people know about horses, riding, and training, the quicker they are to shout "Abuse!" There are people who will accuse you of abusing your horse if you keep him in a field instead of in a stall or (with more justification) vice versa. There are people who will accuse you of abusing your horse if you don't put shoes on him and others who will accuse you of abusing him if you do. One person may think you cruel because you don't put blankets on your outdoor horses in winter; another may tell you that blankets are unnatural and unhealthy. (I've been asked whether horses in a field wearing fly masks were being punished by being "blindfolded"!)

A truly caring individual should *ask* you what you were doing and why you were doing it. A concerned horseman who saw you doing something that was clearly wrong should try to educate you or to persuade you to do something differently, but should not accuse and attack you. To make life better for someone else's horse, you have to convince the owner she *wants* to do things differently rather than trying to force or humiliate her into changing her behavior. If someone is demonstrating bad riding and a lack of horsemanship and you make that person angry, she is very likely to take her anger out on the horse.

All that said, I like *your* attitude very much. If someone accuses you of something, it can't possibly hurt to take a hard look at whatever it is you are doing, just in case you may have overlooked or forgotten something. Willingness to learn and change is essential to horsemanship.

> *"Desensitizing" doesn't mean that the horse no longer feels the kicks, it means that he no longer responds to them.*

Meanwhile, you need to get along with the people at your barn, so something has to change. What do you think would happen if you approached one of your critics and said, "It really hurts my feelings when you call me a horse abuser. Can we talk about this, please?" If there's any chance of establishing some sort of dialogue, you might be able to manage a quiet exchange of ideas. You could also approach the barn manager and say, without necessarily naming names, that you have been accused of horse abuse, that you are upset and feel unhappy about coming out to the barn, and that you would appreciate some help in making the atmosphere more congenial.

Perhaps you and your trainer could offer to give a little demonstration or explanation of your discipline and training methods for the other people at your barn. Once they understand that you aren't hurting your horse with the whip, that your horse is not afraid of the whip, and that its use is limited and becoming more limited every day as his understanding grows and his new habits develop, perhaps they'll be able to relax and focus on their own horses and their own riding instead of calling you names.

Spurs, Western Riding, and Hollywood

Q I have recently been certified as a beginning Western riding instructor and trail guide, and it seems the more I learn, the more there is to learn. I work with both children and adults at a conference center and ranch. Based on Hollywood's portrayal of the American West, the question often comes up: Who should wear spurs, under what circumstances, and how are they used?

The policy at the guest ranch is that no one wears spurs, neither guests nor staff. All of our horses (44 at last count) are well trained and very manageable. As a result, none of the instructors, even the advanced ones, use spurs or know much about them. This information will help us all.

A Hollywood has a lot to answer for! People all over the world imagine that Western riding means leaping onto a horse from a second-story window, yanking his head around, jabbing him with enormous spurs, running at full gallop for miles and miles over rocky, treacherous terrain, and finally jerking him to a rearing stop in front of the saloon. These B-film Westerns have convinced several generations of movie-watchers that Western riders spend most of their time at a gallop, that a horse's normal reaction to a bit is to throw up his head and open his mouth in pain, and that spurs are a sign of cowboy competence — the bigger and fancier the spur, and the larger and sharper the rowels, the more authentic the cowboy must be. Nothing could be farther from the truth.

On the range and on the ranch, riding was not an art, a sport, or a pastime. It was a critical part of the job, and horses were working partners and flesh-and-blood all-terrain vehicles. Cowboys needed their horses to understand who was in charge. Spurs allowed cowboys to make their orders very clear, especially when the cowboys needed their hands free for roping. Ranch horses wouldn't have understood subtle leg pressure, even if the cowboy knew how to give such pressure and even if the horse could feel such pressure through the heavy saddle.

There were practical reasons for the size and design of spurs. Old-fashioned cowboy saddles had so much physical bulk between the rider's legs and the horse itself that long spurs were needed just to reach the horse. Cowboys were sometimes tall and long-legged, while most cowhorses at that time were quite small — before large horses became fashionable, working ranch horses (as opposed to Hollywood horses) were sturdy, balanced, tough animals standing around 14.0 or 14.2 hands.

A man on a small horse, especially a man sitting in a Western saddle with his legs stretched down long, will find his feet and boot heels hanging below the horse's belly. This isn't a problem, unless the rider wants to use a spur. Because spurs attach to the boot just over the heel, most cowboys would be spurring empty air if their spurs weren't designed to curve in an arc, with the rowels not much lower than the top of the boot heel. And because real cowboys didn't spend all of their time on horseback, low-hanging spurs would have been an invitation to trip. With this design, the combination of high boot heels and curved spur shanks was dangerous only if the cowboy forgot to remove his spurs before he squatted by the campfire.

As for the rowels, there is a lot of variation, and many spurs have no rowels at all. The smallest, thinnest rowels with just a few sharp points look deceptively innocent; like a wire-thin bit, these pieces of hardware cause much more pain than the thicker, larger ones. A larger rowel with many points — sharp or rounded — or even no points looks impressive to the novice, but, like a heavier, thicker bit, is much easier on the horse because any pressure applied is spread over a much larger area.

Parade-outfit spurs may be inlaid and engraved and carry the rider's initials or the ranch brand and they may have large, ornate rowels, but those spurs, like

Good dude ranches protect their horses.

the enormous silver-trimmed parade saddles, are for show and the rowels are unlikely ever to touch the horse. Working spurs tend to be less fancy and more utilitarian. Most cowboys customize their spurs to some degree, either by custom-ordering them or by filing down the rowel points of store-bought spurs.

Among real cowboys, spurs are an accepted part of the working wardrobe, but part of the "code" is that a good hand doesn't leave spur marks on a horse. And true Western horsemen don't leap on the horse and gallop until they stop. Cowboys do most of their ranch work at walk and trot, and, like all good horsemen, they walk the first mile out and the last mile in.

Western tack has changed over the years as well. The trend in Western saddles, over the last 20 years, has been toward a lighter saddle that balances the rider better over his legs and puts much less bulk between the rider's leg and the horse. As a result, the rider's legs lie closer to the horse's sides, and the horse can feel subtle changes in leg pressure.

This means that many Western riders now use leg cues rather than spurs to communicate their wishes to their horses. With the rider's legs closer to the horse, spurs become both more effective and less necessary. The horse learns to respond to the rider's leg, and the spurs are used only as reinforcement if the horse fails to respond to the leg. If the horse ignores a brief leg squeeze or bump with the rider's calf (which one is used would depend on how much leather is between the rider's legs and the horse's body), the correction would be the same squeeze or bump, followed immediately by a nudge — not a kick — from the spurs. This is the equivalent of the dressage rider using the whip to reinforce a light leg aid; since cowboys need to keep one hand free, it's more practical for them to wear spurs than to carry a whip.

Today's Western horses, especially those used for dude ranch work like the trail rides you describe, are fully trained, quiet, and obedient. And "dudes," many of whom are quite unfamiliar with horses and riding, or with Western saddles and Western riding, should never be permitted to wear spurs. Your ranch's "no spurs" rule is a good policy. The string of horses and the people who look after them are the backbone of the dude ranch, and most of a ranch's reputation rides (literally) on the healthy, cheerful, well-trained, comfortable horses that visitors enjoy riding and recommend to their friends.

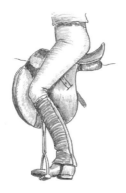

CHAPTER 16

When Your Tack Gets in the Way

RIDERS WHO CAN'T GET COMFORTABLE in their saddles or who can't sit correctly in their saddles generally blame themselves for being incompetent, unfit, or just "built wrong." Many riders accept constant pain as a normal part of their riding experience, but that shouldn't be the case. If a rider has the benefit of good lessons but still experiences discomfort, or is unable to maintain a balanced position, it's very likely that the fault lies with the saddle. Stirrup size and design, stirrup leather adjustment, and the type of reins can also affect rider security and comfort. Riders must be comfortable and balanced in order to focus on their horses, their riding, and their progress.

Finding a Saddle that Fits

Q My half Arabian-half Saddlebred horse and I are at Training Level. I'm looking for a good dressage saddle and I want to learn as much as I can before I spend a lot of money. I tried out a lot of different saddles at a tack shop, but I have a question: How do I know what size saddle I need?

I am 5'0" and have medium-sized bones for my height. I have a narrow pelvis, short legs, a big bottom, and heavy thighs. I thought I needed a 17.5 or an 18 because of the size of my "sit-upon," but a 17 just felt more "secure." How do I know what is right? Maybe my idea of being "secure" means being too confined. Perhaps I'm looking at saddles that hold me too tightly in place.

A This is a very common question. Let's divide saddle fit (for the rider) into several different subject areas, because you'll need to consider all of them.

First, there is the actual fit between the rider's seat and the all-purpose or dressage saddle itself. Don't go by the size of your rear end, as that can be very deceptive. The most relevant measurement is the length of your femur bone (i.e., your thigh). Put one end of a measuring tape on the protruding end of your hipbone and put the other end in the middle of your kneecap. (You'll probably need help with this.) This length determines, to a great extent, what size saddle you need. The measurement in inches between hipbone and kneecap corresponds (roughly) to the saddle size that would probably suit you best.

As a general rule, if your thigh length is 16 inches, you'll be lost in a 19" saddle and happier in a 17" model, whereas if your thigh length is 20 inches, you might be more comfortable in an 18.5" or a 19" saddle. If your thigh measures 20 inches and your bottom is tiny, you might need a custom-built 17.5" or 18" saddle with extra-long flaps. If you have very long thighs, then you will need a larger saddle and/or a saddle with longer and/or more forward-cut flaps, even if you have no rear end at all. If you have short thighs, you will need a smaller saddle; if you have short thighs and a padded bottom, you may need a larger saddle with shorter flaps. You'll need to try different models.

English saddles are measured from either button (not the center of the pommel) to the center back of the cantle. Standard sizes range from 12" for small children to 19" for large/tall adults. Other saddles are measured differently; a rider might need a 17" hunt seat or dressage saddle, a 15" Western saddle, and a 21" saddle seat saddle.

It is almost impossible for an adult to have a too-large saddle. If your saddle *is* too large, you'll float about and may find that you end up chronically behind your leg because of the distance between the stirrup bars and the lowest point of the saddle's seat. If your saddle is too small, however, you'll always either be jammed up against the pommel (painful for you) or sitting on the cantle (painful for your horse). Either way, you'll have a terrible time keeping your balance over your legs and feet. When in doubt, a saddle that's slightly too large rather than slightly too small is better for your horse, yourself, and your riding. Think of it in the same way you would think about a pair of shoes: If you wear a size 7, you can probably wear a half size larger in some styles and you can at least move around reasonably comfortably in shoes that are a bit too big. There's not much chance of your ever being comfortable in a pair of too-small shoes.

The saddle should fit your body. In a properly fitting saddle, you can place the width of your flat hand between your backside and the end of the cantle. You should also be able to shift your position forward without crashing into the pommel. The length of the seat should allow you plenty of room to relax and move your lower body; the width of the seat should fit your pelvic conformation comfortably; the flaps should be sufficiently long and full to accommodate your leg (adjust the stirrups higher and lower than you think you will ever want them and see if the flaps still accommodate your leg); and the stirrup bars should be placed so that you can easily maintain a correct position with head-hip-heel alignment.

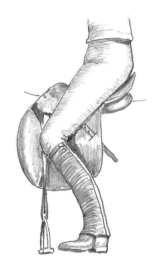

If you are a rider of average height looking for a saddle with a long seat, pay great attention to stirrup-bar placement. Most saddles with long seats are intended for tall riders, and the stirrup bars may be positioned too far forward for you. You will never be able to achieve good balance and a correct position if your stirrup bars are set wrong; you will always find yourself behind your leg and you won't be able to catch up. If you look for a saddle with a long seat, look for a longer stirrup bar as well.

A too-small saddle with badly positioned stirrup bars won't allow correct position.

If the stirrups are correctly positioned, your hip-heel alignment will not change whether you sit in your saddle with or without your stirrups. If the stirrup bar is in the correct place, you will be able to shift easily from a full seat to a half seat and back again without any movement of your lower leg. If your lower leg swings, or if you must make a great effort to move into a half-seat position, then the stirrup bars are probably placed too far forward.

Second, there's the question of the twist or "waist" of the saddle (the narrowest part of the seat). Women with round thighs tend to be most comfortable in a saddle with a narrow twist, as this design creates some room on the saddle for the thighs. Women riders also need to consider how the width of the twist relates to the distance between their seat bones (this varies quite a lot from rider to rider). If your pelvic arch is high and the distance between your seat bones is narrow, you will be comfortable in most saddles. But if your pelvis is wide, with a lower arch and more distance between your seat bones, you will be more comfortable in a wider saddle.

Be careful not to get too wide a saddle, though! A too-wide saddle can force your legs into a position that prevents you from using your leg aids correctly or even sitting comfortably. A too-wide saddle can also force you to carry too much weight in your thighs, keeping you from using your seat bones.

Third, there's the question of the seat itself: padded or hard, deep or flat? Your answers reflect your personal preferences, individual conformation, and regular riding habits. People who ride occasionally are usually happiest in a deeper, softer saddle seat. They depend on the saddle to help them maintain a good position and they can become very sore when forced to ride in a saddle with a flat, hard seat. Riders who are in the saddle for several hours each day often prefer a flatter, harder seat, because they don't want to be held in any particular position; they want the freedom to move around more and they don't need the extra padding on the saddle.

The saddle should fit your style and type of riding and your level of experience. If you are show jumping exclusively, you'll want a longer, flatter seat and minimal padding; if you are galloping and jumping cross-country, you'll want a softer, slightly deeper seat with more padding. If you're doing dressage only, you'll want a saddle that allows you to sit deep with a long stirrup and slight knee bend, but that still allows you freedom of movement. It's not necessary to purchase something that looks like a jousting saddle, with a high pommel, deep seat, and high cantle. Many excellent dressage saddles have fairly flat seats, and many upper-level riders prefer the free-dom that such saddles provide.

Individual conformation is also a factor. If you have a good deal of personal padding between your seat bones and the saddle, you may be quite happy with a harder, flatter seat. If you have very little padding between seat bones and saddle, you may appreciate the softness of a more heavily padded seat.

The best way to find out which saddles suit you is to do exactly what you've been doing: *sit in them.* Sit, and preferably ride, in as many saddles as you possibly can, and take notes. Riders sometimes sell new saddles after just a few weeks because they aren't comfortable, which can be an expensive decision. If your body needs a narrow or wide twist,

Saddle fit is much more directly related to the length of your thigh than the size of your "sit-upon."

big or small knee-rolls or thigh-blocks, a deeper or shallower seat, a softer or harder seat, a particular length of flap, or deeply recessed stirrup bars, find out before you buy.

Look for a comfortable saddle that lets you assume and maintain a correct position, balance yourself easily, use your aids correctly, shift readily between full seat and half-seat, and open and close your hip angle without affecting your lower leg or foot position.

If you're like most good riders, you'll end up searching for a saddle that fits your horse really well, and when you've found it, you'll try to find a version of that saddle that also fits *you.*

Stirrup Length for Dressage: I'm Confused

Q I've ridden Western and hunt seat and am now riding dressage, and I am completely confused about stirrup length. I understand that the dressage ideal is a leg that is almost perfectly straight, but I feel very insecure when I drop my stirrups down three or four holes. Maybe this is because I am used to hunt seat and having my knee bent and my heels down? I feel tippy and wobbly without a bend in my knee, and I can't break the habit of having my heels down.

Can you explain why dressage is supposed to be ridden with a level foot or with the toes down? Also, what can I do to achieve this without my legs going stiff (when I try to put my heels down) or wobbly (when I remember to keep my feet flat or toes down)? I don't have an instructor. I am learning dressage from two friends at the barn and I'm not getting this whole "long leg" idea. Or are there some riders who just can't do dressage?

A To answer your last question first: Any rider who is interested in learning dressage can do so, provided she receives competent instruction! You are confused because you've been given some wrong information and you're trying to make sense of something that doesn't actually make any sense at all.

There's no such thing as one correct stirrup length that applies all the time. The stirrup length that's right for you will vary according to the sort of riding you are doing and the kind of terrain over which you are riding. It will also vary according to your riding skill level, your fitness, your conformation, the saddle you use, and the horse you ride.

Instead of looking for a single, absolute, fixed stirrup length, think in terms of a range of stirrup lengths, all of which will work for you at one time or another. If you are like most riders, your normal, everyday, "using" range will vary within one or two, possibly three, holes. If you change saddles or horses, you may need to change your stirrup length to allow your leg to be comfortable and effective. Go with what works.

If you make it a project to "earn" a longer stirrup by developing a longer leg, remember that changes should always be incremental. Unless you've been riding with your stirrups at jockey height, dropping them three or four holes all at once will only make you uncomfortable, insecure, and tense.

There *should* be a bend in your knee. A straight leg is almost always a stiff leg, and your knee must bend to allow your leg to rest against your horse properly so you can use it correctly. Your heel should always be the lowest part of your body and, as you've already discovered, you can't drop your heels if your legs are straight.

To check your stirrup length, sit in the saddle with your legs hanging down naturally, and your feet out of the stirrups. Where are the stirrup treads? The "default" position is for your stirrup treads to be level with your anklebones. If your stirrups are much higher than your anklebone, they are too short. If they're much lower than your anklebone, they are too long. Just over the anklebone is a good length if you're riding a green horse, riding at speed over terrain, or jumping. At or just barely under the anklebone is a good length for flatwork and dressage.

When you've adjusted your stirrups, spend a few minutes riding at all three gaits and see what is happening with your feet, ankles, knees, thighs, and hips. Your heels should be down — not pushed or forced or "jammed" down, just allowed to drop lower than your foot. (Push them down as a test, and you'll find that your buttocks will tense, your seat bones will come off your saddle, and your hips will lock.)

Your knees should have a definite bend in them. If you pop up like a jack-in-the-box when you post, then your stirrups are too short. If you can't stand up in your stirrups and clear the pommel of your saddle, or if you can do this only by standing with straight legs or (horrors) on your toes, then your stirrups are too long. If you can keep your legs relaxed and your heels low at all times, and you can post easily when you trot without popping up or straightening your leg and standing on your toes, then your stirrup length is just right.

You can do exercises to loosen your hips and to relax and stretch your inner thighs. There are also breathing exercises that will help you relax in the saddle. If you do both types often and well, you will eventually want to lower your stirrups because your legs will be "longer." That's how you "earn" a lower stirrup. Dropping your stirrups too low and trying to ride on your toes with a straight leg will not give you a "dressage leg." When you've made your legs hang lower because they are more stretchy and supple, and because your hips and pelvis are more relaxed and

There should be a bend in your knee. A straight leg is almost always a stiff leg.

allowing you to sit more deeply into your saddle, you will need to drop your stirrups (but never more than one hole at a time) so that you can keep the same good, effective, correct leg position.

Please take some lessons with a good dressage instructor! Your friends undoubtedly mean well, but you shouldn't follow their advice or try to emulate their leg position, because unfortunately they've got it all wrong.

Safety Stirrups for Adults

Q I am wondering about the use of safety stirrups for adults. It seems to me that making sure your foot doesn't get caught could actually lead to a fall if your stirrup releases during a sudden, unexpected movement by your horse, when you most need your foot to be secure. In the normal course of events there are probably more sudden movements than there might be times you would fall off.

Which type of safety stirrup is best for adults — the ones with the rubber bands, the ski-design ones with the hinge right above the stirrup, or the ones with the curvy outside branch? I would like to know the pros and cons of all these. Also, if the point is to not get caught in the stirrup, wouldn't it be just as safe to ride in extra-large stirrups?

A The Peacock safety stirrup — that's the one with the rubber band — is a great design for children because their weight is often insufficient to detach an English stirrup leather from the saddle, even if the stirrup bar locks are in the "open" position (as they always should be, by the way). Even a lightweight child, though, can pop the rubber band off the outside of the stirrup on her way to the ground, which means she'll have a much better chance of falling away from the horse and a much smaller chance of getting dragged. You could use the larger, heavier versions of these stirrups, but there are several other designs that I find to be more useful for adults.

The Australian pattern safety stirrup is the one with the extra S bend in the outside branch. It takes a little while to get used to riding in these, but it's worth making the effort. An even more useful stirrup is the Icelandic safety stirrup. This design has the eye offset at a 90-degree angle, which causes the stirrups to hang perpendicular to the horse's side instead of parallel to it, enabling riders to find, pick up, and keep their stirrups in position easily. The Icelandic stirrup also has both inside and outside S branches. These are excellent, affordable safety stirrups for adults.

A recent and welcome addition to the available options is an extremely practical and comfortable English stirrup (the MDC Intelligent Stirrup) that offers an ideal combination of flexing branches and an adjustable offset eye. The offset eye provides more than the ability to pick up a dropped stirrup easily. Like the flexing branches, the offset eyes allow the stirrup leathers to hang straight. This is a boon to riders with stiff or painful feet, ankles, or knees. The combination of flexing branches and offset eyes can help relieve uncomfortable pressure all the way up the rider's legs — not only in the feet, ankles, and knees but also in the hips, seat bones, and lower back.

These stirrups, and the others you mentioned (the ones designed to work like ski-binding releases are not often seen these days), are all meant to help the rider's foot come loose *only* if the rider is hanging off the horse's side, with the pressure on the *outside* of the stirrup. If all stirrup leathers came sliding off the saddles when they should, there would be no need for safety stirrups, but you can't always count on your stirrup leathers to cooperate. Rusty stirrup bars, stiff saddle leather, new, thick stirrup leathers — there can be a lot of reasons for the stirrup leathers not sliding off the bars, so it's useful to have a second line of defense in the form of safety stirrups.

All that said, your best security equipment doesn't come from the tack store: It's good position and good balance. Open safety catches and purpose-designed safety stirrups add to your security and can help in emergencies, as they were designed to do, but on a day-to-day basis, your personal balance in the saddle matters much more. It's possible to lose a stirrup or even to have a stirrup leather come off during normal riding, but if you're balanced and secure, this will be a brief annoyance rather than a crisis.

Many riders lose their stirrups because they have adjusted them to hang far too low and have to point their toes to reach them, but even when the leathers are correctly adjusted, riders can still lose their stirrups if they are unable to maintain a balanced, secure position. Beginner riders frequently lose their stirrups because they haven't yet learned to keep their legs stretched down and their heels low at all times.

Riders who grip with their knees will probably lose their stirrups at the trot. As their knees dig into the saddle, their lower legs begin to swing and lift, their heels come up, their toes point down, the stirrups begin to shift about, and at some point the stirrups slide off the riders' toes.

At the canter, riders who sit stiffly will find themselves drawing their legs up. This will cause their feet to float in their stirrups, and the stirrups will eventually slide or bounce off their toes.

Riders can lose stirrups when they jump — in fact, the stirrup leather and the stirrup can pop right off the saddle. When this happens, it's almost always because the rider is standing in her stirrups and kicking her legs down and back, instead of staying in place and simply folding her body as the horse takes off.

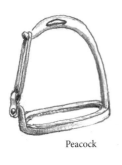

Peacock

Australian S-bend

Icelandic

Add the stirrup pad of your choice for comfort and traction.

If this ever happens to you, one incident will be enough. It's very educational, and will do more for you than all of your instructor's repeated reminders to "Stop standing in your stirrups on the way to the jump!" And even if you come off the horse, it's better to be off the horse than to be bouncing along at the horse's side or under his belly. Horses will do their best to avoid stepping on humans (or, indeed, on anything squashy and noisy), but in that situation, it's just about impossible.

As for extra-large stirrups, they actually detract from your safety. Stirrups must be correctly sized for both safety and comfort. The tread should allow enough room for you to insert a pencil between your boot and the stirrup branch on each side of your boot. Buying too-small stirrups is dangerous; they increase the possibility of your foot becoming trapped in the event of a fall and may rub your toes painfully. Overly large stirrups are equally dangerous because a twisting fall might force your foot all the way through the stirrup. Many saddles for very small children have stirrup covers to keep the rider's foot and lower leg from going through the stirrup. Similarly, endurance riders often add "cages" to their stirrups for safety's sake, and the tapaderos used by working cowboys help prevent their boots from being caught in the stirrups.

Stirrups should be adjusted so that the ball of your foot rests comfortably while your weight is in your heels. The stirrups aren't there for you to tap on with your down-pointing tippy-toes, but they're not intended to take the full weight of your body while you push hard against them, either! They're there to help you maintain the same correct leg position that you would maintain without any stirrups while giving you a place to rest the front part of your foot and reminding you to think "toes up."

Make sure that your stirrups support the point where the short axis of your foot meets the long axis. Draw a line with chalk on the sole of your boot from the center back of your heel to the division between your second and third toes. Then draw another line across the ball of your foot (the widest part). The spot where these two lines cross *must* be on the stirrup tread in order for you to feel truly secure in your stirrups.

Finally, it's easy to lose stirrups if you suffer from any condition, such as arthritis, that limits your ability to (a) flex your ankles and (b) hold your stirrups in the correct position while you ride. The new flexing stirrups with offset eyes are ideal for riders with foot, ankle, knee, or hip problems, as they promote both safety and comfort.

Special Stirrups for Painful Knees and Ankles

Q I am 53 years old and some days I feel fine, but other days I feel 10 or 20 years older! As a young athlete, I broke toes, cracked my right anklebone twice, and messed up my knees. I started taking riding lessons several years ago because I had always wanted to learn.

Last year I was beginning to jump and loving it, but I started to get pain in my legs. I can ride for just so long before my ankles begin to hurt. I have ACL damage in both knees, and for the last three years my doctor has been trying to get me to have my knees replaced. I'm just not ready for that yet! My knees don't hurt much when I am *on* the horse, but they feel horrible when I dismount, and I can barely walk for the next 12 to 16 hours. I usually ride for about two hours, three or four days a week, and I have a lesson every Saturday.

My instructor is nice, but she thinks I should have the surgery. We've tried adjusting my stirrups higher and lower and even making them uneven because my right leg hurts more than my left and I "toe out" more on the right. I put pads on the treads, but nothing is working. I'm always afraid of losing a stirrup because it hurts so much to pick them back up.

I need to do something different: Riding hurts so much that I can't even drive the next day because I'm in too much pain to be a safe driver and if I have a long drive on one day, I'm too stiff to ride the next. At this point I'll try anything if I think it might help. Do you have any ideas to make riding less painful? I understand that you know from personal experience about riding with bad knees. If you could only tell me how to get my bones unbroken and my ligaments back in my knees, you would be perfect!

A Believe me, if I knew how to unbreak bones and make knee ligaments sound again, I'd be much more comfortable myself. You're quite right, I do have bad knees and I completely understand your "ride on Monday, can't drive on Tuesday" issues. What I've learned is that when cartilage is bad and ligaments are overstretched to the point of being useless, the only thing that gives real, round-the-clock knee stability is your own leg muscles. Bandages and braces can help, but you're unlikely to be able to wear them all the time, whereas your own muscles, once you've made them strong, are always there.

You might want to have a serious talk with your doctor about those knee replacements. You're experiencing almost constant pain — why continue to "tough it out" if surgery is an option? The interesting thing about knee (and hip) replacements is that I haven't yet met anyone who regrets having had the surgery. Everyone makes the same comment: "I just wish I'd done it a lot sooner." It would be nice for you to be out of pain and to have the option of driving several hours and then riding the next day or vice versa.

In the meantime, I can make some suggestions that might help reduce your knee pain and allow your riding to become more comfortable, and I can tell you about some new and quite helpful stirrups that have recently come on the market.

You probably already know that it helps to drop your stirrups periodically and move your feet around, circle your ankles in both directions, pull your toes up and push them down, and generally restore circulation to your lower legs. And no matter what kind of riding you do or what type of stirrups you use, you should *not* twist your ankles or knees. If your toes and knees don't point straight ahead,

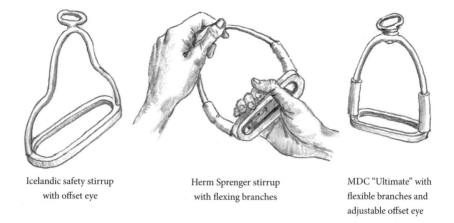

Icelandic safety stirrup
with offset eye

Herm Sprenger stirrup
with flexing branches

MDC "Ultimate" with
flexible branches and
adjustable offset eye

don't try to force them into an "ideal" riding position. Everyone's conformation is different; everyone's soundness and history of injuries is different. Your knees and ankles will be much less painful if you check regularly to be sure they are pointing in the same direction. If your knees are pointing away from the saddle and your toes are pointing straight ahead, you are probably twisting your legs and putting a lot of torque and pressure on your knees in an attempt to keep your feet parallel with the horse's sides.

When you ride, think about your base of support and monitor your level of relaxation throughout your body. Riding with your weight distributed through your seat bones and your thighs puts much less weight in your stirrups and allows your lower legs to remain more flexible. Don't try to put all your weight into your stirrups, as this just stresses your knees (and your ankles and your hips) unnecessarily, especially if you are also trying to hold your lower legs in a particular position. Riding is all about balance, not *grip;* as soon as you try to hold on to the horse with your legs, you're using much more energy and force than you need and making yourself tense and stiff. Keep a bend in your knee, keep your body alignment correct (ears-shoulders-hips-heels), but instead of pushing your heels down or gripping with your lower legs, try stretching your upper body tall while allowing your weight to drop into your heels. If you can ride with a long, stretched, relaxed leg, your correct body alignment and the bend at your knee will allow you to drop weight into your heels without causing tension or stiffness.

You have adjusted your stirrup length; you should also check your stirrup leathers. Don't just look at the holes or numbers — remove the leathers from the saddle to compare their lengths. This is particularly important if the saddle isn't your own, or if you haven't been changing your leathers over each week (putting the left one on the right side of the saddle and the right one on the left side). If you've gone a long time without doing this, you may find that the left stirrup leather is considerably longer than the right one, which would put your whole body off balance and force your body to bend the right knee more than the left knee. You may put even *more* weight into your right stirrup knee if you are trying to sit straight and balanced when a too-long left stirrup leather is tipping your entire body to the left.

The more time you spend in the saddle trying to compensate for an unbalanced position, the more pain you are likely to experience at the end of your ride. Compensation involves muscles and joints from your toes all the way up to your neck! After your long rides, your whole body is probably twisted like a pretzel.

Finally, the stirrup itself can make quite a difference to your riding comfort.

I have long recommended two types of English-style stirrups: those with the "flexing" sides (e.g., the Herm Sprenger stirrups and the newer ones from the MDC Corporation) and those with the eye set at a 90-degree angle to the stirrup (e.g., Icelandic safety stirrups). The flexing stirrups make riding much more comfortable for anyone who has foot, leg, or joint damage due to age or injury, and are justifiably popular with older riders. The Icelandic stirrups make riding more comfortable in a different way; they don't have the "flex" feature, but that offset eye (the part that the stirrup leather goes through) means that the stirrups hang in a position that makes it much easier for riders to pick them up.

The new stirrups that may make all the difference for you are the MDC "Intelligent" Stirrups, which combine the best features of the other types of stirrups. With these stirrups, the eye is not offset in a fixed position but instead adjusts to three different positions. You can adjust them to hang flat against the horse's sides (traditional position) or to hang at a 90-degree angle, perpendicular to the horse's sides (as the Icelandic stirrups do), or to hang at a 45-degree angle.

This solves several problems at once. You can pick up these stirrups easily, without twisting your ankles or knees and without making two or three attempts before your foot finds the stirrup. The 90-degree and 45-degree angle options make life better for riders whose natural conformation causes them to "toe out" a little, and those options also allow stirrups to be set individually (one at 45 degrees, one at 90 degrees) for riders like yourself who have one foot that "toes out" much more than the other.

Riders who are made uncomfortable by the pressure of the leathers themselves against their boots or shins will also benefit from these "Intelligent" stirrups. At the 45-degree angle, you feel only half of the usual pressure from the stirrup leathers; at the 90-degree angle, you feel no pressure at all from the stirrup leathers. This may seem like a small and unimportant change, but any incremental increase in your comfort can have a big effect on your enjoyment of your ride.

Reins for Hands that Won't Close

Q I cannot close my hands on my reins. I try, but I have had arthritis for 15 years and my hands just won't close tightly anymore. My instructor has finally accepted this and has stopped reminding me to close my fingers. The only way I can get a really secure hold on my reins is to grip as hard as I can, which I can't do for very long. When I relax my hands at all, the reins begin to slip through my fingers. My instructor loaned me a pair of her show gloves (which I am afraid I stretched out rather badly), but they didn't help much. I tried a pair of reins with "rein stops" on them, but the only difference is that when those slide through my fingers they do it by "bumps" instead of smoothly. I can deal with this in the arena, but I don't dare go out on the trail and I hate to think that I cannot ride on trails anymore.

A   I think that your instructor's suggestion was a good one and that the right kind of gloves could help you a great deal. I wouldn't expect show gloves to help, however, especially if they were a bit too small. Thin, smooth leather enhances one's grip, but a too-tight glove won't allow you to grip, so any benefit from the extra friction will be canceled out.

Go to a tack shop that has a wide selection of gloves and look for ones that are easy to put on and remove and that offer some friction. The best gloves for you will probably be made of stretch material (polar fleece for winter and perhaps a cotton knit for summer) and will have rough suede or rubber reinforcements on the palm and the insides of the fingers. Make sure the fingers are long enough: If the fingers of your gloves are even a tiny bit too short, you won't be able to hold your reins correctly (snugged up against the base of your fingers) and you'll find it even *more* difficult to close your hands.

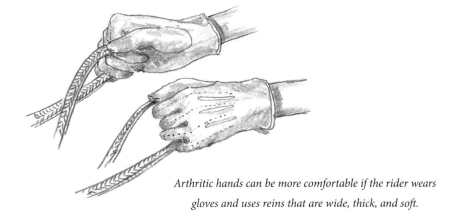

Arthritic hands can be more comfortable if the rider wears gloves and uses reins that are wide, thick, and soft.

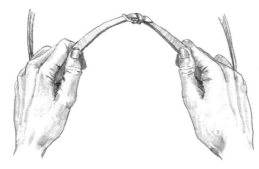

With ordinary reins at a comfortable length for a long-necked horse, the rider may be left with nothing between her hands.

Extra-long reins allow both horse and rider to be comfortable.

The best reins for you may not be on the English side of the tack shop. Over on the Western side you should be able to find wide, thick, flat-braided reins made from cotton. These won't slide so easily and they won't require as much "active grip." They will probably come with scissor snaps to attach them to the bit, but you can go to a leather shop and ask someone to remove those and install leather ends with proper hook studs or buckles. The combination of good, comfortable "grippy" gloves and thick, wide, textured reins should allow you to ride — even on trails — with more comfort and security.

Longer Reins for a Long-Necked Horse

Q My horse is almost 16 hands and has a very long neck. His name is Rafi but we call him Giraffe because his neck is so long. At a clinic last year, you told me that the reason I rode with my reins too short is that my reins were in fact too short, and that I needed longer reins for him.

Rafi is comfortable if I hold the reins with my hands just on the sides of the buckle part, but I don't like the way it feels and I always end up shortening them so that I have about a foot of rein between my hands. But when I do that, Rafi starts shaking his head and backing up again.

I am using reins made from parachute cord, but they are too light and not flat. I miss my webbing reins with the leather stops. Do you know of a place that sells extra-long reins? I love my Courbette bridle and wish I could find long reins to match it, but the local tack shop only carries 54" reins. You solved our riding problem last year; can you solve our tack problem?

A This one is easy: just go right ahead and order your new reins from Courbette. You're right, the standard rein length is 54", but the better makers of strap goods usually sell a 60" version of the same rein. It's called an extra-long or Warmblood length, but either way, the 60" length is very popular. The extra length will give you the additional foot of rein that you want at your end. Many riders in your position simply take the amount of rein that makes them feel comfortable, without realizing how much it cramps their horses' necks. Good for you for considerately giving Rafi the amount he needs at his end; no wonder he's happier now.

If you order the reins through your local tack shop, remind the owner, politely, that Courbette *does* make those extra-long 60" reins (and that most other manufacturers do too). He was probably just looking at his current inventory, not at his catalogs. When you order longer reins, be aware there's often a 10 percent surcharge added on. The comfort and convenience is well worth that extra expense.

CHAPTER 17

When Your Clothes
Get in the Way

FROM HELMET TO BOOTS, problems caused by rider clothing can range from annoying discomfort to real pain. The wrong clothing can make riding a miserably uncomfortable experience; the right clothing can dramatically improve a rider's comfort and performance. Sometimes the saddle itself is the problem, causing pain that won't allow a rider to relax. If replacing the saddle isn't an option, seat pads and purpose-made riding underwear can make riders more comfortable. Riders too often blame themselves for their own discomfort without considering that a change of clothing or properly broken-in boots might make all the difference.

Pain from New Boots

Q My granddaughter is going to a big equestrian show where she will perform a precision synchronized routine to music over jumps with a team of girls. I bought her a new pair of tall boots. She had them fitted at a local tack shop but says they are killing her, and we are wondering if you have any tips on breaking them in faster. We already questioned the tack shop, and they remeasured her and the boots are the proper size. They say she just has to tough it out until they break in.

A Breaking in boots can be a painful process; your granddaughter has my sympathy! Blisters and sores are very common during the breaking-in process. One of my old riding instructors used to say that she had a pair of scars for every pair of new boots she had ever owned. New tall boots are stiff, and until the leather softens and the boots develop creases at the ankle, it's possible to be extremely uncomfortable in them.

I'm going to assume that her boots fit comfortably in the foot, the heel, and the calf area, because if they *don't*, they probably aren't the right size! New boots ought to be comfortable across the instep, and there should be room for the ankle and heel to flex and slide. They ought not to be super-tight in the calf. The only major cause of discomfort from a pair of new boots that fit well should be the painful rubbing behind the knees that's caused by the excess height.

New boots are always a bit too tall (by at least an inch, sometimes more) so that they will be the ideal height when they break in at the ankles and drop lower on the leg. The painful breaking-in period can be made more bearable by wearing heel pads inside new boots. In fact, I generally recommend that riders break in new tall boots by using two heel pads or lifts in each boot. They can

Brand-new tall boots can cause painful rubbing behind the knees.

remove one set as the boots begin to drop after a week or two of riding and then remove the second ones when the boots are truly broken in. This will make the rider much more comfortable and will help avoid the unsightly "dog-eared" look that results when the back of a tall boot folds over.

Meanwhile, your granddaughter should fasten her boot laces loosely and spend a few minutes each day working boot cream into the ankles of her boots so that the leather will soften a little more quickly and so that she can control the depth and location of the creases.

Putting Folds into Tall Boots

Q I just bought my very first pair of good (semi-custom) tall dressage boots. I've been riding for 20 years and taking dressage lessons for six years, and this is a very big thing for me. I haven't worn my gorgeous new boots yet because my instructor warned me to break them in and put folds into them before I begin wearing them every day.

Apparently there is a "good" way to put folds into tall boots and there are a lot of "bad" ways to put folds into tall boots. My instructor said that *her* instructor was a military man who always said to stand in water until the boots were soaked and then walk around in them until they "broke" at the ankles. This seems extremely scary to me — what if I ruined the leather and they literally "broke"? Horrifying! Can you suggest some less dramatic way for me to do this?

A A lot of old-style cavalrymen used that method. They would stand in a stream until their very stiff new boots became waterlogged and pliable, and once the boots had dried on their legs and conformed to their shape, they would do their best to restore the integrity of the leather through nightly applications of leather conditioner. It usually worked, but I agree with you that new boots are too costly to risk in that way! So here's a method that works very nicely and just requires a little effort and patience for about a week.

As tall boots inevitably develop creases at the ankles no matter what you do, it's in the rider's best interest to avoid spontaneous creases that might be uneven, uncomfortable, and unsightly (accordion-like pleats do *not* look good). The best way to avoid this is to put creases into the boots before wearing them so that you can be quite sure that the folds aren't in areas where they'll cause painful rubs.

Military men must have devised this method as well (instead of the uncomfortable alternative you mentioned!), because I know it as the Cavalryman's Crease. It involves using your own hands (and some bits of furniture) to create *good* folds in new boots. Begin by standing your boots on a flat surface and admiring them in profile. The legs look almost vertical: nice and tall and standing straight. You're going to change all that, starting right now.

Remember that all new boots drop an inch or more, and consequently they are invariably too tall at first.

Dress boots have a clearly defined area just front and center, where the uppers are attached to the feet. With the front of the boot facing you, put both thumbs into that area just above the ankle and push the leather inward, into the cavity of the boot, until you create a long horizontal dent or fold.

At this point, the leather above this area should be bulging forward. While pushing the dent inward, try to pull and roll this part of the boot (the shin area, just above the ankle) toward you and down toward the foot of the boot. Keep bending and rolling and pulling this part of the boot until you've created a fold that crosses the entire front of the boot and continues on both sides almost all the way to the back of the boot.

Don't fold all the way to the seam that runs up the back of the boot! You want the deepest part of the fold to be just in the front-and-center area directly over the front of the ankle, and you want that deep front-and-center fold to decrease as it extends along the sides of the boot, until there is *no fold at all* at the back of the boot (where the seam is).

Place your boots back on the flat surface and look at them in profile again. They should show a deep crease at the front, tapering on both sides to become no crease at the back of the leg, and they should now be angled forward, with smooth backs, lightly creased sides, and a deep horizontal crease in front of each ankle. If you like, you can now use a small sponge to apply a generous amount of good leather conditioner to the creases. This will help soften the leather and make it easier for the creases to become established.

Now observe your boots. Are they remaining in position, like good, quiet, well-behaved boots? If so, leave them alone for a week or two. If the tops begin to creep upward, place them under a piece of furniture to hold them in position and keep them from popping up or falling over and losing their lovely new creases. Some boots resist being creased and persist in trying to pop back into their original configuration.

After a week (two, if the leather is very thick and heavy), work any remaining leather conditioner into the new creases or add more if necessary, put on a pair of thick, soft ankle socks under a pair of nylon knee-highs, and put on your boots but don't ride in them. Just walk around your house in them. The longer you can stand to do this, the better, because the combination of the conditioner, the warmth (you know how heat builds up inside riding boots!), and the activity will help set the creases and encourage the boots to soften and drop correctly. If the creases aren't in precisely the right place and you need to re-crease the boots, or if the boots haven't quite committed to those creases yet, find out while you're still in your comfortable home and can remove the boots, implement the change, and put the boots back under that chair or bench. It's not a perfect system, but it's much better than going out on horseback and discovering the problem when you're several miles from home.

When you *do* begin wearing your boots, for heaven's sake remember that all new boots drop an inch or more, and consequently they are invariably too tall at first. They *should* be too tall. If they aren't, then after they drop, they will be too short, and you will be sad. But the extra height means that until they are broken

Once you've established the crease you want, the best way to maintain it . . .

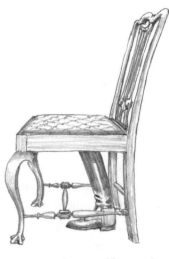

. . . is to put the creased boot under a chair to set the crease.

in and fully accept their new creases, your new boots can cause incredible pain and bruising behind your knees.

This suffering isn't necessary. Buy heel inserts and use them. In fact, buy *two* pairs of heel inserts and begin by wearing both at once. As your boots soften at the ankles, they will drop a little and you can get rid of one pair of inserts. When the boots are completely relaxed at the ankles and have become form fitting, you'll be able to remove the second pair of inserts. If the inserts slide around or if you're having trouble slipping in or out of your boots, sandwich them between thin socks and nylon knee-highs to hold them in place. It helps to pull the nylons over your breeches, not under them.

Finally, someone with very slender legs came up with a good idea that would be easy to implement if you already wear knee-high stockings over your breeches: Before you pull your boots all the way up, place a small, soft sponge behind each knee, between the breeches and the knee-highs. The sponges should provide enough cushioning to keep you comfortable.

Riding Jeans

Q My husband and I are planning to take a dude ranch vacation in Colorado with my siblings and their spouses. My sister-in-law and I have done some English riding, but nobody else in the group rides at all. We are all taking lessons to get ready, so I think we'll be okay for our riding skills.

My question is about riding jeans. I know better than to go out west with English britches and boots. We are all going to get some jeans so that we can feel Western (though we *will* wear helmets, of course). What can you tell us about different kinds of jeans and what kinds are best for riding? Are the ones in the tack catalogs worth the money or are they just regular jeans with little horse tags on them? We want to be comfortable on our special vacation!

A What fun to vacation at a dude ranch, and how wise of you to prepare by taking lessons. Not only will you feel much more at home and in control of your horses, but you'll be much less sore after a day's riding. That can make all the difference between a day consisting of ride-shower-liniment-bed and a day consisting of ride-shower-change-swim/dance/play tennis/explore the area. Good for you!

As for riding attire, you could show up in breeches and boots if you wanted to, and I'm sure that nobody would turn a hair. Most dude ranches have seen much stranger outfits. And there is a good bit of English riding, and even polo, in Colorado, so nobody is likely to point and giggle. If you have comfy boots and breeches, by all means take them along.

Jeans designed for riding *are* different. Ordinary jeans usually have heavy seams along the inside of the legs and smooth seams on the outside. That's fine for street wear but not very practical for riding. The currently fashionable wide-legged jeans and those with low rises are totally impractical, not to mention uncomfortable, in the saddle. You don't want heavy seams on the inside of the thigh or a lot of fabric in the upper calf and knee area. Wrinkles there can rub enough to cause nasty sores by the end of a long ride. Look for "cowboy cut" or "boot leg" jeans; "relaxed fit" is fine, but no baggies or bell-bottoms, please.

Jeans that are just a little bit too long when you're standing on the ground and sag a little under the calf will be just the right length when you're in the saddle.

If you have any doubts about the fit of your jeans, or if you have sensitive skin (or if you must wear jeans that have unsuitable seams or are too loose in the leg), consider wearing pantyhose or tights or leggings underneath. This goes for the men in the group too. Men can be funny about this, but really, it can make all the difference between a comfortable and an uncomfortable ride. Ask the men who ride in endurance competitions — they wear tights.

Wrangler jeans are ideally suited for riding: They have high pockets, and the heavy seam is on the outside of the leg where it's much less likely to cause painful chafing. You may want to buy jeans with a slightly longer inseam than you would usually select. Jeans that are just a little bit too long when you're standing on the ground and sag a little under the calf will be just the right length when you're in the saddle. Put a chair near a mirror, put one foot up onto the chair, bend your knee and let your heel drop as though your foot was in the stirrup, and you'll see that those too-long jeans are suddenly just right. (If you're shopping in a tack store, there may be a saddle or saddle stand you can sit on to check the jeans for fit. Ask before you sit on anything, though — only a few specialty saddle stands can take the weight of a human, and you don't want to wind up on the floor!)

There are all sorts of riding jeans, including snugly fitting ones made from stretch denim. The give in the fabric can be helpful, but if you buy stretch jeans, do not try to squeeze into a smaller size. For one thing, you'll use up all the stretch just getting into them. For another, you'll turn your legs into tight round sausages that can't relax and flatten against the saddle or the horse's sides, making you uncomfortable the entire time you're in the saddle. Buy your usual size and let the stretch fabric make mounting and dismounting easier. Riding is never fun if your clothes cause you pain.

Choose your underwear carefully too. These days most tack shops carry a selection of underwear designed specifically for riders (both male and female). Padded biking shorts can help provide a softer ride on a hard saddle seat.

Still Bouncing with Two Sports Bras

Q I am a beginner rider, 51 years old, and I am large-busted. None of my bras keep me from bouncing painfully. My instructor suggested a sports bra, but that didn't work either. Then she told me that some riders wear *two* sports bras at a time, which helps enough that I will keep wearing them if there's no other solution. But wearing two bras at once makes me sweaty and itchy and uncomfortable, and worst of all, it doesn't stop the bouncing, just reduces it. In addition to being large-busted, I have some long-term damage to one shoulder due to a rotator cuff injury, so I'm not able to wear the kind of sports bra that pulls over the head. I am learning dressage and right now there is no way I could sit the trot even for half a minute. Is there anything I can do, short of wrapping my chest with tight elastic bandages to make my bust entirely flat? I'm almost ready to try that.

A You're in luck. As the demand for really effective, bounce-reducing sports bras has grown, manufacturers are offering more and better choices.

It used to be there were only two choices in sports bras: those that compressed and those that encapsulated. The compressing kind — the sort that you want — is the most effective. There's a trade-off, of course. Most sports bras that compress create what is sometimes called the "uni-boob." You won't bounce, but you won't have any shape either. If you feel strongly about keeping a shape, you'll have to sacrifice some of the bounce control, which is not a good choice if you're large-busted.

In the past, it's true that these bras were made only in pull-on styles, but that's no longer the case. There are several sports bras designed specifically for riders, and you can check equestrian catalogs and Web sites for different types. For full support *and* bounce reduction (compression), the Minimal Bounce bra from Sporteze is probably the best option. It's available in a zip-front model, which should make it manageable even with a troublesome shoulder. And any large-busted dressage rider will find the manufacturer's description compelling: *"Inspired by the sitting trot."*

Comfort for Male Riders

Q I have been taking English lessons twice a week for two years and frequently find myself banging my "male equipment" on the saddle. Much of the time I'm sure my poor riding is responsible, and my female instructor is helpful in trying to alleviate the causes. It does seem, however, that male riders have special problems due to their anatomy. I have asked a number of men at the barn and various tack shops about this issue with little success, but there aren't nearly as many of us as there seem to be women riders. Another issue is that many people aren't eager to discuss this subject. And finally, while I have seen products and articles about equestrienne undergarments, I've not seen any for men.

Do you have any recommendations for the proper underwear? I can't ride in two-point forever!

A No wonder we have fewer male riders, if nobody is willing to explain to them what they should wear and how they should adjust themselves to avoid pain! Fortunately, it won't be necessary for you to spend your entire riding life in two-point.

The first thing you should know is that in an English saddle of any variety, you should be able to put one flat hand between your crotch and the pommel and another hand between your backside and the cantle. If you have to squeeze up against one end of the saddle to get a flat hand (approximately four inches) between your body and the other end, then the saddle is too small for you, and you will *never* be able to sit correctly and comfortably, no matter how talented you are or how hard you try.

A too-small saddle that crushes you against the pommel will send your body scooting back against the cantle in self-defense. This will make your horse very uncomfortable and will put you into a "chair seat" that makes it impossible for you to balance your body over your feet. This isn't an exclusively male issue, by the way; it's just as true for women. Maintaining the vertical alignment of your ears, shoulders, hips, and heels is only possible if you use a saddle that allows you to sit in balance.

Fortunately, it won't be necessary for you to spend your entire riding life in two-point.

As for clothing, the male riders I know and every male student I have ever taught agree that good underwear is the key to riding in comfort. You need proper support, especially during the first year or two of lessons, when you are learning correct body alignment and how to maintain a balanced, flexible position on horseback. For some riders, snug briefs and dressing "up" rather than right or left is enough, but you'll almost certainly benefit from some padding and you may need to experiment with different types of undergarments. Take the time to do this, because if you're uncomfortable in the saddle, you won't be able to focus on your riding skills or your horse.

Many instructors automatically tell a male student to wear snug briefs, but this is not the answer for all male riders. If the briefs are too snug, they can interfere with rider comfort and position. For both men and women, tight, restrictive underwear causes more riding problems in the long run than it solves in the short run. Riders need to be able to protect delicate areas while leaving the abdomen and buttocks free to relax. A tense abdomen makes for a tense lower back, locked hips, and shallow breathing, all of which make good riding impossible.

A jockstrap may work better for you than tight briefs because it will allow you to relax your abdomen. Some riders find that a dance belt (worn by male dancers to stay safe and comfortable without spoiling the line) is more comfortable than a jockstrap, but again you'll need to experiment with different ones. Some styles have very wide waists that might interfere with abdominal relaxation, and some have full bottoms while others have thongs. Since dancewear sizes are not the same as street-wear sizes, buy according to actual measurements. If you guess at your size, you may find the results uncomfortable.

Other options you can explore include bike shorts (the snug kind with the padded crotch), equestrian tights (yes, they make them for men as well as women), and pantyhose (I'm not joking). A lot of working cowboys will tell you that pantyhose are a real boon to riders. On a long trail ride, they can make the difference between comfort and misery.

I think that your best bet is to buy some purpose-designed underwear or tights, such as the "original cowboy underwear" designed and produced by The Saddle Bums Company. The owner of that company, Stan Dill, originally designed these to protect his own assets and soon discovered that the world was full of men who were desperate for some way to avoid the crushing, chafing, uncomfortable dampness, and eventual saddle sores that seemed to go with riding. Now the company makes all sorts of padded riding tights, including English-style ones, for both men and women. The padding is strategically positioned (you may not even need a jockstrap) and made from materials that wick moisture away from the body.

Getting back to saddles: If you buy your own, or if your riding school offers you a choice of saddles, you could select one with a cushy, padded seat. You can also add padding to the saddle seat in the form of an on-the-saddle pad made from gel, foam, gel-foam (a thin layer of gel over a thicker but much lighter layer of foam), sheepskin, or synthetic fleece (very useful for those of us who are allergic to wool). This option has the advantage of being easily changed if you find you need more or less padding.

In addition to underwear, saddle fit, and on-the-saddle pads, keep your posture and position in mind. Part of the problem that some riders experience when they first sit in a saddle is that they try to literally *sit* in the saddle. When you're on a horse, you don't place all of your weight squarely on your seat as you would in a chair. Your position in the saddle should be a straddling one, not a sitting one. You can approximate it on the ground by separating your feet to shoulder-width or a little wider and bending your knees. This is your riding position — it's not sitting at all. In the saddle, this position allows you to rest some of your weight in your heels and lower legs with a tiny bit in the stirrups, some on your seat bones, and a little on your buttocks, but most of your weight should be carried by your thighs.

People who don't ride find it difficult to understand how just sitting on a horse could possibly make you tired or sore. Until you've learned how to sit correctly, in balance, with your weight distributed properly, you can tire very quickly. Keep this in mind, because distributing your weight properly (that is, *not* putting all of it onto your seat bones) requires conscious effort at first, until your balance and your muscles have adjusted. Short rides are better than long ones when you're

A combination of good position and proper underwear allow this rider to jump in comfort.

first learning, because you can keep reminding yourself to sit correctly, and then dismount before you become so tired that you begin to sit incorrectly from sheer fatigue.

Proper position and a balanced seat allow you to keep most of your weight in your thighs, and a combination of proper position and good muscle tone will allow you to achieve good body control. This is essential, because body control lets you post lightly and easily, for example, performing a series of deep knee bends with your body touching the saddle very gently (without squashing any part of you) instead of slamming up and down in a way that's an invitation to pure pain.

By the way, "protecting the package" is understandably the single issue that most male riders find compelling, but just in case you're interested, it's only one difference between male and female riders. There are many others. The length and position of the seat bones, the length and position of the tailbone, the dimensions of the pelvis, and the way the femurs (thigh bones) fall from the hip bones all create very significant differences between male and female riders, affecting everything from rider position in the saddle to the design of the saddles themselves.

Saddle Sores

Q I am having a problem with saddle sores. I believe the problem originated from the elastic in my panties rubbing in the crotch area (this was in a Western saddle). The sores were open and bleeding and have never really healed. I have stopped riding for several weeks sometimes, and they go down quite a bit but never really go away. My doctor told me to put antibiotic ointment on them and cover them with adhesive bandages, but they still haven't gone away. I did purchase a "tush cush" for my Western saddle, which helps on trail rides.

I recently started English lessons. We are working on my balance and sitting the trot properly, which I obviously cannot do very well, so my sores immediately flared up again. I know this sounds funny, but trust me, it's really difficult to relax and sit the trot when you're in pain.

I've tried riding without underwear, but the sores are there now and any rubbing makes them flare up. I've also tried the padded underwear sold in the tack catalogs but it was no help either. Please tell me I am not the only one with this problem and if you have any suggestions on what I should do.

A This is definitely not an amusing problem, and I'll bet that some other readers are groaning in sympathy.

First, you should avoid riding long enough to allow those sores to heal properly. As long as the sores are there, they will probably become more painful and take longer to heal every time you ride, so take some time off. Three weeks may not be enough; it may take six.

Your doctor's ointment suggestion was probably wise, but I'm not so certain about the adhesive bandages, which can wrinkle, fold, and shift out of position, making a bad situation worse. Many people also react badly to the adhesive, especially in sensitive areas. Baby powder, cornstarch, or similar products may help more than bandages.

If I were you, I would go to a second doctor, one who specializes in sports medicine. That way, you'll get a second opinion, which is often an excellent idea, and you'll benefit from the advice of someone who may have more experience with the sort of injuries that afflict riders and cyclists.

In the meantime, riding without underwear probably isn't the answer either. Once the sores have healed, try underwear with covered elastics. You may also find that part of the problem relates to your riding clothes. Some jeans are not suitable for riding because the seams will make you uncomfortable and eventually cause sores to develop. Some riding breeches can rub too; be sure that whatever you wear fits snugly, so that there are no wrinkles and loose areas. Pay particular attention to the length of the rise (the distance from crotch to waist). A too-short rise will make you uncomfortable immediately; a too-long rise will wrinkle at the crotch, which can lead to more sores. Wearing pantyhose under breeches can virtually eliminate chafing, so if you can tolerate pantyhose, you might give this a try.

Now, since I know perfectly well that you're going to ride in spite of the above advice . . .

Tack stores have their own version of the lingerie counter.

If you've just begun English lessons, you probably shouldn't be trying to sit the trot quite yet anyway, and you certainly shouldn't even *think* about sitting the trot as long as you have any sores. The discomfort will only cause you to sit badly and learn an incorrect position. Instead, your condition presents a perfect opportunity (with built-in incentive) for you to develop a long, strong leg by doing a lot of work in your two-point position.

There are gel pads designed to be placed on top of the saddle, and these can make some riders more comfortable. These pads aren't cheap, but if you're determined to ride with sores, then get one — otherwise you'll spend just as much on medication and bandages!

Seat Bone Pain When Riding

Q At age 46, I am a relatively new rider. I am working toward my lifelong dream of owning a horse by taking lessons and leasing a horse for a year before I buy. I have had one year of lessons and thought that I was doing very well. But now I am leasing a horse and things are going badly, in a strange way.

The horse, a 16-year-old Quarter Horse gelding, is very sweet and obedient. I have no problem handling him or tacking him up or riding him. The problem is the area of my body that sits on the saddle!

I used to hear other riders talk about crotch pain or sore seat bones when I first started my lessons, and I thought that I was really lucky not to experience any of that. But now that I am leasing Dakota, I feel those sore seat bones at every ride. I thought that the saddle might be too small for me, but it fits fine. (I am 5'3"and short-legged, and the English saddle is a 17.5 size.)

Is there anything I can do? I tried a fleece seat-saver that helped a little bit, but I don't know if this is something I should do. Dakota's owner says that the saddle doesn't hurt her (it's her saddle and it fits the horse) and she doesn't see why it should hurt me. She has watched me ride and so has my instructor, and nobody can figure it out. All I know is that it's making me reluctant to ride, which is horrible because this is what I've wanted all my life!

A It sounds to me as though you've been very sensible so far. Don't hesitate to use a seat-saver if it helps. In addition to fleece seat-savers, like the one you tried, there are seat-savers made from genuine sheepskin, from foam, and from the sort of gel that's used in bicycle-seat pads. There's no point in making yourself miserable, and trying to tough it out won't help your riding either. When something hurts, the normal human reaction is to wriggle and twist and compensate, so if you are suffering from sore seat bones, your riding position will suffer too, as will your effectiveness.

One thing that you haven't checked is the position of your seat bones and how their placement relates to the placement of the saddle seams. There's probably nothing wrong with you or the saddle, but it's quite possible that the two of you aren't compatible. The twist or "waist" of the saddle is the narrowest part at the top, where you can see a sort of "hourglass" shape (the top of the saddle widens at the pommel and the seat). Seat bones are variable, and if yours are aligned so that they are just on top of those seams as you ride, you are guaranteed to be miserably uncomfortable.

If this is the case, a foam or gel seat-saver will probably do the trick. Special padded riding underwear might help too.

Keep all of this in mind when you start looking for your *own* saddle. Saddle-seam placement is just one more factor to think about as you shop.

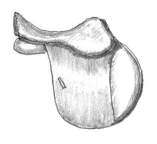

If you lack natural padding, you can buy comfort
at the tack shop in the form of a seat-saver.

Helmet Fitting

Q I bought a new helmet last month because my old one was almost five years old and I had done some of the things you say not to do. I kept it in my car for two years and it fell off the top of the car quite a few times, so it probably was not in the best shape.

My new helmet is a Troxel, which I have heard is a good brand. It is very lightweight and comfortable, but it doesn't stay on when I fall off. I discovered this when my horse stumbled when I wasn't really paying attention and I just kind of fell off sideways. After I hit the ground I waited a minute to see how I felt, then I got up, but my helmet was nowhere near me. A friend who saw me come off said my helmet was going one way when I was going the other way, so I didn't even have it on my head when I hit the ground. It's a good thing I landed on my butt in a sand arena!

What good is a helmet if it doesn't stay on my head when I fall off? I thought it was properly fitted, as it was the right size for me and I had the harness fastened. The harness was still fastened when I picked up my helmet. How could this happen, and is there something I should be doing so that it won't happen again? My old helmet never came off my head no matter what I did. Should I look for a different brand?

A That's a scary situation. Your helmet certainly can't protect you if it isn't on your head. Something was obviously wrong here — either the helmet was not, in fact, the correct size or shape for your head or the harness wasn't properly adjusted before it was fastened. Size evaluation and harness adjustment should be dealt with at the time of purchase, but it's a sad fact that many of the people who work in tack shops simply don't know how to help customers select or fit a helmet or adjust a harness. Since these issues speak directly to rider safety, it's important for riders to understand them clearly.

Let's begin with helmet size and shape. Both vary from model to model and from manufacturer to manufacturer, so try several makes and models before making up your mind. Some sizes are precise (like hat and shoe sizes), while others are more general (small-medium-large). Some styles are a particular shape (e.g., round, oval, long oval). There's no right or wrong helmet shape or head shape, but for the sake of safety and comfort, it's important to achieve as close a match as possible between the shape of your helmet and the shape of your head. It's a good idea to try several helmets in different sizes and shapes from each manufacturer, because even tiny design differences can make a huge difference to helmet fit.

Shop in person. Online shopping and catalog shopping are very convenient, but you must try a helmet on if you want to be sure that it fits. The same size from two different companies may fit entirely differently, and the new version of the model that *used* to fit you may no longer have exactly the same contours, so spend some time visiting tack shops and trying on helmets. Also, the day before the show or the day before you leave for riding camp is *not* the moment to begin looking for a helmet. If you only have an hour to find a new helmet, you won't necessarily buy the one that fits best, and that's just not the way to shop for something that's designed to protect your brain.

By the way, your hair can affect helmet fit. Before you begin shopping, arrange your hair in the way that you usually wear it when you ride. If you try on a helmet in the store with your hair down and loose, then try to ride with your hair in a high ponytail or French braid, the helmet may no longer fit! If you always school with your hair braided and tucked into your helmet, but like to wear it in a bun at the nape of your neck for competitions, or if you school with a braid down your back but like to have your hair up under your helmet for competitions, you may need two different helmets or a single helmet with an adjustable-fit system. And if you're planning to have your long hair cut short, do it *before* you go shopping for your new helmet.

If a helmet isn't approved or lacks the ASTM/SEI label, don't even bother trying it on. When you've found a few approved safety helmets that seem likely to fit, you can begin. Start by putting the helmet on your head straight and level, so that the visor (if any) points forward and the brim of the helmet is an inch above your eyebrows. Don't fasten the harness yet — you're checking for basic helmet fit. In this position, the helmet should feel snug from front to back and from side to side but not painfully tight.

With the harness still unfastened, put one hand on top of the helmet and wiggle it backward and forward, up and down, and from side to side. If it stays snugly on your head and moves your eyebrows and scalp when you move it up and down, good. If it doesn't move at all, and you're beginning to feel that your head is caught in a vise, it's too small — try the next larger size. If it moves easily without shifting your eyebrows and scalp with it, it's too large — try the next smaller size. Don't compromise on fit. A too-tight helmet will give you headaches and a too-loose one will slip.

It's a good idea to try several helmets in different sizes and shapes from each manufacturer, because even tiny design differences can make a huge difference to helmet fit.

Evaluate the fit. Does the helmet seem to fit all around your head or does it fit better in some places than in others? The shape of the helmet might not match the shape of your head. Minor adjustments can be made with optional padding, and some helmets come with built-in adjustable padding that allows you to customize the fit in front, in back, and on the sides. If a helmet feels snug across your forehead but shifts easily from side to side, it's probably too round for your (oval) head, and a pad on each side may do the trick. If it's just a little bit too oval for you, a pad in the back or one in the front may be the answer. If the helmet doesn't fit well after a small adjustment to the padding, you may need an entirely different helmet with a different basic shape.

(**NOTE:** If a helmet seems to fit snugly and comfortably at the sides, but can be rocked forward and backward easily, then it may be too oval for your head, but since an improperly adjusted harness can allow a helmet to rock like this, be sure to adjust the harness correctly and try the helmet again before you cross it off your list.)

Now fasten the harness, bend over from the waist, and shake your head vigorously. The helmet ought to stay on without shifting. If it moves around, something is wrong with the fit or the padding or, very likely, the adjustment of the harness. *This is key.* Make sure you actually read the manufacturer's instructions and adjust the harness correctly before fastening it. If you only changed the length of the chinstrap, you didn't actually adjust the harness properly. Do this now and then bend over and shake your head again. The feel may be very different.

Harness adjustment is an essential but often-overlooked part of helmet fitting, helmet safety, and helmet shopping. Harnesses, like the helmets themselves, vary from manufacturer to manufacturer and from model to model and are subject to design changes over time. Every time you buy a new helmet, read the directions and be sure that you are adjusting the harness correctly. Although you will need to follow the directions exactly for each helmet you try on, here is some basic, generic information about harness adjustment.

The harness (sometimes referred to as the retention system) involves much more than a mere chinstrap. Whatever its design, it should fit snugly against the back of your head. Any ASTM/SEI helmet has a harness that adjusts in several different areas: the back of the harness, the sides of the harness, and the strap that fastens under the chin.

When the helmet is on your head correctly (straight and about one inch above your eyebrows), check the following:

- ► Is the back of the harness snug enough to keep the helmet from moving forward?
- ► Do the side straps meet just below and in front of your earlobes?
- ► Is the throat strap under your chin and fitting snugly, even firmly, but not too tightly?

You should end up with a harness that feels snug but not uncomfortably tight, and that fits well in the back, over and around the ears, and under the jaw.

Once your helmet is properly adjusted, always wear it correctly. Keep it straight — don't push it back on your head so that your forehead is exposed. Keep the harness adjusted snugly and keep it fastened! Riders who loosen the chinstrap so there is no longer contact between the strap and the skin are putting themselves at risk. Like a badly adjusted seatbelt, a badly adjusted helmet can't do the job it was designed to do. And don't take unnecessary risks: always fasten your helmet harness before you mount, and unfasten it after you dismount.

As for your particular situation, it sounds as though your helmet doesn't fit as well as you thought it did or the harness wasn't adjusted correctly. Go through the helmet-fitting and harness-adjusting process again to see if you need to make some changes. If you've lost the instructions, check at a tack shop or contact Troxel directly; the company is very responsive to customers.

If you determine that your helmet simply doesn't fit your head and can't be made to fit securely, then you probably need a helmet of a different shape. I suggest that you pay another visit to the tack shop and try on as many different helmets as possible. Don't limit yourself to one particular model of helmet — try several different styles from the same manufacturer. Also, don't limit yourself to a single manufacturer, but try as many models as possible from as many different manufacturers as possible. It's important that your safety headgear be both protective and comfortable, so keep looking until you find the equestrian helmet that's right for you.

Keep trying different helmets until you find the one that's most comfortable for you.

Wearing a Hat under a Helmet

Q I've asked this question at two tack shops and haven't managed to get what I consider to be a good answer. I want to know if it is good or bad to wear hats like knit caps under equestrian helmets that are too large? And also, is this a good way to keep riders warmer in winter?

My children both ride in schooling helmets, but the helmets are definitely too big for them, and I also worry about their heads being too cold in winter when the wind can go right through those vents in the helmets! I don't think that a pull-on knit cap under a helmet would hurt its protection, do you?

A I *do* think that wearing any kind of a hat under an equestrian helmet risks diminishing its effectiveness, and I don't think it's a good gamble. The stakes are simply too high.

It's true that in winter, cold air can come through the vents of a schooling helmet. If that becomes a problem and the rider's head is cold, the solution isn't

Fight winter cold with a warm cover that goes over the helmet.

to put a hat under the helmet but to put a cover over the helmet! Several equine accessory companies sell stretchy, polyester fleece covers that go over the helmet itself plus the rider's neck and ears. I'd suggest investing in a couple of these for your children's winter riding.

I'm curious — why are your children's helmets too large for them? It's really not a good idea to buy a child a too-large helmet so that she can "grow into it" over a year or two. During those years, the child is wearing a helmet that doesn't fit and therefore cannot protect her brain properly.

Adding a knit cap to the child's head won't make the helmet safer, although it may seem to fit more snugly. Part of what makes equestrian helmets so useful is the way they stay in place when they are properly fitted to the rider's head and the harnesses are properly adjusted and fastened. Putting an extra layer of any kind between the rider's head and the helmet can cause the helmet to slip out of position in the event of a fall. I know it must be very frustrating to be buying clothing, boots, and helmets for growing children who seem to change sizes every few weeks, but helmets are such basic safety equipment, and correct (snug) fit is so essential, that it's best not to take any unnecessary chances.

Your children ride in equestrian helmets — that's good. Help them be as safe as possible by purchasing helmets that fit them correctly. If you need to purchase new helmets in six months or a year, the cost of the new helmets will still be trivial compared to the cost of a single visit to the emergency room. Truly, schooling helmets are one of the best deals around.

PART IV

Getting Better
All the Time

INSTRUCTORS AND LESSONS

GOING TO CLINICS

GOING TO COMPETITIONS

YOU ARE NOT ALONE

CHAPTER 18

Instructors and Lessons

RIDING INSTRUCTORS HAVE GREAT INFLUENCE on both horses and riders, not just because they teach the mechanics of riding but because they act as interpreters for the horse until the rider achieves the ability to understand the horse and communicate with him directly. Lessons are essential for riders who want to improve their skills, and riders need to take great care when selecting — or staying with — an instructor. Not everyone can teach and not everyone *should* teach. Every rider needs and deserves the full, focused attention of a competent, kind, qualified instructor with proven teaching skills.

Adult Beginner Lessons

Q I am a 39-year-old mother of four who took up riding six years ago. After some sporadic riding lessons with a not-so-great instructor, I started riding at a nearby hunter/jumper facility that buys Thoroughbreds off the track in New York and retrains them. The instructor there is quite young but very knowledgeable. I am not interested in jumping but love flatwork and want to learn dressage. I have taken lessons on two different horses: a 7-year-old gelding that scared the pants off me and a 20-something 17-hand gelding that bites when you groom him.

I have had some scary experiences in my weekly lessons. Two other women around my age have had bad falls, including one that put the rider under the horse with a hoof hitting her cheek and nearly crushing her back. I have not been back to ride there since witnessing that injury. I know it is not the instructor's fault — the horse tripped in the middle of cantering — but I am nervous nevertheless. The majority of students are young girls who show and board their horses there or are very experienced adults who have owned horses forever.

I cannot afford to injure myself. I really love riding but do not want to deal with the constant fear of being severely hurt. Am I riding at the wrong facility? It is less than a mile from my house and that makes it convenient, but at what cost?

A Alas, the convenient location of this barn may be the most appealing thing about it. Some of the problems you are experiencing could be due to the age and experience level of your instructor. She may well be a wonderful rider with years of experience in the saddle, but it's unlikely that someone so young has had enough teaching experience to be a really good instructor. She also may not have many, or any, teaching skills. Riding and teaching involve very different skill sets, and there's often little or no overlap. It takes time, effort, and experience to create a good teacher even when the basic talent is there. That's why young instructors should serve as apprentices for several years to good teachers who can help them learn *teaching* skills.

Another point is that young instructors, even certified ones (and I would hope that yours is certified by the American Riding Instructor Certification Program or the U.S. Dressage Federation or both), are not necessarily good instructors for adult beginners. With limited experience and limited knowledge of the adult world, they simply aren't in a position to understand the physical, mental, and

Bucking and rearing horses don't belong in lesson programs.

emotional issues that affect adult beginner riders. It's difficult, if not impossible, for an instructor in her early 20s to understand the concerns of a beginner rider in her 40s, 50s, or 60s, particularly as those concerns relate to physical, mental, and emotional fear. A young woman who has been riding since childhood simply cannot understand what goes on in the mind of an adult beginner who is the mother of four children.

Look for a facility with slow, steady school horses that will allow you to relax and learn, and where the instruction is aimed at adult beginner riders. Suitable horses and appropriate instruction will go a long way toward helping you learn and feel more secure.

Having said that, I do need to point out that *accidents happen.* Lessons shouldn't involve riders hitting the ground on a regular basis, but horses do trip, riders do become unbalanced, and every once in a while a rider comes off, even in a lesson. There are many things you can do to minimize the risk. You can purchase and wear proper headgear and footgear. You can take lessons in falling off. Emergency dismount lessons on horseback or fall-tuck-and-roll lessons at a martial arts or gymnastics studio can be very useful, as they teach you to keep thinking and *do* something when you fall off. It's important to know how to avoid a fall and how to fall if you have no other choice. You can take lessons from a good, experienced instructor who uses steady, reliable school horses. You can work at home to increase your fitness and flexibility; walking, for instance, is easy and inexpensive and wonderful exercise for riders.

But there is no way to guarantee that you'll never fall off and no way to ensure that you won't get hurt if you do. When parents ask me if I can guarantee that their child will never fall off a horse, I say, "Yes, I can, if you promise that your child will never get *on* a horse." That's truly the only way you can be absolutely sure that you'll never fall off.

You can't learn if you can't relax, and you can't relax if you are constantly frightened. Try to find a quieter facility that's more suited to your needs; if it adds 20 miles to your drive, so be it. If you can find a place where you're able to relax and learn, you won't mind the longer drive.

Questions to Ask Prospective Instructor

Q I found a trainer/instructor in my area through a newspaper ad and am wondering what type of questions I should ask and what signs would clue me not to use this instructor. I am a fearful beginner, and my horse is an older hormonal mare set in her ways but a sweetheart just the same. I would appreciate any input because I do not want to make matters worse for my horse or me.

A First of all, check out the facility where this instructor teaches. Horses in poor condition, dangerous fencing around the arena, and riders without helmets would all be "no go" indicators. So would overcrowded lessons — in fact, individual lessons are best for beginner riders. When you are more experienced, you will benefit from sharing lessons with a few other riders.

Asking questions is always an excellent idea. Here are some I would ask; I'm sure you will think of others.

Is the instructor certified, and if so, by which program and in what specialty area? To learn a particular style of riding, such as stock seat or hunt seat or dressage, you need an instructor who is qualified and competent to teach it. The American Riding Instructors Association (ARIA) maintains a list of certified instructors, together with their levels, specialties, and contact information.

Does she carry insurance? Like certification from a reliable organization, this is a good sign because it tells you that the instructor regards herself as a professional and takes her work seriously.

What are her safety equipment rules? A good instructor will ask you to wear safe footgear on your feet and an ASTM/SEI-approved equestrian helmet on your head, even if she doesn't care what you wear elsewhere on your body.

What are the names and telephone numbers of some of her adult students? You can learn a lot from them, if you listen carefully! For instance, "She's great; she doesn't make us wear helmets" or "She's so much fun; we get to do anything we want in lessons" would be warning signals, not recommendations.

After you've asked some questions, arrange to watch this instructor teach a lesson to another beginner rider of your age. Observing a lesson will answer questions you might not even think to ask. You'll learn the instructor's teaching techniques and philosophy, and observe her attitude toward riders and horses.

While you watch, ask yourself if the horse looks healthy and happy and under control. Or does he look nervous or depressed or uncomfortable or out of control? Does the rider look relaxed and comfortable and secure? Or does she seem fearful or uncomfortable? Does the rider seem to understand what the instructor tells her and is she able to act on what she's being told? Or does the rider seem confused and unable to make sense of what the instructor is telling her?

When you watch a well-taught lesson, you will wish that you were the one on the horse.

If you enjoy watching the lesson and can easily imagine yourself in the student's place, this may be the right instructor for you. If you are glad that you're *not* the rider, then this isn't the instructor for you.

A good instructor knows her subject in depth. She knows about particular styles of riding, she knows about riding and horses and horsemanship in general, and she knows about human and equine learning styles. A good instructor communicates effectively with her students. Above all, a good instructor always speaks for the horse.

My Instructor Hates My Horse

Q I am 43 years old and have been riding for several years. I bought my gelding, Chance, two years ago. Based on his conformation and intelligence, he seems to be part Quarter Horse and maybe part Arabian. He is 15.1 hands with a stocky build. His gaits are okay, nothing fancy, not very rough or super-smooth, and he has an average stride. I think he is just about perfect!

At first, I wasn't sure that I could take care of a horse, even at a good boarding stable, but he has been no problem! He is never sick or lame or unwilling, and he always looks interested and eager when he sees me coming or hears my footsteps, so I know he likes me and the things that we do together.

My instructor has been teaching me basic riding skills and some dressage for four years. I would like to get serious about dressage and I have read in many books, including yours, that dressage is good for all horses and will help them improve. My instructor says that if I want to do dressage, Chance's limitations are going to get in the way, and I should buy a horse with better movement and more potential. I just want to work with Chance, because I really love him and want to ride him forever. I wouldn't feel the same about another horse and I can't afford to keep two horses.

I've tried to tell my instructor how I feel, but she says that I'll see it her way when I get serious about dressage, and that she'll know when I'm serious because I'll ask her to find me another horse. I started riding late in life and I don't care about showing, but I *do* care about dressage and I *am* serious. I just want to do it with my own horse that I love. But when I ask her to teach me something like turn on the forehand or turn on the haunches, she shrugs her shoulders and says, "He'll never be able to do what you want." I don't think that's true, but I've only been riding four years, so maybe I'm wrong. Or is my instructor trying to say something about my own abilities? Please tell me if I'm wrong, and if not, how I can make her understand?

A I would be very surprised if your instructor actually hates, or even dislikes, your horse. A true professional, especially in dressage, might like some horses much more than others, might feel very sorry for some horses, and might not wish to purchase, train, or ride certain horses, but wouldn't have it in her to hate any horse, especially a sweet, kind horse like your Chance.

If your instructor truly doesn't like your horse, however, it's going to be hard for you to work with her and it's going to be impossible for her to put her best effort into working with your horse. Someone who dislikes a horse is unlikely to give him the benefit of the doubt, which is something that all horses deserve. But don't just assume that your instructor doesn't like your horse: *Ask* her, get those communication lines open, and let her finish stating her whole sentence or whole thought before you break in. You may be surprised at what you learn. Sometimes the instructor who says, "This horse isn't suitable" is only saying that the horse isn't suitable for a particular purpose. She may like the horse very much but honestly find him unsuitable for a specific task.

If your instructor wants you to replace Chance because she really believes that only competition and show results matter, and he isn't likely to win in competition, then you and she obviously have completely different ideas about the meaning of dressage and about your own reasons for riding. But before you give up on your instructor, make one more attempt to talk to her. It's possible that you can go on working together, and it's worth making an effort to find out.

You are correct that any horse can benefit, physically and mentally and emotionally, from dressage training. The same is true of any rider. Having said that, let me point out that I mean dressage as "the systematic progressive development of the horse's body and mind," not as a competitive sport. Those are two very different things.

Think of some other discipline — figure skating, say, or ballet. Any human can benefit from learning the discipline, balance, breathing, and movement skills of these activities, but very few actually make skating or ballet the focus of their lives. Any horse can benefit from dressage, but very few become successful national or international dressage competitors. Students are not always realistic about themselves or their horses. Instructors want to encourage their students, but an ethical instructor will not encourage any student to pour her heart, money, and effort into trying to become a star performer, if the best that student can possibly achieve is a workmanlike competence.

Instructors and trainers are accustomed to thinking of riders and horses in terms of their potential.

Instructors, too, have anxieties and insecurities. They want their students to do well, they want the horses they work with to improve, and they often see show results as proof of their teaching skills. Young and inexperienced instructors, especially, may feel insecure about their teaching abilities. If your instructor is very secure, knows the value of what she is teaching, and cares about you and your horse's progress whether or not you ever put one hoof into the show arena, her attitude will be more relaxed. If your instructor is depending on *your* show results to make *her* feel good about her teaching, then she will be much less relaxed about your work and your progress.

Many riders are in a hurry to make it into the show ring. They care about competition results more than they care about the process of learning to ride and training their horses. They too believe that the proof of good instruction is show-ring success. These riders and their instructors are constantly in search of a competitive edge. They're not interested in simple "sweat equity" — hard work and focused attention. The competitive edge can take the form of the latest, most expensive bit or browband, a new saddle that "puts the rider's leg in just the right place," or a new horse that moves really well.

If your instructor is used to riders like this, she may not be hearing your words accurately. When you say "I love dressage; I want to do dressage," she may hear "I want to go to dressage shows and come home with ribbons and trophies." If that's what her other students mean when they say "I want to do dressage," and if that's what she thinks you mean, then her answer — "You're going to need a fancier, bigger-moving horse" — makes sense in that context.

Instructors don't want their riders to be unhappy or frustrated. Many riders who have average skills, an average amount of time to ride, and an average horse with ordinary gaits become unhappy and frustrated when they attend competitions and discover that badly behaved, badly ridden horses with naturally spectacular gaits typically score better than obedient but more limited horses. Let your instructor know that this doesn't matter to you, because you're interested in improving, not competing.

Your instructor may not understand just how much you love your horse.

Instructors and trainers are accustomed to thinking of all riders and horses in terms of their potential. Before you start analyzing yourself and your horse in terms of abilities and potential, ask yourself "potential for *what?*" If you are discussing potential and your instructor hears "potential for high scores at competitions," whereas you mean "potential to become a stronger, more coordinated, and more flexible horse with better gaits," then you aren't talking about the same thing. Before you can have a coherent discussion, you have to agree on what the terms mean. When your instructor says, "Chance will never be able to do what you want," she doesn't mean that he can't learn to do a turn on the forehand, a turn on the haunches, or a half-pass. Of course he can; any reasonably sound horse can achieve these things. What she probably means is that he's unlikely to perform those things in a way that would allow him to beat fancier-moving horses at a competition.

If, as is typical of many adult riders, you are overworked, overtired, and barely able to find time to ride a few days a week, then let your instructor know that you don't expect her to perform miracles. Tell her that you will take responsibility for keeping your body and your horse's body gymnasticized between lessons and able to work in lessons.

Instructors often worry that a student expects too much or that they can't give a student what she wants or needs. Your instructor may be concerned that because of your horse's limitations, you won't be able to meet your expectations and she won't be able to help you meet those same expectations. She may be worrying that she is shortchanging you by allowing you to work toward a goal (e.g., competitive success) that you're unlikely to reach. She may simply be trying to spare you frustration and distress.

Tell your instructor what you want from yourself, what you want from your horse, and what you want from her. Make it clear that you want to learn the discipline and skills of dressage because you love dressage, not because you love ribbons. Explain that you want to make your imperfect self into the best and happiest rider you can possibly become; and that you want your horse to move as well as he can, use his body to the best of his ability, last as long as possible, and enjoy his life as a riding horse; and that you see dressage as the way to accomplish these goals.

Make it clear that what you want from her is guidance through the levels of dressage. If you make all of this clear, and she *still* disagrees, listen to her reasons with an open mind. Then decide whether you want a new horse and a new focus or a different instructor who can help you with your own ideals and goals.

Same Lesson Over and Over

Q My instructor is knowledgeable, and I like her a lot. But I feel like I am taking the same lesson over and over again and I don't know what to do about it. Some of it is probably my fault because I don't ride very often. I work full-time and I don't have much time for riding. Most days I just have time to clean the stall and feed my horse. Some weeks I don't ride at all and some weeks I might get to ride once. In the summer when it's light longer I can sometimes ride two or three times a week, but not all that often.

I take a lesson whenever the weather is good, my instructor is in town, and my horse doesn't need shoeing. That means I have a lesson every month when I'm lucky, otherwise every two or three months. Whenever I have a lesson, I feel like it's the first one all over again, and my instructor is still telling me to balance properly in my saddle, stretch my legs down, close my fingers, and all that. I can always see some progress during the lesson, but when it's time for my next lesson, we start from the beginning again. I'd like to move on.

If there are several months between my lessons, I don't feel like I should be doing the exact same things I was working on three months ago. I need to try something different or I won't make progress. Please tell me if I'm right or if I'm wrong, and if I'm right, how can I tell my instructor that she needs to give me different lessons, not the same one every time? I don't feel that I know enough to design my own lessons, but I'm tired of doing the same lesson over and over.

A Believe me, I sympathize with your frustration, having been in similar situations myself. Working full-time, looking after a horse, and trying to find riding time — especially when the days are short — is never easy.

I have to sympathize with your instructor too, though. It's frustrating for a teacher to work with someone in your position. Students who take lessons once a month (or less often) *can* make progress, but only if they are able to practice regularly between lessons. Without practice, there's no way for students to build their skills, confirm their technique, or create new habits, and these are the building blocks that enable students to progress.

Could there possibly be a valid reason for your instructor always giving you the same lesson? Pretend that you are someone else taking an objective look at you. Take a good look at yourself, your level of preparedness, and your physical and mental readiness, and ask yourself whether this student is truly able to build on a lesson and improve to the point at which she is ready for a second lesson. Riding involves both physical and mental skills. Are you bringing improved skills to each lesson or are you bringing exactly the same skills each time?

Learning to ride is a process of skills acquisition: Students are introduced to each skill, taught how to do it, then helped to practice until (a) they can do it correctly, (b) they don't have to think about it while they do it, and (c) they've done it correctly so often they can't possibly do it *incorrectly.* Meanwhile, they should also be taught the theory behind the skill and how the skill fits into the overall lesson plan.

All of this takes time and requires focused, productive effort. If a student masters the skills introduced in Lesson One well enough to build on them, then the teacher should proceed to Lesson Two. But if the student is still struggling with the material in Lesson One, it would be *wrong* to try to move on as if the student had mastered the first lesson. If you've ever been in a class where the teacher was determined to cover a set amount of material every day, regardless of whether the students understood it, you'll understand just how hopeless it can be to try to learn from someone who teaches exclusively by the clock and the calendar.

If you think that your instructor simply doesn't have a plan for you, talk to her! While you're busy being frustrated with her, she might be just as frustrated with you. Clear the air and work out a way for you to improve your skills and make progress. You may want to ask your instructor for an overview of her lesson plan for the next six months or the next year. If either of you feels that you aren't making progress because you aren't practicing effectively between lessons, ask for "home-work assignments" in the form of exercises that you can do on and off the horse.

Some riders are not at all ambitious. They may be happy to have a lesson every few months, not because they particularly want to make progress, but because they enjoy "checking in" with the instructor periodically just to socialize a little and be sure that they aren't actually backsliding. There's nothing wrong with that, as long as both the rider and the instructor understand that the "lessons" are primarily social in nature.

Other, more ambitious, riders become frustrated when their riding schedules don't permit them to make the kind of progress they want. If you're one of these riders, let your instructor know. There are exercises you can do on horseback and there are hundreds of exercises that you can do *without* the horse, in your home or hotel room, to increase your strength and flexibility and stamina.

Here's one example: If you're always standing on your toes in your stirrups, because your hamstrings and Achilles tendons are short and tight, and you know that you could change this with a daily or even three-times-weekly session of riding in a half-seat at walk and trot, ask your instructor to suggest alternative forms of stretching exercises that you can do at home, without a horse. When you do find time to ride, you'll feel the benefit of those exercises immediately. You will have a more secure seat and leg, and your instructor will have more to work with in your lesson.

Are you bringing improved skills to each lesson or are you bringing exactly the same skills each time?

Similarly, you can do exercises to learn to keep your fingers closed, even if you're at home. Tie a set of reins to a leg of your coffee table, and practice holding the reins when you watch TV. You can use this to get yourself in the habit of holding your reins correctly, with closed fingers, and it really will take just 10 or 15 minutes a day.

If balance is a problem, doing yoga or tai chi will work wonders; even a few minutes here and there during your workday will help immensely. Don't give up just because you can't ride every day. There's so much you can do to improve your riding even if you're nowhere near a horse. Show your instructor that you're determined to make progress in spite of your schedule, and I'm sure that she will find ways to help you.

"Jerk and Shout" Instructor

Q I am a beginning adult rider who started lessons a few months ago and just bought a nice gelding on which I will continue my lessons at the stable where he's boarding. My problem concerns my instructor's attitude toward and way of dealing with my horse. She seems to be of the "jerk and shout" school of horse handling. I know it's important not to let my horse take advantage of me or develop bad habits, but I'm not comfortable with, nor convinced of, the necessity of so much harshness. My horse is basically a mellow guy. Can he be trained without a lot of jerking and shouting?

A I'm going to tell you what you already know: You need a different instructor. This may entail taking your horse to another barn. Investigate your options as soon as you can, for the sake of your horse and your riding.

The "jerk and shout" school isn't one you need to attend. All you will learn are behaviors, techniques, and an attitude that you will have to lose later on if you want to learn good riding and horsemanship. If you've ever tried to relearn a skill, you know how hard it is to change the way you've learned to do something. It's much better to find someone who can teach you to do it right the first time around. When horses are involved, it's even more important to learn things right the first time! If the subject is tennis or typing, you'll only hurt and inconvenience yourself by learning badly and having to relearn later. When the subjects are riding and horsemanship, you'll also hurt your horse — something I am quite sure you do *not* want to do.

Horses develop bad habits through being treated badly. They don't sit up at night planning how to annoy and inconvenience their owners and riders. Horses don't have an interest in getting away with things, but they will learn bad habits if they are handled by unkind humans, and the lessons will be learned just as well whether the unkindness is deliberate or based on pure ignorance.

Your instincts are good. Trust them. You know that the way to teach a horse to be relaxed and quiet in a given situation has to involve something other than yelling and hitting. Horses aren't all that different from humans, cats, dogs, or any other animal — they quickly learn where they feel safe and where they feel unsafe. You need to teach your horse to trust people and to be confident and calm, and he can't learn this when someone else is busy teaching him to be nervous and afraid.

Your horse doesn't sound as if he has a problem, and neither do you, apart from the one *big* problem of having an inappropriate instructor. I wish I could tell you that you would be able to learn good riding and good horsemanship from someone who has this sort of attitude, but I can't. It just doesn't work that way. You wouldn't put your child in a day-care center run by someone who disliked children, and if you were interested in becoming a child-care worker, you wouldn't want to be trained by someone like this. Think about what you want from your riding lessons — I'm guessing that you are genuinely fond of your horse and that you want horses to be part of your life forever. You need to get the best possible instruction from a teacher who actually likes and understands horses. The student-teacher relationship is a complex one, and you can't learn well from someone you don't trust.

Horses will learn bad habits if they are handled by unkind humans, and the lessons will be learned just as well whether the unkindness is deliberate or based on pure ignorance.

You may be feeling that you don't know enough to evaluate your instructor, that you don't know enough about horses to know what's right, and that she's a "professional" and who are you, a mere novice, to question her? The answer is simple: you are an adult and you *do* know enough. The advantage of learning to ride as an adult is that you bring important assets to the project, including emotional maturity, good sense, and the ability to evaluate your instructor. The disadvantage is that you have less leeway and less time to recover from major mistakes.

If you stay with this instructor, *you will become like her,* because you will absorb her attitude and beliefs along with her instruction. If that happens, you'll say good-bye to any hope of becoming a horseman because you'll be embracing the concept that the relationship between horse and rider is fundamentally adversarial. ("Make him do this!" "Don't let him get away with that!") Staying will change you as a person, and not in a good way. It will also change that nice, mellow gelding, and you don't want that.

Go out and find a good, competent, safety-oriented, horse-loving instructor *now.* Set yourself up for success instead of failure. I'll tell you the same thing that I tell riders at lessons, clinics, lectures, and demonstrations: Don't take even one step down a path that's leading somewhere you don't want to go.

New Instructor, New Ways

Q I have had a few instructors and never been very happy with them, although my current one seems perfect.

My horse is a 17.3-hand Thoroughbred that I purchased off the track about eight months ago. After several silly accidents in the paddock, he is finally in work. I had one instructor who tied his head to his tail to get him to listen to the rider's hands and then used a rope to pull his head down. He reared and carried on until even the trainer got a bit worried. I really didn't like it, but at the time was friends with some rather nasty horse people who were telling me how the horse needed this. I guess I was pretty stupid.

My next instructor told me to seesaw my horse's mouth to get him down on the bit. She also insisted that he go deep into the corners and told me to use a martingale because when I was trying to get his head down he would chuck it up as a resistance.

My new instructor is great, but I just wanted to know what you thought because I have not had a very good run so far. She does not care where his head is but tries to get me to have a steady contact on the reins. He seems to be bringing his head down quite nicely with this but only some of the time (not that I would expect any more). He leg yields well in the walk, and we are working in an egg shape until he learns more balance. We are mainly working on halt-walk-trot transitions. She says as soon as he loses his balance to bring him back to walk and then push him on again so he does not learn to run on his forehand or hang on the bit, which he did a lot before.

This instructor says that it will take about a year to give him sound basic training that will give me a good-quality horse for life. He has the best temperament and is really trainable. He puts his heart into everything I ask him for and is a total sweetie on the ground. My instructor also said that I should work him only three or four times a week for a few months and then give him a few weeks off so he can come into his body. She said to do this for at least the next six to eight months and preferably for the next year. He is only five years old — do you think this is a good idea?

Do you think what I did with the other instructors could have damaged him, considering it was only about three lessons with each? I am feeling very guilty.

A You've been through the mill with those two earlier instructors, neither of whom should ever be allowed anywhere near another horse! But it sounds as though "third time lucky" applies in your case. Your new instructor appears to have a good understanding of horses, riders, and training. Every suggestion and practice of hers that you've described is solid classical training — you seem to be in good hands at last.

You've also discovered one of the worst feelings in the world: the feeling of guilt because you've hurt your horse or let him down. I'd have to say that yes, you hurt and confused your horse by doing (and allowing) the tying, pulling, and seesawing, but as you didn't take many lessons from the bad instructors, and as your horse is only five years old, and as you've now got a proper instructor with a sensible plan to help you both, with any luck the damage will have been temporary. Your new instructor's plan of time on and off work should help give your horse a chance to recover, and you'll be ready to learn more effectively when you begin riding again.

I think you should relax and look ahead to a long and enjoyable relationship with your horse and your new instructor. Don't look back, except to remind yourself that certain practices should never be employed with any horse — they're not in the best interest of the horse and thus are simply incompatible with horsemanship. If you've learned a lesson from your earlier experiences, it should be this: It's *your* responsibility to do what's right for your horse.

If an instructor wants you to do something that's wrong, you need a different instructor. If your friends want you to do something that's wrong, you need different friends. Your horse can't speak for himself or defend himself against

Always make your horse's welfare your top priority.

unacceptable treatment, but you can refuse to do things that are wrong, and when the horse involved is your own horse, you can also refuse to let anyone else do things that are wrong. Remember, your horse needs to be educated, not forced, and if he doesn't enjoy his training, something is very wrong.

Finally, the "new ways" your new instructor is teaching you are actually very old ways, and they're also the very best ways, designed to help your horse develop over time, mentally and physically, until he's the best horse he can be. If you follow the classical principles, your horse will enjoy his training and so will you.

Riding Lesson Etiquette?

Q Your advice on selecting stables and instructors saved me a lot of heartache when I decided to get back into riding after a long hiatus. It was helpful to have a list of things to look for and to do. Once you do find an instructor who "clicks" with you, how should you deal with problems that come up in the lessons? As in all relationships there are bound to be some rough times, but what is the proper etiquette for addressing one's frustrations in a situation where you are paying for a service?

Let me list some of the things that have happened in some of my past lessons.

▸ The instructor tells me to "continue trotting around the ring" and then goes to the rail to talk to someone. The conversations may last only a minute or two, but I feel that detracts way too much from a 30-minute lesson that never goes over time.

▸ The instructor routinely starts lessons late.

▸ The instructor asks me to do something I don't feel comfortable with or asks me to ride a horse I feel is too much to handle.

How would you recommend discussing such problems with an instructor? What is the best way to express frustration or disappointment without seeming hostile or overly demanding?

I'm also wondering if such subjects should be discussed up front once you select an instructor. Should you mention the things you feel uncomfortable about or find frustrating? It seems like a sensitive issue because even the nicest instructors with the best of hearts probably don't want to hear "I will not put up with this; I don't like that."

Would you shed some light on this and also mention what you feel would be appropriate responses from the instructor?

A What I see in your question is really two separate topics. One is whether your previous instructors behaved in a professional manner (they didn't) and whether you were right to leave them (you were). The other is whether you might have been able to change their behavior (it's possible) and whether there is some way to ensure that you and your current instructor keep communicating well and stay on the right track (there is).

Once you have found the right instructor for you, it's worth investing some effort to keep her and to keep your lessons running smoothly. Honesty is generally the best policy, but honesty should be diplomatic. It's always a good idea to find the best way to phrase a request, a comment, or a criticism.

When you hire a professional, you have the right to expect her to behave in a professional manner. You also have the right to discuss problems with her and to try to arrive at a mutually agreeable solution. If you aren't satisfied, you have every right to take your business elsewhere, which you've already done. I understand that you want some assurance that this time things will be different and that you've found "your" instructor at last. Here are my suggestions.

To begin, assume that your new instructor is professional and wants to help you and intends to give you a good lesson. Approach her on this basis, and do it soon instead of waiting until something happens that reminds you of a previous bad experience. If this happens, you may be too frustrated and upset to talk rationally, so accomplish more by having a good *preventive* conversation.

There's no need to antagonize her (or any prospective instructor) by announcing that you "will not put up with" this or that behavior or situation. Instead, invite your instructor for a cup of coffee and tell her how much you enjoy her lessons and how frustrated you were in the past when your other, less professional, less focused instructors did this, that, or the other. It will get your message across very clearly but in a friendly context. Trust me, there's not an instructor alive who would object to hearing that you are impressed with her competence, caring, and professionalism.

Good instructors want to know about their students. If you have a physical disability of some kind, or a medical condition, or if you take pills that make you a bit unsure of your balance, your instructor *needs* to know. If you are dead terrified of jumping, or of losing control of the horse, or of falling off, or if you get sick before each lesson out of fear of working without stirrups, your instructor

A good instructor will watch her students, not chat with other people.

needs to know that also. Her interest is in keeping you safe, teaching you well, and having you feel pleased with yourself, the horse, and your progress at the end of the session. The better she knows you, the more easily she can look out for you.

Your instructor won't think she's being warned off (which she isn't; you've already said that you like her and that she is a truly good instructor)! She *will* think that you are a particularly thoughtful sort of student, that you care very much about your lessons and your progress, and that you have a clear understanding of her part in your progress — and aren't those exactly the points you wanted to make?

Should Beginners Ride Many Different Horses?

Q I have been taking riding lessons for almost two months. I have heard that to be a good rider you should ride a lot of different horses. So I always ask for a different horse at my lesson, but the teacher doesn't seem very happy about that. She wants me to ride the same horse. I have been insisting on riding different horses. What do you think?

A When you have been riding for a long time it will be important for you to ride different horses. Right now, though, while you are just beginning to learn to ride, it would help you more if you rode the same horse at every lesson.

Here's why: When you are just learning how to sit and move with the horse and signal him to stop, start, and turn, it's easy for you to track your progress if you ride the same horse every week. If the horse is very slow to respond at your first lesson and becomes quicker to respond and more attentive at successive lessons, you will know that the difference is *you* — that you are sitting better, following his motion better, and making your signals more clearly.

If you ride Trigger this week and Spot next week and Prince the week after that, you won't know whether your skills are improving, staying at the same level, or going backward! If Spot responds more quickly than Trigger, you can't be sure that it's because your riding has improved; perhaps Spot is just a more sensitive horse.

Stay with the horse your instructor suggests you ride, at least for a few months. Then talk to your instructor and ask what horse you will be riding next. Instructors generally have a plan for each student, and you'll probably find that you'll be assigned a different horse when you've reached a certain standard.

Weekly, Biweekly, or Monthly Lessons?

Q I'm a city-dwelling horse lover and get most of my "horse contact" though books, magazines, and the Internet, instead of with the real thing. I know a lot of theory but next to nothing of the practical. I am moving soon to study and will have access to several riding schools, but my finances will be limited. I would like to know what kind of lessons I should take.

I know that one-on-one lessons are best, but I can afford only one a month. Would an hour group lesson every two weeks or a half-hour group lesson a week be better? How much can be done in half an hour, especially in a group? I've also thought of having a half-hour lesson the first week and an hour hack the second to practice what I did in the lesson. Would I just teach myself bad habits? Wouldn't it be better than having lessons with some 16-year-old who says "Just hit him harder!"?

A In an ideal world, you would have daily private lessons with a brilliant instructor. But in your circumstances, it's more realistic to think in terms of a single weekly lesson. It would still be best to have at least the first few lessons to yourself, because beginners really do need, and benefit from, the full attention of the instructor. You will probably pay more for a private lesson than for a group one, but for the first few months at least, you will truly get much more from those private sessions. Ideally, you would have at least 30 private sessions under your belt before you began taking group lessons, and when you did begin taking group lessons, the group would be small (three or four riders at most), riding at the same level.

The quality of the instruction should be your top priority. You'll learn more in one lesson with a good instructor than you would in 10 lessons with a poor one, and you'll learn more in a group lesson with a truly good teacher than you would in a private lesson with a poor one. Frequency matters, so if your only choices are the half-hour weekly group session and the hour-long session every other week, the weekly lesson probably is preferable.

This is why the idea of a half-hour lesson one week and an hour hack the second is, sadly, *not* a good idea for you right now. In a year or two, it may be a very good thing to do. Because your knowledge is largely theoretical at this point, you need time and experience (and a good instructor) to help you acquire riding skills and also to help you learn to monitor yourself.

It's important to avoid putting yourself into a situation where you'll be learning bad riding and bad habits of thinking about horses, because unlearning, or relearning, any skill (or way of thinking) is infinitely more difficult, and takes infinitely longer, than learning it properly from the very start. So if you find that the instructor at the nearest and most attractive riding school *is,* in fact, a 16-year-old who says "Just hit him harder!," say "Thank you" to the person who gave you the tour, and go and inspect another school.

More Lessons = More Confusion

Q I have been riding in a casual way, mostly trail rides, for a long time. As I became more interested in good riding, I decided to learn dressage and some jumping. I want to be a good rider and get it right.

I took a "package" of 10 dressage lessons with someone who said that she taught classical dressage, but after reading articles you have written on the subject of dressage, I realized that she was not telling the truth! Everything was all about the hands and the reins, and controlling the horse's legs with the reins. She used bungee cords to set the horses' heads. She never taught anything about body position at all.

I stopped those lessons after the fifth one (and couldn't get my money back) and I took some hunt seat lessons instead. She was a better instructor, but I really wanted to focus on dressage. I took two lessons with another dressage instructor who was just like the first one. Finally, I found someone near me who gives lessons sometimes and I have been taking dressage lessons with her for the last three years.

The problem is that I am not making the kind of progress I want to make! After four years of dressage lessons I should be getting reasonably good at lower-level stuff, I think. But I still can't really follow the horse's head movement, I can't sit the trot, sometimes I can't even sit the canter, and whenever my horse goes from trot to canter or canter to trot, I get thrown around in the saddle. I used to square dance a lot when I was younger and I played tennis when I was a kid, so I know that I am pretty well coordinated.

Also, you wrote that horses trained in dressage should get better looking. Well, mine haven't (I have three horses now; it's a long story!); they look just the same, even the one I have been riding for years. I have owned the others for one year and two years, but they haven't muscled up nicely; in fact they have developed muscles in the wrong places, mostly under their necks.

Please advise me. I spend a lot of money on lessons and clinics. I know how important it is to learn from a lot of people and I take all different kinds of clinics, probably 25 or 30 a year: natural horsemanship, dressage, and hunt seat, and so on. I am intelligent and college-educated and have nice horses and an outdoor arena to ride in at home. I always learn something, then I come home and try to apply what we did at the clinic, but after a day or two it begins to fall apart. I don't understand what I am doing wrong. What is it about me that won't let my riding improve? It seems that the more help I get, the more confused I get. Is it impossible for some people to learn to ride well? Am I just hopeless and should I give up? I love horses so much and I don't want to stop, but it seems like the more I do, the worse I get.

A You've obviously invested a lot of money and effort and you're right that you're not getting much of a payback in terms of improvement. First, let me commend your energy and your commitment! I don't think that you're hopeless and I don't think that you should give up. I think that you should try a different approach, because your problem isn't that you're doing things wrong, it's that you are trying to do too many things.

You're probably familiar with the expression "Don't work harder, work smarter" — that's what you need to do. You're doing too much, and you're getting thoroughly confused — all of you! Your body, your mind, your emotions, and your horses are all confused. It's time to back off a little bit, take a much-needed break, and regroup.

It is useful to learn from many people, or at least to expose yourself to the methods and ideas of many people, but this should happen *after* you have achieved good skills and good understanding. At that point, you'll have a solid foundation and you'll be proficient within one method or system. Then you'll be in a position to wander through the "information mall" by participating in many different clinics. When you have a solid foundation, you have a clear idea of what you want, where you want to go, what obstacles are in your way, and how you can get there in spite of them. When you know enough, you'll be able to attend a different clinic every weekend, if that's what you like to do, and you won't become confused because you'll be very selective about what you choose to incorporate into your own riding and training.

So choose one good system, find a good teacher, and learn that system thoroughly and well.

In addition to trying too many things at once, it sounds as though you don't really have a good foundation in any one system. With all your running from instructor to instructor and from clinic to clinic, you've accumulated a lot of bits and pieces and tips and tricks, but those aren't what you need.

You'll do yourself, your horses, and your ambitions a favor if you settle on one good teacher and learn one good system. Then add *one* good clinician — one whose philosophy and methods are compatible with those of your instructor — with whom you can work several times a year. You need to work with people you can trust, who will learn to know you and your horse over time. You and your horses need consistency, which is something you simply cannot get when you go from one instructor to another and one clinician to another.

It's hard to get a proper start if there aren't any good instructors in your area, because at first you need both quality time and quantity time. A good instructor will benefit you more than any number of clinics, but if you can't find one, you'll be better off working several times a year with one really good clinician. Don't worry that you'll miss something — you won't. Take the time to learn one thing really well so that it can be the foundation for all the rest of your learning. Then learn something else, and so on. This is the only way to get what you want.

Think of riding in terms of a language, which it is. If you want to learn another language, an intensive course is a good idea and total immersion is even better, because you won't really know the language until you can read it and write it and carry on a conversation in it. If you want to learn several languages, learn them one at a time, mastering each one before you move on to the next. Otherwise, you'll get nowhere, even if you try very hard. You can't become fluent in French and German simultaneously by learning a handful of French nouns and a handful of German verbs and trying to string them together as sentences. Not only will *you* be confused, you won't make sense to anyone else.

This is what's going on with you and your horses. You should be learning the same language together, but instead you're getting a German verb here, a French noun there, perhaps a few Italian prepositions. It doesn't add up to a clear language that you can speak fluently, so you can't make sentences or even phrases that make sense to your horses.

So choose one good system, find a good teacher, and learn that system thoroughly and well. This doesn't mean that you'll be locked into a single system forever. Once you've mastered the first one, you can begin to investigate others. Over the years, you'll be able to identify and claim useful, compatible bits and pieces of different systems. As you continue to learn, your preferred style of riding may change, but if you begin by learning a single complete, logical, progressive system from someone who can give you consistent information and help you progress over time, you'll find it very easy to learn another system.

Based on what you've said, I think that you will know when you've found the right system and the right instructor. If classical riding is your choice, congratulations — you're taking on the most complex and artistic form of riding, but also, in my opinion, the one that is ultimately the most rewarding. Be sure to find someone with whom you can work happily and who always puts the horse first. (Hint: Any true classical instructor does this — it's a fundamental part of the classical tradition!)

Trust your judgment, trust your own good sense, trust your horses, and trust your eye. Your observation that your horses aren't getting better looking is a very good one. You're right — if they were being properly trained and worked, they *would* be getting better looking. Never stop observing your horses and monitoring their development. We humans can become confused or distracted by grandiose claims or fancy equipment, but our horses cannot be fooled. By paying attention to their development over time (appearance, movement, and attitude), we can know whether our work is correct.

In your case, you may find it more practical to select just one of your horses — either the calmest, quietest one or the one with the most training — and work exclusively with that horse. Just for a few months, give your other horses a vacation. Working with (but not overworking) just one horse will help you become more attentive to that horse's needs, reactions, and development.

You're already working quite hard enough; you should relax a little. Select a single system and a good teacher, and narrow your focus for at least the next few years. Your riding, your understanding, and your horses will all benefit greatly from the change.

Old, Scared Lady Wants to Ride

Q I have "inherited" a wonderful 14-year-old Thoroughbred gelding. He's very calm and tolerates it when I make mistakes on him. It has been years since I rode on a regular basis, and I want to ride him correctly and comfortably, for his sake and mine. I can't afford riding lessons and live about an hour from the nearest stables. I don't want to ride dressage or anything of that sort; I just want to ride him for pleasure.

I am, however, terrified. Two years ago I was riding a friend's 4-year-old Arabian mare that decided she wanted to go home. (It's important to let you know she wasn't ridden nor exercised often! In fact, she was rarely taken out at all.) Well, this mare took off home with me on her back trying to slow her down. I panicked, she stumbled on some asphalt, and we went down. She rolled over me and got a few scratches, whereas I broke my collarbone, shoulder blade, and three ribs.

I want to ride for pleasure, I want to ride correctly, and I don't want to fall. I'm hoping you can tell me how to properly ride this fellow without bumping his poor back or falling off.

A Please don't feel that you're being picked on. What you are about to read is (oh, dear, you knew I was going to say this) for your own good. You *must* manage to get lessons from a good instructor. It will be less expensive and more convenient to get them now than to get them later, after a preventable accident.

Not all instructors are competition-oriented and not all are devoted to a specific discipline. Some instructors specialize in casual riders who just want to go out and enjoy themselves safely on horseback. The American Riding Instructors

Association (ARIA) certifies instructors in many specialties, and one of these is recreational riding, so you are obviously not the only rider in the world who wants to ride for fun. You still need an instructor, though, because whether your interest is competitive or recreational, your horse's needs must be met, and one of those needs is to have a reasonably well-balanced and coordinated rider with a reasonably stable seat and an understanding of the fundamentals of riding. Without that minimum level of accomplishment, you won't be able to ride in a way that will be comfortable or safe for you or your horse.

Imagine someone asking you, "Please tell me how to ride a bicycle. I don't want to ride in the Tour de France, I just want to have fun and be safe! I want to be able to stop and start and change directions and not wipe out on gravel and not get hit in traffic and not fall off, but I don't want *lessons*. Just tell me what to do and I'll teach myself."

Good lessons are not a luxury or an indulgence; they're essential to your enjoyment and to your safety.

Horses are far more complicated than bicycles. A bicycle stays where you put it and isn't constantly on the alert for Things That Are Scary. A bicycle won't buck or rear no matter how badly you adjust the seat or how tightly you grip the handlebars. Riding horses properly and well is a complicated matter. Unfortunately, it's not a skill you can acquire by just going out and doing it. You need someone to show, to tell, to explain, and to answer your questions, and you need to put in time practicing *correct* riding. No matter how many miles you log, if you are hanging off one side of the saddle or hanging on your horse's mouth, your horse will be miserable, and you will be unbalanced and ready to go flying off at the first stumble — and a stumble is very likely to happen under those circumstances. Riding for pleasure works only if the horse is a pleasure to ride, if the rider is a pleasure for the horse to carry, and if the whole experience is a comfortable one.

I know this sounds harsh, but I don't know any better way to say it: If you absolutely don't want to fall off a horse, never get *on* one. You can minimize your chances of falling by choosing a nice, quiet horse, and it sounds as though you've done just that. But any horse can trip or spook or become fed up with tack- or rider-caused pain. Your safety and security have to be protected in every possible way, and a steady horse is just one factor. Your balance, coordination, and physical fitness greatly affect your security in the saddle. These are things you can work on at home — yoga and tai chi are ideal, but any exercise program will help. Knowing how to fall without breaking body parts is useful and is something an instructor can help you learn. You also need to understand tack and equipment as well: Learn what fits, what doesn't, what's in good enough shape to be used, what should be replaced. You can learn a good deal of that on your own. But in the end, your safety comes down to your ability and confidence in the saddle, so please find someone to help you with your riding!

You may be able to "earn" some of your lessons by doing barn chores or by arranging an exchange of professional skills, but don't say, "I can't afford lessons" and leave it at that. Good lessons are not a luxury or an indulgence; they're essential to your enjoyment and to your safety. Once you've acquired the necessary skill base, you'll have more fun than you can even imagine right now. At that point, you'll be able to get by with an occasional lesson and with what you've learned and your own good sense. Your horse sounds wonderful, and it would be lovely to know that you were able to keep and enjoy him safely for many years to come.

Beginner, Intermediate, or Advanced?

Q I'm a 40-year-old adult beginner who started riding four years ago. I ride in a lesson once a week, all year-round, though I don't have my own horse yet (non-horsey husband, full-time job, 8-year-old daughter who is getting into horses too). Last week at my lesson I heard my instructor refer to my 16-year-old lesson partner and me as her "beginners." I don't really consider this girl a beginner like me; she's much braver for one thing! And she can jump a nice hunter round of four or five jumps cleanly (2'6"). I am wondering what criteria instructors use to classify a rider as a beginner or intermediate rider.

A I can't give you a specific, all-purpose answer, but I can give you some ideas on the subject and tell you what my own definitions are.

As you suspected, there are beginners and then there are *beginners*. A person taking her very first riding lesson is clearly a beginner, but so (usually) is a person beginning her second year of lessons.

Anyone who has ever run a commercial stable, whether renting hacks by the hour or leasing horses by the month or year, will tell you that people tend to misrepresent their riding ability. The less someone knows about horses and riding, the more likely that person is to overestimate her skill and experience. A beginner rider is very likely to describe herself as intermediate. The more someone knows about horses and riding, the more likely that person is to underestimate his or her ability, skill, and experience. Many Olympic-level riders, for instance, would describe themselves as intermediate rather than advanced. This isn't false modesty; it's a matter of knowledge and perspective. The more you know, the more you become aware of how much there is to know and how much more there is for you to learn.

Every instructor has individual criteria that can be very subjective. The higher the standards, the longer a rider will be a beginner; the lower the standards, the more rapidly a rider will lose beginner status. At the Spanish Riding School, a rider might achieve intermediate status only after several years of intensive daily work. At a children's summer camp in the United States, a beginner might be someone who had never been on a horse, an intermediate might have been on several trail rides, and an advanced rider might be able to get her horse to trot.

Instructors' definitions may also vary according to their specialty and according to their student's ambitions. The young girl you describe probably rides just

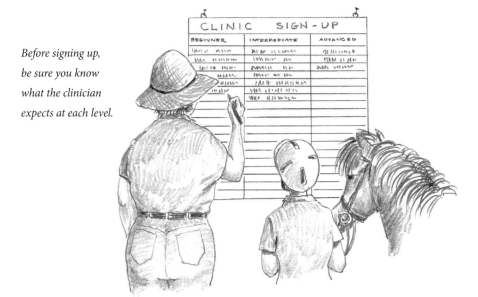

Before signing up, be sure you know what the clinician expects at each level.

as well as many much older people who have owned horses for years but who sit sloppily in their saddles and have no desire to improve their riding technique or their understanding of the sport. For these people, riding is an enjoyable way to wander through the woods and fields without making much effort. But for someone like your partner or yourself, who *are* making an effort to learn to ride correctly and well, being a beginner means just that: being at the beginning! You do intend to continue to learn and improve, after all.

When I have to divide riders into categories (beginners, intermediate, and advanced) at home or at clinics, my divisions look something like this:

Beginners are learning to follow the horse's movements, move with the horse, and not interfere with the horse. When they have achieved those things at walk, trot, and canter, they become intermediates.

Intermediates are learning to put a trained school horse through its paces and can ask correctly for walk, trot, canter, and halt. Depending on their interests and discipline, they may be able to jump courses of low jumps (say up to 3'6" or so) and some individual higher jumps, or they may be able to do First or Second Level dressage work. In either case, they can get from the horse what someone else has put into it in terms of training and conditioning. If they achieve all this and keep going (though intermediate is a very respectable category that not many riders achieve), they can work their way, eventually, to advanced.

Advanced riders can do all of the above, plus improve the horse's performance when he knows how to do something and teach the horse how to do more advanced things.

Visualize a pyramid! The rider pyramid is like any other skill pyramid (think tennis, think ballet, think figure skating), with masses of beginners at the bottom, a much smaller group of intermediates in the middle, and a very small group of truly advanced riders at the top.

"Beginner" isn't a bad word — it just means that you're at the beginning of something you mean to continue. You can have fun all the way, no matter how far you want to go or when you choose to stop.

CHAPTER 19

Going to Clinics

GOOD CLINICS CAN CREATE A SENSE OF COMMUNITY, provide a wonderful educational opportunity, and help riders and their horses attempt a new skill or take an existing skill to a new level. To get the most from any clinic experience, it's important that riders know something about the clinician — as well as something about themselves and their own values and standards. Sign up for clinics only with clinicians you *know* you like or who are highly recommended by your trusted instructor.

"Not Good Enough" for a Clinic?

Q I keep my horse at a wonderful boarding barn where there is a good instructor and a regular clinician who is simply marvelous. I have been riding for three years but just began riding dressage seriously a year ago. I could not be happier with my lessons and I also enjoy watching the clinics. The clinician is a wonderful teacher who explains things clearly and is always very kind to the horses and the riders.

I would love to ride in one of her clinics, but I am not ready to sign up because I know I am not good enough yet. I hope that in another year, if I work hard, I will be ready. My instructor is very sweet and encouraging and keeps telling me that I ought to ride in the next clinic, but I cannot bring myself to do this. I think I would feel out of place, but it's hard for me to explain this to my instructor.

A I understand your reluctance to sign up if you feel out of place, but I'm not sure why you are uncomfortable. I think you might misunderstand the whole idea of a clinic. Clinics, whether for riding, skating, or dancing, are designed to help you improve your knowledge, your understanding, and your skills. They are not competitions. You're not participating so that you can be judged; you're participating so that you can *learn* and so that you can get help and suggestions from an expert.

If your instructor feels that you would enjoy and benefit from riding in a clinic, by all means sign up and have a wonderful time.

Clinic Costs

Q I have been wondering about the cost of taking a lesson in a clinic. My instructor charges $30 for an hour of private instruction. The clinicians who come to my area seem to charge at least two or three times this much, and some of them charge each rider $300 or $400 for a weekend clinic (two group rides, one hour each, sometimes with five to ten riders in a group). Can this experience possibly be worth the price?

My instructor says that clinicians charge less at home than they do when they go somewhere else to teach. Why is this? At clinics, they don't have to use their own horses or maintain their arenas. Do farms just sponsor clinics to make money? I would love to participate in a clinic or two, but I am annoyed about the cost and would like to understand the reasons. Because you are a clinician, I'm sure you can tell me exactly why clinic lessons are so expensive! I don't mean to be rude, but I have been wondering about this for a long time.

A This is an excellent question, and I understand why you are wondering about clinic lesson prices.

Clinics are the way clinicians make their living, so the clinician has to be able to make a certain amount of money per clinic, whether it's a weekend session or a six-day intensive training program. You're right about the school horses and the arena, but consider this: A clinician who travels on Friday, teaches on Saturday and Sunday, and travels home again on Monday has put four days into that clinic but been paid for only two of them. And those four days away from home cost money — if the clinician has an active home farm, someone else has to be in charge there (and get paid). The horses still have to be fed and exercised, and the stalls mucked out. The arena still has to be watered and raked, and the barn aisles still have to be swept. Almost everything at a barn goes on whether the clinician is there or not. Lessons are the exception; with the clinician away, either they don't take place and the clinician loses that income, or someone else gives them and again, the clinician loses income.

Most clinicians don't get rich from clinics. A few at the top do quite well, making, as you say, $300 or $400 per rider for one weekend and working with very large groups of riders. Some who give "demonstration" clinics can collect $30,000 to $50,000 for a single weekend's work. But these are the exceptions, and they are invariably the "showmen," not teachers who work one-on-one with individual horse-and-rider combinations.

At most conventional clinics — the ones involving six to eight hours of individual lessons each day — the amount the clinician makes is necessarily limited. You may pay anywhere from $75 to $300 for your lesson, but not all of your money goes to the clinician. Clinic organizers usually add to the clinician's suggested lesson charges so that they can cover their expenses. Your $85 lesson check for example, may represent $75 for the clinician and $10 for the host barn.

This doesn't mean that the host barn is making a profit. It's not uncommon for a host barn to make nothing at all from a clinic. The organizers usually cover the clinician's travel expenses, food, and lodging, and there are other expenses, such as special-event insurance. While the clinic is in progress, the barn manager or owner is usually present to ensure that everything runs smoothly. Organizing a clinic requires work: Assigning stalls, checking Coggins tests, providing feed and bedding for incoming horses, grading and watering the arena, renting toilets, setting up concessions, and more. And someone has to answer all the questions — everything from "Does the clinician allow martingales?" to "My horse eats straw bedding; do you have shavings?" (or "My horse is allergic to shavings; do you have straw?").

Many barn owners host clinics not to make money but because they want to offer their boarders and other local riders the benefit of a particular clinician's ideas and insights. A good clinician benefits a host barn in many ways: providing publicity, bringing in potential students or boarders, and attracting local riders who have a particular interest in that clinician's ideas or methods.

Many experienced riders who are looking for a boarding or lesson barn ask "Do you hold regular clinics?" or "Who are your regular clinicians?" when they are comparing several local facilities. This is good information to have. Regular clinicians are likely to be people whose style and methods are compatible with those of the barn's regular instructors, so a potential client might choose, for example, a barn that has regular Centered Riding clinics or a barn that has regular jumping clinics with a specific clinician.

As for the issue of whether the clinic can be worth several hundred dollars for a weekend, especially if the riders are in groups, I think they can be worth that price, but you are wise to be careful with your money. Always *audit* before you ride. An individual's techniques, methods, philosophy, and personal style can make your lesson a wonderful experience or can leave you feeling that you never want to ride with that person again. If you audit a lesson or two and find that you dislike a particular clinician's style, then you know that for you, the clinic would not be worth the money. But if you decide that you would like to work with this person, you'll be able to sign up with confidence. Even if a clinician comes to your area only two or three times a year, it's still a good idea to attend your first clinic as an auditor.

Clinics for "the Rest of Us"

Q I ride mostly for pleasure and recreation, but I have always been interested in attending a clinic. For some reason I just feel there is something "special" about a clinic. In the last few years I have become more interested in dressage and eventing, and my husband has marked an arena for me at home and built me a few jumps. I will probably never compete, but I would still like to attend a clinic.

I live in an area that is not exactly full of big boarding stables. Most people who ride keep one or two horses on their own land, which is one reason we moved here. There are lots of trails and people are nice and not snooty, but without the big stables we don't have any clinics. When I see signs for clinics that I can't go to because they are so expensive and held several hours away, I feel wistful and frustrated.

Are there clinics for people like me who don't have a lot of money and don't care about showing? How do people organize a clinic? Do the clinicians just call the stables and tell them they are coming? How do you get in touch with clinicians? I don't want to drive for five hours to pay a lot for stabling and a hotel plus hundreds of dollars to ride for one hour, but I really want to attend a clinic. Does anybody give clinics for "the rest of us"?

A I had to smile at the idea that clinicians call stables and announce that they're going to come and teach there — I could just hear my colleagues shouting "I only *wish!*" Usually it's the other way around. The stable manager or owner contacts the clinician about scheduling and availability, and the conversation goes on from there. Or the stable manager might have heard that the clinician is good and will ask for more information about his or her teaching methods, subjects, and style. And it's always a good idea to talk to other people who have ridden with the clinician.

As for whether there are clinics for "the rest of us" — of course there are! Some clinicians, like some riders, are strongly show-oriented. But many are quite happy to work with riders who just want to improve their riding for the sake of improving their riding. I teach a lot of clinics like this and I enjoy the recreational riders just as much as I do the upper-level dressage and eventing riders. I'm interested in teaching *anyone* who wants to improve in any way: riding skills, training skills, communication with horses, you name it. Many other clinicians feel the same way.

If your area is full of people who keep a few horses on a few acres, why not talk to as many of them as you can about your clinic idea? It's quite likely that some of these riders would like to attend a clinic, too. From a practical standpoint, if you can find seven other people who want to take two lessons each, and you take two lessons yourself, you will fill a two-day, eight-lessons-per-day clinic.

The best clinics provide information, education, and a positive experience.

When you are signing up riders, be sure to give them an accurate idea of the cost. Most clinicians charge a daily fee plus expenses, so don't just compare their fees! A nearby clinician with a higher daily fee might actually prove to be *less* expensive than a faraway clinician with a lower daily fee and a more expensive plane ticket. That said, there are ways to reduce the cost of bringing in a clinician from a distance. Many of us are willing to teach multiple clinics in a certain area or along a certain route, and it's often possible for organizers of separate clinics to share the travel expenses of a single clinician.

Another consideration is the cost of the care and feeding of the clinician. If the clinician wants to stay in a hotel or B&B and eat at restaurants, it will cost more than if s/he stays at your home and eats with your family or with the clinic riders. Some clinicians are happy to spend extra time with the riders, answering questions and sharing meals. Others want to arrive just before the first lesson and return to their hotel as soon as the last lesson ends.

Before you start your financial planning, however, find out what the riders in your area would enjoy and figure out which clinician or clinicians seem most appropriate. Think about what you'll be getting for your money — cost and quality aren't the same thing. Information, education, new ways of looking at what you're doing, and a positive experience? Those are worth a lot. A chance to watch someone else do something with or to your horse, without getting the kind of help that will allow you to understand the process or repeat the results? That's not worth anything at all. Look for the very best clinician you can possibly afford, because quality *must* be your first priority.

As for facilities, you do not have to have a fancy stable, miles of white fencing, or an arena with mirrors on the walls. I've taught jumping clinics in a field with five jumps, and dressage clinics in not-quite-flat fields from which the jumps had been removed the night before. Depending on where you live and what your weather is like, and whether it's predictable at certain times of year, you may not even need an indoor or covered arena. If you can find any large arena (indoor, covered, or outdoor) with reasonably good footing, you've got a venue.

You'll have to arrange water and shade for participants (human and equine) and you may need to find some seating for spectators, but people who really want a clinic can be very resourceful, from bringing their own marquees and their own folding chairs, to tying horses to trailers (pretend it's a show), to organizing a potluck lunch for the entire group (don't forget tables).

One final thought: Clinics don't have to be about riding. If you want to appeal to a lot of riders in different disciplines without breaking the bank, I suggest that you offer just a few actual riding clinics, so that riders have time to recover financially! That doesn't mean that you can't offer *other* sorts of clinics, though. Bring in someone to teach riding-related skills. Sponsor a group class in body awareness such as the Feldenkrais Method or Alexander Technique, or a few yoga or tai chi lessons, or an introduction to one of the martial arts. Most riders could benefit immensely from learning how to improve their posture and balance and breathing when they are *off* the horse, and it will have a wonderful effect on their riding.

Another idea is to organize a clinic on saddle fitting; that's information that *all* riders need. Or bring in an equine dentist to discuss equine mouths and teeth and let that lead into a discussion of bits and bitting. I'm sure you can think of other topics. Expand your definition of "clinic" — a clinic can be whatever you want it to be!

If you take your time, find the right clinician, and organize it carefully, it will be lots of fun and a great learning experience.

Clinician's Comment on Riding Corners

 I haven't been able to find a good local instructor, so I go to as many clinics as I can and get lessons whenever a good clinician comes to the area. The clinician who came last month was a well-known trainer with a good reputation, but I was very unhappy with my lesson and with something he said. I want you to tell me if I am right to be upset or if I misunderstood something!

Here is the situation. My horse is a 12-year-old Thoroughbred, and we have been working for about a year on the U.S. Dressage Federation (USDF) First Level tests. I don't show, but I care very much about doing dressage and I always ride as well as I can at every clinic. According to the clinicians I rode with a couple of years ago, we did good Training Level work. After a year of hard work, I thought I was doing good First Level work. When I asked this man when he thought we would be ready to move up to Second Level, however, he said, "You won't be ready for Second Level until you learn how to ride corners." The rider was already in the ring for the next lesson, so I couldn't ask him to explain.

My feelings were very hurt. I thought I was riding well and my horse was doing well. Why would he say something so unkind? And what do you think he meant by that? Was he just trying to make me feel bad or did he truly think that I was such a horrible rider that I couldn't even ride around a corner? Dressage means so much to me, and I'm afraid that I am hopeless because I obviously can't even do something as elementary as ride around a corner. Maybe I should just give up.

A   Take a deep breath and try not to worry, even when I tell you that what he said was right. Think about it. He may not have said it constructively or even very nicely, but he was right.

The quote was: "You won't be ready for Second Level until you learn how to ride corners." I can't argue with that. Try to take it less personally — change the sentence to "A rider isn't ready for Second Level until she learns how to ride corners." Make the *riding*, not your personal self, the subject of the sentence.

Now that you've done that, think about the phrase "how to ride corners." It's not riding "around" a corner, which anybody can do even on a first pony ride. The horse goes to the end of the wall, turns when he runs out of wall, and goes down the next wall. Just because the rider stays on, does that mean that she rode a corner? Not at all. It means that the pony meandered around a corner, and the rider went with him.

"Riding a corner" means quite a lot. It's something that beginner riders can't do, because it requires too many skills and too much knowledge and far too much coordination! A correct corner isn't trivial. To ride one, you must be able to:

- Keep your horse moving forward evenly, with no change of pace through the turn
- Keep your horse bent correctly; that is, flexed ("in position"), then flexed and bent going into the corner, then flexed and bent and turning smoothly and evenly *through* the corner
- Reverse the process as you leave the corner, with your horse first turning, then bending, and finally just flexed ("in position") as you return to your straight line

While your horse is stepping forward evenly and rhythmically and moving from position to bend to turn to bend to position, *you* should be riding every step, very quietly adjusting your own position by shifting the position of your hips and shoulders to parallel the positions of your horse's hips and shoulders, looking around your turn, feeling every movement of the horse and encouraging him to step through with the inside hind leg and to reach into the bridle by stretching the outside of his neck (a stretch that your position will, of course, allow).

Riding a corner correctly means having the ability to deal with pace, rhythm, position, balance, turns, and straight lines, and dealing with them smoothly and all at once. *A well-ridden corner is the beginning of collection.* That, I suspect, is what your clinician meant when he said "You won't be ready for Second Level until you learn how to ride corners."

Please don't be insulted or give up. You're obviously not hopeless and you weren't being criticized unfairly or picked on; you were being treated like a serious rider and reminded of something that you need to know, and need to be able to do consistently, if you're going to make the shift from First to Second Level. Take it as a compliment to your progress and determination, and keep on riding and learning. Above all, keep on enjoying it.

Should the Clinician Ride Your Horse?

Q What is the right thing to do if the clinician insists on riding your horse and you don't want him to? I made the mistake of not auditing a clinic with someone before riding with him and was faced with a very awkward and embarrassing situation. About halfway through my lesson, when I had already come to the conclusion that this man was not someone I ever wanted to ride with again, he wanted to get on my horse. My mare is 17 years old and a little stiff in her hocks; usually she works out of it after half an hour, but we had trailered for three hours that morning to get to the clinic (another mistake, I should have planned to arrive the night before), and she was much stiffer than usual.

The clinician was working on shoulder-in with us (he had all the riders work on exactly the same thing, so we all got more or less the same lesson), and my mare was not supple enough to do it the way he wanted her to. I knew what he wanted and tried to do it, but she just didn't have it that day. She is a sweet mare, always tries hard, and never tries to pull any tricks or avoid work, so I tried to ignore his comments about how I needed to get tough with her and make her obey. We did what I really believe was the best shoulder-in she could do that day, but he called us into the center and said, "Get off that horse. I'm going to have to show you since you're obviously not capable of understanding what I'm saying."

I did not want him on my horse, but I didn't want to be rude, so I said, "Please, let me try it again." He became very angry and yelled at me, shouting that I would never be a rider, and that I could either get off and give him my horse, or I could leave. I was shocked and embarrassed, but I had seen him ride two other horses in earlier lessons, and he was quite rough with them, really almost brutal, so I chose to leave. This ended my lesson 20 minutes early. While I was taking off my mare's tack and putting her into her stall, I could hear his loud voice making comments to the other riders and auditors about "spoiled amateurs and their pet horses."

I didn't stay to watch the rest of the lessons, just packed up and went home. Could I have handled that situation better? Is it "clinic etiquette" that riders have to let the clinician ride their horses? I feel stupid for wasting my money, and even more stupid for not knowing what to do.

A The answer to both of your questions is "No." Riders do *not* have to let clinicians ride their horses, and I think that you handled a difficult situation very well indeed.

Some clinicians never get on the riders' horses; some insist on riding every horse; some will rarely get on a rider's horse, and when they do, it's just for a moment, usually to get a more accurate feel for what the horse is doing.

If you've never had the opportunity to watch a particular clinician at work (teaching, riding, or both), you may have no way of knowing whether you should allow that person to ride your horse. In this case, you were able to form your own conclusions about the clinician's riding and his attitude toward horses during the course of the clinic, and you did exactly the right thing.

Whenever a clinician asks to get on your horse to do something (or, for that matter, asks *you* to do something with your horse), you need to ask yourself, "Will this be good for my horse?" If you would be honored and thrilled to have your horse benefit from the clinician's kind attitude and soft, subtle techniques, then your answer will be "Yes, please." If you are dubious about the clinician's attitude or riding skills, or if, as in your case, you are horrified by the clinician's behavior, you should say no.

After all, what's the worst that can happen if you say no? As you discovered, you may not get your full lesson. Given this clinician's approach to teaching, riders, and horses, I'd say that having less time with this person was probably a good thing.

You have to think about your horse's soundness and happiness and about your own long-term training and riding goals.

You also lost some money, and I'm sure that you could have found at least 50 better uses for it, but consider this. The money you spend on any clinic is gone, whether you had a good, bad, or mediocre experience. Oddly enough, if you feel that you wasted your money and will absolutely not ride with this person ever again, this is only a bad outcome, not the *worst* outcome.

The worst outcome leaves you feeling sick to your stomach because, against your better judgment, you did something wrong to your horse or allowed someone else to do something wrong to your horse. Leaving a bad lesson is sometimes the only thing you can do. Don't look at it as throwing away money — in the long term, staying in a lesson that causes your horse to lose confidence in you and sets your training back several months is much more costly and can make you angry and sick. It isn't worth it.

Never forget that after the clinician goes down the road, you will still be working with your horse. You have to think about your horse's soundness and happiness and about your own long-term training and riding goals, not about what would make a clinician happy in the short term. This incident reflects badly on the clinician, but it reflects very well on you — in spite of pressure and embarrassment, you did the right thing and protected your horse. This means that you know something that the clinician will probably never understand: the meaning of true horsemanship.

Learning from Watching

Q I don't have enough money to ride in a lot of clinics, but I try to watch as many as I can and take notes. My problem is that I'm not always sure what I'm seeing at a clinic. Sometimes it seems that the clinician is saying one thing and doing something completely different. I saw this at a dressage clinic where every other word in the advertising was "classical" or "lightness," but the clinician just made everyone pump with their back and yank on the reins until the horses put their heads practically between their front legs and the riders had sore hands afterward.

At a "natural horsemanship" clinic, the clinician talked and talked about kindness and gentleness and communication, but all he did was chase horses around in deep sand until they were almost too tired to stand up. Neither one of these clinics was cheap, by the way!

The last clinic I went to was better, but it wasn't great. Two friends (less experienced riders than I am) who came with me to all three couldn't understand why I thought the first two were awful and the third one was just okay. I tried to explain, but what it came down to was really my *feeling* that I didn't like what was going on and that it wasn't good teaching or training.

I would like to know — not just inside myself, but truly know so that I can explain it to other people — what to watch for at a clinic, what's a good sign, what's a bad sign, and basically how to tell a good clinician from a bad one.

A You've obviously got a good sense of what really matters: not what people say to other people but what effect their actions have on the horses.

The horse world is full of people who can talk the talk just fine. They know which words to use and as long as they use them by the (manure) bucketful, many people are fooled by the words and don't look at the substance that may or may not exist behind them. The solution is simple: Learn everything you can and always check it with the *horse*. The horse is the ultimate authority on what works and what doesn't and whether certain techniques are suitable or not.

Horses care whether their trainers make sense to them and are kind; they don't care whether their trainers are good-looking or famous or wealthy. People, however, often care very much whether the trainers and clinicians they choose are good-looking or famous or wealthy, and quite often they don't even think about whether those trainers make any sense to the horses or whether they are kind. Some trainers, as you've found out, make a big show of talking about kindness, but their actions and the horses' reactions tell a very different story.

When you're at a clinic, don't leave your judgment at home. Watch and listen and learn, and if a trainer's "audio" doesn't match his "video," believe the video. So no matter what you *hear*, keep watching the horses and listening to them too. It's clear that you are already listening to the horses, whether you know it or not — good for you!

Here are some signs of a good clinic or lesson:

The horses and riders are comfortable. As the clinic progresses, the riders become more relaxed, quieter with their aids, and more focused on their horses; the horses relax and begin to move better.

The clinician's audio and video match. The riders and the audience receive clear and accurate explanations describing exactly what is happening with each horse and rider, and how and why each improvement is being made.

You can take the information home. When you try those things with your own horse, you see him become happier, more relaxed, more comfortable, and able to perform better.

Warning signs of a bad or dangerous clinic or lesson:

The clinician is in a hurry. Training a horse takes time. A trainer who wants to improve the *horse* will take things slowly and gently; you may sit in utter boredom (or, if you know a great deal about horses, in utter fascination) while the trainer carefully teaches the horse what is expected. A trainer who is more interested in impressing the crowd will move along quickly, make a fuss, and often use harsh tactics and/or harsh equipment to create the effect he wants.

The clinician uses too much (or wrong) equipment. Equipment that is designed to keep the horse safe and comfortable, like a proper longeing cavesson, a long enough longeing tape, and a longe whip, is one thing, but too much equipment or the wrong kind of equipment is a bad sign. Look for a simple saddle that fits the horse correctly, a simple bit that fits the horse comfortably, and a simple bridle that keeps the bit in the horse's mouth without tying his mouth shut.

Simple equipment is designed for communication and comfort; yes, it can be misused, but it's not necessarily a sign of trouble ahead. If simple equipment is used unsuitably, be wary. If you see extra ropes, pressure halters, twitches, auxiliary reins such as draw reins, inappropriate or severe bits, or tack that doesn't fit or suit the horse, be very wary. If the trainer or clinician doesn't seem to be aware of the effects of equipment fit and equipment adjustment, be extremely wary.

Some people make riding and training complicated through ignorance. If one trainer says "A longe whip is kind; a rope is nasty" while another one says "A rope is kind; a longe whip is cruel," but both of them use the items to send the horse out and away in the round pen, you can probably safely assume that the first one doesn't know how to handle a rope and the second one doesn't know how to handle a longe whip. It's natural for people, even professionals, to fear and criticize what they don't understand. If they understand the equipment and use it well, you can learn from them. If they don't, they serve as bad examples, and you can still learn something.

A longe whip serves to make the trainer's arm longer and is used to signal the horse. A rope, used by a Western trainer in the same context, is just the piece of equipment that he uses to make *his* arm longer. The longe whip isn't for beating the horse, and the rope isn't for beating the horse.

If someone uses either of those items to scare or punish the horse, then that person is misusing those items, but the whip and rope are not to blame. A bad trainer can scare or punish a horse with a bare hand, a toy bunny, or an oven mitt. It's the trainer's intention and actions that determine whether tools are employed for communication or for abuse. You'll need to watch closely, because a horse that's being "sent away" with a longe whip may be quite happy because he understands the message and knows what he's supposed to do, while a horse that's

At a good clinic, both horse and rider should be comfortable and relaxed enough to learn.

being held tightly while someone rubs him forcefully between the eyes or pats him very loudly on the neck is a horse that is frightened and/or resigned, *not* a horse that is comfortable or pleased.

The clinician makes wrong assumptions and displays an adversarial attitude. The goal of any trainer, instructor, or clinician should be to *educate* a horse, a rider, or a horse-and-rider combination. Education is teaching, and teaching *cannot* involve abuse or wrong assumptions or an adversarial attitude toward the student, whether that student is human or equine. The student must be given the benefit of the doubt, not just once but over and over again, especially if the student is a horse. If a trainer "explains" that horses are sneaky and deceitful and spend all their time and energy trying to outmaneuver humans so that they can win a power struggle, then you are unlikely to hear anything helpful at that lesson or clinic, because that person has absolutely no idea how horses' minds work.

An adversarial attitude often goes along with the above-mentioned assumptions. But it's complicated by the fact that a trainer can be extremely adversarial while smiling at the audience, patting the horse, and talking about kindness. This is where you must become a keen observer, watching the horse and its reactions while developing your own judgment.

Don't regard any of the clinics you attended as a waste of your money. You may not have gained good, useful, educational clinic experience, but you found something just as valuable: support for your critical sense, and a clear idea of what you do not want and will not accept for yourself or your horse. Because you were auditing, you learned all of that without putting your horse in harm's way.

I hope that you will continue to audit clinics. Eventually you'll find a clinician who makes you feel that *you* need to be in that ring with your horse, and then you'll be ready to sign up the next time that person comes to town. In the meantime, auditing can let you learn what clinicians are like (as opposed to learning what their advertising is like) without hurting yourself, your horse, your bank account, or your principles.

If you can possibly manage it, always audit before you ride with someone! If you *know* that a clinician is absolutely wonderful, then go ahead and ride without auditing, but no good clinician will be angry or offended if you choose to audit first.

CHAPTER 20

Going to Competitions

COMPETITION SHOULDN'T BE REGARDED as the be-all and end-all of riding, but horse shows can be enjoyable for riders who approach the experience in the right spirit. It's no coincidence that the riders who have the most fun at horse shows are always those who are most relaxed and best prepared. Many riders have strong feelings about what they would do if they were in charge of a competition. Organizing and running a horse show is an educational experience that is invariably challenging.

I Want to Show, but I'm Terrified

Q I'm 39 and I've waited my whole life to own my first horse. Now that I have him, I want to take him to shows. Competing in horse shows has always been my second biggest dream, right after owning a horse. This summer I went to three shows and I was a total disaster. The minute we get to the show grounds, I'm frightened, I feel lightheaded, and I have cold sweat dripping down my back. I can't breathe, I get stiff, and I feel that I can't ride at all. I'm scared of everything, including falling off (I did fall off at the second show, but at least it wasn't in the show arena).

The problem is definitely me. My instructor is great, and a lot of her other students did well at these shows, so I know it's not her. The students help each other, and my instructor helps all of us, so I'm not alone, but I feel incompetent and uncomfortable and I know I ride badly. My horse is a sweetheart at home, and it upsets me to know that I make him nervous and edgy at shows because I'm such a terrified mess. I also know that I'm supposed to be enjoying myself, but I just can't! I still want to show, I'm not ready to give up, but I'm so sad and disappointed that my dream is a failure.

A I don't think that your dream is a failure, and I don't think that *you* are a failure, but I do think that you are expecting far too much of yourself. You've participated in exactly three competitions in your life — that's not enough to make you feel relaxed and comfortable with the experience. You wouldn't treat a horse this way! If you took a completely inexperienced horse to his first few competitions, where every sight and sound was unfamiliar, and he became nervous and agitated, you wouldn't be angry or frustrated. You would realize that he needed time to become familiar with and comfortable in this very different environment, and you would do everything in your power to help him learn to *enjoy* that environment. That's exactly what you need to do for yourself.

Start now to act and think in a way that will help make next summer's competitions more enjoyable for you.

First, prepare! You and your horse should both be able to do, easily and without thinking, whatever you'll be expected to do in competition.

Second, check all possible sources of physical discomfort. Ride in your show clothing at home and notice how it affects you. Feeling uncomfortable and riding badly at shows isn't always a matter of psychology and nerves; it can be purely physical, caused by your reactions to unfamiliar, uncomfortable, restrictive clothing. Too-tight breeches and/or boots can make you miserable and cause your balance, relaxation, and position to deteriorate badly, so be sure that you're at ease in your show clothing before you blame yourself.

At the show, sign up for easy classes, not challenging ones. Both you and your horse should be doing things that you do comfortably and well at home. The show ring is not the place to begin schooling at a higher level; it's a place to *show* how well and comfortably you and your horse can perform at your *current* level. If you are learning to jump 3'6" courses at home, good for you — but at the show, sign up for classes where the jumps are 3' or even 2'9". The difficulty level will be increased by the unfamiliarity of the venue, the jumps, the crowds, the loudspeakers, and the presence of a judge. Similarly, if you're schooling First Level Test 4 at home, sign up for First Level Test 1 or 2, or even for Training Level tests. You need to be completely at ease with the task itself, so that you can focus on keeping your horse happy and enjoying the day.

Prepare in other ways too. Try to get some sleep the night before the show. At the show, eat sensibly — bring your own sandwiches, vegetables, and fruit so that you can avoid the high-grease, high-salt food that's generally sold on the show grounds. The wrong food can upset your stomach, but you need to eat and drink because low blood sugar can make you feel dizzy and faint, as can dehydration. Take care of yourself so that you can take care of your horse.

Put a smile on your face, breathe, and pay positive attention to your horse. By helping him enjoy the experience, you'll help yourself enjoy it too. Pay attention to your fellow students (and other riders too) and congratulate them on their good efforts. Keep smiling, stay positive, and you'll discover how helpful other people's positive outlook and actions can be. When it's your turn to go into the ring, your fellow students will be there for you.

Getting Help at Shows

Q I really need help when I go to shows because I get so nervous and tense and there's so much to do. My husband used to help me, but he won't come with me anymore because we just fight all weekend. My daughter helped me at one show, but she got mad at me for the same reason. I know that being nervous and tense makes me sound angry, but I'm just trying to stay totally focused on my riding. I don't want to have to explain things, so if I ask someone to do something, and they don't do it right or they ask questions about how to do it, I just repeat what I said or say, "Oh, forget it." I never mean to sound unkind or sharp, but I guess I do. A friend has offered to come to shows with me, but I'm worried that I'll make her angry too. I don't think I can show without someone to help out, but how do I get that person to understand what to do and why I don't want to hear a lot of questions?

A It would be easy to say, "Just relax and have fun; it's only a show," but I don't think that would help you much. So, here are my suggestions:

Prepare yourself for the show ahead of time so that you feel more organized and more competent to cope with whatever happens. Feeling more competent will make you feel more confident.

Prepare your helper before the show: Walk her through the tasks you need help with, show her the equipment you use, and make sure she's familiar with everything she will be handling (braiding equipment, rub rags, and fly spray, for instance).

Don't assume that your helper will automatically know exactly what you need and want, even if she shows in the same discipline or at a higher level than you do. If she does compete, she probably has her own routine based on what she and her horse need, which may not correspond to what you and your horse need.

If she doesn't compete, she may have no idea what you need or what kind of time will be involved in helping you. If you want her undivided attention from the time you load the trailer at home to the time you return, *tell her.* Otherwise, she may assume that she'll help a little here and there, watch the show, meet you at the stabling area when the show is over, and go home with you.

Describe exactly what your plans are; it's not overkill to discuss the day minute by minute. Otherwise, she may stay with you when you don't need her, then take the wrong moment to visit the concession stand or the toilet. If you are scheduled to ride at 10:00 a.m. and you plan to groom and braid at 9:00 and then tack up and warm up for half an hour before your test, tell your helper what you need her to do in what order and at what times.

Explain that you'll need her to help with the grooming and braiding, that you'd like help with tacking up, that she'll need to stay with the horse while you change your clothes and visit the toilet, that you'd like her to watch you (or not) in warm-up, and that you'd like her to meet you at the end of your warm-up with a rub rag in hand to give your boots a last once-over before you enter the arena.

A good helper can keep you hydrated by bringing you water at every opportunity.

Don't forget to tell your helper to be prepared for both rain (raincoat, waterproof boots, a towel) and for intense sun (sun hat, sunglasses, sunblock, bottles of frozen water), as well as for insects. She should wear comfortable clothing that allows her to move quickly if she needs to, and sturdy shoes that protect her feet. Both of you should wear watches synchronized to the show clock.

Give her copies of the tests, in case you want to be reminded at some point. In fact, keep copies in your towing vehicle so that she can quiz you on the tests while you drive. Alternatively, if your idea of preparation is to *think* each test through in detail, warn your helper that you don't want to chat or listen to music while driving to the event. It's a useful way to get the day off to a good start, without hurting anyone's feelings.

The more complete and detailed the discussion before the show, the fewer misunderstandings you will have at the show. There will be fewer reasons for you to become nervous and tense, your helper will feel more useful, and your experience will be more positive. At some point during your discussion, be sure to warn her that when you're at a competition, your focus and your nervousness combine to make you sound curt, brusque, even angry. Tell her that both your husband and your daughter have experienced this, and that it's likely that she will, too. Finally, agree that you will do your best to remain calm and pleasant and that she will not take it personally if you seem impatient and rude. Don't let her *discover* your "show persona" — warn her about it in advance.

I'm Never in the Ribbons — Why?

Q Last year I took my horse to four shows. We didn't place in any classes, but I thought that it was probably because he was green and wanted to look at everything. This year he is much calmer, and I have taken him to six shows, where I think I've done some good riding. These are not big shows with top-level competitors; they are local or area shows where all the competitors come from boarding stables or are like me and keep their horses on five acres at home.

I need to know what I'm doing wrong. Is it me, is it my horse, is it my clothes or tack? Why don't the judges ever place us? I don't have a particularly fancy horse and I'm not the best rider in the world, but I've ridden for a long time and I ought to be able to get ribbons at local shows.

A I don't have enough information to make specific suggestions about your riding or training, and I know how hard it can be to analyze yourself when your horse lives on your own property and you do most of your riding and schooling alone. But I can offer two suggestions:

1. You probably know the riders who *are* winning the ribbons in these shows. Ask them where they take lessons and then schedule a few lessons with one of their instructors. If all or most of the winning riders have the same instructor, you'll know exactly where to go for your lessons.

2. If you don't win a ribbon at the next show, talk to the judge. Judges aren't unapproachable; in fact, most of them are very happy to talk with you if you approach them nicely at a moment when they aren't busy. You might say, "Hi, I'm the rider of the gray gelding in classes 4, 5, 7, and 9, and I've been trying to figure out why we don't do better at these shows. It would help me if I could understand why my horse and I are always out of the ribbons. Would you mind telling me what we need to change and what I should be focusing on when I school?" This kind of approach generally works very well, and you should be able to get the information you need.

Interpreting Dressage Scores

Q With show season about to begin, I am already worried about my dressage scores. Last year I went to 10 shows and saved all my tests (I ride at

Training Level) and planned to study them over the winter so that I would know what to work on. When I started reading them again I realized that I didn't really understand what the judges were talking about!

Part of the problem is that it's hard to remember my rides after I finish them and compare them with the test later. But I thought some rides were really good in parts where the judges didn't. My score totals went up and down, and my first show scores were better than my last ones, which is very upsetting. Help!

How can I know what the scores mean so I can do better this year? I want to improve, but I'm not sure I even understand the number scores. If I get a 6 on a circle from one judge and a 5 from another at the next show, what happened and what am I doing wrong? I want to understand.

A Test scores aren't all that mysterious, although comments can be, especially if the scribe's handwriting is less than clear. You're right to save your tests — they're very useful. Obviously not all judges will agree on everything, and equally obviously, you and your horse will have good days and less good days, brilliant moments and less brilliant moments. But if you go to 10 shows, you'll have 10 or 20 tests by the end of the season and you can learn a lot by reviewing and comparing the scores for the movements and, perhaps more important, the various judges' comments.

The number scores are fairly simple: Tests are divided into movements, and each movement is marked between 0 and 10. Every test sheet has the list and definitions of the marks.

In theory, your scores will range from 0 to 10. In practice, especially at the lower levels and at schooling shows, you're far more likely to receive scores in a more limited range; from 3 to 8, for example. I've been at shows where the range appeared to be even narrower, with no scores below 4 or higher than 7. This can happen because the judge is insecure and wants to stay in a "safe" range. Some judges always mark high, especially at schooling shows where they want to encourage beginning dressage riders. Other judges typically mark low. A change in your test score doesn't necessarily indicate a change in your riding. This is why it's important to study both your number scores and the comments on your test.

Here's a quick explanation of what the marks mean.

A score of 10 is a rare sight, even though it doesn't mean "perfect" as some riders (and judges) seem to believe. It means "excellent," and if you do see one awarded, it's likely to be for an outstandingly good entry and halt.

A score of 9 indicates that you and your horse performed extremely well indeed. It is also comparatively rare.

A score of 8 is often the top mark awarded. An 8 on a movement indicates that your horse's engagement, energy level, outline, and obedience were entirely appropriate for the level of competition, and that you demonstrated not just quality but also accuracy (making your transitions precisely at the letter, for example).

A score of 7 is a good mark, and you'll need to pay close attention to see just why a judge marks a 7 instead of an 8. If the movement were performed with just a little bit less accuracy (making your transition just before or just after the letter, for example) or there was a brief moment in which the horse hurried or got above or behind the bit, a score of 8 would drop to 7.

A score of 6 means that your horse was obedient and executed the movement reasonably well, making the required transitions, performing the required gait, and going steadily from letter to letter, but there was nothing outstanding about his performance.

A score of 5 indicates that your horse did what he was supposed to do, and was probably obedient, but may have been above the bit, on the forehand, or lacking in energy.

A score of 4 reflects something noticeably wrong with the execution. Your horse might have bent the wrong way on a circle, been very late or very early with a transition, or thrown up his head and made a rough transition. Other possibilities could be a complete lack of energy or an inverted silhouette, with a high head, dropped back, and trailing hindquarters.

A score of 3 shows serious trouble with a movement. For example, if the horse performed a late transition as above, but also showed marked resistance, the score would drop from 4 to 3. A very disobedient horse, a very resistant horse, or a very stiff horse would tend to get a good many 3s.

A score of 2 is rare, and if you receive one anywhere on a test, you'll know why!

DRESSAGE SCORES	
10	Excellent
9	Very Good
8	Good
7	Fairly Good
6	Satisfactory
5	Sufficient
4	Insufficient
3	Fairly Bad
2	Bad
1	Very Bad
0	Not Performed

If your horse bucked, reared, or shied dramatically across the arena, you have probably found the source of that 2.

A score of 1 is another unusual mark that you'll tend to remember because it means that something happened that was even worse than whatever got you the 2! If your horse bucked halfway around a circle or shied across the diagonal or otherwise showed great disobedience and used up most of the movement, you might well find a 1 on your test.

A score of 0 means that the movement wasn't performed at all. Either there was a severe problem with the horse or it was entirely the rider's fault. Even the most unbalanced, resistant, counter-bent, inverted, bucking horse can manage a 2 on a circle, but if he fails to complete any sort of a circle at all, that would be a "movement not performed."

Another common cause of movements not being performed is a rider memory blip! If you simply *forget* to perform the indicated movement, you'll get a 0, but don't take the score as a comment on your riding or your horse's behavior or training. Some judges will ring the bell for an "error of course" if a movement is left out, whereas others will simply mark it 0 and keep going.

Most low-level tests show a lot of 5s, because judges feel more comfortable working in the middle of the range and because many tests *are* midrange; that is, average and acceptable. It's also very common for judges to go easy on beginning competitors so that they will enjoy competing and feel encouraged to go on competing. This can be nice, but it can also backfire. Riders who earn all 5s for their first few shows and then begin to see 4s instead, and riders who receive 5s at first and then *more* 5s after months of practice, can be very upset and disappointed and wonder what they are doing wrong.

There are two factors involved here. One is the wide range of quality that many judges consider to be represented by 5, and the other is the kindness of judges who don't want to give discouraging 4s. The use of 5 as a sort of catchall "middle" mark can cause confusion. The rider who deserves a 4 but is given a 5 "to encourage her" will probably not understand that the 5 she gets four months later on the same (and clearly improved) movement is now an "honest 5" or a "5 that's very close to a 6" instead of a "5 that really should have been a 4."

Judging is hard work. If you get a chance to scribe for a judge at a show, take it — you'll learn a lot about the complexities and difficulties of judging. You'll also learn that most judges hope to give good marks. Don't worry that the judge wants to "catch you" in order to lower your mark. Most judges say, "Oh, no!"

not "Hurrah!" when a 7 movement suddenly turns into a 6 or a 5 because of a moment of stiffness or inattention.

Don't compare your *overall scores* from test to test and show to show. Some judges score consistently higher, some lower, and if you try to train according to what you think you understand from comparing one test score with another, you'll only be frustrated. Even the same judge may score differently on different days — more generously at a schooling show, perhaps, and less generously (and more accurately?) at a recognized competition. Instead, look for the high and low *areas* of your tests and notice whether they stay the same during each test and from test to test and show to show. That will tell you what to work on, and why.

Focus on the comments and the quality of the various movements. If the lowest marks in each test are invariably your canter departs, say, or your canter circles to the right, then you have something definite to work on. If you find that your halts are always marked down for "lack of immobility" or that your entry is consistently wobbly or that no judge can tell the difference between your horse's free walk and medium walk, you'll know where you need to focus.

> *Forget the specific numbers and look for trends and patterns. One judge's 7 walk may be another's 6.*

Read your collective marks carefully too, and compare them with the marks for movements. If your horse scores well on the test, but the collectives are a mark or two lower, your horse is probably very obedient and very accurate but perhaps not engaged or energetic or round. If your marks for movements are just adequate, but the collectives are high, your horse probably moves well and you should work on accuracy. Improving your accuracy is an easy way to improve your performance scores. Be precise. "At C" means "when the rider's leg is at C," not "when the horse's nose or tail is somewhere in the vicinity of C."

Transitions matter: There are more transitions than any other movement in every dressage test. If your transitions are sloppy, stiff, early, late, or just not quite at the letter, you're sacrificing marks. Don't sacrifice quality for accuracy. A good judge will award a higher mark for a smooth, late transition than for a rough, resistant, prompt one. But any judge will award the best marks for a transition that is both smooth *and* accurate, so once you've mastered the smoothness, spend some time refining your accuracy.

Look at your own collective marks, too. If you are a wonderful rider and your horse is stiff or sluggish, you may find that he gets low marks for his gaits and submission, whereas you get high marks for your position and aids. But if your horse's marks are consistently good and your own marks not so good, again, you know what to work on — your position and aids.

Forget the specific numbers and look for trends and patterns. One judge's 7 walk may be another's 6; it doesn't mean that your horse or your riding has deteriorated. But if you keep seeing the same comments ("halt not square," "transition late," "rushing," or whatever), take those comments seriously and work to improve the *reasons* for the comments.

Above all, don't forget to have fun and to be sure that your horse is having fun, too. We do this for our own reasons, and our horses do it to please us. Let your horse know that you're pleased with his effort no matter what your scores are. You obviously care about improving; with attention and careful, correct work, your scores will only get better.

Organizing a Horse Show

Q I am the president of our local riding club, and the members have voted to have a show this summer. It will be the first show since I have been president, and I wasn't here when they had the last one a few years ago. I would like to do things right so that everything will run smoothly, but I am concerned that there are just too many "cooks" involved!

This is a big club, and there are about 20 people who want to help with the show. I have a planning group of five other people. I don't want to turn anyone down, but we have lots of volunteers and I don't want to have too many people involved. I have some idea of what needs to be done, but I'm not certain what I ought to do myself and what I should try to delegate!

A A successful show entails a great deal of work, so the earlier you begin your planning and delegating, the better. If each person in your core group runs a committee, you will be free to do other things or oversee the larger picture. But don't turn *anyone* down. You're going to need as much help as you can get. There is no such thing as too much help, especially with a big show. There is such a thing as disorganized, ineffective help, and that's what you can avoid by delegating.

If I were you, I'd start with your core group. There are a lot of different responsibilities associated with shows. You can divide those into rough categories, then let the committee chairmen subdivide the categories. That way, everything will get done, everyone can be useful, and you won't have to spend all of your time assigning and tracking specific tasks. The important thing is to create an organization chart and then start delegating jobs. There are usually more jobs than individuals, so plan ahead in case people need to wear more than one hat.

So, just what is involved in planning a show? Here are the major categories and responsibilities.

Money and Paperwork

This includes finances (how much will go into the show and how much will come out of it?), publicity (press releases for the local newspaper and radio stations, posters, flyers), printing and processing entry forms, and producing a program and prize list.

Supplies and Logistics

This includes determining the venue (rental, insurance, and management on the day, plus jumps, judges' stands, on-site transportation, etc.), renting portable toilets (you can never have too many of those!), and purchasing trophies and ribbons.

Even a small show needs a sound system for the announcer. Do you need to rent one? Can it be moved around? Are there enough speakers hooked up to let people all over the grounds hear the announcements?

If you are going to go all out with flowers and flags and such, assign a subcommittee to do the decorating. If they are very nice, you may be able to persuade the same people to act as your maintenance or concession crew.

A key job in this category is concessions! People at shows expect to

Many details go into organizing a show.

find food and beverages for sale. Cleanup is also essential: Where there are people and food, there will be litter, so you'll need a large supply of well-marked trash cans and a maintenance crew.

A horse show entails certain legal requirements and emergency precautions. Careful checking of Coggins tests is one requirement you know about, but there are others. There should be a first-aid station at any show. If your show is small, then you probably won't have an ambulance waiting, but you should have quick access to emergency services. Be sure that everyone on staff carries a cell phone or can find the telephone at the venue. Post signs with the numbers of local emergency services and directions to the venue so that in case of an emergency, anyone could ring for an ambulance and give accurate directions.

Fire and police protection may be necessary; call your local services and find out what is required. Even if no formal arrangement is needed, inform your local police and fire department of the dates and times of your show, its location, simple directions, and the numbers of people and trailers you are expecting.

Even a small show must carry liability insurance. If you are putting a great deal of time and money into this show, you may also want rain insurance so that you can recoup your expenses if the show is rained out. Your club's regular insurance may cover a certain number of events each year, but talk with your insurance carrier and find out exactly what is and isn't covered.

A well-run show allows riders to relax, enjoy themselves, and appreciate their horses.

Show Officials and Staff

This includes your judge(s), announcer, show secretary (who will need assistants if the show is big), and scorer. If the show is large, you'll want ring clerks and additional scorers. If it's a dressage show, the judge will need a scribe and someone to check the bits. For a dressage or combined training competition, you'll need runners to collect each rider's score sheet and take it to the show scorer.

For a large show, you'll want a farrier and a veterinarian on-site. Even if your show is tiny, you will need to know how to reach a local veterinarian (talk to him in advance, so that you can truthfully claim to have a veterinarian "on call").

Other jobs include selling programs and tickets, registering entries, and assigning stalls to incoming horses. Have people to direct spectators to the appropriate parking and to oversee trailer parking for participants. Someone must check that each horse has a current negative Coggins test before the horse gets off the trailer. You'll also need a ring crew to set up courses for jumping classes, rebuild fences that horses knock down, rake the arena during the lunch break, and so forth.

It takes a lot of work and a lot of people cooperating to put on a successful show. This is why I say that you can *never* have too many volunteers! Encourage all of your club members to participate, and don't forget to thank them afterward. A combination of food and certificates of thanks can keep exhausted, footsore volunteers happy enough to come back the next time and help you again.

CHAPTER 21

You Are Not Alone

THESE SUBJECTS ARE VARIED, but they're not at all random. Dozens of letters like these have arrived in the *Horse-Sense* mailbox every month for the last 10 years. Each writer obviously feels unique and alone, as well as harried, harassed, inept, and incapable.

In fact, few, if any, riding problems are truly unique. Most concerns are shared by hundreds, thousands, or even hundreds of thousands of riders around the world. Fitness, fear, finances, injuries and illnesses, and aches and pains are universal concerns.

Can't Let My Friends See Me Ride

Q I hope I'm not the only person in the world with this problem, but I have a huge fear of riding in front of people, and it's getting worse all the time. I am in my 40s and have taken some lessons but not very many. I have owned horses for years, and right now my husband and I keep five horses on our farm. I do most of my riding there, by myself. I mostly did trail riding, but about 10 years ago I got interested in dressage. So I took a few lessons and practiced what I learned and read some books.

Instead of taking more lessons, I started reading more and more books about dressage and pretty soon I had a bookshelf full. I know a lot of terms and a lot of techniques to do, at least in my head, and I can discuss and argue about dressage with my friends on the phone and on the Internet. But here is the problem: I can't relate what I *know* to what I *do* when I'm riding a real horse!

My horses aren't fancy warmblood dressage horses, but they are nice riding horses, and I should be able to practice some of this stuff with them. But even though it makes sense to me when I am reading or talking with my friends, when I get into the saddle it's like some other person takes over my body and my brain, a person who doesn't know anything about dressage and can't even ride very well.

This has been getting worse and worse. I can't stop reading about and discussing dressage – it's so interesting, and I really do want to learn. At this point, I am ashamed to let anybody see me ride, so I don't know if I could take lessons even if we had a good dressage instructor around here. When my telephone and Internet friends come to visit, I always find some excuse not to ride, because I don't want to lose their respect and friendship. I miss riding with friends, and I would like to become a better rider, but I don't know what to do. I'm sure my friends are starting to wonder why I don't ride with them and why I never sign up for clinics. I have talked so much about all this technical dressage stuff that I'd be too embarrassed to sign up for a lesson at my real level, but if I tried to take one at my "talking" level I would be even more embarrassed.

I know this is my own stupid fault, but I don't know what to do! I don't want to be a lonely old lady with no friends to ride with, but how do I fix this? I feel like I told everyone I have a wonderful palatial home and now I can't let anyone come to my house and see that I live in a doublewide trailer! It really does feel like that!

A   You are absolutely *not* the only person who has ever done this, and I'm sure that you will not be the last. This has become far too important in your mind. It really is not such a big deal.

Many riders experience something like this at some point during their lives. If you like to read and think and talk about riding, and you have, for one reason or another (weather, injury, work, travel), spent more time reading and thinking and talking than actually riding, it's understandable that your physical skills will lag behind your intellectual understanding of the subject.

Dressage *is* compelling, and there's a big technical and theoretical side to it. But without lots of time in the saddle, you end up talking about dressage in the same way that I talk with some of my friends about figure skating. We know quite a lot about it, but since we can't do it, we don't make all of the necessary connections. We can explain what should be done to make it better; that's all theory and technique. But we cannot explain *how* to improve the performance. That's where actual practical experience comes in.

You don't need to e-mail or telephone everyone you know and confess that you're a great big phony! Lots of people, not just riders, exaggerate their abilities to one degree or another. I bet that if you took even one lesson with a good instructor, then announced to your friends that you don't know nearly as much as you thought you did, and that you need to start over with your new understanding and your new ambition to do everything correctly this time, they would understand and applaud you. And you'd be telling the truth.

Alternatively, you can say that you have to begin again as rehab. Resist the temptation to invent a terrible accident! If they want to know why you are in rehab and what happened to you, you can say that you tripped over your ego and hurt your pride. Every honest rider should be able to relate to *that*.

I know this seems like a big problem to you, but really it doesn't have to be. You haven't done anything terrible and you haven't hurt anyone except yourself. Your friends will sympathize, and it's entirely possible that many of them will also empathize. Many, many riders get so caught up in theory that they get ahead of themselves. Life is too short not to have fun. Don't waste any more time worrying about what you can do and how it compares with what your friends may *think* you can do, or to what *you* think that your friends think that you can do. Just go out, ride, and have fun with your friends.

If you continue to find reasons (or invent excuses) not to ride with them, they probably aren't going to figure out that you're embarrassed because you've oversold

Friends ride together to enjoy each other's company.

your riding abilities; they'll just think that you don't like them as much as they like you or that you've lost interest in riding. Since your friends are obviously happy to visit you, invite them on a trail ride where you'll be on familiar ground. They will be happy to see you on horseback, and you'll probably talk about all sorts of things other than dressage. Give yourself a chance and give your friends some credit. Friends don't tear each other down; they support and encourage one another. Would you stop liking *them* if you discovered that their riding isn't exactly to the very highest standard, as per their discussions with you online and on the telephone?

I'm going to bet that you won't be the only person in the group who rides better in her head than she does in the saddle. It's very common, and there really isn't anything wrong with it. Until you overcome this worry, you won't be able to begin to close the gap between theory and practice. It takes a lot of time in the saddle for any rider to relate theory to reality and become adept at putting principles into practice. Wanting to be a better rider should cause you to spend *more* time in the saddle, not *less*, and it certainly shouldn't keep you off your horse entirely!

Dressage for Occasional Rider

Q I can't ride my horse every day like I used to. I just started working with a new dressage trainer, and dressage is very new to both my horse and me. Is it okay to try new things when I can only ride once or twice a week?

A As long as you don't push too hard during your lessons and rides, this is a good time for you and your horse to learn new things. Time off between rides doesn't mean wasted effort or backsliding — it just means that you'll always have time to think about what you did in the previous session.

This works for your horse too. He may not "think" about the session consciously, but I often find that horses exhibit excellent latent learning. You can begin work on something new, go away for a few days, come back, try again, and find that the horse does it easily and may even have taken it a step beyond the point at which you left off!

There may also be a real advantage to your situation: If your horse gets any small injury, perhaps a strain or a sore back, during one ride, he will have a couple of days to relax and recover in turnout before the next session.

As long as the lessons are pleasant, you and your horse enjoy each other, and your horse has exercise (at least some turnout) on the other days, your schedule shouldn't get in the way of your progress. You won't build habits and reflexes (in either of you) as quickly as you would if you could ride every day, but there's no reason that you can't both make steady progress. If you have a good dressage trainer, your lessons will be geared to the horse's physical and mental development in any case, and you won't be pushed too fast or feel that you're falling behind. Many good riders began by riding once a week, in a lesson, over a period of time. If you and your instructor both understand the situation, and agree about your goals and the program that will help you achieve them, you should be fine.

Frustrated Adult Beginner

Q For the last year, my 13-year-old Thoroughbred and I have been working with a wonderful trainer on the basics of dressage. She trains Simon twice a week, and I take two lessons a week. Simon gets at least two days off each week, and we try to get out on the trails as much as we can. Prior to buying him I had only ridden Western, off and on, and had no formal instruction.

Simon has really progressed, having originally arrived at the barn traveling hollow in his back with his head held high and needing a *lot* of leg. Now he works from behind, has muscled up, has a cresty neck, and goes on the bit. He is smart, though, and does not have a terrific work ethic. The rider must constantly use her leg to remind him to move on and must really keep wiggling the bit to keep him from popping his head up. My trainer is doing lateral work with him, and he is becoming more supple. She makes him look like a million bucks, and I love watching her ride him. It takes a lot of energy, and I appreciate how much effort she has put into him.

Measuring my own progress, however, is a problem, because I am very hard on myself. When I first came to the barn my riding was quite a sight to behold. I have made lots of progress in many respects but can't seem to put all the pieces together consistently. I am learning how to use my aids independently and still have trouble keeping my reins steady enough to keep my horse, who likes to evade, on the bit. Keeping him moving is a job unto itself, so I have trouble putting the whole package together in my head so it flows.

I question my progress. Every lesson is a major learning experience with some things improving and others not. One day I am good at one thing and the next day another! It is frustrating. Is dressage that hard to learn? Should I, as an adult, expect to be further ahead after a year? Am I being too hard on myself? Today someone suggested that maybe I'd be a better rider on a different horse, but I love Simon more than anything in the world, and I promised myself when I bought him that I would learn to ride him no matter what. My trainer says that I definitely will, and it just takes time.

Do adults take longer to learn than children? Is dressage something that comes along at a slow pace? Over the summer I was in several schooling shows and won my very first blue ribbons, one in dressage and one in long stirrup, walk/trot, so how badly can I be doing?

A I agree — how badly could you be doing? You've taken on two difficult and complicated tasks: learning to ride really well, and learning on a challenging horse. As long as every lesson is a learning experience and you are improving overall, you are doing very well.

Adults and children learn in different ways and at different speeds. Adults may take longer to learn *some* things because they are generally stiffer, more fearful, and have more bad habits than children do. Children who are just beginning riding lessons are often riding for the first time in their lives and don't have years of bad riding (casual or organized) and incorrect habits to overcome. For adults who have had some experience on horseback but never had lessons (or never had good lessons), the process takes longer because they're beginning with a handicap. But either way, there's no timetable involved.

When the subject is dressage, adults have some advantages over children, because in addition to the physical side of dressage, there's the intellectual side. Adults have an easier time understanding theory than children do. The tricky thing about dressage is that you need it all: physical skills, technique, and theory. And it is essential to put the horse *first*. Without true horsemanship, there is no dressage, there's only riding.

Learning to ride well takes time, and the more ambitious you are, the longer the process will be. If you're satisfied with "one leg each side, kick to go, yank to stop," as some people are, you can take 10 lessons and announce to the world that you now "know how to ride." If you have, say, Olympic ambitions, you'll be taking lessons and clinics all your life and working hard every day to perfect your skills and timing and communication.

Becoming a good rider is a *process*. Trying to rush through it and become an "instant rider" simply doesn't work. No matter what you're trying to achieve in the short term — backing without using your reins, performing a subtle half halt, jumping an oxer, getting a good trot-canter transition — getting it done and crossing it off the list and moving on isn't the point. Doing it correctly, with understanding, and then repeating it correctly hundreds and thousands of times so that it becomes a habit that you can do smoothly and easily and beautifully every time — *that* is the point. Without that key concept of correctness, real improvement is impossible.

> *Becoming a good rider is a process, and the more ambitious you are, the longer the process will be.*

As for your rate of progress, every rider and every situation is different, so it's generally not a good idea to compare yourself with someone whose physique, opportunities, and situation are unlike yours. It's also not a good idea to compare yourself with some imaginary ideal student. Just compare yourself with *yourself* and be fair. Being self-critical in a positive way is useful; for example, if you say, "I'm still not quite there when it comes to posting trot, so I'm going to ask my instructor for some new exercises that will help me improve," then you're helping yourself. If you say, "I'm a disaster. I'll never get the hang of posting; I should be able to do it by now and I can't," then all you're accomplishing is making life unpleasant for yourself and your horse. When you have a problem, try to analyze it in terms of what's going wrong (timing? strength? flexibility? endurance?

preparation? recovery? communication?), then discuss it with your instructor and ask for help to make it go right.

As you work on dressage, I suggest that you keep a riding/lesson journal — it's the best and most effective way to track your progress. Before every lesson and every ride, write down your goals for that session. Afterward write a description of the session, what you did, what the horse did, what the instructor said, what you thought and felt. If you do this every time, you'll soon be able to look back at earlier entries, read about problems you were having a few months ago, and say, "Oh, I can't believe there was a time when I couldn't do *that!* I must have improved, because now I do it easily without even thinking about it!"

Every few months, review your long-, medium-, and short-term goals, discuss them with your instructor, and record that information in your journal as well. Once you're able to see that you *are* making progress in many different areas, you'll be able to relax more and enjoy the process of learning to ride, and once you can do that, you will improve much more quickly.

Finally, don't focus on shows. Schooling shows can be fun, but what matters is your actual progress, not whether you win a ribbon. Enjoy a schooling show as a day out and as a chance to acquire some experience riding away from home, but don't take the results too seriously, and above all, don't let them determine the course of your riding. If you are too strongly affected by the results of schooling shows, you may want to avoid them entirely for a few years. Some riders find themselves tied in emotional knots because they interpret a first- or second-place ribbon as proof that they've perfected something, or a seventh-place ribbon (or no ribbon at all!) as proof that they're hopeless. Neither feeling is true 100 percent of the time.

Now that I've said all that, there are three things that worry me in your question. The first is the notion of the horse's work ethic — more about that in a minute. Then there are the comments that you have to use your leg strongly all the time to keep your horse moving and that you have been told that you should wiggle the bit to keep his head down.

Simon should be learning to respond to lighter and lighter leg aids, and you should be using less pressure, less often, from month to month as you both improve. Wiggling the bit constantly is simply *wrong*. His head will come down naturally when he is using his hindquarters with energy, his belly muscles are working, and his back is lifted and stretched. The only correct way to achieve the head and neck position you want is to train and ride him in a way that develops his strength and balance until he's physically capable of doing what you want him to do.

If you develop him correctly, he will *offer* what you want as soon as he's strong enough, because it will be the most comfortable option for him. If you demand something that he isn't physically capable of, such as a particular head position, you won't get it. Pulling his head down with draw reins or seesawing the bit to make him curl his neck and duck behind the bit will create a painful parody of the silhouette you want. Instead of becoming stronger, more flexible, and happier about his work, your horse will become stiff and lame and very unhappy about being ridden.

And that brings me to the question of a work ethic. Horses are straightforward animals with relatively simple agendas. They are typically willing to learn and eager to please. "Work ethic" is a human concept generally invoked by humans who are trying to justify forcing a horse to do something when he's in pain, afraid, or confused. If you want a horse to be eager to work for you, first eliminate all possible sources of pain, fear, and confusion, and then *make the work fun.* "Fun" for the horse means that he feels physically and mentally comfortable with whatever the rider is asking him to do, and he feels liked and appreciated by the rider. That's it.

If you want to become a truly good rider, you'll stop worrying about your horse's work ethic and focus on making his working conditions as pleasant as you possibly can.

It's a good idea, however, for riders to pay attention to their *own* work ethic — not just occasionally but all the time. If you are aware of your goals and make a conscious effort to learn everything you can about riding and horses and horsemanship, if you focus on your horse and always make the effort to ride and communicate as accurately and correctly as possible, and if you don't allow yourself to become sloppy during practice rides or on the trail, I promise you that your riding will continue to improve, not just this month or this year but forever, and your enjoyment will improve right along with your riding and your horsemanship. That's really not such a bad deal.

Riding Clubs

Q Some of the people at my barn and other boarding barns in our area have been talking about starting a riding club. I guess I'm not quite sure what that is, but I don't see the point in having a club since we're all riding anyway. I would like to know your opinion of riding clubs and if they have a purpose or are just something snobby?

A I like riding clubs, and I don't think they are snobby at all. Riding clubs can help local riders do things that they can't do on their own or even with the help of a barn owner. Most of the riding clubs I know have regular meetings, dues, and a newsletter. They use club money for books and videos for a riding club collection (any member can borrow the books or tapes), and to bring in people who can lecture or teach lessons or clinics — I do a lot of both for various riding clubs!

Why not go to a meeting and find out what the plans are for this particular club? It will need officers and volunteers; if you're interested, why not join in the planning and have some input of your own? Perhaps there's a particular clinician you would like to have come to your area or a particular book or tape you would like to have in a club library. If you work for the club, your voice will be heard when those sorts of decisions are made. I say it's worth a try; after all, if you don't like it after six months or so, you can always stop going to meetings.

Riding clubs can be a good resource for people with common interests.

Limited Riding Time during the Winter

Q What's the best way to keep my horses from completely forgetting about me during the winter? I ride as often as possible, but I work full-time and have a house to maintain and a young daughter who needs me. In winter, I can only ride on weekends because of limited daylight time. I feel bad because they're only getting ridden once, maybe twice per week.

Is this going to absolutely "kill" them as far as the stuff they learned last spring, summer, and fall? They're both nearly six years old and sweet horses. Are my job and daughter going to take too extreme a toll on my equine partners?

A Don't worry; your horses aren't likely to forget anything over the winter even if you can't ride them *at all*. Horses rarely forget anything! They have wonderful memories, which is why we can train them and also why we must handle them kindly and correctly.

Your horses will probably surprise you. Riding once or twice a week isn't ideal, of course, but it can work out very well, even for horses in training. Some horses actually learn their lessons much more effectively if they have a few days off between sessions. Many horses (and riders!) exhibit latent learning: You might work hard one day to teach your horse the rudiments of a turn on the forehand, then come out several days later and have him show you that he's figured it out in the meantime. This happens a lot, and it will probably happen with your horses, too.

Rising six is just coming into adulthood for horses; you aren't going to lose any ground. They can still make progress even if you're only riding once or twice a week. It may not be as rapid as you like, but your horses will *not* backslide. Just be patient, because they may need to be reminded of what you were working on, and realize that after a winter of reduced exercise they won't have the strong muscling and quick reflexes they would get from more regular work. But the memory and the understanding will be there, and you can add the muscling and develop the reflexes and habits when you have more time to ride.

Please — drop the guilt load! You don't need it, and it isn't appropriate. Your horses are having a perfectly good time being horses, just hanging out in their field. When you have time to work with them, work with them and *enjoy* them. When you don't have time, don't worry about what you "should" be doing. They're fine, they're healthy, they're happy, and they aren't going to forget anything.

"My Way is the Only Way"

Q I am very new to the horse scene, even though I grew up around horses. I never learned to ride, but now, at almost 30, am doing just that. It is a dream come true for me, and I'm learning so much all the time. I read extensively and file it all away for when I will be able to have a horse of my own.

One thing I've noticed when discussing horses or riding trails with other people is that many horse people are very much of the opinion that their way is not just the best way, but the *only* way. Because I don't work with horses on a regular basis, I've had a lot of people look down on me, even though I don't claim to be a horseman or to know much about horses. I just love the animals and feel that I have the ability to be very good with them given time.

I've been very discouraged lately because every time I want to talk about a horse issue, people act like I'm not worthy of such a discussion or that I should automatically be in awe of their way of doing things. I agree with some of what they say and disagree with some of it. It seems to me that should be okay. Why are these people so defensive every time I ask a question or proffer something I've just read? I'm just trying to get a bunch of opinions together so that I can come up with what I believe. Now I'm wondering if I want to spend a large amount of time and money on horses if the other people involved are so ornery.

My instructor is very pleased with my progress and says that I have a natural way with horses and that with time and experience I'll be a great horsewoman. Can you help me understand the human factor behind all the defensiveness and the know-it-all attitude? I just want to learn about horses and riding.

A Congratulations on starting to live your dream. You probably appreciate your time with horses all the more because you had to wait so long for the opportunity! Relax; you don't have to give up your interest in horses just because of some didactic people. You *will* need to get used to the phenomenon, though: There's an old saying that if you put 10 horsemen in a room, you'll hear at least 11 opinions. It's quite true.

Keep reading everything you can find, but try not to draw a lot of carved-in-stone conclusions until you've accumulated a few years of experience with horses and riding. Remember that not every source of information is reliable. You seem to have a pleasant, encouraging instructor: That's an excellent beginning. Ask her what books she recommends, which clinicians she admires, and which local riders might be a good source of information or conversation.

The human factor is always the most difficult one. Horses are easy, simple, and clear. Their motivations are easy to understand, their language is primarily physical, they're direct about their feelings, and they don't lie. People, however, are rarely easy, simple, or clear, and as for their motivations . . . ! Put 10 people in a room and ask them why they ride, and you'll get at least 11 different motivations (and those are just the ones of which they're *aware*).

One way to evaluate a source of information is by doing what you are doing: Ask a question, mention something you've read, and see what the reaction is. A person who is both well informed and interested in helping you will give a detailed answer to your question, or a detailed reaction to whatever you're quoting. People who react defensively to straightforward, honest questions and who react defensively to hearing another person's opinion are usually angry because they feel that they have been challenged. The less they know about the subject, and the less able they are to explain the reasoning behind their own beliefs, the more angry and defensive they will be. So remember two things:

1. If someone reacts defensively and nastily to your question or quote, that person probably doesn't know much about the subject. Well-informed people don't see questions as attacks. Knowledgeable people will also say, "That's an interesting question, and I don't know the answer" when they don't know, instead of making something up or being rude.

2. If someone doesn't know much about a subject and feels challenged by a question or quote, that person will probably react by putting down the question or the questioner. This is a time-honored way of avoiding the actual subject of discussion. If you ask someone "Why did you fasten your girth that way?" or "Why did you tie that kind of knot in the lead rope?" and there's an actual reason, that person will probably be happy to tell you the reason. If there's *no* reason, the response may be "That's how I do it" or "That's the only way to do it" or even "You're ugly, and your mother dresses you funny."

What can you do about these people? *Nothing.* Don't waste your time on them. There are obnoxious people in every area of human endeavor. Riding is no exception. What makes riding special are the kind, knowledgeable, helpful people involved with horses. Keep looking, and you'll find some or they will find you. Whatever you do, don't give up on horses and riding just because of a few silly people.

Ground Work *and* Riding — You Need Both

Q I've had my 16-year-old Quarter Horse mare for a year. During that time, I've helped her overcome health problems, bad feet, and fear of humans. I follow the training methods of natural horsemanship. Much of the initial training takes place on the ground, and I'm enjoying that immensely. I now have a horse I can catch easily and that leads well and actively participates in all the ground work. However, whenever it comes to putting a saddle on my horse, I hesitate. I am a beginner and need to put in the hours, but I just can't get on and ride. Whenever I do, I find it puts me in the "leader" role so strongly that I fear I lose my horse's respect. I'm not heavy-handed and wouldn't dream of hurting or forcing my horse into anything she isn't ready for. But I still hesitate.

I keep thinking, "I have this horse that all these other people want to ride; why don't I?" I'm an oddity at my barn — most people only ride on weekends, while I am there daily, grooming, cleaning her buckets, doing ground work, just hanging out, etc. I admit I am sort of possessive about my horse. I'm not crazy about anyone else riding her. I've been accused of being too close to my horse and treating her like a friend or pet.

In one year, my horse and I have come a long way. She used to be terrified and pretty nasty. I used to be terrified and, I'll admit, pretty meek. We now seem to be at a standstill, both fairly happy but ready for the next step.

A   Perhaps you'll find it comforting to know that a lot of other people are in very similar situations. You've actually answered your own question: You don't want to ride your horse because you don't like the kind of person you become, or the way your horse reacts to you, when you get in the saddle. The good news is that this is not only a common problem, it's a very fixable problem.

One of the great benefits of the popularity of natural horsemanship is that horse owners are paying more attention to their horses on the ground and becoming more aware of the ways in which they interact with their horses. Unfortunately, this only takes you so far, because establishing a relationship with a horse on the ground, and learning to interpret his body language and use your own body language to direct his movements, does not necessarily have any direct carryover when you're in the saddle. That makes perfect sense, when you think about it. The "language" of ground work and the "language" of under-saddle work are, all too often, completely different.

If you are somewhat fearful and nervous and not entirely certain that you *want* to be in the saddle, it's natural to want to preserve the comfortable relationship that you have with your horse on the ground. If you feel competent to understand, direct, and handle your horse from the ground, but are not at all certain that you are in charge when you're on her back, it makes sense that you would prefer to stay *off* her back.

From your point of view, getting into the saddle means that your happy, cooperative, controllable horse suddenly changes and becomes a tense, unpredictable

*Both horses and riders need
variety in their work and play.*

animal. From your mare's point of view, her friendly, kind, understandable human suddenly changes and becomes a tense, unpredictable, and aggressive animal as soon as she is in the saddle.

In the round pen, large gestures and movements allow you to be quietly authoritative. Your arm-waving and stepping this way and that way are signals that make good sense to a horse that is 20 or 30 feet away from you, where she can see you very well and can accept your authority and your signals without feeling threatened. But get into the saddle and make similarly large gestures and movements, and two things change completely: You've "turned up the volume" to loud or *very loud*, and your horse, who can no longer see you, interprets the increased volume as aggression.

What happens then? Typically, the rider gets "louder" because of worrying about being unable to control the horse. The horse reacts badly to the perceived aggression of the rider. Both horse and rider become more and more uncomfortable — emotionally, mentally, and physically. When the rider dismounts, both parties heave great sighs of relief. The horse says, "Oh, *there* you are, you're back, how nice, there was a really nasty scary person here a moment ago!" And the rider says, "Oh, *there's* my nice quiet horse. I think I'd much rather prefer to work you on the ground. Riding is overrated, I hate having to be a bully, but if I'm not a bully, I can't control you at all." If you reduce each reaction to its essence, the horse is very happy to have the rider off its back; the rider, who is more and more afraid to ride, is very happy to have her feet on the ground again, and both are happy to be back in a familiar situation where they understand one another and can be friendly.

What is the solution? There are several; I'm going to suggest the two most logical and practical ones.

Best solution: Take riding lessons from a good instructor who understands that horsemanship and riding cannot and should not be separate subjects. A good instructor will help you interpret your horse's reactions and will help you learn to control your own body and use it in a way that won't frighten, worry, or interfere with your horse. With someone to help you focus on good communication and positive feedback, you and your horse will quickly learn to have a good relationship when you're in the saddle.

Second-best solution: If you don't have such an instructor, and you have to find your own way, try this: Spend at least six months working *only at the walk*. It's a good way to avoid feeling frightened and frightening your horse, and no, you won't get bored and neither will she. If you are physically and mentally and emotionally right there with your horse, keeping your (positive) focus on her and existing in the moment as she does, you'll find that walking is both a challenging and an interesting activity. You need to practice staying still and quiet in the saddle and giving gentle signals that direct her without intimidating her.

You also need to practice staying focused on your horse in a positive way. Working at a walk will let you do those things while building your own confidence and your horse's confidence. It will also help your body, especially your core muscles, become stronger. As you become stronger and better able to control your own body, you'll be better able to direct your horse with quiet, subtle signals that will let you ask for her cooperation instead of demanding action.

Six months of *riding* at the walk, not just meandering around thinking about other things, will build up your body, your competence, and your confidence. It will do the same for your horse and it will help the two of you build the same trusting relationship under saddle that you have on the ground. Only then will it be time for you to go faster. If and when you want to, you'll be able to trot and canter with much more comfort and confidence (on *both* sides of the saddle).

I think that you're on the right track. Take things slowly, stay relaxed, stay positive, get the best lessons you possibly can, and if you can't find a good instructor, just saddle up, mount up, and *walk* for at least six months. Not one second of that time will be wasted, because you'll be able to build a strong, solid, mutually trusting under-saddle relationship with your horse. When you are in control of yourself and feeling strong, competent, and confident, you'll be able to become the kind of leader you want to be: not a loud, crude, dictatorial *boss,* but a quiet, inspiring leader that your horse will *enjoy* following. When you're able to ride correctly and effectively, there will be every reason for you and your horse to continue to be friends.

Am I Letting My Horse Down?

Q I am a first-time horse owner and was lucky enough to find a really wonderful mare for my first horse. I love Peekaboo very much, and she seems to be very fond of me too, which makes me happy. She is a real friend.

Before I bought Peekaboo, I had some bad lessons from an instructor who rushed me into things before I was ready, mostly because she was in a hurry to have me join a group lesson. The others in the group were more experienced; I was the only one who was completely new to riding. The instructor sent me down a line of jumps and the horse ducked out after the second one and I fell off and got hurt and very frightened. When I healed I was too afraid to go back to that instructor, who is apparently well known for damaging riders!

I found another instructor who teaches a few people at a small private farm with two school horses and practically no facilities, but it is much more low-key and offers much better-quality teaching. After two years with her, I was still a bit nervous of jumping, but able to do it safely. Then I bought Peekaboo, who was also nervous about jumping, and we rode on the flat for another year, just going over a few cross rails or very low single jumps once in a while. Peekaboo is such a sweet mare that I don't think anything could frighten me as long as I was on her back. She trusts me too, and we have begun jumping real jumps this year.

Last week I went to my first jumping competition. It was just a local schooling show that I thought would give both of us a pleasant low-pressure experience. We placed in two classes! Peekaboo was so good, and I felt confident on her. Then a woman I didn't know came over to me and asked me why I was putting her in classes that were so far below her ability. At first I thought this was a compliment and was thanking her, but she made it clear that she thought I was a bad rider and had no business with such a nice horse and that my mare could do much better if she had a good rider. She even gave me a card and said, "You can call me if you decide to give that horse a chance."

I was crushed — I felt like we had come so far together and we were getting to be a real team that trusted each other. It hurt me so much to think that I could be hurting Peekaboo and holding her back from what she could do and that I am letting her down just by owning and riding her. I went from so happy to so sad, arrived home in tears, and ever since then I have been trying to decide what is right.

I am not going to call that woman, because I think she was horrible, but I worry every night that she might be right and I should sell Peekaboo to a better rider. I feel that I have been making progress with my jumping, but maybe I can't keep up with my horse. I don't want to let her down, but the thing is, I trust Peekaboo and I am starting to enjoy jumping with her. I don't think I could ever jump another horse, but I want to do what is right for her. Please help me do the right thing.

A You're already doing the right thing, so please stop worrying. You certainly do *not* need to sell your horse — what you need to do is relax and enjoy her. Your instincts are good; you and Peekaboo obviously have a partnership, you are a team, and you should stay together. Your instincts about that woman were good too, and "horrible" is a fair description. I don't know what motivated her to say those things to you, but I could make a few guesses. Let's just say that some people get so caught up in their drive to compete and win (or to make money by selling horses to other people who want to compete and win) that they completely lose sight of what riding should be about, which is the development of a true partnership between a horse and rider.

Riders who aren't really sure of themselves often worry that they are "not good enough" for their horses, and that they are "letting their horses down." Ask yourself these questions: Does Peekaboo come to you when you arrive at the pasture gate and call her? Does she work, and jump, willingly and cheerfully? Does she seem to enjoy the time you spend together?

From what you've said, I'm sure that your answers are yes, yes, and yes, so stop worrying and do what you and your horse enjoy!

If you want to improve your own skills, take lessons, take clinics, read books, watch videos. Do everything you can to make yourself the best and kindest rider you can be and to make your horse the healthiest, soundest, and happiest horse she can be. Enjoy your time with Peekaboo and do everything you can to ensure that she enjoys that time as much as you do. If you focus on keeping your horse healthy and happy while you improve her training and your own skills, *you cannot possibly let her down.*

Don't worry about what some stranger with heaven-knows-what agenda says to you or what she thinks, or indeed what anyone thinks, other than your trusted instructor! The question is: What does Peekaboo think? You are *not* "letting her down" by providing her with a sport she enjoys and a partnership with a person she likes and trusts. You would *not* improve her life or her happiness by selling her just so that she could belong to someone who would make her run faster and jump higher. If she could talk, she would tell you that. Ribbons don't mean a thing to horses. Partnerships, on the other hand, mean everything. You've given your horse trust in you and confidence in her own ability to jump (which, if you think about it, is also what *she* has given *you*), so don't allow anyone to frighten or bully you into giving up your horse and your partnership.

Remember that competition is optional. You don't *need* to compete, and you certainly don't need to compete in order to "prove" anything about your horse or yourself. As long as you're making progress, who cares how slow or fast that progress is? If you enjoy competing, and Peekaboo enjoys competing, then go out and compete at a level that's comfortable for both of you. Push yourselves a little bit, because it's good to stretch, but don't push yourselves so hard that you stop enjoying the process. The important thing about riding, and the thing that some people forget (how sad for them!), is this: *We do it for fun.* You and Peekaboo had fun at your competition, at least until that woman interfered, so by all means go to competitions if you enjoy them. Just remember that it's your *horse's* opinion of you that matters most, and your mare has made it clear that she considers you a friend and a totally suitable partner. Hold that thought!

The opinion of your horse is the one that should matter the most to you.

Appendix: How to Build a Mounting Block

IF YOU'RE AT ALL HANDY, the mounting block that you've been seeing throughout this book can be yours. If you are new to woodworking or power tools, contact your local building suppliers, as they may offer helpful how-to sessions to teach beginners about safety and the correct use of tools. Or you can enlist the help of a handy friend or family member or hire a professional to do the job for you. The end result will be a sturdy and durable mounting block that will help protect your horse's back, your own back, and your saddle tree while making mounting and dismounting much easier and more pleasant for both you and your horse.

SAFETY TIP: When you've completed your project — and this applies to *any* woodworking project that you do in or near any habitat for horses, be it a barn, pasture, or arena — take a large magnet and do a slow, complete sweep of your work area and a foot or two beyond the perimeter. If any nails escaped during the construction process, you and your magnet should find them before a horse does.

Tools needed:

- Circular power saw
- 12" Speedy Square or builder's square
- 12' tape measure
- 16 oz. claw hammer
- Pencil

Material list:

- Three 10' lengths of 2×8
- One 8' length of 2×8
- One 12' length of 2×8
- One 8' length of 2×4
- Two 10' lengths of 1×6 decking
- One 8' length of 1×6 decking
- Two small boxes nails — 16d coated sinkers
- Two small boxes nails — 8d coated sinkers

*All wood should be treated for exposure to ground

STEP ONE: Cutting the Pieces

- Mark and cut eight 26"-long risers from two of the 10'-long 2×8 boards. Four will be end risers and four will be step risers.
- Mark and cut side risers as follows:
    a. Two 56 ½" pieces from the remaining 10'-long 2×8
    b. 2 pieces, each 46 ½" long, from the 8'-long 2×8
    c. 2 pieces, each 36 ½", and 2 pieces, each 26 ½", from the 12'-long 2×8
- Cut 2 pieces, each 28", from the 8'-long 2×4
- Cut eleven 30" treads from the 1×6 decking boards

STEP TWO: Assembly

1. Lay four side risers (one of each size) on edge on a flat surface, such as a garage or patio floor. Position the end of one 26" riser perpendicular to the edge of each side riser (as shown below) and nail into place with three 16d nails driven through the side into the cut edge of the step.

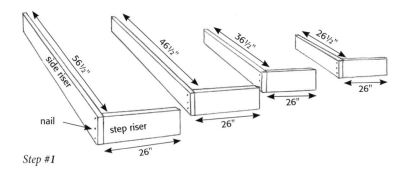

Step #1

2. Turn the side risers so that the step risers are pointing upward. Line up the bottom ends of the side risers so they are flush and push them together tightly. Measure 21" from the flush end. Position a 28" 2×4 across all four boards and fasten with 8d nails all the way along to join the four side risers (see illustration).

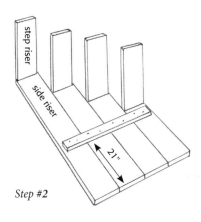

Step #2

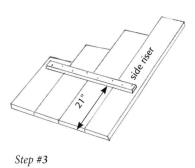

Step #3

3. Lay the remaining four side risers flat on the floor, flush at one end. Measure 21" from flush edge; position a 28" 2×4 across all four and nail in place (see illustration). Ensure that the 2×4 supports end up *inside* the mounting block by placing the sides so that they face in the same direction with the longer boards next to each other.

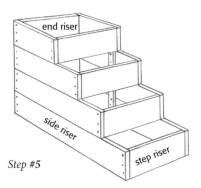

Step #5

4. Stand the two side riser sections on edge, positioning the unconnected side riser edges across the ends of the step risers. Nail into place with three 16d nails driven through each side riser.

5. Position the end risers across the back of the stacked steps and nail each into place with 8d nails, thus completing the "box" of the mounting block (see illustraton).

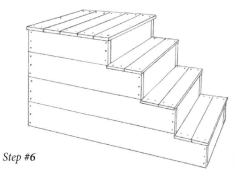

Step #6

6. Position two treads across each step and five across the top so that there is a ½ inch overhang on the front of each step and on each side. Nail into place with 16d sinkers (see illustration).

INDEX

Page numbers in *italics* indicate illustrations

canter, 62
  walk, 30–32, *31*, 33, 34
forgiving nature of horses, 188–89
forward movement of posting, *45*, 45–46
four-beat lope vs. canter, 73
frame, false, 181–83, 184, 224
friction grip, leg, 86–87
friends, riding with, 343–45, *345*
front-to-back riding, 181–84
frustrated riders, 200–203, 312, 346–50
full-seat (three-point), 43, 44
fun rides, 184–87

Gag bit, 224, 226
gaited horses and body soreness, 139, *139*
galloping on trail ride, 93–96, *94*
gloves for arthritic hands, 258–60, *259*
goals and horse comfort, conflicts, 170–73, *172*
good clinics, signs of, 325, 326, *326*
good enough for a clinic, 314
gripping legs, 86–87
grip vs. balance of rider, 19, 253, 257
ground, mounting from the, 3–5, *5*
ground poles and walk, 38–39
ground work, 145, *145*, 146, 354–58, *356*
group vs. private lessons, 303–4
guilt about bad instructors, 298–300, *299*

Hackamores, *169*, 169–70, 179
half-halts for rebalancing, 63, 64, 66–67, 69–70
half-seat (two-point)
  body soreness and, 127, *127*, 128, 131–32, 134
  jumping, 80, 86
  position, rider's, 18–19, 20
  trail riding, 90–91, 92, *92*, 98
  trot, 44–45
hands
  arthritic hands, reins for, 258–60, *259*
  position, rider's, 23–25, *25*, 221
  walk, moving hands at, 30–32, *31*, 34
hard mouth, 163–65, *165*
harness (retention system) of helmet, adjusting, 279–80
hat, wearing under a helmet, 281–82, *282*
heavy riders, 105, 109, *109*, 110–16, *114*
heel inserts for new boots, 263–64, 267
helmets, safety
  ASTM/SEI helmets, 148, 149, 185, 278, 288
  fear and, 148, 149
  fitting, 277–82, *281–82*
  harness (retention system), adjusting, 279–80
  hat, wearing under, 281–82, *282*
  trail riding with, 95

help at shows, getting, 330–32, *332*
Herm Sprenger stirrups with flexing branches, *256*, 258
hills, riding, 91–92, *92*, *96–97*, 96–98
hill work, walk, 38
hindquarters, engaging the, 37–39
hips, rotating legs from
  body soreness and, 128, *129*, 129–30, 135
  position, rider's, 20, 21, 43, 50
"hips toward hands," trot, 46
holding reins
  how to, 34, *34*, 219–22, *220*
  mounting and, 8–10, *9*
Hollywood riding, 242
horse (your)
  clinician riding your horse, 321–23
  instructors and lessons, 289–93, *292*
horse problems, 161–73. *See also* size, horse and
      rider; thinking right about horses
  bit alternatives, 168–70, *169*, 179
  bucking, 162–63, 286, *286*
  conflicting goals, 170–73, *172*
  "feel," 166–67
  goals and horse comfort, conflicts, 170–73, *172*
  hackamores, *169*, 169–70, 179
  hard mouth, 163–65, *165*
  instructors and, 162, 171, 173
  leg contact, too sensitive to rider's, 162–63
  longe lessons for, 162
  nervousness in horses, 165–67, *167*
  racehorse, retraining, 163–65, *165*
  stretching exercises, 171
  "tuning out" by horse, 166–67
  voice commands, 162
horses (different) for lessons, 302–3
horses vs. ponies, jumping, 109–10
Horse Trail Skills, Top 10, 98–100, *100*
hula image for sitting trot, 51–52
hunt seat equitation, 84, 85, *85*
hunt seat vs. cross-country position, 83–85, *85*
hydration importance, 137

Icelandic safety stirrups, *254*, *256*, 258
image for sitting trot, 51–52
improving riding problem solvers. *See* clinics;
      competitions; instructors and lessons;
      universal concerns
impulsion for canter, 73–75
inconsistent, sad rider, 200–203
independent seat, trot, 49–51, *50*
injury, fear of, 143–50, *145*
inside-leg contact
  body soreness and, 128, *129*, 129–30, 135

OTHER STOREY TITLES YOU WILL ENJOY

The Horse Behavior Problem Solver, by Jessica Jahiel. Using a friendly question-and-answer format and drawing on real-life case studies, Jahiel explains how a horse thinks and learns, why it acts the way it does, and how you should respond. 352 pages. Paperback. ISBN 1-58017-524-4.

Riding for Kids, by Judy Richter. This complete learn-to-ride program is the perfect companion to lessons in the ring, with a focus on English riding skills and techniques. 144 pages. Paperback. ISBN 1-58017-510-4.

Storey's Horse-Lover's Encyclopedia, edited by Deborah Burns. A comprehensive, user-friendly, A-to-Z guide to all things equine, this book covers breeds, tack, facilities, daily care, health issues, riding styles, shows, and much more. 480 pages. Paperback. ISBN 1-58017-317-9.

Storey's Illustrated Guide to 96 Horse Breeds of North America, by Judith Dutson. This first-ever photographic tribute to all horse breeds that call North America home captures the spirit of these noble animals and provides a wealth of information about each breed's particular history, special uses, conformation standards, and much more. 416 pages. Paperback. ISBN 1-58017-612-7.

Stable Smarts, by Heather Smith Thomas. Gathered in this readily accessible handbook, Thomas's hundreds of useful tidbits — gleaned over a lifetime of working with horses day in and day out — will generally improve and simplify the quality of life on a horse farm, while saving time and money in ways you never thought possible. 320 pages. Paperback. ISBN 1-58017-610-0.

Horsekeeping on a Small Acreage, by Cherry Hill. This thoroughly updated, full-color edition of the best-selling classic details the essentials for designing safe and functional facilities whether on one acre or one hundred. Hill describes the entire process: layout design, barn construction, feed storage, fencing, equipment selection, and much more. 320 pages. Paperback. ISBN 1-58017-535-X.

Becoming an Effective Rider, by Cherry Hill. Develop your mind and body for balance and unity using a range of techniques that help riders reach full mental and physical potential, whether in recreational riding or formal dressage. 192 pages. Paperback. ISBN 0-88266-688-6.

Easy-Gaited Horses, by Lee Ziegler. Discover the pleasures of riding a horse that is calm, obedient, relaxed, and sure-footed with this comprehensive guide to training and riding a variety of horses in specific gaits. 256 pages. Paperback. ISBN 1-58017-562-7.

Trail Riding, by Rhonda Hart Poe. This comprehensive resource with fundamental instruction and detailed advice on every aspect of trail riding is essential reading for everyone who rides anywhere other than in the ring. 320 pages. Paperback. ISBN 1-58017-560-0.

These and other Storey books are available wherever books are sold and directly from Storey Publishing, 210 MASS MoCA Way, North Adams, MA 01247, or by calling 1-800-441-5700. Or visit our Web site at www.storey.com